New York Burning

New York Burning

LIBERTY, SLAVERY, AND
CONSPIRACY IN EIGHTEENTH-
CENTURY MANHATTAN

JILL LEPORE

Alfred A. Knopf   New York   2005

THIS IS A BORZOI BOOK
PUBLISHED BY ALFRED A. KNOPF

Copyright © 2005 by Jill Lepore

All rights reserved. Published in the United States by
Alfred A. Knopf, a division of Random House, Inc., New York,
and in Canada by Random House of Canada Limited, Toronto.

Knopf, Borzoi Books, and the colophon are registered trademarks of
Random House, Inc.

ISBN 1-4000-4029-9

Manufactured in the United States of America

For Tim

Liberty is to live upon one's own Terms; Slavery is to live at the meer Mercy of another; and a Life of Slavery is to those who can bear it, a continual State of Uncertainty and Wretchedness, often an Apprehension of Violence, and often the lingering Dread of a violent Death.

—John Trenchard and Thomas Gordon,
Cato's Letters, reprinted in Zenger's *New-York Weekly Journal,* September 15, 1735

Let by *My* specious Name no *Tyrants* rise,
And cry, while they enslave, they civilize!
Know *LIBERTY* and *I* are still the *same,*
Congenial!—ever mingling Flame with Flame!

—Richard Savage, "Of Public Spirit in Regard to Public Works," 1737

I know not which is the more astonishing, the extreme *Folly,* or the *Wickedness* of so base and shocking a Conspiracy; for as to any View of Liberty or Government you could propose to yourselves, upon the Success of burning the City, robbing, butchering, and destroying the Inhabitants; what could it be expected to end in . . . but your own Destruction?

—Daniel Horsmanden, sentencing Quack and Cuffee to be burned at the stake, May 29, 1741

I am a dead man.

—Adam, from his jail cell, June 27, 1741

CONTENTS

	Preface	xi
PROLOGUE	*The Plot*	5
CHAPTER ONE	*Ice*	15
CHAPTER TWO	*Fire*	40
CHAPTER THREE	*Stone*	64
CHAPTER FOUR	*Paper*	93
CHAPTER FIVE	*Water*	129
CHAPTER SIX	*Blood*	170
CHAPTER SEVEN	*Ink*	198
EPILOGUE	*Dust*	221
	Appendices	233
	Source Notes and Abbreviations	275
	Notes	279
	Acknowledgments	309
	Index	311

Preface

"LIBEERTY and SLAVERY! how amiable is one! how odious and abominable the other!" wrote James Alexander in the pages of the *New-York Weekly Journal* in 1733. When Alexander championed liberty and condemned slavery, he meant the liberty of the press and the slavery of tyranny. "No Nation Antient or Modern ever lost the Liberty of freely Speaking, Writing, or Publishing their Sentiments," he warned, "but forthwith lost their Liberty in general and became Slaves."[1] By slaves, Alexander meant a nation ruled by a despot; he did not mean the two thousand men, women, and children who toiled as human chattel in the bustling city of eighteenth-century Manhattan, a number that included not only the five people who lived in Alexander's own elegant house but also the one black man who had escaped from its attic, carrying a pass he had penned himself, in an act of forgery that defined, better than anything Alexander could put to paper, the liberty of freely writing.

Political liberty was the most cherished blessing in the British realm, and political slavery its most dreaded specter. "Rule, Britannia, rule the waves; / Britons never will be slaves," wrote an English poet in 1740, in lines that became the empire's anthem. But throughout that empire, and especially in its American colonies, dark-skinned people lived under worse than the slavery of tyranny; they lived in the slavery of human bondage. In the colonies, "liberty" and "slavery" tripped off tongues, and nearly slipped into meaninglessness. "Though Liberty and Slavery are words which incessantly vibrate on the ears of the Public," wrote one colonist, "yet we have few terms in the English Vocabulary so generally misunderstood."[2] Everywhere, liberty was passionately celebrated, and slavery just as passionately condemned, by men like James Alexander, Americans who owned Africans.

That calls for liberty came from a world of slavery has been named the central paradox of American history. Eighteenth-century observers did not fail to remark upon it. "How is it that we hear the loudest *yelps* for liberty among the drivers of negroes?" Samuel Johnson famously complained in 1775, in a reply to American revolutionaries' protest of parliamentary taxation. Nor have historians quieted their astonishment, and rightly so. "The paradox is American, and it behooves Americans to understand it if they would understand themselves," wrote Edmund Morgan in 1975.³ Three decades and Thomas Jefferson's twenty-three chromosomes later, Americans are now quite aware of the American paradox, but it remains, somehow, impossible to understand. That abject bondage contributed to the creation of the world's first modern democracy, however true and even self-evident, is, finally, so painful a truth as to be nearly unfathomable.

This book tells the story of how one kind of slavery made another kind of liberty possible in eighteenth-century New York, a place whose slave past has long been buried. It was a beautiful city, a crisscross of crooked cobblestone streets boasting both grand and petty charms: a grassy park at the Bowling Green, the stone arches at City Hall, beech trees shading Broadway like so many parasols, and, off rocky beaches, the best oysters anywhere. "I found it extremely pleasant to walk the town," one visitor wrote in 1748, "for it seemed like a garden."⁴ But on this granite island poking out like a sharp tooth between the Hudson and the East rivers, one in five inhabitants was enslaved, making Manhattan second only to Charleston, South Carolina, in a wretched calculus of urban unfreedom.

New York was a slave city. Its most infamous episode is hardly known today: over a few short weeks in 1741, ten fires blazed across the city. Nearly two hundred slaves were suspected of conspiring to burn every building and murder every white. Tried and convicted before the colony's Supreme Court, thirteen black men were burned at the stake. Seventeen more were hanged, two of their dead bodies chained to posts not far from the Negroes Burial Ground, left to bloat and rot. One jailed man cut his own throat. Another eighty-four men and women were sold into yet more miserable, bone-crushing slavery in the Caribbean. Two white men and two white women, the alleged ringleaders, were hanged, one of them in chains; seven more white men were pardoned on condition that they never set foot in New York again.

What happened in New York in 1741 is so horrifying—"Bonfires of the Negros," one colonist called it—that it's easy to be blinded by the brightness of the flames. But step back, let the fires flicker in the distance, and they cast their light not only on the 1741 slave conspiracy but on the American paradox, illuminating a far better known episode in New York's past: the 1735 trial of the printer John Peter Zenger.

IN 1732, a forty-two-year-old English gentleman named William Cosby arrived in New York, having been appointed governor by the king. New Yorkers soon learned, to their dismay, that their new governor ruled by a three-word philosophy: God damn ye. Rage at Cosby's ill-considered appointment grew with his every abuse of the governorship. Determined to oust Cosby from power, James Alexander, a prominent lawyer, hired Zenger, a German immigrant, to publish an opposition newspaper. Alexander supplied scathing, unsigned editorials criticizing the governor's administration; Zenger set the type. The first issue of Zenger's *New-York Weekly Journal* was printed in November 1733. Cosby could not, would not abide it. He assigned Daniel Horsmanden, an ambitious forty-year-old Englishman new to the city, to a committee charged with pointing out "the particular Seditious paragraphs" in Zenger's newspaper. The governor then ordered the incendiary issues of Zenger's newspaper burned, and had Zenger arrested for libel.

Zenger was tried before the province's Supreme Court in 1735. His attorney did not deny that Cosby was the object of the editorials in the *New-York Weekly Journal.* Instead, he argued, first, that Zenger was innocent because what he printed was true, and second, that freedom of the press was especially necessary in the colonies, where other checks against governors' powers were weakened by their distance from England. It was an almost impossibly brilliant defense, which at once defied legal precedent—before the Zenger case, truth had never been a defense against libel—and had the effect of putting the governor on trial, just what Zenger's attorney wanted, since William Cosby, God damn him, was a man no jury could love. Zenger was acquitted. The next year, James Alexander prepared and Zenger printed *A Brief Narrative of the Case and Trial of John Peter Zenger,* which was soon after reprinted in Boston and London. It made Zenger famous.

But the trial of John Peter Zenger is merely the best-known episode in the political maelstrom that was early eighteenth-century New York. "We are in the midst of Party flames," Daniel Horsmanden wryly observed in 1734, as Cosby's high-handedness ignited the city. Horsmanden wrote in an age when political parties were considered sinister, invidious, and

A brief Narrative of the Cafe and Tryal of *John Peter Zenger*, Printer of the *New-York weekly Journal.*

AS There was but one Printer in the Province of *New-York*, that printed a publick News Paper, I was in Hopes, if I undertook to publifh another, I might make it worth my while ; and I foon found my Hopes were not groundlefs: My firft Paper was printed, *Nov.* 5th, 1733. and I continued printing and publifhing of them, I thought to the Satisfaction of every Body, till the *January* following; when the Chief Juftice was pleafed to animadvert upon the Doctrine of Libels, in a long Charge given in that Term to the Grand Jury, and afterwards on the third *Tuefday* of *October*, 1734. was again pleafed to charge the Grand Jury in the following Words.

' *Gentlemen* ; I fhall conclude with reading a Paragraph or two out of the ' fame Book, concerning Libels ; they are arrived to that Height, that they ' call loudly for your Animadverfion ; it is high Time to put a Stop to them ; ' for at the rate Things are now carried on, when all Order and Government ' is endeavoured to be trampled on ; Reflections are caft upon Perfons of all ' Degrees, muft not thefe Things end in Sedition, if not timely prevented? Lenity, ' you have feen will not avail, it becomes you then to enquire after the Of- ' fenders, that we may in a due Courfe of Law be enabled to punifh them. ' If you, *Gentlemen*, do not interpofe, confider whether the ill Confequences ' that may arife from any Difturbances of the publick Peace, may not in part, ' lye at your Door ?

' *Hawkins*, in his Chapter of Libels, confiders three Points. 1*ft. What fhall* ' *be faid to be a Libel.* 2*dly. Who are lyable to be punifhed for it.* 3*dly. In what* ' *Manner they are to be punifhed.* Under the 1*ft.* he fays, *§. 7. Nor can there be* ' *any Doubt, but that a Writing which defames a private Perfon only, is as much* ' *a Libel as that which defames Perfons intrufted in a publick Capacity, in as much* ' *as it manifeftly tends to create ill Blood, and to caufe a Difturbance of the publick Peace;* ' *however, it is certain, that it is a very high Aggravation of a Libel, that it tends to* ' *fcandalize the Government, by reflecting on thofe who are entrufted with the Admini-* ' *ftration of publick Affairs, which does not only endanger the publick Peace, as all other* ' *Libels do, by ftirring up the Parties immediately concerned in it, to Acts of Revenge,* ' *but alfo has a direct Tendency to breed in the People a Diflike of their Governours,* ' *and incline them to Faction and Sedition.* As to the 2*d.* Point he fays, *§. 10.* ' *It is certain, not only he who compofes or procures another to compofe it, but* ' *alfo that he who publifhes, or procures another to publifh it, are in Danger of being* ' *punifhed for it ; and it is faid not to be material whether he who difperfes a Libel,* ' *knew any Thing of the Contents or Effects of it or not ; for nothing could be more*

A   *eafy*

Opening page of A Brief Narrative of the Case and Tryal of John Peter Zenger, *1736. Collection of The New-York Historical Society.*

destructive of good government. As Alexander Pope put it in 1727, "Party is the madness of many, for the gain of a few." Or, as Viscount St. John Bolingbroke remarked in his 1733 "Dissertation upon Parties": "The spirit of party . . . inspires animosity and breeds rancour." Nor did the distaste for parties diminish over the course of the century. In 1789, Thomas Jefferson wrote: "If I could not go to heaven but with a party, I would not go there at all."[5]

Parties they may have despised, but, with William Cosby in the governor's office, New Yorkers formed them, dividing themselves between the opposition Country Party and the Court Party, loyal to the governor. Even Cosby's death in March 1736 failed to extinguish New York's "Party flames." Alexander and his allies challenged the authority of Cosby's successor, George Clarke, and established a rival government. Warned of a plot "to seize his person or kill him in the Attempt," Clarke retreated to Fort George, at the southern tip of Manhattan, "& put the place in a posture of Defence." In the eyes of one New Yorker, "we had all the appearance of a civil War."[6]

And then: nothing. No shots were fired. Nor was any peace ever brokered; the crisis did not so much resolve as it dissipated. Soon after barricading himself in Fort George, Clarke received orders from London confirming his appointment. The rival government was disbanded. By the end of 1736, Daniel Horsmanden could boast, "Zenger is perfectly Silent as to polliticks."[7] Meanwhile, Clarke rewarded party loyalists: in 1737 he appointed Horsmanden to a vacant seat on the Supreme Court. But Clarke proved a more moderate man than his predecessor. By 1739, under his stewardship, the colony quieted.

What happened in New York City in the 1730s was much more than a dispute over the freedom of the press. It was a debate about the nature of political opposition, during which New Yorkers briefly entertained the heretical idea that parties were "not only necessary in free Government, but of great Service to the Public." As even a supporter of Cosby wrote in 1734, "Parties are a check upon one another, and by keeping the Ambition of one another within Bounds, serve to maintain the public Liberty."[8] And it was, equally, a debate about the power of governors, the nature of empire, and the role of the law in defending Americans against arbitrary authority—the kind of authority that constituted tyranny, the kind of authority that made men slaves. James Alexander saw himself as a defender of the rule of law in a world that, because of its very great distance from England, had come to be ruled by men. His opposition was not so much a failure as a particularly spectacular stretch of road along a bumpy, crooked path full of detours that, over the course of the century, led to American independence. Because of it, New York became infamous for its "unruly spirit of independency." Clarke, shocked, reported to his superiors in England that New Yorkers believe "if a Governor misbehave himself they may depose him and set up an other." The leaders of the Country Party "trod very near" to what, in the 1730s, went by the name of treason.[9] A generation later, their sons would call it revolution.

IN EARLY 1741, less than two years after Clarke calmed the province, ten fires swept the city. Fort George was nearly destroyed; Clarke's own mansion, inside the fort, burned to the ground. Daniel Horsmanden was convinced that the fires had been "set on Foot by some villainous Confederacy of latent Enemies amongst us," a confederacy that sounded a good deal like a violent political party. But which enemies? No longer fearful that Country Party agitators were attempting to take his life, Clarke, at Horsmanden's urging, turned his suspicion on the city's slaves. With each new fire, panicked white New Yorkers cried from street corners, "The Negroes are rising!" Early evidence collected by a grand jury appointed by the Supreme Court hinted at a vast and elaborate conspiracy: on the outskirts of the city, in a tavern owned by a poor and obscure English cobbler named John Hughson, tens and possibly hundreds of black men had been meeting secretly, gathering weapons and plotting to burn the city, murder every white man, appoint Hughson their king, and elect a slave named Caesar governor.

This political opposition was far more dangerous than anything led by James Alexander. The slave plot to depose one governor and set up another—a *black* governor—involved not newspapers and petitions but arson and murder. It had to be stopped. In the spring and summer of 1741, New York magistrates arrested 20 whites and 152 blacks. To Horsmanden, "it seemed very probable that most of the Negroes in Town were corrupted." Eighty black men and one black woman confessed and named names, sending still more to the gallows and the stake.

That summer, a New Englander wrote an anonymous letter to New York. "I am a stranger to you & to New York," he began. But he had heard of "the bloody Tragedy" afflicting the city: the relentless cycle of arrests, accusations, hasty trials, executions, and more arrests. This "puts me in mind of our New England Witchcraft in the year 1692," he remarked,

"Which if I dont mistake New York justly reproached us for, & mockt at our Credulity about."[10]

Here was no idle observation. The 1741 New York conspiracy trials and the 1692 Salem witchcraft trials had much in common. Except that what happened in New York in 1741 was worse, and has been almost entirely forgotten. In Salem, twenty people were executed, compared to New York's thirty-four, and none of Salem's witches was burned at the stake. However much it looks like Salem in 1692, what happened in New York in 1741 had more to do with revolution than witchcraft. And it is inseparable from the wrenching crisis of the 1730s, not least because the fires in 1741 included attacks on property owned by key members of the Court Party; lawyers from both sides of the aisle in the legal battles of the 1730s joined together to prosecute slaves in 1741; and slaves owned by prominent members of the Country Party proved especially vulnerable to prosecution.

But the threads that tie together the crises of the 1730s and 1741 are longer than the list of participants. The 1741 conspiracy and the 1730s opposition party were two faces of the same coin. By the standards of the day, both faces were ugly, disfigured, deformed; they threatened the order of things. But one was very much more dangerous than the other: Alexander's political party plotted to depose the governor; the city's slaves, allegedly, plotted to kill him. The difference made Alexander's opposition seem, relative to slave rebellion, harmless, and in so doing made the world safer for democracy, or at least, and less grandly, both more amenable to and more anxious about the gradual and halting rise of political parties.

Whether enslaved men and women actually conspired in New York in 1741 is a question whose answer lies buried deep in the evidence, if it survives at all. It is worth excavating carefully. But even the *specter* of a slave conspiracy cast a dark shadow across the political landscape. Slavery was, always and everywhere, a political issue, but what happened in New York suggests that it exerted a more powerful influence on political life: slaves suspected of conspiracy constituted both a phantom political party and an ever-threatening revolution. In the 1730s and '40s, the American Revolution was years away and the real emergence of political parties in the new United States, a fitful process at best, would have to wait until the last decade of the eighteenth century. (Indeed, one reason that colonists only embraced revolution with ambivalence and accepted parties by fits and starts may be that slavery alternately ignited and extinguished party flames: the threat of black rebellion made white political opposition palatable, even as it established its limits and helped heal the divisions it created.) But during those fateful months in the spring and summer of 1741, New York's Court Party, still reeling from the Country Party's experiment in political opposition, attempted to douse party flames by burning black men at the stake. New York is not America, but what happened in that eighteenth-century slave city tells one story, and a profoundly troubling one, of how slavery destabilized—and created—American politics.

EVEN BEFORE the fires died to embers, New Yorkers began to wonder whether the city had suffered "in the merciless Flames of an Imaginary Plot." More than a few began "to think it all a Dream, or a Fiction." Some even *"took the Liberty to arraign the Justice of the Proceedings,"* declaring "that there was no Plot at all!" Daniel Horsmanden, who had staked his reputation on the investigation, was outraged. Inspired by Alexander's success in publishing the record of Zenger's trial, Horsmanden decided to bring the evidence before the public. In 1744, he published his *Journal of the Proceedings in The Detection of the Conspiracy Formed by Some* White *People, in Conjunction with* Negro *and other* Slaves, *for Burning the City of* NEW-YORK *in America, And Murdering the Inhabitants,* containing (as advertised on its title page) "A Narrative of the Trials, Condemnations, Executions, and Behaviour of the several Criminals, at the Gallows and Stake, with their *Speeches* and *Confessions;* with Notes, Observations and Reflections occasionally interspersed throughout the Whole." It is one of the most startling and vexing documents in early American history.

Daniel Horsmanden's *Journal* is many things: a diary, a mystery, a history, and maybe one of English literature's first detective stories. By publishing it, Horsmanden hoped to persuade New Yorkers *"of the Necessity there is, for every One that has Negroes, to keep a very watchful Eye over them, and not to indulge them with too great Liberties."* More, he sought to illustrate the brilliance of his investigation of this "Master-piece of Villainy." Yet Horsmanden has convinced his few modern readers of nothing so much as his own unreliability to report on a conspiracy hatched by people he considered "degenerated and debased below the Dignity of Humane Species." On every page of the *Journal,* Horsmanden's fiery racial hatred testifies to his inability to offer justice to each black man and woman who came before his court, making it all too easy to conclude that New Yorkers did indeed suffer "in the merciless Flames of an Imaginary Plot."[11]

But the plot cannot be so easily dismissed, just as Horsmanden's *Journal* cannot be so carelessly tossed into the trash bin of history. To place

A *James Beekman*

JOURNAL

OF THE

PROCEEDINGS

IN

The Detection of the Conspiracy

FORMED BY

Some *White* People, in Conjunction with *Negro* and other *Slaves*,

FOR

Burning the City of *NEW-YORK* in AMERICA,

And Murdering the Inhabitants.

Which Conspiracy was partly put in Execution, by Burning His Majesty's House in Fort GEORGE, within the said City, on Wednesday the Eighteenth of *March*, 1741. and setting Fire to several Dwelling and other Houses there, within a few Days succeeding. And by another Attempt made in Prosecution of the same infernal Scheme, by putting Fire between two other Dwelling-Houses within the said City, on the Fifteenth Day of *February*, 1742 ; which was accidentally and timely discovered and extinguished.

CONTAINING,

I. A NARRATIVE of the Trials, Condemnations, Executions, and Behaviour of the several Criminals, at the Gallows and Stake, with their *Speeches* and *Confessions* ; with Notes, Observations and Reflections occasionally interspersed throughout the Whole.

II. AN APPENDIX, wherein is set forth some additional Evidence concerning the said Conspiracy and Conspirators, which has come to Light since their Trials and Executions.

III. LISTS of the several Persons (Whites and Blacks) committed on Account of the Conspiracy ; and of the several Criminals executed ; and of those transported, with the Places whereto.

By the Recorder of the City of NEW-YORK.

Quid facient Domini, audent cum talia Fures? Virg. Ecl.

NEW-YORK:

Printed by *James Parker*, at the New Printing-Office, 1744.

Opening page of A Journal of the Proceedings in The Detection of the Conspiracy, *1744. Collection of The New-York Historical Society.*

both liberty and slavery, and not just one or the other, at the center of American history requires much more than a casual reading of what the *Journal* contains: page after page of what eighteenth-century lawyers called "Negro Evidence," testimony elicited from slaves. "Negro & Spectre evidence will turn out alike," that anonymous New Englander warned, predicting that the confessions of New York City's slaves, like teenage girls' visions of witches flying over Salem, would turn out to be nothing more than lies and delusions. By 1693, spectral evidence had become an embarrassment in Massachusetts courts; "Negro Evidence" was legally dubious from the beginning. But without recourse to such evidence, much of early American history, and especially of the tangled paradox of liberty and slavery, is probably unrecoverable. Getting to the truth of the 1741 conspiracy means taking the "Negro Evidence" in Horsmanden's *Journal* seriously.

Daniel Horsmanden never failed to set his sights high, as a writer, as a politician, as a judge. His *Journal* was no exception. In it he boasted that the Supreme Court's tireless inquiry into the events of 1741 solved the problem of evil, the "Mystery of Iniquity," the biblical *Mysterium iniquitatis*, by which he meant the slave conspiracy. Like Horsmanden, I think there's more to this mystery than the conspiracy. There's the iniquity of slavery, and the mystery of why it thrived in Britain's American colonies, even in the North, even among English settlers passionate about liberty. "LIBEERTY and SLAVERY! how amiable is one! how odious and abominable the other!" Perhaps the paradox, the mystery, of liberty and slavery can never be solved. But a lantern can be held up to it, on a walk that might begin at the slave market on Wall Street and end at the Negroes Burial Ground near the Collect Pond, a long, cold walk through the harsh and beautiful and unfamiliar past of what would become America's most important city, a city that slavery built, and nearly destroyed.

New York Burning

David Grim's Plan

In this plan of Manhattan made in 1813, a seventy-six-year-old New Yorker
named David Grim mapped the densely settled city of the 1740s—
with some eleven hundred houses—complete with references to sixty landmarks,
including the "Plot Negro's burnt here," the best remembered event of the
mapmaker's childhood. Grim was just four years old in 1741, but he had "a perfect
idea of seing the Negroes chained to a stake, and there burned to death."

Detail from David Grim, "A Plan of the City and Environs of New York as they were in the years 1742 1743 & 1744,"
1813. Collection of The New-York Historical Society.

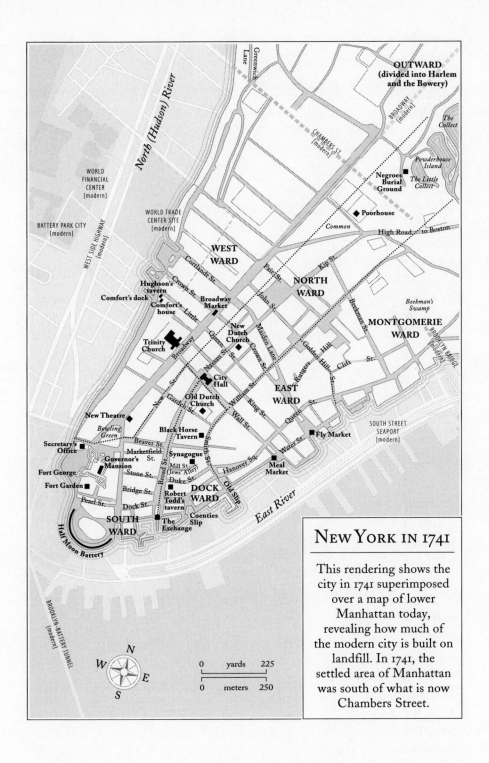

OUTWARD
(divided into Harlem
and the Bowery)

BROADWAY [modern]

The Collect

North (Hudson) River

Greenwich Lane

CHAMBERS ST. [modern]

Powderhouse Island

Negroes Burial Ground

The Little Collect

WORLD FINANCIAL CENTER [modern]

WORLD TRADE CENTER SITE [modern]

BATTERY PARK CITY [modern]

WEST SIDE HIGHWAY [modern]

◆ Poorhouse

Common

High Road "to Boston"

WEST WARD

Cortlandt St.

Hughson's tavern

Crown St.

Comfort's dock

Comfort's house

Little

Broadway Market

Fair St.

Kip St.

NORTH WARD

John St.

Beekman St.

Beekman's Swamp

MONTGOMERIE WARD

New Dutch Church

Broadway

Queen St.

Maiden Lane

Crown St.

Golden Hill St.

Golden Hill St.

BROOKLYN BRIDGE [modern]

Trinity Church

Nassau St.

City Hall

Old Dutch Church

Smith St.

William St.

King St.

Clift St.

Rutgers

EAST WARD

Queen St.

New Theatre

Bowling Green

Black Horse Tavern

New St.

Garden St.

Wall St.

Fly Market

SOUTH STREET SEAPORT [modern]

Secretary's Office

Governor's Mansion

Beaver St.

Marketfield St.

Stone St.

Synagogue

Mill St. (Jews' Alley)

Broad St.

Duke St.

Water St.

Hanover Sq.

Meal Market

Fort George

Fort Garden

Bridge St.

Robert Todd's tavern

DOCK WARD

Old Slip

Pearl St.

Dock St.

The Exchange

Coenties Slip

SOUTH WARD

East River

Half Moon Battery

BROOKLYN-BATTERY TUNNEL [modern]

N
W   E
S

| 0 | yards | 225 |
| 0 | meters | 250 |

NEW YORK IN 1741

This rendering shows the
city in 1741 superimposed
over a map of lower
Manhattan today,
revealing how much of
the modern city is built on
landfill. In 1741, the
settled area of Manhattan
was south of what is now
Chambers Street.

The Plot

VEAL, DUCK, SALT PORK, a quarter of mutton, two loaves of bread, at least one goose, a flask of rum, two bowls of punch. It was a fine feast. Planks were balanced on low wooden tubs to make benches and a cloth was laid over three tables pushed together, like cobblestones down a narrow lane.

The guests began arriving at four o'clock in the afternoon, on a bitterly cold Sunday in January 1741. They came from all over the city. Bastian trudged up from Jacobus Vaarck's bakery on Broad Street. Captain John Marshall's slave Ben headed north on Broadway and then west to Gerardus Comfort's dock, where he called out to Comfort's slave Jack, "*Brother go to Hughson's.*" In the Trinity churchyard, Emanuel, owned by a cordwainer named Thomas Wendover, met Quash, who worked at a brewery on Maiden Lane, and together they walked along the waterside, staring out at the meringue of ice on the Hudson River, to John Hughson's tavern on the edge of the city.[1]

It had been a doleful winter. The "hard winter," it was called, the worst anyone could remember. And the "great snow" of that hardest of winters had come at Christmastime, three feet on a single night; seven more in the days that followed. "Our Streets are fill'd, with confused Heaps of Snow," the *New-York Weekly Journal* reported on December 22. Two weeks later, a canoe carrying "one Woman and a Child at her Breast and 5 Men" was "Jamm'd in with the Ice" and driven to Coney Island, where its passengers died of the cold. The Hudson was frozen for thirty miles upriver, while in the harbor abandoned ships creaked, their masts rising up from the glacial sea like inverted icicles. Birds and squirrels froze to death. Cows and deer, "unable to browse or escape through the depth of the snow," simply starved, their carcasses sinking under the white.

Stuck in their city that winter, New Yorkers were marooned on the tip of their tiny island. They had barely cleared paths to walk down the streets and there was so much snow—drifts buried dozens of houses—that even sleds and sleighs were dangerous. In the winter of 1740–41, ten thousand New Yorkers, two thousand of them slaves, tried to stop shivering, and they failed. "While I am Writing in a Warm Room by a good Fire Side," wrote a correspondent for John Peter Zenger's *New-York Weekly Journal,* "the Ink Freezes in the Pen."[2]

As Cato, owned by city alderman John Moore, trudged to Hughson's that afternoon from his owner's house at Whitehall Slip, on the East River, he must have ached for the warmth of the tavern. Cato had come by invitation, but by the time he arrived there were already forty or fifty guests in the parlor of what was a suspiciously large house for such a poor cobbler as the Englishman John Hughson. Nearly all of Hughson's guests were men, men born into bondage in Jamaica, Antigua, or Barbados, and traded to New York, or born in Africa, kidnapped or captured in warfare, marched to the Guinea Coast, packed in cargo holds, shipped to the Caribbean, and finally sold at auction in New York, at the market on the dock at the base of Wall Street. A few were born slaves on the banks of the Hudson. Now, they all felt the chill seep out of their bones as they sat in Hughson's house, listening to the popping and spitting of his fierce fire.

Hughson, his wife Sarah, their daughter, and a lodger named Peggy Kerry sat at one end of the table; next to them sat six dark-skinned Spanish-speaking sailors, "Spanish Negroes," who had been sold into slavery after being captured by English privateers. Kerry, an Irish prostitute, was seven months pregnant, carrying a child fathered by Caesar, who was owned by John Vaarck, Bastian's owner's son. Hughson's wife, Sarah, who had given birth to ten children, probably nursed a newborn. Ben sat "at the Head of the Table." Jonneau, another of Jacobus Vaarck's slaves, "stood at the Door a pretty while," but when the meat was served, he came in and took a seat. The other men shifted their weight on the benches, making room, keeping warm. Finding no place for himself, Cato sat at a makeshift side table. "The Room was so full," Emanuel said, "that several of the Negroes stood."

When Bastian entered the crowded tavern, he must have nearly fainted at the sight of the feast. Meat, by God. The slave of a baker, Bastian was better fed than many New Yorkers, but he, too, felt the hunger that plagued the city's poor that winter, when even bakers ran out of grain. Later, in March, ravenous New Yorkers would taste flesh for the first time in months, when flocks of pigeons darkened the sky and were "taken in nets in such plenty" as to "greatly contribute to the relief of the poor." No one understood why the pigeons arrived so early, migrating from the south six weeks sooner than usual, their craws still full of undigested Carolina rice. Nor did anyone wonder for long; instead, while the birds roasted on the spit, the poor gave thanks for one of the hard winter's few mercies.

Before Bastian, his mouth watering, could reach for the veal, or the duck, mutton, pork, or goose on John Hughson's table, Caesar pointed a pistol at his chest. Would Bastian "join along with them to become their own Masters?" he demanded. "What would he have him join with him in?" Bastian asked. "In the Plot," Caesar answered, "to take the Country." At first Bastian refused. Caesar poured rum down his throat and warned that he "should not go alive out of the House." Finally, Bastian, "very much daunted," consented to the plot: to burn the city, kill the white men, and take the white women for their wives. He's "*but a weak-hearted Dog,*" Caesar called over to Hughson, but "*set his Name down.*"

OR AT LEAST that's what Bastian, Jack, Cato, and Emanuel confessed when questioned by their masters, by magistrates, and by a grand jury, after being jailed in the dungeon below City Hall in the spring and summer of 1741. And they, and many others, confessed to more, much more. Not only at the "Great Feast" but on other days and nights, John Hughson had fed them lavishly, and served them drinks: cider, rum, punch, and beer. Juan, the Indian slave of a Dutch sailor, "drank a Mug of Beer, and paid for it"; more often the drinks were free. York, the slave of an English miller, said "*Hughson* made him so drunk that he could not stand." Cajoe, owned by a Portuguese Jewish merchant named Mordecai Gomez, complained that the drinks were spiked: Hughson mixed a mug of punch that was two-thirds rum "and made it so sweet, that he did not immediately feel the Strength of it."

At Hughson's—they confessed—they played cards and dice. They held cockfights. They danced. A man named Fortune had heard "they had a Dance there every other Night," with music supplied by African drummers from the city's militia and fiddlers from as far away as Long Island. "After Supper, were dancing," Joshua Sleydall's slave Jack recalled, "and Mr. PHILIPSE's Cuff plaid on the Fiddle." Thomas Ellison's slave Jamaica fiddled at Hughson's, too, and Mary Burton, the Hughsons' sixteen-year-old indentured servant, said that Jamaica promised to play his fiddle for the city's whites "while they were roasting in the Flames; and said, he had been Slave long enough."

Hughson's guests ate and drank, fiddled and played and danced, and they plotted. Jack, owned by attorney Joseph Murray, had barely entered the tavern when he heard talk "of burning the Houses and killing the white people, and of taking all the Gentlewomen for their Wives." "After they had done dancing, they made a Bowl of Punch," another man confessed. "And having for some Time drank, they said one to another, *Let us set Fire to the Town and kill the white People.*"

Next they swore. There were inducements: Hughson told his guests that if they swore, "they should never want for Liquor whether they had Money or not." And there were threats. "Boy will you stand by it?" Hughson asked York, a slave of Charles Crooke, the day after Christmas, in the warmth of the tavern. York said he would. Hughson said if he didn't, "he would stick him with a Sword, and pointed to one in a Corner of the Room." York said he would. "Boy, if you stand by it," said Hughson, "you must *kiss the Book.*" York pressed his lips to it, and declared he would not be a coward. They swore oaths by God and by thunder "*of Damnation to Eternity to the Failers.*" They were "*not so much as to tell a Cat or a Dog.*" Vintner Robert Todd's slave Dundee cursed, "*The D—l fetch him, and the D—l d—n him if he did.*"

John Hughson kept a list. When Joseph Murray's men Adam and Jack arrived at the tavern, Hughson "*produced a Paper, and said it was an Agreement of the Blacks to kill the white Folks,*" and added their names to it, the ink, no doubt, freezing in his pen. Primus, owned by a French distiller named James DeBrosses, said Hughson "*put his Hand on a Paper, which he told him was a List of the Names of those who were to rise.*" Hughson used it to call roll.

Hughson swore, too. "By G-d, if they would be true to him, he would take this Country." How would they do it? Albany, the slave of an English butcher's widow, told Will, owned by a Dutch cordwainer, "he believed an Hundred and Fifty Men might take this City." They were to begin by burning Fort George, the city's crucial defensive outpost, behind the Half Moon Battery on the southern tip of the island. At this signal, each man was to kill his master and "*such of the Negroes as would not assist them.*" Hughson was collecting guns: he told Brash and Ben, slaves of the French merchants Peter and Augustus Jay (the father and grandfather of founding father John Jay), "that they should get what Guns, Swords and Pistols they could from their Master's, and bring them to his House; but if they could not get any, that he could furnish them with them himself." Still, guns were scarce. And knives were silent. Pedro, a "Spanish Negro" owned by Peter DePeyster, knew that "*the Report of a Gun would immediately alarm*" the *People*," but with knives and swords, "*they might stab many before they were found out.*"

Not every recruitment succeeded. "D—n it," cursed Robin, when asked his opinion of the plot. "I'll have nothing to say to it; if they burn their Backsides, they must sit down on the Blisters." But most men eagerly agreed to cut their masters' throats. Jack and Adam were keen to "*destroy Mr. Murray, Mrs. Murray, and all the Family, with Knives.*" Dundee volunteered "to cut his Mistress's Throat in the Night."

After the butchery, the men would set fire to their masters' houses. Some of the Spaniards "had *black Stuff to set Houses on fire,*" but live coals would serve just as well. A man named London agreed to burn down Peter Marschalk's house (no mean trick, since Marschalk served as one of the city's firemen). Dundee was to set fire to his owner's tavern on Broad Street. Joe, owned by a dancing master, agreed to torch the city's only theatre, on the corner of Broadway and Beaver. Asked to burn his master's tall house on Broadway, Ben refused. "No, if they conquor'd the Place," he said, he would keep that house "to live in himself."

Their owners dead, the city in flames, the men who pledged to the plot were to assemble just north of the fort, into companies under their appointed captains—Ben, Jack, York, Dundee, and Othello—and burn their way up Broadway.

How would they know when to begin? "*Now was the best Time to do something,*" Hughson told his guests that winter, for it was a time of war. England's war with Spain, the War of Jenkins's Ear, had begun in the fall of 1739 and was even then merging with a broader conflict, the War of the Austrian Succession, pitting England against France. By autumn 1740, most of Manhattan's force of British regulars and provincial soldiers had been sent to fight against the Spaniards off the coast of Cuba, leaving the island nearly defenseless. Not only were the city's military ranks thinned, but the men who gathered at Hughson's expected England's enemies to come to their aid. At the "Great Feast" just after Christmas, they "agreed to wait a Month and half for the Spaniards and French to come," and if they did not, "they were to do all themselves."

And to what end? "*After they had conquered,*" Hughson told Tom, the slave of a French silversmith, "*they would know what it was to be free Men.*"

OF THE 152 enslaved and free black New Yorkers arrested in the spring and summer of 1741, 80—more than half—confessed to conspiring to destroy the city. (And one more man confessed who had never been arrested.) From those confessions, prosecutors pieced together a composite of what happened at Hughson's. As Daniel Horsmanden was keen to point out, the confessions agreed both "minutely in the Circumstances of this Conspiracy"—the "Great Feast" at Christmas, the tablecloth, the rum punch, the veal—and broadly, in "the principal Things aimed at, *the burning the Town and assassinating the Inhabitants.*"

It made for an effective prosecution. In his closing argument in the conspiracy's first trial, attorney William Smith offered the jury a summary of this "most horrid conspiracy":

> *Gentlemen,*
> No Scheme more monstrous could have been invented; nor can any Thing be thought of more foolish, than the Motives that induced these Wretches to enter into it! What more ridiculous than that Hughson in Consequence of this Scheme, should become a *King!* Caesar . . . a *Governor!* That the White Men shou'd be all killed, and the Women become a Prey to the rapacious Lust of these Villains! That these Slaves should thereby establish themselves in Peace and Freedom in the plunder'd Wealth of their slaughter'd Masters! 'Tis hard to say whether *the Wickedness* or *the Folly* of this Design is the Greater: And had it not been in Part executed before it was discovered; we should with great Difficulty have been persuaded to believe it possible, that such a *wicked* and *foolish Plot* could be contrived by any Creatures in Human Shape.

It was horrid. It was monstrous. It was wicked. It was inhuman. But it was also hackneyed.

What those eighty-one New Yorkers confessed to was a plot dripping with plot, ripe to bursting with familiar characters and contrivances. Smith delivered his speech in the very era in which the novel was born; not surprisingly, his argument echoed conventions established not only in early English novels but also in England's vast store of quasi-fictional tales of rogues and pirates, whores and mutinies, and ruthless gangs of highway robbers, as well as in a growing literature of alarming reports from the colonies of rebellious slaves and bloodthirsty Indians.[3]

"What more ridiculous than that Hughson in Consequence of this Scheme, should become a *King!* Caesar . . . a *Governor!*" Ridiculous, but by no means unfamiliar. English ideas of what a slave plot looked like were fully elaborated as early as 1676, in a conspiracy detected by colonists in

Barbados and related in a pamphlet published in London that same year. The island's slaves had allegedly formed a conspiracy whose "grand design was to choose them a King," who would lead them in killing white men, burning their houses, and taking white women as wives. In London, the account of the Barbados rebellion was sold stitched together with a narrative not of suspected but of actual rebellion: a violent Indian uprising in New England known as King Philip's War. In 1675 and 1676 Philip, an Algonquian "king," had plotted and conspired with Indian confederates to burn over half the towns in New England, killing one out of every ten colonists as they fled from houses set ablaze.

The plot detected in Barbados in 1676 looked like an Indian war. But in 1741, William Smith more easily called to mind more recent slave plots, published accounts of which were readily at hand. In the spring of 1737, John Peter Zenger had printed in his *New-York Weekly Journal* the *"full and particular Account of the Negro Plot in Antigoa,* as reported by the Committee appointed by the Government." It was so long that Zenger used an extra small font to set it; even then, the tiny type cluttered the entire front page of three consecutive issues and spilled over several pages more. Readers of Zenger's newspaper learned that in Antigua in 1736, black men "had formed and resolved to execute a Plot, whereby all the white Inhabitants of this Island were to be murdered, and a new Form of Government to be established by the Slaves among themselves, and they entirely to possess the Island." Court, the leader of the conspiracy, "assumed among his Country Men . . . the Stile of KING." During "Entertainments of Dancing, Gaming and Feasting," he recruited conspirators who swore to a plot to set a fire to signal the start of the wholesale murder of the island's whites.[4]

Prosecutors called the 1736 Antigua conspiracy an "unparallel'd Hellish Plot," but, hellish or not, it was hardly unparalleled. By 1741, it was utterly conventional. In Barbados in 1676, slave rebels sent signals using trumpets made of elephant tusks; in Antigua in 1736, dancing plotters swished an elephant's tail. The New York confessions seem so formulaic that, if pachyderm tusks and tails were plausibly to be had on the banks of the Hudson, they might have made an appearance in John Hughson's tavern, and in Daniel Horsmanden's *Journal.*

THAT SAID, there's no need to travel a thousand miles and more from Manhattan to places as far away as Barbados and Antigua to find disorderly men drinking, feasting, dancing, crowning kings, and plotting to overthrow the government. New York's slave plot bore a striking resemblance not only to earlier well-publicized Caribbean slave rebellions but also to what went on in New York's own fashionable gentlemen's clubs, just blocks away from John Hughson's house.

"New-York is one of the most social places on the continent," wrote William Smith, Jr., in his 1757 *History of the Province of New York;* "the men collect themselves into weekly evening clubs."[5] (Smith, Jr., was the son of the William Smith who prosecuted slaves in 1741.) By the early eighteenth century, club life was the central social activity of urban gentlemen. "By *Clubs* I mean those societies, which generally meet of an evening, either at some tavern or private house, to converse, or look at one another, smoke a pipe, drink a toast, be politic or dull, lively or frolicksome, to philosophize or triffle, argue or debate, talk over Religion, News, Scandal or bawdy, or spend the time in any other Sort of Clubbical amusement," wrote the physician Alexander Hamilton in his "History of the Ancient and Honorable Tuesday Club," a club he had founded in Annapolis in 1745. "The main Intent and purpose of the meeting of these Clubs, was to drink and be merry, and among them all, it was hail fellow, well met." At "Royalist Clubs," whoever could drink the most was crowned king, and held "an absolute power to command any of his Subjects, to drink as often and as much as he pleased," although, as Hamilton wryly noted, "the Reigns of these monarchs were Commonly very short, for, they might perhaps hold up an hour or two, and then be fairly knocked under the table."[6]

When Hamilton visited New York in 1744, he dined with Daniel Horsmanden and the Chief Justice of the Supreme Court, James DeLancey, and other members of the Hungarian Club, which met at Robert Todd's tavern on Broad Street, "next Door to the Coffee-house." "There was nothing talked of but ladys and lovers, and a good deal of polite smutt," Hamilton wrote in his diary after an evening at Todd's at which two toasts were raised, "the first was to our dear selves, and the tenour of the other was my own health," leading Hamilton to dub Todd's place "the Selfish Club."[7]

Gentlemen joining clubs had first to be initiated. After nightfall, they were taken into a private room, asked a series of questions, and required to write their names in the book of rules. Freemasons, a mystical gentlemen's club whose first New York lodge was founded in 1737, required initiates to "kiss the book" to swear to secrecy. At Hamilton's own club, in Annapolis, a club rule prohibited talk of politics, and if anyone dared raise a political topic, every man in the room was supposed to laugh "in order to divert the discourse."[8] But such was far from the case in New York, where even the taverns were divided along party lines. At Todd's, Horsmanden, De-Lancey, and other Court Party members convened meetings of the Governor's Council. One block east, at the Black Horse Tavern on Smith Street, the General Assembly, dominated by the Country Party, held committee meetings, and it was there that James Alexander and his allies had plotted a strategy to remove Governor William Cosby from power. (Not for nothing was Zenger's printshop just across the street, "opposite to the Sign of the Black Horse.") In New York's fashionable taverns, men who dared to speak of politics were never laughed into silence.

DRINKING, FEASTING, kissing a book, swearing an oath, crowning a king, holding meetings, talking of politics, plotting a strategy. It was all uncannily like what Bastian said happened by the warm fire at Hughson's tavern in the hard winter of 1741, when snow blanketed the city. Except that at Hughson's, all the roles were perversely reversed. In a winter blighted by famine, black men feasted on veal and goose, as if they were gentlemen; they pledged themselves to a secret society, as if they were Freemasons; they plotted to appoint a new governor, as if they were party politicians; all the while flirting with young white women who laid a tablecloth before them and served them meat and poured them drinks. What Bastian and every man who confessed described was a world turned upside down. A world where whites served blacks, the vulgar affected refinement, and slaves would be free.

Maybe what looked to white New Yorkers like an "unparallel'd Hellish Plot" was in fact play, a topsy-turvy parody of gentlemen's clubs and politicians and Freemasons so insulting and unsettling to whites, still reeling from their own experiment in political opposition, that they mistook it for rebellion. Or maybe it really was a rebellion, inspired in part by all the talk of liberty in the city's newspapers and on the streets. Or maybe there never were any meetings at Hughson's and the whole plot was merely the awful product of Daniel Horsmanden's anguished imagination.

Maybe. But the truth can only be found in telling the story from the beginning, since what is wit and what is not cannot be discerned at a distance. Meanwhile, it is worth remembering that although Horsmanden easily saw the political dimensions of the feast at John Hughson's house—he called the slave conspirators "infernal Politicians"—the humor was lost on him. More, it troubled him. It bothered him so much that he was at pains to keep it out of the official proceedings. One of only a handful of lines Horsmanden expurgated when he copied the manuscript confessions for publication were the very last words uttered by Cato, owned by John Shurmur: if asked about the plot, the conspirators were to say "they were only Joking."[9] And out of all the slaves Horsmanden interrogated in 1741, no one vexed him so much as a man named Othello, owned by Chief Justice James DeLancey. When told about the plot and asked to join, Othello said he would, "and laughed." What was so funny?

CHAPTER ONE

Ice

A FTER TEN FEET OF SNOW over Christmas, the skies cleared in January. In the brightening sun, poor widows and orphaned children hobbled through the snow to a house on Smith Street, across from the Black Horse Tavern, where a charity promised "To Feed the HUNGRY & Cloath the NAKED," or at least those "in Real Need of Relief." But in February, the fierce weather returned. "We have now here a second Winter more Severe than it was some Weeks past," Zenger's *Weekly Journal* reported on February 2, the feast of Candlemas. "The Navigation of our River is again stopp'd by the Ice, and the poor in great want of Wood." At Peter DeLancey's farm outside the city, his "Spanish Negro" Antonio de St. Bendito, whose "Feet were frozen after the first great Snow," was still unable to walk. In the city, coals were passed out to the poor to help heat their humble homes. At John Hughson's tavern, his Irish servant girl, Mary Burton, dressed herself "in Man's Cloaths, put on Boots, and went with him in his Sleigh in the deep Snows of the Commons, to help him fetch Firewood for his Family." At David Machado's house, in the East Ward, his black slave Diana, driven to desperation by the ferocity of the cold and by the hopelessness of bondage, "*took her own young Child from her Breast, and laid it in the Cold, that it froze to Death.*"

The first week of February, New Yorkers stared helplessly from piers along the East River as a boat was "taken by a large Cake of Ice in our Harbour, and carried by it through the Narrows, and out of sight." Watchers wondered, but could not discover, what happened to the people on board. Six more ships lay frozen in Long Island Sound, and another, sails set, crashed against the ice, abandoned. Meanwhile, from Charleston, South Carolina, came the shocking news that slaves had nearly destroyed that city, burning three hundred houses to the ground. But this turned out to have been only a rumor. On February 9, Zenger printed a quiet retraction: "The report of the Negroes rising was groundless."[1]

Even while the weather worsened, there were still city pleasures to be had. "ON *Thursday*, Feb. the 12th at the new Theatre in the Broad Way will be presented a Comedy call'd the Beaux Stratagem," announced a back-page ad in the *New-York Weekly Journal*, in the hard winter of 1741. Tickets for a box: 5 shillings; for the pit: 2 shillings and 6 pence.[2]

For those who ventured out by the light of lanterns to attend the New York debut of George Farquhar's late Restoration comedy, it was a cold walk down "the Broad Way," a wide, straight street, paved with cobbles, slick with snow, and thickly canopied with the overburdened, icy branches of the beech and locust trees that lined it. The theatre lay just across from the Bowling Green, a triangle of land at the wide base of Broadway fenced in in 1734 "for the Beauty & Ornament of the Said Street as well as for the Recreation & delight of the Inhabitants."[3]

An evening at the theatre must have been delightful distraction for those who could scare up the shillings, and whose boots were warm enough to keep frostbite at bay. *The Beaux' Stratagem*, first staged in London in 1707, was not only George Farquhar's best play but also the most successful comedy of the age. From its debut to the close of the eighteenth century, it was performed in London during every season but one; and in the 1730s alone, it was staged over a hundred times.[4]

The appeal of *The Beaux' Stratagem* to eighteenth-century audiences lay chiefly in its dizzying reversal of roles and fortunes. The play tells the tale of "two gentlemen of broken fortunes," Aimwell and Archer, on a trip to the town of Lichfield. Having spent their small inheritances on the pleasures of London, the two friends travel from town to town, each taking a turn at pretending to be his companion's servant in order to help his "master" impress and seduce gullible country women. In Lichfield, the ruse works well until Aimwell falls in love with Dorinda, the wealthy daughter of Lady Bountiful, and Archer is taken with Dorinda's married sister-in-law, Mrs. Sullen. Intrigues abound, as Aimwell decides to pass himself off as his elder brother, a viscount, in hopes of securing Dorinda's hand, while a host of still sillier characters—a dishonest innkeeper, Bonniface, and his clever daughter, Cherry; Lady Bountiful's dim-witted son, Squire Sullen; Sullen's dunderheaded servant, Scrub; an amorous French count; a nefarious French priest; and a gang of particularly feckless robbers—pursue their own schemes, stage their own impostures, and plot their own plots, their *beaux' stratagem*, leading Archer to conclude at the end of Act II, "We're like to have as many adventures in our inn as Don Quixote had in his."

At the New Theatre on Broadway, New York's gentry—merchants, bureaucrats, lawyers, and naval officers—paid for the box seats. Everyone else—servants, artisans, sailors, soldiers, and a handful of free blacks—sat in the pit. Joe, the slave of dancing master Henry Holt, probably worked backstage. James Alexander, a Freemason, may have walked down the aisle in procession with his brother lodge members, to sit together in a row, as Masons liked to do. Attorney Joseph Murray, an avid collector of English drama who happened to live more or less across the street from the theatre, must surely have attended with his wife, Grace, daughter of the former governor, their clothes for the evening laid out, perhaps, by their house-keeper, Mrs. Dimmock; their handsome house's front steps swept clean of flurrying snow by one of the Murrays' slaves: Jack, Congo, Dido, Adam, or Caesar. Perhaps Cuba, one of attorney John Chambers's slaves, entered the theatre quietly, before the curtain rose, to place a warming pan beneath the skirt of her mistress, Chambers's wife, Anna.[5]

The playhouse on Broadway had much to offer in the way of conviviality, but the production on the night of the twelfth was not particularly polished; eighteenth-century New York, like the rest of the colonies, was a theatrical backwater. A 1709 decree by the Governor's Council had forbidden "play acting and prize-fighting," and the city's first recorded production did not take place until 1732, when another of Farquhar's comedies, *The Recruiting Officer*, was performed, with "the Part of *Worthy* acted by the ingenious Mr. Thomas Hearly," the mayor's barber and periwig maker. Nearly a decade later, the hairdressing thespian was no longer available. In 1741, for the New York debut of *The Beaux' Stratagem*, the part of Aimwell was "perform'd by a Person who never appear'd on any Stage before."[6]

Still, the crowd, coming in from the cold, must have relished Farquhar's comedy, at once a pretzel of plot twists, a farce of love and deceit (and of the deceitfulness of lovers), a slightly bawdy parody of eighteenth-century courtship, and a rather bold critique of marriage. In Act IV, after having been wooed by Aimwell and Archer, Dorinda and Mrs. Sullen compare their suitors:

Dor: . . . my lover was upon his knees to me.
Mrs. Sul: And mine was upon his tiptoes to me.
Dor: Mine vowed to die for me.
Mrs. Sul: Mine swore to die with me.
Dor: Mine spoke the softest moving things.
Mrs. Sul: Mine had his moving things too.
Dor: Mine kissed my hand ten thousand times.

MRS. SUL: Mine has all that pleasure to come.
DOR: Mine offered marriage.
MRS. SUL: O Lard! d'ye call that a moving thing?

If Daniel Horsmanden attended the New Theatre on the night of February 12, he would have seen much that was familiar, uncomfortably familiar, in Aimwell and Archer, two men on the make, willing to say anything and to pass themselves off as wealthier than they were, plotting to marry rich women. Horsmanden was born in England in 1694, the eldest son of the rector of All Saints Church, in Purleigh, Essex. As a young man, he declined to inherit his father's position and determined instead on a legal career. In his twenties, while studying law in London, Horsmanden pursued his own *beaux' stratagem* on a trip to the fashionable resort town of Tunbridge Wells with his cousin, the Virginian William Byrd II, a widower in his forties who was desperately seeking a marriage alliance that might rescue him from debt. In Tunbridge Wells, Horsmanden courted "Miss B-n-y." Byrd, having recently failed to win the hand of Miss Mary Smith (in spite of boasting of his Virginia estate of 43,000 acres and 220 slaves), scouted about for another suitable wife while composing *Tunbrigalia*, a book of poems celebrating the charms of several pretty Englishwomen of his close acquaintance, including Horsmanden's older sisters, Susanna (or "Suky") and Ursula (delightfully known as "Nutty Horsmanden"):

> Thrice happy Wells! where Beauty's in such store,
> When could'st thou boast an *Horsmanden*, a *Hoar*,
> A *Borrel, Lyndsey, Searle*, and Thousands more?

William Byrd fancied himself a wit: after he and Horsmanden returned to London, Byrd wrote a love letter for his tongue-tied cousin Daniel. When Horsmanden told Byrd he "was going to Tunbridge again to endeavor to get Miss B-n-y," Byrd "lent him thirty guineas for his expedition." But Byrd's pen and pocketbook failed to win Horsmanden his suit. The mysterious Miss B-n-y turned him down.

In the 1710s, Horsmanden and Byrd dined together, drank together, attended the theatre together, and spent endless hours gossiping in London taverns and coffeehouses. And they went whoring together, as is made abundantly clear in Byrd's secret diary (written in an obscure shorthand and kept under lock and key), in entries like the one from June 26, 1718:

"After dinner I put some things in order and then took a nap till 5 o'clock, when Daniel Horsmanden came and we went to the park, where we had appointed to meet some ladies but they failed. Then we went to Spring Gardens where we picked up two women and carried them into the arbor and ate some cold veal and about 10 o'clock we carried them to the bagnio, where we bathed and lay with them all night and I rogered mine twice and slept pretty well, but neglected my prayers."[7]

William Byrd neglected his prayers more than once; he was a shattered man, compulsively rogering whores. During these painful, dissolute years of Byrd's life, young Daniel Horsmanden was his boon companion. By the diary's end, it's difficult not to raise an eyebrow at the homonym in *Tunbrigalia,* "When could'st thou boast an *Horsmanden,* a *Hoar . . . ?*"[8]

Byrd, for all his sexual bravado, was mortified by his dependence on cheap prostitutes. He once wrote of himself, "The struggle between the Senate and the Plebeans in the Roman Commonwealth, or betweext the King and the Parliament in England, was never half so violent as the Civil war between this Hero's Principles and his Inclinations." Visiting prostitutes gave Byrd nightmares. In September 1719 he confided in his diary, "Daniel Horsmanden came again and we went to visit a whore but she was from home. . . . I dreamed I caused a coffin to be made for me to bury myself in but I changed my mind." What gave Byrd nightmares made Horsmanden sick. Six weeks after his first visit to a prostitute, the young law student was confined to his lodgings with "a sore leg." After another episode, he "had a swelled face."[9] The "leg" might have been a euphemism: Horsmanden may have contracted syphilis, whose symptoms during the first two years after exposure include joint pain and markedly swollen glands—the "swelled face." In any event, Horsmanden's own rather tortured relationship with prostitutes, whom he tried in vain to give up, might explain why he didn't marry until 1747, at the age of fifty-three, and never fathered any children.

In 1720, the year after William Byrd left England for Virginia, Horsmanden lost his fortune, what little was left of his inheritance, in the South Sea Bubble. It was an awful blow. He continued to study at the Inns of Court but failed to earn much of a living or to recover his considerable South Sea losses by practicing law. He was broke. Eventually, as Horsmanden later explained, "I was Oblig'd to leave England."[10]

In 1729, Horsmanden bought a book entitled *A New Survey of the Globe,* by Thomas Templeman. Templeman, true to an Englishman's sense of geography, reported only two kinds of information in his curious book:

Southwest Prospect of New York, 1756. Collection of The New-York
Historical Society.

the size of landmasses and the distance of every important city in the world from London. Horsmanden, penniless and aimless, made his own survey of the globe, attempting to determine in what direction to head. He studied Templeman's figures closely. Finally, he decided to sail for Virginia, where his cousin William Byrd was a member of the Governor's Council.

But Horsmanden failed in Virginia, too. He was unable to gain admission to the bar, and he left after less than two years.[11] By 1731, Daniel Horsmanden was on his way to New York City. Miles from London: 3,471.

"HAVE I BEEN traversing the Ocean for so many weeks, to be sett down again in the country I quitted?" wondered another Englishman when he arrived in New York. "This cannot be a new town, in a new world, for such must be attended with many new objects, new faces, new manners, new customs, but here I can find nothing different from what I have quitted." More than three thousand miles from London, New York struck English visitors as uncannily familiar. "The dress and external appearance of the people is the same. The houses are in the stile we are accustomed to; within doors the furniture is all English or made after English fashions. The mode of living is the same." One visitor was flustered: "Where then shall I find any difference?" He found only one: "the greater number of the Blacks."[12]

There was, of course, another difference. Compared to London, New York was no city at all. It was only a mile long and half a mile wide. In population, New York in 1741 was second only to Boston among colonial cities (and neck and neck with Philadelphia), but against London it was a hamlet. By Thomas Templeman's reckoning, "London contains about 105,000 Houses, 840,000 Souls." In 1741, New York boasted more like 1,500 houses and 10,000 souls.[13] But nearly 2,000 were the souls of black folk, and their numbers almost always grabbed travelers' attention. (There were probably only about 15,000 blacks in eighteenth-century London, less than 2 percent of the population, compared to New York's 20 percent.)

Despite how almost entirely English the city may have at first appeared, New York was a jumble of cultures, languages, and religions. By 1731, it even had its own synagogue, the first in Britain's colonies. Peopled with Dutch, English, Welsh, Irish, Scots, and German settlers, French Huguenots, Portuguese Jews, and African slaves and "Spanish Negroes," New York was a frenzied, factious place. "The inhabitants of New York," a visiting English vicar observed, were more than half of them Dutch and therefore "habitually frugal, industrious, and parsimonious," but the rest were of so many "different nations, different languages, and different religions, it is almost impossible to give them any precise or determinate character."[14]

The Dutch had settled Manhattan in 1626; in 1664, the English took possession, peacefully, of a motley city. "Our chiefest unhappiness here is too great a mixture of Nations, & English ye least part," one Englishman complained in 1692.[15] While the Dutch retained considerable political influence for decades, anglicization proceeded swiftly. By 1730, just under 40 percent of the city's white population was Dutch, 8 percent French, 2 percent Jewish, and 1 percent German. Nearly 50 percent of the city's whites were British, their origins recorded in the names they gave to their chattel slaves: among the black men suspected of conspiracy in 1741 were Scotland, Windsor, Sterling, London, York, Galloway, Cambridge, Warwick, Sussex, Worcester, Hereford, Dublin, and Dundee.

Under the terms of its 1731 charter, the city of New York was divided into seven wards, unevenly populated: the fashionable and densely settled Dock, South, and East wards, along the bustling East River waterfront; the less well populated and less posh North and Montgomerie wards; the remote and isolated West Ward, along the Hudson River, where John Hughson kept his tavern; and the quite rural Outward of rolling farmlands to the northeast, divided into the Bowery and Harlem. Every January, ward tax collectors estimated the value of real and personal estates. In the well-heeled East Ward, where the average tax assessment was £26, blacks comprised 25 percent of the population; in the poorer Montgomerie Ward, where the average tax assessment was £10, blacks made up just 13 percent of the population. The richest New Yorkers, in short, owned the most slaves.[16]

"The city of New-York consists principally of merchants, shopkeepers, and tradesman," wrote William Smith, Jr., in 1757. City life was dominated by the port's busy trade: at the height of the shipping season, when masts rose up in the harbor like a forest of trees, the ceaseless rumble of barrels pushed over cobblestones from slips along the water was deafening. Compared to other American cities, New York had a certain buzz. "I found this city less in extent but, by the stirr and frequency upon the streets, more populous than Philadelphia," wrote Dr. Alexander Hamilton. But much of the city, for all its buzz, still had the feel of the frontier; the year Horsmanden arrived, a panther was killed in the street.

"With respect to riches, there is not so great an inequality amongst us, as is common in Boston and some other places," Smith, Jr., boasted. But there were still paupers begging on the streets, starving families sheltered in the Poorhouse just beyond the Common, and debtors imprisoned in the garret of City Hall. And New Yorkers who were as debauched as Daniel Horsmanden had been in his youth could find whores—"a good choice of pritty lasses among them, both Dutch and English"—at the Half Moon Battery after sunset. In 1734, the wealthiest 10 percent of taxpaying New Yorkers owned 39 percent of the city's taxable property, while the poorest 30 percent owned only 7 percent. But these figures don't count households too poor to be included on the tax rolls, nor do they include slaves, who owned less than nothing. When Smith talked about the slight "inequality amongst us," he meant among whites. Poor whites and slaves disagreed. The Irish prostitute Peggy Kerry said the goal of the plot hatched in 1741 was "*to murder* every one that had Money." A slave named Cuffee said much the same thing. "A great many People had too much, and others too little," complained Cuffee, whose master, Adolph Philipse, the seventy-six-year-old former Speaker of the provincial Assembly, kept a house in the city, where Cuffee lived, and also a vast estate in Westchester, Philipsburg Manor, where he kept twenty-seven slaves.[17]

The Dutch began importing Africans to New York in the 1620s, mostly men and women from West and Central Africa they called "Angolans," or sometimes "Congos," farmers from the Kikongo-speaking Kingdom of

Kongo and the Kimbundu-speaking Ndongo. Many of these people had first been taken captive during civil wars, both on the coast and in the African interior. After capture, they were sold to coastal Portuguese traders and seized by the Dutch when they pirated Portuguese trading vessels. In 1638, the Dutch began buying Africans directly; by the mid-seventeenth century, under the auspices of the Dutch West India Company, they conducted an extensive coastal slave trade, having captured several principal Portuguese trading forts. Still, the men and women they brought to New Amsterdam, many of whom spoke Portuguese as well as one or more African languages, bore names that bespoke their origins: Simon Congo, Paulo d'Angola, Anthony Portuguese.[18]

After the English took possession and renamed New York in 1664, they continued the Dutch policy of importing Africans as a source of cheap labor, but they turned, generally, to the Upper Guinea Coast, where the Royal African Company traded. "I should advise the sending for negros to Guinea," the governor of New York wrote to the Lords of Trade in 1699, "I can cloath and feed 'em very comfortably for 9*d.* a piece pr. day sterling money, which is 3*d.* pr. day lesse than I require for the soldiers." Before 1741, the English imported about one hundred and fifty slaves each year. It was cheaper for New York slave traders to import directly from Africa; buyers in New York paid customs duties of only 40 shillings "For every Negro and other Slave, of 4 years old, and upwards, imported directly from *Africa*," compared to £4 (or 80 shillings) for those "From all other Places." Despite this discount, less than 30 percent of slaves imported to New York before 1741 came directly from Africa, while 65 percent came from the English sugar islands, mainly Barbados and Antigua and above all Jamaica, which supplied 30 percent of the city's slaves. (These places, too, became names: in the 1730s and '40s, black men named Jamaica and Barbados walked the streets of New York.)

Slaves came to New York in very small numbers, just a handful on any given ship, almost always on the return leg of voyages made by New York–based trading vessels. New York merchants exported grain and lumber to the Caribbean in exchange for sugar and sometimes slaves. Although Manhattan merchants preferred to be paid in bills of exchange, their West Indian trading partners preferred to pay in goods, and were especially likely to use the opportunity to rid themselves of unwanted slaves by sending them to New York. These unwanted slaves were either notoriously rebellious, or too sick or old to bear the backbreaking work of sugar cultivation. New York merchants, faced with slaves that were too expensive to re-export, but having, in the city, little use for their labor, often sold them to farmers in the countryside. A 1732 law decreed that any New Yorker who imported more than one slave ("to attend on their Person") was required to pay the import duty; many merchants, having paid the duty, decided to keep a handful of slaves with them in the city in order to realize a profit by hiring them out, by the day, to fellow New Yorkers needing workers on the docks or on building projects.[19]

Although, under the English, New York's slaves generally came from the Caribbean, many were themselves new arrivals from the Akan-speaking region of what is now Ghana. The English usually called these Akan speakers "Coromantees." A few retained Akan "day names," given to mark the day of the week on which they were born: Quash (Kwesi, or Sunday), Cudjoe (Kwodwo, Monday), Quack (Kwedu, Wednesday), Cuffee (Kofi, Friday), and Quanimo (Kwame, Saturday). But just as often these names were anglicized: Cudjoe became Joe, Quack Jack. And many other African names, having no easily pronounceable English equivalent, did not survive at all.[20] One man arrested in 1741 was named, simply, Africa.

In the Caribbean, Africans were "seasoned": exposed to the plague of diseases, and the sheer exhaustion, malnutrition, and despair that confronted them on sugar plantations. For every one hundred Africans seized in the African interior, only about sixty-four survived the journey to the coast and only about forty-eight or forty-nine made it across the Atlantic's Middle Passage to arrive in the New World. Of those few, only between twenty-eight and thirty were still alive after a three- to four-year period of "seasoning." Most of the West and Central Africans in early eighteenth-century New York had witnessed and endured extraordinary suffering. In the New World, faced with catastrophic mortality and profoundly disorienting separation from family and community, they forged new bonds that drew on linguistic and cultural similarities, and even on shared military experience (many Coromantees had been soldiers). While the Africans who ended up in New York came from dozens of independent states, Coromantees shared a common language and Angolans a broadly similar cultural background. In the New World, these bonds could transcend political divisions that had mattered more in Africa. Meanwhile, the very endurance of seasoned slaves in the face of demographic devastation only increased their value: on the New York slave market, having survived smallpox was a particular selling point, frequently mentioned in advertisements of slaves for sale, as in that for "a Young Negro Woman, about 20 Year old" who "had the small Pox in *Barbados* when a Child."[21]

In London, Daniel Horsmanden had lived in a world of ranks, ranks of title, ranks of learning, ranks of estate. But the chief division in that world marked the line between men of property and propertyless men. There were, of course, the miserably destitute, but even these souls owned at least their selves or, if they were servants, they expected to own their labor when their indentures expired. New York, like all slave societies, was different. "It rather hurts a European eye to see so many negro slaves upon the streets," one Scottish traveler complained.[22] In New York, Horsmanden found an entire class of people who had not even the property of their own flesh, and never would. They served, instead, as markers of other men's wealth. Even their smallpox scars were counted by the shilling. Joseph Murray outfitted his liveried slave Adam with silver-buckled shoes. And four men arrested in the 1741 conspiracy—two of whom were hanged— had been named by their owners "Fortune."

"EVERY MAN of industry and integrity has it in his power to live well," William Smith, Jr., wrote, speaking of white, not black, New Yorkers, "and many are the instances of persons, who came here distressed by their poverty, who now enjoy easy and plentiful fortunes." In 1732, Daniel Horsmanden, thirty-eight and still a bachelor, landed in the city with very little in his pocket, but he came with credentials, and with William Byrd's recommendation for an appointment in the administration of the incoming governor, William Cosby, who had succeeded John Montgomerie. (Montgomerie died of an "Appolecktick fit" in the summer of 1731.) Almost as soon as Horsmanden arrived he was admitted to the bar, a distinction he had failed to achieve in either Virginia or London, and one which he greeted with pomp: in March 1732, Horsmanden contributed to "a good part of the Discourse of the toun" when he insisted on wearing his formal lawyer's "barr gown," an ostentation never before seen in New York.[23]

On the day after William Cosby's own arrival in the city the following August, his first public act was to have a man whipped for not moving his wagon out of the way of the governor's coach quickly enough. His second move was no less audacious: Cosby attempted to claim half the salary of his predecessor, the Dutch merchant Rip Van Dam, who had served as interim governor in the thirteen months between Montgomerie's death and Cosby's arrival. Cosby appointed Horsmanden as one of his attorneys in this suit. When the learned sixty-two-year-old Chief Justice Lewis Morris ruled against him, Cosby summarily dismissed Morris from the bench, promoting thirty-year-old James DeLancey to his position. Meanwhile, Cosby recommended Horsmanden for a position on his Royal Council—a twelve-man appointed body that served at once as a governor's cabinet and the upper house of the provincial legislature—and tried to remove James Alexander, Morris's political ally. Alexander was "very unfit" for the Council, Cosby wrote to his superiors, the Lords of Trade in London, declaring that Alexander was "stuff'd with such a train of tricks and oppressions to gross for Your Lordships to hear." (When the governor's request was refused, he simply stopped sharing the Council's meeting times with both Alexander and Van Dam, who also served on the Council.) Of Cosby's flurry of appointments and dismissals Alexander wrote, "The Promoters of Justice & humanity are banish'd far from such an Administration and in their Room flattering Parasites Indigent wretches courting power & fit for the worst purposes are thrown into the Offices of power and trust."[24]

New York, like most American colonies, had suffered under corrupt governors before. Governors "do not come here to take the air," one New Yorker remarked; instead, they come "either to repair a shattered fortune, or acquire an Estate." Almost from its birth, New York had been notoriously factious, as clusters of wealthy men, often connected by family ties, had rallied themselves both for and against earlier governors, forming what some called "factions" and others "parties." In late seventeenth- and eighteenth-century political thought, the distinction between "faction" and "party" was slight. Viscount Bolingbroke wrote that "The creeds of parties vary like those of sects; but all Factions have the same motive, which never implies more or less than a lust of dominion." "Faction" was a more despicable form of "party," but both implied a potentially violent challenge to the existing government, and thus overlapped with "sedition" and "treason." In England, where there were Tories and Whigs, competing factions were sometimes called "parties": in New York, those in power were typically called the "Court Party," those not in power the "Country Party."[25]

"It is the Governour's desire to be of No Party," Cosby's few defenders insisted. But William Cosby fueled partisan passion like no other governor before him: "No Man was ever so universally hated as he is," Morris remarked. "We have a Perfect war here," New Yorker Abigail Franks wrote to her son in London in 1733; or, as Daniel Horsmanden put it a few months later, "We are in the midst of Party flames." With Cosby in the Governor's Mansion, New York politics moved beyond the conventional wisdom of the perils of party, advancing the innovative argument that parties were a necessary evil and, even more radically, that they were a necessary good, preserving not tyranny but liberty. By 1734 the view, almost unheard of in England, that parties might be *necessary* for liberty, was printed in the pages of the *New York Gazette:*

> A free Government cannot but be subject to *Parties, Cabals,* and *Intrigues:* This perhaps may be form'd into an Objection against free Governments by the Advocates for absolute Power, but for that Reason it is of no Weight . . . some Opposition, tho' it proceed not entirely from a public Spirit, is not only necessary in free Government, but of great Service to the Public. Parties are a check upon one another, and by keeping the Ambition of one another within Bounds, serve to maintain the public Liberty. Opposition is the Life and Soul of public Zeal, which without it would flag, and decay for want of an Opportunity to exert itself. It rouses and animates the Heart, raises Emulation, quickens and improves the Capacity, gives Birth often to national Integrity, and instead of clogging, regulates and keeps in their just and proper Motion the Wheels of Government.[26]

In the 1730s, newly willing to tolerate and even to celebrate parties, New Yorkers consolidated their two political parties through meetings held at separate city taverns. The Country Party men met at the Black Horse Tavern at the south corner of Smith and Garden streets, to plot against William Cosby, while Court Party men gathered at Robert Todd's tavern on Broad Street, two doors north of the Exchange Coffeehouse on Broad, between Water and Pearl streets, to toast His Excellency. In October 1735, on the occasion of Cosby's return from a trip to Albany, his supporters held "a very splendid Entertainment" for him at Todd's, complete with an illumination display. Not to be outdone, Cosby's opponents, the very next night, held a ball at the Black Horse for Rip Van Dam, with as much elegant food, as many toasts, and just as many lanterns. In January 1736, the two taverns again held rival balls, this time marking the Prince of Wales's birthday: at Todd's on Monday, at the Black Horse on Tuesday. One weary New Yorker scoffed, "They are happy that have the least to doe on either side."[27]

INTO THIS MAELSTROM came Daniel Horsmanden, who quickly became a target for partisan attacks. Rip Van Dam included Horsmanden's appointment as Article 14 on a list of grievances against Cosby, challenging

Horsmanden's appointment on the grounds that he was "a Man of no visible estate in this Province and in necessitous circumstances." Lewis Morris understood all too well that Van Dam's complaint against Horsmanden's appointment "lookes like pique," but it was nonetheless legitimate, since the law required that Council members be "not necessitous people or much in debt."[28] And Daniel Horsmanden was a man who, until he married a wealthy widow in 1747, was hardly ever "not necessitous."

Horsmanden arrived in New York decidedly short of cash. Not long after landing in the city, he had attended a public auction of the estate of the governor whom Cosby had been sent to replace, John Montgomerie. For £6, Horsmanden outfitted himself with gentlemanly attire: Montgomerie's sword belt, and three new ruffled shirts, which he bought on credit. Unlike his peers, Horsmanden could ill afford to buy any of the late governor's luxurious household goods, his card tables, beaver hats, parrot cages, silver pistols, feather bolsters, and over 2,000 gallons of Madeira. (Montgomerie had been a wealthy man; as governor of New York, he held the most lucrative governorship in the colonies, a position full of perks; simply for the honorific title of commander of Fort George, he pocketed £2,600 a year.)[29] James Alexander spent £70 on Montgomerie's wine, cloth, and plateware, while James DeLancey spent more than £140 on curtains, bed lace, and leather chairs. (DeLancey, who had lent the city the £1,000 necessary to draw up the new city charter in 1731, was possibly the wealthiest man in the colonies.) Of these housewares, Horsmanden bought not so much as a spoon.

Slaves were sold at the Montgomerie auction, too. Cosby himself dominated the bidding on Montgomerie's slaves, carrying away Betty for £56, Jenny, £30, and "2 Cradles for Negroes," while DeLancey's brother-in-law, Captain Peter Warren, won the bid for "a Negro Boy Named Othello" at £36.[30] Horsmanden could hardly have afforded one.

From Montgomerie's library Horsmanden did buy a handful of law books, including John Calvin's *Lexicon Juridicum,* a history of Japan, and Samuel Purchas's *Pilgrimage.* But he ruefully passed over the governor's impressive collection of history and belles lettres: Defoe and Plutarch, Swift and Shakespeare, Hobbes and Machiavelli, Pope and Milton, Homer and Plato. Joseph Murray bought volume after volume of plays and poetry and fiction. James DeLancey bought a stack of law books and a copy of James Harrington's utopia, *The Commonwealth of Oceana.* The young lawyer John Chambers bought *Paradise Lost, Paradise Regain'd,* and a copy of *Cato's Letters*—the collected essays of the English political theorists John Trenchard and Thomas Gordon. James Alexander bought more books than anyone else in the city, including *The History of the Art of Print-ing* and John Toland's *The Art of Governing by Partys* (not a how-to-manual but a meditation on the "ill effects of partys on the people in general, the king in particular, and all our foren affairs"). Alexander, a dedicated collector and avid reader, also bought the collected works of Rabelais, the philosophy of Bacon, and dozens more histories, dictionaries, and law books, disappointed only that he had been outbid by his law part-ner, William Smith, for two folio volumes of Cicero (asked to sell them, Smith refused, on the admirable grounds that he "loved Books better than Money"). Alexander hired a cartman to crate and carry his sixty-four titles.[31] Horsmanden stuck his books in a sack and headed home.

To read over Montgomerie's library catalogue is to be reminded that New Yorkers lived in a world of enlightenment, of exuberance in the arts, of confidence in man's capacity to reason the ways of nature and of nature's God, and of ardent embrace of political liberty in the face of tyranny's slav-ery. To read the list of their slaves' names is to place that world of ideas against the reality of human bondage: at Montgomerie's auction, where Shakespeare's *Works* were sold, a young boy named Othello was offered to the highest bidder. And while James Alexander read Julius Caesar, Joseph Murray read Aphra Behn's novel *Oroonoko* about a Coromantee slave rebellion in Dutch Surinam, and John Chambers read *Cato's Letters,* slaves named Caesar and Oroonoko and dozens of Catos walked the streets of New York.

TWO YEARS IN the city failed to improve Daniel Horsmanden's finances. By 1734 he owned a modest house (assessed at £30) in the South Ward, a garden (£20) in the North Ward, and personal property totaling £20. For a gentleman, it wasn't much. Although he had been admitted to the bar, he hadn't found many clients and was "Eclipsed by his Contem-poraries Alexander Murray Smith and Chambers who ingrossed all the Business." To improve his position, Horsmanden actively courted the province's surveyor-general, Cadwallader Colden, in an attempt to secure a land grant through a series of machinations so bold that, while he eventu-ally gained a stake in 6,000 acres near Albany, he almost lost Cosby's favor. By the mid-1730s, Horsmanden had earned a reputation as "a Person unsafe to Converse with." Lewis Morris suspected Horsmanden of falsely reporting to England that he, Morris, "was dead & applying for his place," a charge Horsmanden denied, complaining that the mere suspicion of it had given Morris's son "Such a Spleen against me that nothing less than my Destruction could, I Suppose Satisfy his Resentment."[32] Meanwhile, as a consequence of yet another imprudent investment "as my Ill Stars would have it," as Horsmanden put it, he fell into debt to Morris's son-in-law, Richard Ashfield. "Mr Horsmanden . . . is a Gentleman of breeding and sence," Lewis Morris wrote to the Lords of Trade, "but has no real Estate that is known, & I fear no personal neither, that being all mort-gaged to a gentleman of my acquaintance, and payable this month, which, how he will discharge is a mistery I wish he may be able to discover, he having no means known but his practice to do it, and (tho' a Barister) that is not much."

In 1734, Ashfield sued Horsmanden, demanding payment within twenty-four hours and threatening to sell the books Horsmanden had given him as security. (Ashfield, apparently, loved money better than books.) Cosby intervened, promising to pay Ashfield and sparing Hors-manden the indignity of debtor's prison. The governor's last-minute rescue wasn't as gratifying to his henchman as it might have been; by now Hors-manden had come to agree with Lewis Morris's judgment that Cosby was essentially a "mad man"; even Horsmanden nicknamed his patron "Machiaval."[33]

In 1735, the desperate Daniel Horsmanden did what any Aimwell or Archer might: he courted a wealthy widow. "We have as various reports of your fate with the widdow there, as there are about peace & war in En-gland," his cousin William Byrd wrote to him in early 1736. Byrd tried to lure Horsmanden back to Virginia, since the death of two lawyers there had finally "made room at the bar," but Horsmanden was unreceptive. "All these allurements I laid in your way," Byrd wrote, "but to as little purpose as Peg Smart us'd to spread her charms at Tunbridge."[34] In 1735, Cosby, res-cuing Horsmanden from debt, named him to the powerful and lucrative office of City Recorder. It was no mean clerical job. The Recorder was attorney for the Corporation of the City of New York and the only unelected member of the city's Common Council, second in authority only to the mayor. As the crucial link between the provincial and munici-pal government, the Recorder was, in effect, the governor's man in City Hall.[35] By the time Horsmanden received Byrd's letter, he had far too much at stake in New York to flee to Virginia, and he could ill afford to start again.

IN THE FINAL, romping act of *The Beaux' Stratagem*, the two scheming gentlemen rescue their lovers from a gang of robbers, prove their undying devotion, and reveal their true identities, only to discover that Aimwell's older brother has died, leaving our hero his title—turning him into "Lord Aimwell" after all—and making it possible for him to marry Dorinda. Role reversals that began as impostures turn true. Meanwhile, Lady Bountiful's brother convinces the loathsome Squire Sullen to divorce his delightful, wealthy wife so that she can wed Archer, who, she now realizes, is no footman but a gentleman. All of which leads Archer to muse, not without cause, "This night's adventure has proved strangely lucky to us all."

In the 1730s, Daniel Horsmanden was not nearly so fortunate: no dying brother left him a fortune; no rich widow was willing to marry him. Unlike his chief political rival, James Alexander, Horsmanden found neither love nor fortune in New York. The year Van Dam objected to Horsmanden's appointment to Cosby's Council on the grounds that Horsmanden was "in necessitous circumstances," James Alexander ranked as the wealthiest lawyer and the second wealthiest taxpayer in the city. In 1734, Alexander owned two houses and a stable in the Dock Ward (valued at £265) and a much smaller house (£20) in the East Ward. Many of the province's wealthiest men lived outside the city: Lewis Morris in his manor at his 1,000-acre estate, Morrisania; Cadwallader Colden in his 3,000-acre country seat, Coldengham; Frederick Philipse at Philipsburg Manor. Alexander, unlike these men, was an inveterate urbanite. In 1739 he would build for himself another house in the Dock Ward, on Broad Street, with a garden extending to Jews' Alley (so named because it led to the synagogue), a house "sumptuously furnished" after the finest English fashion: "There was the great dining room and the lesser dining room, the room hung with blue and gold leather, the green and gold room, the little front parlour and the little back parlour and the great tapestry room above stairs; besides red rooms and green rooms and chintz rooms up stairs and down, furnished with damask hangings, costly carpets and buffets set off with massive plate."[36]

James Alexander was a very rich man indeed. Born in Scotland in 1691, he had arrived in New York in 1715, was admitted to the bar in 1720, appointed to the Governor's Council in 1721, and greatly improved his position that same year by marrying the widow Mary Spratt Provost, by whom he had seven children. Mary brought two sons to the marriage, along with her late husband's import business, which she continued to run out of a shop in Alexander's house, even during bouts of illness. "If she is able to crawl she will be in the shop," Alexander once wrote of his wife. During breaks in his own business, Alexander occasionally tended the shop as well. By 1745, his fortune was estimated at £100,000.[37]

James Alexander, *by John Wollaston, c. 1750. Oil on canvas. Courtesy of the Museum of the City of New York.*

Alexander, a stout, rosy-cheeked man with a dimpled chin and a contented smile, was the astute and learned owner of the best library in the province and a founding member of Benjamin Franklin's American Philosophical Society. "In these parts of the World," one contemporary remarked, "few men surpass him either in the Natural sagacity and Strength of his Intellectual powers or in his Literary Acquirements." James Alexander was also a slaveowner. In June 1729, one of Alexander's six slaves, a "Negroe Man named Yaff, about 35 Years old," ran away. In an ad placed in the *New York Gazette,* Alexander offered £4 reward for "whoever takes up the said Negroe, and secures him so that his said Master may have him again." It was a hefty sum—the going rate for runaway slaves was 40 shillings—one that is justified in Alexander's description of Yaff's useful-ness: "He was born in this Country, and reads and writes. He is a sensible cunning Fellow."[38]

Alexander's papers—his letters, account books, receipts, and journals, and even swatches of fabric sold at his wife's shop—are collected at the New York Public Library and the New-York Historical Society, most of them donated by his great-grandson, Lewis Morris Alexander, in 1884. They fill folder after folder, box upon box. Even his great-grandson's name tells a story about the family's history. Against this vast archive stand the 107 words of Alexander's ad for Yaff in the *New York Gazette* on June 23, 1729:

> Run away about the ninth of this Instant June from James Alexan-der of New-York, a Negroe Man named Yaff, about 35 Years old; he formerly belonged to Mr. Trent and before him to Coll. Ingoldsvy; he was seen at Elizabeth-Town after he run away with a gray Coat trimmed with Red, and an old white Fustian Coat: He was born in this Country, and reads and writes. He is a sensible cunning Fellow, and probably has got a pass forged. Whoever takes up the said Negroe, and secures him so that his said Master may have him again, shall have four Pounds Reward, and all reasonable Charges.

But for this brief biography, Yaff might never have entered the historical record at all. He was unusual in this, and in three other respects: he was born in New York, he could read and write, and he ran away.

Most blacks in colonial New York were born someplace else. They bore marks of both the Old World and the New. One 1730 runaway bore them literally: he was "remarkably Scarrified over the Fore head"—with orna-mental African facial scarring, an Old World adornment—and "branded *R N*," for "runaway," upon his shoulder, a New World punishment. (He was also barely clothed, his owner having given him "a Pair of trowsers only.")[39] Even without scars, many African-born New Yorkers were easy to spot: they had teeth chiseled to the shape of a point, or an hourglass—signs of beauty, signs of belonging.

Maybe the two men named "Albany" and the seven men named "York" accused of conspiracy in 1741 were born in the colony, too. But they, like Yaff, were in a distinct minority. New York's black population did not grow by natural increase until the end of the colonial period. Young women, and especially "seasoned" adolescent girls, were highly sought after. In 1737, women of childbearing age constituted 35 percent of the city's black population. But they bore very few children, partly because at least the African-born among them breast-fed their children until age three or four. Most enslaved women were dead by forty, and their mortality rates peaked between the ages of thirty and thirty-four; they died of disease or complications of childbirth, exacerbated by poor nutrition and years of toil. Some were simply driven mad. In 1749, "a Negro Girl of about 15 Years of Age," who "had been for sometime disordered in her Sences," fell or, more likely, jumped "out of a Garret Window three Story, of which unhappy fall she was so Bruised, that she dyed in a few Hours."[40]

The low fertility of their slaves failed to concern their owners. Indeed, on the New York City slave market, female sterility was a selling point: "To Be Sold, a young Wench about 29 years old, that drinks no strong Drink, and gets no Children, a very good Drudge." Infant mortality was high, and infanticide not uncommon. In the hard winter of 1741, Diana put her newborn out to die in the snow. Five years earlier, the *New-York Weekly Journal* printed this chilling news: "Yesterday Morning was found in the Negroes Burial-place, a small Infant in a Wigg Box, and partly buried under-Ground."[41]

Discouraged and even prevented from having children of their own, black women in New York cared for their masters' children. Cadwallader Colden's wife asked him to buy "a negro Girl of about thirteen years old. . . . Chiefly to keep the children." For whites, leaving the care of a black nurse and the company of black children marked a transition out of childhood. Of his eleven-year-old son, Colden wrote his wife: "I hope he no longer looks on himself as a Child & that he'l be ashamed to play about the Doors with the Negro Children."[42]

That young black women looked after white children did not mean they were necessarily beloved or even especially valued. Nowhere is this more brutally illustrated than in a short piece of local news printed on September 12, 1737: "Saturday last a Boy about 14 or 15 years old, in this City was handling a gun, a Negro Girl sitting in the yard, with a Child in her Arms, at the outside of the Window, the Boy, in a jesting manner said, *I'll shoot ye,* and the Gun went off and shot the Negro's Brains out." But, the *Gazette* hastened to add, "the Child in her Arms [was] not hurt." The boy went unpunished.[43]

Those few black children born in New York generally lived with their mothers at least until weaning, and developed strong ties of family and friendship: as an adult, Cuffee (owned by Adolph Philipse) knew both his father and his brother; as a boy, attorney Joseph Murray's slave Adam had played marbles with his friend Quack. But slave childhood was short, especially because New York slaveowners considered separating mothers and children as much a disciplinary as an economic necessity. Selling a thirty-three-year-old woman and one of her children to Barbados in 1717, Cadwallader Colden explained: "I could have sold her here to good advantage but I have several other of her Children which I value & I know if she should stay in this country she would spoil them."[44]

Most New York slaves who ran away went to visit family, to maintain ties their owners hoped to sever. About 10 percent of runaways were literate. Knowing how to write made running away easier: Yaff forged a pass. Other men relied on other guises. One ran off in a soldier's clothing; another wore a wig. But one eighteen-year-old runaway had no hope of disguising himself as a free man: he wore "an Iron Ring about his Neck and one about his Leg, with a Chain from one to the other."[45] How he must have stumbled as he fled.

BEFORE THE CURTAIN fell at the New Theatre on February 12, 1741, there was a dance, of the sort James Alexander carefully recorded in a small notebook he kept to help him remember dance steps, for he and his wife Mary loved to dance.[46] The dance, the "Beaux Stratagem," was, like all English country dances, a coming together, parting, and coming together again of paired couples, assembled in two lines. As it progresses, the couple at the top of the line exchanges places with the couple below, and so on, all the way to the bottom of the line so that, when the music stops, the couple at the top has moved to the bottom. The high become low, the low become high. And back again. In the final scene of *The Beaux' Stratagem*, the lovers, Aimwell and Dorinda, and the divorcing couple, Squire and Mrs. Sullen, glide across the stage, while Archer delivers the play's closing line:

> 'Twould be hard to guess which of these parties is the better pleased, the couple joined, or the couple parted; the one rejoicing in hopes of an untasted happiness, and the other in their deliverance from an experienced misery.

Applause broke out, and the audience stirred, gathering their coats, bracing for the cold walk home through the icy, lantern-lit city.

New Yorkers who watched *The Beaux' Stratagem* that night must have reveled in its celebration of romantic love, and the orderly pairing of couples expressed in this final dance. And if New York's theatregoers were anything like the crowds in London, they relished the comic role reversals, especially that of the gentleman, Archer, posing as footman to his friend Aimwell. It was a difficult part to play well. When David Garrick took up the role in London, Samuel Johnson complained, "The gentleman should break out through the footman, which is not the case as he does it."[47] A role reversal was only funny as *pretense,* not as transformation.

New York's theatregoers also cherished the plots-within-plots. And they must have laughed at one of the funniest scenes in the play, when Scrub, Squire Sullen's stupid servant, pledges to uncover a plot: "Ay, sir, a plot, and a horrible plot. First, it must be a plot because there's a woman in't; secondly, it must be a plot because there's a priest in't; thirdly, it must be a plot because there's French gold in't; and fourthly, it must be a plot, because I don't know what to make on't."

WITHIN DAYS of the debut of *The Beaux' Stratagem,* the "Great Negro Plot" began to unravel: first the gold (actually silver), then the woman, and only much later, months later, the priest.

On Thursday, February 26, a young English sailor named Christopher Wilson, nicknamed "Yorkshire," walked the short distance from his docked ship, a man-of-war called the *Flamborough,* to a shop owned by Robert Hogg. Hogg's shop fronted Broad Street, just next to James Alexander's sumptuously furnished house, but it had a side door that opened onto Jews' Alley, a street known not only for its synagogue but for its "idle Houses," frequented by sailors. Wilson bought some linen and paid with Spanish coins; Hogg's wife made change for him by opening a drawer full of Spanish pieces-of-eight. "She soon reflected that she had done wrong in exposing her Money to an idle Boy in that manner . . . and immediately shut up the Bureau again, and made a Pretense of sending the Money out to a Neighbour's to be weighed."

Rebecca Hogg was prone to hysterics (her husband believed that "a good mowing was a cure for such complaints"), but this time she was wise to be alarmed, although she would have been wiser still to have actually sent the money to her neighbor, Mary Alexander.[48] Christopher Wilson, meanwhile, walked to the outskirts of town to John Hughson's tavern to speak with Hughson and three black men he knew he would find there: Caesar, owned by the baker John Vaarck; Prince, owned by the merchant

John Auboyneau; and Adolph Philipse's Cuffee, a man who spoke English and Spanish, and could read and play the violin. Together, they hatched a plan to rob Hogg's shop.

On Saturday afternoon, Wilson returned to Hogg's to buy rum. While Rebecca Hogg was busy with other customers, Wilson shoved back the bolt on the shop's side door, undetected. Later that night, under cover of darkness, Caesar and Prince slipped in through the unbolted door and stole not only an abundance of coins but also "diverse Pieces of Linnen and other Goods" and "wrought Silver" worth more than £60. Caesar hid the coins in John Hughson's cellar and buried the linen and silver plate under the kitchen floorboards at Vaarck's house.

In the morning, Sunday, Caesar went to Hughson's to see the twenty-one-year-old Irishwoman Peggy Kerry, who only days before had given birth to his child, "a Babe largely partaking of a motley Complexion," as Horsmanden described it. Horsmanden said Kerry "pretended to be married" but was actually "a Person of infamous Character, a notorious Prostitute, and also of the worst Sort, a Prostitute to Negroes." For bearing a bastard, Peggy Kerry, if discovered, risked being sent to the city's Poorhouse—a bleak brick building just north of the Common, crowded with beggars, captured runaways, "unruly and ungovernable Servants and Slaves," and "parents of Bastard Children," and equipped with a whipping post, fetters, and shackles. In 1738, in a summary judgment before a juryless municipal criminal court headed by the mayor and Recorder Daniel Horsmanden, another city prostitute, Mary Lawrence, had been stripped to the waist and received thirty-one lashes at the hands of the public whipper, after which she was sentenced to a year of hard labor at the Poorhouse.[49]

The money Caesar stole may have been meant to help Peggy Kerry avoid this fate. He paid for her lodging and frequently slept with her at Hughson's, climbing in through her window at night. As Peggy had only just delivered, Caesar worried about how she and the baby would fare, and how she could escape the Poorhouse. At Hughson's, he offered Mary Burton "a Piece of Silver, which she supposed was to engage her to look after Peggy Kerry in her lying in," but Burton refused. She would have "look'd after White People's" infants, she told Caesar, but not Peggy's "black Child."

Just before noon, Christopher Wilson returned to the scene of the crime to gossip with Rebecca Hogg. Betraying his comrades, he revealed to her that, earlier that morning, he'd seen just such a collection of coins as the ones she had lost at John Hughson's house in the possession of a soldier named John Gwin. Rebecca Hogg sent for the magistrate, but James Mills, deputy sheriff and jailkeeper, and James Kannady, constable and wigmaker, searched Hughson's house in vain. By nightfall, Mills learned that "John Gwin" was an alias Caesar sometimes used. Mills returned to the tavern and promptly arrested him. On Monday, Mills arrested Prince and brought John Hughson and his wife, Sarah, in for questioning. Sarah carried with her a nursing baby.

Prince and the Hughsons denied everything.

On Tuesday, March 3, sixteen-year-old Mary Burton walked to Ann Kannady's house in the South Ward "to buy a Pound of Candles for her Master." Ann Kannady, like Rebecca Hogg, ran a small shop. She sold Burton the candles and "gave her motherly good Advice," promising her that if she told all, "she would get freed from her Master."

Burton, known for her "warm hasty Spirit," "had a remarkable Glibness of Tongue, and uttered more Words than People of her supposed Education usually do." To Ann Kannady, she dropped vague but ominous hints about a plot. Later that evening, James Mills and Ann and James Kannady went to Hughson's. Burton pulled a silver coin out of her pocket and told them Caesar had given it to her on Sunday morning to buy her silence—or (as was reported in another version of the story) to pay her for caring for Kerry and her newborn.

The next day, Wednesday, March 4, Burton offered her first deposition at City Hall. She talked about the stolen goods. She said nothing about a slave plot. But she did reveal that Caesar "usually slept with the said *Peggy*, which her Master and Mistress knew of." Kerry was arrested but denied any knowledge of the robbery. So did Caesar, although he freely admitted to his relationship with Kerry. Meanwhile, John Hughson dug the coins out of his cellar, turned them in, and confessed to receiving stolen goods, only to refuse to sign his statement when it was read over to him. Instead, he called Burton "a vile, good-for-nothing Girl" who "had been got with Child by her former Master," a charge that was never investigated.

By the end of the day, Rebecca Hogg had her silver and linen back. Mary Burton, who feared "she shou'd be murdered or poisoned by the *Hughsons* and the Negroes," was taken into protective custody and housed with Mills in his lodgings in the garret of City Hall. Caesar and Peggy Kerry were imprisoned in the dungeon below. (Possibly with their baby, who, if it hadn't already died, would have been jailed with its mother. In any event, the baby was never mentioned again.) Prince and John and Sarah Hughson, with her own baby, were released on bail. Cuffee had yet to be accused. What remained unresolved—Burton's fear of being poisoned, her unwillingness to help Kerry during her lying-in, Hughson's calling Burton a "good-for-nothing Girl"—seemed as much a household squabble as a criminal case. A routine trial for burglary was set for the next regularly scheduled meeting of the provincial Supreme Court, the third Tuesday in April.

But before that, the city would begin to burn.

CHAPTER TWO

Fire

S LOWLY, THE HARD WINTER began to melt. A sloop from South
Carolina and a brigantine from Lisbon broke through the ice and
into the harbor. On March 12, the *Royal Ranger,* a sleek ship that had
sailed from Kingston in just four weeks, dropped anchor in New York. Her
captain brought news of a grand fleet of more than thirty ships launched
from Jamaica in January, in the chief engagement of the War of Jenkins's
Ear, the trade war between England and Spain that, the summer before,
had nearly emptied New York of the ablest of its men.

New Yorkers avidly followed news of the war, brought to the city in
salty packets of wax-sealed letters written by homesick soldiers and sailors
to anxious family and friends and delivered by the master of every ship that
docked along the city's wooden piers. James Alexander corresponded with
his stepson, David Provost, a captain in Colonel William Gooch's regiment in Jamaica. James DeLancey awaited letters from his brother-in-law,
New York's most celebrated and daring naval commander, Captain Peter
Warren, who had married DeLancey's sister Susannah in 1731. On March
16, Zenger's *Weekly Journal* reported that Warren, on duty patrolling the
Caribbean, had seized a French ship bound for Cartagena loaded with
flour and iron, in whose hold he found concealed "the *French* contract
for Supplying the *Spaniards,* with Provisions." The document, proof of
French collusion with Spain, seemed to make England's declaring war
with France all but inevitable, although news brought by a ship from London the same week reported that "the talk of a War with *France,* was not
so hot as it had been."[1]

Two days after the *Weekly Journal* reported on Warren's exploits, while
New Yorkers were still busy pondering the latest news of fleets, skirmishes, prizes, and lines of battle on the high seas, the city's fort went up in

flames. Fort George stood on a hill commanding a view of the harbor and the island of Manhattan. It was built as Fort Amsterdam in 1626; after the English took possession in 1664, it had as many names as England had monarchs: Fort James, Fort Anne, and, beginning in 1714, Fort George. Names were about all that England provided, except for soldiers; year after year, the fort suffered for lack of improvements; it was "but a weak place, and badly contrived."[2] In 1735, under pressure to improve the city's defenses, William Cosby had directed the erection of a half-moon-shaped fortified wall along the water, dubbing it "George Augustus' Royal Battery." This, and the fort itself, were all that stood between the city and foreign invaders.

At one o'clock on a gray, Wednesday afternoon, March 18, 1741, a great plume of smoke rose from the roof of Lieutenant Governor George Clarke's mansion, just inside the fort's thick stone walls. Nearly hidden behind the curtain of smoke, flames danced across the cedar-shingled roof while the bells at the fort's chapel and at City Hall, heard throughout the city, sounded the doleful, urgent alarm. But New Yorkers could easily see

View of Fort George with the City of New York from the Southwest, *by J. Carwitham, c. 1740. Collection of The New-York Historical Society.*

that Clarke's mansion would be utterly destroyed long before the stoutest horses hitched to wagons carrying fire engines could pull them two blocks south on Broad Street, then a block west on Beaver, from the engine house near City Hall. While the horses snorted, their steamy breath trailing like ribbon behind them, "great Numbers of People, Gentlemen and others" raced down the icy streets to the patch of snow-covered grass known as the Fort Garden.

Fire was the greatest danger facing an early modern city, as New Yorkers well knew. "Have not we heard of, and many of us seen great Conflagrations in the City of *London*, and other Cities?" a correspondent asked in the *New York Gazette* in 1729. In the Great Fire of London in 1666, more than thirteen thousand buildings were destroyed in five days. Much of Boston burned in 1711. Two thirds of Rennes was ruined in 1720. "Our News-Papers have almost every Month given us Melancholly Accounts of the half, the 3d. or some considerable Parts of large Cities are reduced to Ashes," the *Gazette* reminded New Yorkers. "*Petersburg* and *Copenhagen* are late Instances of this; nor have we forgot the violent Conflagrations at *Boston;* and its to be fear'd our fate may be like others, if some better Oeconomy is not fallen on, to prevent such a Misfortune." In 1729, New York's firefighting had consisted of little more than a poorly enforced bucket law, far less than the measures taken in London and even some colonial cities, as the *Gazette* writer pointed out: "the City of *Philadelphia* (as young as it is) have had two Fire Engines for several years past; and its a Wonder to many that this City should so long neglect the getting of one or more of them."[3]

In 1731, in response to that impassioned plea, New York had passed "A Law for the Better Preventing of Fire," providing for the purchase of two fire engines and a new bucket law: anyone who owned a house with one or two chimneys was required to hang a three-gallon leather bucket just by the front door, labeled with the owner's name; houses with three or more chimneys needed two buckets, bakeries three, breweries six. When a fire alarm was sounded, these buckets were to be thrown into the street, to be picked up by the fastest runners and carried to the scene of the fire, where two lines were formed: one to pass full buckets from a pump, or the river, to the fire, and one to pass the empty buckets back.

On March 18, when the alarm bell rang, buckets were grabbed and tossed, stacked and toted toward the billowing smoke at the southern end of the island. A bucket brigade lined up in the Fort Garden. "There were Rows made of People in the Garden, Negroes as well as white Men, from

Firefighting in New York. Possibly Henry Dawkins, Certificate of the Hand-in-Hand Fire Company, ca. 1753. I. N. Phelps Stokes Collection, Miriam and Ira D. Wallach Division of Art, Prints and Photographs, The New York Public Library, Astor, Lenox and Tilden Foundations.

the Water Side thro' the Sally Port, in order to hand Water along to the Fire," a cordwainer named Isaac Gardner later recalled. Bucket by bucket, they fought the blaze. Meanwhile, soldiers rescued Clarke and his family and dragged his belongings out of the house, placing upturned chairs and charred tables and broken plates of china on the snow, a ghastly winter garden party.

From a hill at the edge of town, Robert Todd's slave Dundee watched the fire with his friend Patrick, owned by William English. "*Dundee said, he was sorry the Governor's House was burnt; Patrick said he was not.*" Instead, "*he wished the Governor had been burnt in the middle of it.*"

When the last man was out, Clarke's house burned with such fury "that no human power could extinguish it."[4] Not that every human power was marshaled. Gardner, who was standing next to Adolph Philipse's Cuffee, said that "when the Buckets come to *Cuffee*, instead of handing them along to the next Man, he put them upon the Ground and overset them, by which Means the Ground, which was at first dry and hard, became so wet, that [Gardner] . . . was almost up to the Ankles in Mud." And "when the Flames of the House blazed up very high," Cuffee "huzzah'd, danced, whistled and sung." Perhaps, on top of that hill, Patrick did the same.

Colonists celebrated the bucket brigade as a triumph of brotherly solidarity. In contemporary illustrations, bucket brigadiers stand together like so many paper dolls, in quiet harmony. A 1733 editorial by "Pennsylvanus" in Benjamin Franklin's *Pennsylvania Gazette* waxed poetic on the subject: "How pleasing must it be to a thinking Man to observe, that not a Fire happens in this Town, but soon after it is seen and cry'd out, the Place is crowded by active Men of different Ages, Professions and Titles; who, as of one Mind and Rank, apply themselves with all Vigilance and Resolution, according to their Abilities, to the hard Work of conquering the increasing Fire." "Pennsylvanus" measured social order by the bucket: "here are brave Men, Men of Spirit and Humanity, good Citizens or Neighbours, capable and worthy of civil Society, and the Enjoyment of a happy Government." Of "one Mind and Rank," Philadelphians lining up to pass buckets "have a Reward in themselves, and they love one another."

Maybe that's what happened in the City of Brotherly Love. Or maybe not. (One "vagabond Fellow" at a Philadelphia fire refused to pass pails and, "being smartly ask'd by an industrious young Man, why he did not lend a Hand to the Buckets, answer'd, He car'd not if all the Houses in Town were o'Fire: For which he received a Bucket of Water on his impudent Face.")[5] And in New York? "You black Dog," Isaac Gardner hollered at Cuffee, "is this a Time for you to dance?" But Cuffee only laughed, whispered something to his friend Albany, standing on his other side, and kept dancing.

While Cuffee danced, the flames spread from the roof of the Governor's Mansion to the chapel and barracks. In a fierce wind, they threatened to blow even beyond the fort's tall walls and to catch the roofs of the tightly packed houses lining the west side of Broadway, the "handsome Spacious Houses of the principal Inhabitants," Joseph Murray's mansion among them.[6] The whole city might be destroyed, left as desolate as the charred, smoking ruin that was London after the Great Fire.

Eighteenth-century New York was an especially elegant city, known for its opulence and its grand "Broad Way," one hundred feet wide, and its fine buildings, from Trinity Church, with its imposing stone steeple, to the majesty of City Hall, with its triple-arched arcade, to the boxy tower of the massive New Dutch Church. Some parts of the city still had "the general appearance of a Dutch-town," with narrow houses, their gables facing the street, "just as is done in Holland," built of brick of "divers Coullers and laid in Checkers." Newer houses were built to English taste, and "in the Italian stile." By eighteenth-century standards, Manhattan's buildings were unusually tall, four or five stories high. On a granite island teeming with new arrivals too frightened to settle lands far beyond the street that was once a wall, New Yorkers, Dutch, English, and everyone else built upwards. Only slowly were they replacing thatch and wood buildings with stone and brick.[7]

Meanwhile, the city's tall wooden buildings, like those nearest to Fort George, spread fire swiftly. The first structure to the north of the fort was the clapboard Secretary's Office, just over the fort gate. Clarke, desperate not only to halt the fire before it headed up Broadway but also to save the vast archive of documents stored in the Secretary's Office, ordered men inside the building, calling out orders with a speaking trumpet.[8] Shattering the upper-floor windows, they threw down sheaf after sheaf of the governor's papers—official commissions, private letters, newspapers, council records—only to watch them flutter and scatter, a white confetti wind. Almost as soon as the last pile of papers was thrown from the office, that building, too, began to burn. Finally, the engines arrived.

The city had imported its first two engines in 1731, paying the hefty sum of £200 for "two Compleat fire Engines" of "Mr Newshams New Invention of the fourth and sixth Sizes with suctions, Leathern Pipes and Caps." Richard Newsham, a London engineer, introduced the first modern fire engine in England in 1718. Twenty men working its foot treadles, while another team dumped buckets of water into its cistern, could power the Newsham Engine to pump 60 gallons per minute through a copper spout to which was attached a rather unwieldy wire-framed, leather-jacketed canvas suction hose. The Newsham was vastly better than no engine at all, and money well spent (the same model engine, with only slight modifications, was used until 1832). But it was cumbersome, and the hose leaked. Newsham engines also required trained men to work and maintain them. In 1736, the Common Council ordered the building of an engine house, attached to the Watch House on Broad Street, and the following year the Assembly passed a law providing for the appointment of volunteer firemen "to be ready at A Call both by Night as well as by day." In 1738, thirty-five firemen were appointed by a "Law for Regulating and declaring the Duty of Firemen in the City of New York": at the first alarm, "with all possible Expedition" they were to "Repair to the fire Engines and draw them to the place where such fire Shall happen" and "Work & Play the Said Fire Engines, and all Other Tools and Instruments at such Fire, with all their power, Strength, Skill and understanding."[9]

That power and, most of all, those tools and instruments were not always adequate. Although the stalwart firemen showed up and played the engines on the fire at the Secretary's Office, the building was soon reduced to ashes.

A thin drizzle began to fall. Rain tickled hands and faces, and sizzled on burning wood. There was a lull of relief. The rain picked up. But then long-forgotten hand grenades stored in the cellar of the Secretary's Office suddenly exploded and citizens who had valiantly fought the fire now fled in fear, struck with the terrifying realization that the whole fort, with its stock of gunpowder, hay, pitch, tar, resin, and turpentine, might blow up. "The usual alertness of the inhabitants," William Smith, Jr., wrote, "was checked by their dread of the explosion of the magazine."[10] The bucket brigade retreated. At least one soldier, Griffith Evans, was badly burned. In the chaos of paper and mud and flames and a stampeding crowd, one man lost a gold watch; the next week he would advertise for its return. Many more men lost their courage.

And still Cuffee laughed.

When the explosions stopped, and didn't start up again, the men returned. Slowly, the leather buckets and the Newsham engines and, above all, the rain, soaked the fire out. "The Govrs house barracks & Sundry offices in the ffort were almost in an hour reduced to ashes during the time of a high wind which much Endangered the City," James Alexander wrote to his stepson.[11] Too late to save the fort, the rain, in the end, saved the city. New York would not follow London's fate.

By late afternoon, the weary crowd headed home. The drenched, shivering firemen collected all the buckets onto a cart and carried them to City Hall, for their owners to pick up in the morning. The Newshams were hauled back to the engine house on Broad Street. The fort's thick timbers burned through the night, while captain of the militia Cornelius Van Horne, nicknamed "Major Drum," zealously paraded his seventy armed men up and down the streets, keeping watch that the fire didn't blaze up again or spread beyond the embers inside the wrecked fort. Later, Horsmanden would argue that only Van Horne's providential watch had thwarted the conspirators' plans to set more fires that night, saving the city from apocalypse.

The day Fort George burned was a day of utter desolation in New York, one from which the city did not easily or soon recover. For months afterward, Clarke would beg the Lords of Trade in London to send money to help pay for the damage and rebuild the fort, with little success, since the War of Jenkins's Ear had emptied the imperial coffers. (Three years later, when Dr. Alexander Hamilton toured New York, he found the fort still entirely "in ruins.") And there were more urgent problems, such as what to do with the rescued papers; what lessons could be learned from fighting the fire at the fort; and the mystery of how it had started.

On March 19, the city's Common Council held an emergency meeting at City Hall. Acting in his capacity as Recorder, and governor's man, Daniel Horsmanden reported that "in the Dreadful Calamity Which happened Yesterday the Secretarys Office was Entirely Destroyed," and he asked the aldermen to "Assign the Common Council Room for the Keeping the Publick Books and Records of the Province. During the present Exigency." The books were moved to the Council Room on the second floor of City Hall that same day. Meanwhile, five aldermen were appointed to "a Committee to Inspect into the Ladders. Hooks and all other kind of Implements . . . Necessary for Extinguishing fire" and to make sure they were in proper repair. There was also a hint that, at the crucial hour, the good citizens of New York had not provided enough three-gallon leather buckets: before it adjourned, the Common Council placed an order for one hundred new leather fire buckets of its own, painted with the words "City of N. York."[12]

WHAT CAUSED THE FIRE at Fort George? At first, it appeared to have been an accident. Zenger's *Weekly Journal* reported on March 23 that Clarke's mansion had been ignited by a careless plumber using a soldering iron to fix a leak in a gutter that extended from the roof of the mansion to the roof of the chapel. "For some time after the fort was burned I had no other thoughts of it, than that it was an accident," Clarke wrote to the Lords of Trade. George Clarke, sixty-five, was a seasoned politician. Born in England, he had come to New York in 1702, was appointed clerk of the Council three years later, and a member in 1716. "He had genius, but no other than a common writing school education," according to William Smith, Jr. "Nor did he add to his stock by reading, for he was more intent upon improving his fortune than his mind," not least because he had ten children to provide for. Calculating, but not without a strong sense of self-preservation, Clarke had attached himself to Cosby. But by spending most of Cosby's administration at "his rural villa on the edge of Hempstead plains," Clarke had left it to James DeLancey "to enjoy the praise or blame" of being Cosby's henchman. After Cosby's death in 1736, Clarke had done much to quiet the province and to please the populace: at the death of Clarke's wife, Anne, in May 1740, he ordered that a loaf of bread be given to every poor New Yorker.

George Clarke was said to have "a perfect command of his temper." At first, he was willing to believe that the fire at the fort, which occasioned him considerable personal loss, was an unhappy accident. "No one imagined it was done on Purpose," Horsmanden recalled. Instead, the plumber, "carrying his Fire-Pot with Coals to keep his Soddering-Iron hot, to perform his Work; and the Wind setting into the Gutter, 'twas thought, some Sparks had been blown out upon the Shingles of the House."[13]

That explanation was reasonable enough. Fires were far from uncommon in New York City, and they were almost always accidental. In 1733, Gerardus Comfort's workshop and stable, on the North River, had burned to the ground in a fire "occasioned by a Crack in the Oven (which being then heating to bake Bread for the Family)." The next year another New Yorker's house was reduced to ashes by a kitchen chimney fire. In 1737, Rip Van Dam's house went up in flames sparked "by the careless throwing of hot Ashes." Chimneys ablaze in every building, lighted candles by every bed. Daily life was a fire hazard. A list of dangers printed in Franklin's *Pennsylvania Gazette* included many more: shovels full of live coals "carried out of one Room into another, or up or down Stairs"; "too shallow Hearths," "wooden Mouldings on each side of the Fire Place," and "foul Chimneys."[14] It was all too easy to believe that the plumber had let sparks fly from his pot to the governor's roof.

The plumber's pot was plausible. But it didn't last out the week.

On Wednesday, March 25, a house near the Long Bridge, belonging to that daring seaman Captain Peter Warren, went up in flames. Unlike the Governor's Mansion, Warren's house was saved by the bucket brigade and the Newsham engines: the fire "was soon extinguished, without doing much Damage to the House."

Two fires after an especially cold winter (just the kind of weather that dries out wood) were not unusual, and, at first, the fire at Warren's was attributed to a faulty chimney. But exactly a week later, a dockside warehouse owned by Dutch blockmaker Winant Van Zant burned to the ground, with everything in it. The fire at Van Zant's, "an old Wooden Building, stored with Deal Boards, and Hay at one End," seemed to have begun by "a Man's smoking a Pipe there, which set Fire to the Hay." But after three fires on three Wednesdays in a row, it was impossible not to wonder if this, too, were just another accident. And it was impossible not to wonder, what would the next Wednesday bring?

New Yorkers didn't have to wait that long. Three days later, two more fires broke out. The first, at dusk on Saturday, April 4, burned a haystack in a cow stable at the Fly Market in the East Ward, on Maiden Lane at Pearl Street, near the house of Dutch cordwainer Jacobus Quick. (The Fly Market's name was a corruption of the Dutch *vly*, or "valley.") Neighbors raced to respond to the alarm, buckets swinging. Clarke showed up, too. "I went constantly to every fire to give directions and to animate the people," he told the Lords of Trade.[15] Patrick and Dundee again watched the blaze together. "The Fires in Town were not half done yet," Patrick warned. Just as the cow-stable fire was put out and weary citizens headed back to their homes, there was "a Second Cry of Fire, at the House of one *Ben Thomas*, next Door to Captain *Sarly*, on the West Side." Thomas's fire, too, was soon extinguished, not least because the leather buckets were already out on the streets. Now, for the first time, there was proof of arson: "Upon Examination, it was found, that Fire had been put between a Straw and another Bed laid together, whereon a Negro slept."

Early the next morning, Sunday, April 5, coals were found "under a Haystack, standing near the Coach-House and Stables of *Joseph Murray*," on lower Broadway. The coals had gone out on their own, "having only singed some Part of the Hay," but a trail of coals and ashes led from the stables to a neighbor's house, "which caused a Suspicion of the Negro that lived there." That afternoon, a housewife named Abigail Earle was looking out the second-floor window of a house on Broadway when she saw "three Negroes" coming up the street. As they passed the house, one of them, a slave named Quack, owned by the butcher John Walter, shouted, "*Fire, Fire, Scorch, Scorch*, A LITTLE, *Damn it*, BY-AND-BY," and then "threw up his Hands, and laughed."

Monday brought four more fires. At ten o'clock in the morning, the first alarm was sounded when a chimney in George Burns's house, opposite the Fort Garden, began to burn. (Burns was a sergeant in a company of fusiliers.) Two hours later the roof of Mrs. Hilton's house, on the east side of Captain Jacob Sarly's house, went up in flames and, again, evidence pointed to arson; this time, to a man with a very good motive: Sarly's slave Juan de la Silva, who had been seized by an English privateer, John Lush, during an attack on a Spanish ship on which De la Silva served as crew. (Sarly himself had also captained slave-trading ships.) Despite the dark-skinned Spanish sailors' protests that they were subjects of Spain, and therefore prisoners of war, Lush's "Spanish Negroes" were auctioned as slaves in New York. It was said that they pledged to "burn *Lush's* House, and tie *Lush* to a Beam, and roast him like a Piece of Beef."

Jacob Sarly's neighbors charged the arson to De la Silva. More, they began to wonder if *all* of the recent fires had been set by Spanish prisoners wrongfully, or at best dubiously, sold into slavery. News spread that the

"Spanish Negroes" had damned Sarly, who was, like Lush, a privateer, and said "*that if the Captain would not send them to their own Country, they would ruin all the City.*" "*Take up the Spanish Negroes!*" went the cry from street to street. Bucket brigadiers turned into vigilantes and hunted down De la Silva and four other "Spanish Negroes" who had been captured by Lush in the fall of 1740: Antonio de la Cruz, Antonio de St. Bendito, Augustine Gutierrez, and Pablo Ventura Angel. All five were found and dragged to City Hall.

At four o'clock, city magistrates assembled in the Council Room to interrogate the five men. But even as the magistrates took to their seats, another fire alarm was sounded. From City Hall's long windows they saw smoke rising from Frederick Philipse's warehouse on New Street and "a small Streak of Fire running up the Shingles, like Wild-Fire." Before that fire could be put out, "there was another *Cry of Fire;* which diverted the People attending the Storehouse, to the new Alarm." One fireman, Dutch gunsmith Jacobus Stoutenburgh, stayed behind at Philipse's. From the top of the warehouse roof, where he was pulling off shingles, Stoutenburgh looked down inside the building and saw a black man wearing a blue coat lined with red: Adolph Philipse's slave Cuffee.

Cuffee, spying him, took flight. Stoutenburgh gave chase, climbing down through the laths, "but he was hindered by a Nail catching hold of his Breeches." Hanging by his pants, Stoutenburgh watched helplessly as Cuffee escaped by jumping out of one of the end windows, "leaping over several Garden Fences," and hiding in some old stables nearby. "*A Negro; a Negro!*" Stoutenburgh hollered. Bucket brigaders who recognized the fleeing man changed the cry to "*Cuff Philipse, Cuff Philipse!*" A mob "of upwards of a Thousand Men" chased Cuffee to Adolph Philipse's house, between Broad Street and Coenties Slip, where they grabbed him and carried him to jail, "borne upon the People's Shoulders."

And still, across the city, panicked citizens fled their houses in confusion. The women, especially, were "exceedingly frightened . . . so that some Fainted, others Miscarried and one Died of the fright."[16] From street to street New Yorkers began to cry, "The Negroes are rising!"

NOW, EVEN THE most skeptical of men turned suspicious. "Within these five weeks we have had above a Dozen of allarms with fire in this City," James Alexander wrote to his stepson. "Five of these fires happening in one day, with many other strange causes of Suspicion render it likely that all or most of them have bene on purpose." Clarke had once believed the fires were accidental, "but when three or four and once I think five houses were set on fire in a day and some of them apparently by design," he explained, "I soon changed my thoughts and set myself heartily to work to find out the villainy."

Briefly, New Yorkers entertained the possibility of witchcraft. A woman in the city had made "a Prophecy" before several of the fires, including the four fires on Monday, April 6. "The Aldermen of this City made strict enquiry after this Woman," one New Yorker wrote to a friend in Philadelphia, "but can't find her out." But with Cuffee's arrest, the witch was forgotten and never mentioned again. Clarke, for one, was relieved that it had taken so long for New Yorkers to conclude "The Negroes are rising!": "had the suspicion obtained, when those fires begun that the negroes were at the bottom of it, the whole town might have been laid in ashes, for men in that case would have been more intent upon guarding themselves and their families, than upon extinguishing the fires."[17]

The frequency of the fires convinced Clarke and Alexander—and most everyone else—that they were more than accidents. But how, exactly, did suspicion come to fall on the city's slaves?

Nothing "just happened" in the early eighteenth century. There was always a villain to be caught, a conspiracy to be detected. The century was lousy with intrigues. Nearly everyone, and enlightened, reasonable people most of all, spotted plotters lurking behind nearly every shadow, and arsonists in the flicker of almost every flame. This was, in many ways, a departure from the providential thinking that ruled the minds of previous generations.[18] Even into the eighteenth century, providential thinkers like the Puritans of Massachusetts Bay explained fires as God's will. In a 1711 sermon entitled *Burnings Bewailed,* the Puritan minister Increase Mather sought to explain "the sins which provoke the Lord to kindle fires" like the one that had just attacked his city.[19] In New York, where people subscribed to a more familiar, more recognizably "modern" sensibility, blaming the fires in the early spring of 1741 on a vengeful God never occurred to anyone.

That left them groping for an explanation. They could take little comfort in a premodern providentialism. Terrible things no longer happened simply because God willed them to happen; they happened because *someone* caused them to happen. The trick was to figure out just who was behind it all, to track down conspirators. The island of England nearly sank into the sea under the weight of plotting papists, levelers, and anarchists. The colonies were riddled with political plotters, too, nearly all of them men who challenged or usurped the authority of royally appointed governors: Nathaniel Bacon in Virginia in 1675, Jacob Leisler in New York in 1690, James Alexander and Lewis Morris in New York in the 1730s. In 1710, irate Antiguan assemblymen had had their governor *murdered.*

But in the New World, there were also different villains: dark-skinned peoples whose land or liberty, or both, had been taken away. In an empire acquired by conquest and built by slaves, English colonists in the New World had the unnerving and unrelenting impression that they were being watched, and despised, always, and that plots were forever being hatched against them, plots of arson and murder and revolution. Worse even than this consuming fear was the suspicion, only rarely voiced, that the plotters might have right on their side—a point made by the English poet Richard Savage in his 1737 poem "Of Public Spirit in Regard to Public Works":

> Do you the neighb'ring blameless *Indian* aid,
> Culture what he neglects, not His invade;
> Dare not, oh dare not, with ambitious View,
> Force or demand Subjection, never due.
> Let by *My* specious Name no *Tyrants* rise,
> And cry, while they enslave, they civilize!
> Know *LIBERTY* and *I* are still the *same,*
> Congenial!—ever mingling Flame with Flame!
> Why must I *Afric's* sable Children see
> Vended for Slaves, though form'd by Nature free,
> The nameless Tortures cruel Minds invent,
> Those to subject, whom Nature equal meant?
> If these you dare, albeit unjust Success
> Empow'rs you now unpunish'd to oppress,
> Revolving Empire you and yours may doom,
> (*Rome* all subdued, yet *Vandals* vanquish'd *Rome*)
> Yes, Empire may revolve, give Them the Day,
> And Yoke may Yoke, and Blood may Blood repay.[20]

Sometimes, Empire did revolve, and Blood did Blood repay. Slaves murdered their masters, and chopped their corpses up with axes. Indians attacked English towns, and burned them to the ground. The paranoid style of American colonial life might just as easily be termed a realistic assessment of the perils of empire. New Yorkers themselves had seen blood in the streets. On March 25, 1712, a group of New York slaves had met at night to complain about "hard usage" from their masters. Sucking the blood of one another's hands, they pledged to a plot to destroy the city and murder every white. On the night of April 6, between twenty-five and fifty black men and women, many of them Coromantees, met at midnight, carrying guns, swords, knives, and hatchets. They set fire to a building, and when whites raced to the scene, "the slaves fired and killed them." Adrian Hoghlandt's slave Robin stabbed him in the back. Nicholas Roosevelt's slave Tom shot Andries Beekman in the chest. Peter the Porter, owned by Andries Marschalk, killed young Joris Marschalk with a dagger blow to his breast. Before the butchery ended, nine whites had been killed and six more wounded.

Governor Robert Hunter commanded the cannon at Fort George fired to alarm the city and "order'd a detachment from the fort under a proper officer to march against them, but the slaves made their retreat into the woods, by the favour of the night." The next day, Hunter ordered the New York and Westchester militias to "drive the Island." Sweeping Manhattan, the troops captured nearly all of the rebels, although a handful, six men, had sufficient time and fortitude to kill themselves before the soldiers found them. "Had it not been for the Garrison there," most New Yorkers believed, the city "would have been reduced to ashes, and the greatest part of the inhabitants murdered."[21]

New Yorkers knew, too, about more recent rebellions. They knew about a slave conspiracy at the Danish island of St. John's in 1733, in which more than ninety African-born slaves took control of the island and held it for over six months. They followed the news of a slave plot in Antigua in 1736; in 1737, Zenger's *Weekly Journal* had reprinted a full account of the investigation into the conspiracy. They knew about the Stono Rebellion in South Carolina in 1739, in which a group of nearly a hundred armed slaves killed some twenty whites before being defeated by a local militia company. And everyone in New York had heard about what had happened in Jamaica, where, in the 1720s and 1730s, large bands of runaway slaves, led by a charismatic leader named Cudjoe, established rebel towns and fought off repeated efforts to conquer them. Cudjoe's forces not only held their positions, they gained territory. "The Numerous Rebellious Negroes there are very Turbulent, and almost every where Attack the Inhabitants without Fear," reported the *Weekly Journal* in April 1734, "and no Body of Men can be got to withstand their wicked and malitious Designs." The next month, the *New York Gazette* noted that the rebels live "with as much freedom as if they were Settlers." Repeated attacks finally forced the British authorities to sign a peace treaty with Cudjoe in March 1739; this secured for him and all of his followers not only their freedom but also the 1,500 acres of the territory they had conquered.[22] It was a tremendous victory that must have humiliated Englishmen everywhere and sparked the imagination of every slave who heard tell of it.

New Yorkers avidly followed the news from Jamaica in particular not least because Robert Hunter, who served as governor of Jamaica from 1727 until his death in 1734, had been governor of New York from 1710 to 1719. From Jamaica Hunter corresponded with many of his former acquaintances in New York, including his close friend James Alexander, who also served as his personal attorney, and even ordinary New Yorkers took an interest in Hunter's troubles. Jamaica was also the single largest supplier of New York's slaves.[23]

But even if Zenger had never printed an account of the Antigua revolt, even if Robert Hunter had never written to James Alexander, New Yorkers would have heard of the wave of slave rebellions across the Atlantic in the 1730s. From the depths of cargo holds, Caribbean slaves sold in New York brought stories of these uprisings with them. In the 1730s, dozens of black Caribbeans traveled to New York in ships owned by New York merchants whose slaves would be accused of conspiracy in 1741. Those merchants included Rip Van Dam, Peter and Augustus Jay, Nathaniel Marston, William Walton, John Moore, Obadiah Hunt, John Groesbeck, Abraham Van Horne, Mordecai Gomez, John and Henry Cruger, David Provost, Jasper Bosch, Winant Van Zant, Cornelius Kortreicht, David Clarkson, and John Tiebout. And the men who captained slave-trading ships owned slaves accused in 1741, too: Jacob Phoenix, Jaspar Farmer, John Lush, Jacob Sarly. In all, at least thirty-nine of the black New Yorkers accused in 1741 were owned by men directly involved in the Caribbean slave trade.[24] And many more belonged to widows of ships' captains and brothers and cousins of slave merchants: the Bayard, Kiersted, DePeyster, and DeLancey families were all involved in the trade.

Blacks who came to New York from the Caribbean brought with them tales of rebellion. And more than a few brought experience of it. Will, sold to a New York watchmaker, "understood these Affairs very well": in 1733, he had joined the revolt at St. John's; three years later, he had pledged to the plot in Antigua. In both places, he had saved his life by testifying against his supposed co-conspirators. From St. John's he was transported to Antigua; from Antigua he was shipped to New York, probably on Garrett Van Horne's sloop the *Albany*, which docked in New York in May 1737, carrying five slaves for sale. "The Negroes here were Cowards," Will was said to have complained after he arrived in Manhattan, "for that they had no Hearts as those at Antigua." "Will was very expert at Plots," Horsmanden remarked, "for this was the *third Time* he had engaged in them."[25]

BLOOD DID BLOOD REPAY. There were real plots. But almost as often, the plots were imagined. And the circulation of colonial newspapers only further fueled the rumors. In the fall of 1738, English colonists on the island of Nantucket detected "a Conspiracy to destroy all the English, by first setting Fire to their Houses, in the Night, and then falling upon them with their Fire Arms." The plot was led by "the Indians upon that Island," whose explanation for "this cruel Attempt" was "that the English at first took the Land from their Ancestors by Force, and have kept it ever since, without giving them any valuable Consideration for it." It made sense to the English colonists who spread the story—news of the plot appeared in the *Pennsylvania Gazette*—because they lived in an age, and in a place, obsessed with just this kind of conspiracy. But a week later, the *Pennsylvania Gazette* retracted the story: "The News that we had . . . that the Indians of the Island Nantucket had lately contriv'd a horrid Scheme to set Fire to the Houses of the English Inhabitants in the Night, and kill as many as they could, is wholly contradicted. . . . This Report arose by a drunken Indian Woman of that Island, who being in Liquor, reported such Things." The horrible scheme was "but a drunken Story."[26]

If a single drunken Indian woman could come up with a plot and a completely plausible justification so compelling that it terrified an entire island of English colonists and was reported up and down the Atlantic seaboard, even though there were no fires on Nantucket that fall, the degree of panic inspired by actual fires like the ten that blazed across New York in March and April 1741 is hard to imagine.

Conspiracies were horrifying, but the fear of them also ran so deep in the culture that it made for a good joke, as when Scrub in *The Beaux' Stratagem* pledges to uncover a plot: "Ay, sir, a plot, and a horrible plot. First, it must be a plot because there's a woman in't; secondly, it must be a plot because there's a priest in't; thirdly, it must be a plot because there's French gold in't; and fourthly, it must be a plot, because I don't know what to make on't." It was just this kind of obsession with conspiracy that Jonathan Swift mocked in *Gulliver's Travels* in 1726: Gulliver, on a visit to the Grand Academy of Lagado, finds a professor who shows him "a large

Paper of Instructions for discovering Plots and Conspiracies against the Governments":

> He advised great Statesmen to examine into the Dyet of all sus-
> pected Persons; their times of eating; upon which side they lay in
> Bed; with which hand they wiped their Posteriors; take a strict
> View of their Excrements, and from the Colour, the Odour, the
> Taste, the Consistence, the Crudeness, or Maturity of Digestion,
> form a Judgement of their Thoughts and Designs. Because Men are
> never so Serious, Thoughtful, and Intent, as when they are at Stool,
> which he found by frequent Experiment: For in such Conjunctures,
> when he used meerly as a Trial to consider which was the best way
> of murdering the King, his Ordure would have A Tincture of
> Green, but quite different when he thought only of raising an
> Insurrection or burning the Metropolis.[27]

Plots to burn the metropolis flowed freely across the Atlantic, and up and down the seaboard. When they were true, they were terrifying. When they were delusions, they were droll. In June 1738, New Yorkers received word that Jamaicans had been deluded by "a Discovery of a Plot concerted by the Negroes at *Kingston,* but by good Information, we find it to be no more than an intended Meeting, to drink to the Memory of an old Negro Felow, dead some Time agoe, whom they used to call their King." New Yorkers, Zenger's *Weekly Journal* reported, "have been amus'd" by the Jamaicans' credulity.[28] Mistaking black men drinking and toasting a black man "King" for a deadly plot? Now *that* was funny.

IN NEW YORK, the first response to suspicious fire was the three-gallon leather buckets, the unwieldy Newsham engines, the rallying of the heroic, harmonious men of the bucket brigade. But for all the city's bucket laws and tireless firemen, New York suffered from an uncontainable flammabil-ity: the savagery of slavery. While smoke was still rising from the ashes, New York's second response to suspicious fire was, almost always, to place curbs on slaves' liberties. In 1730, on the same day that the provincial Assembly voted an act authorizing funds for the purchase of fire engines for New York City, it also passed "An Act for the more effectual preventing and punishing the conspiracy and insurrection of negro and other slaves and for the better regulating them." In December 1736, the *New York*

Gazette reported that "a Fire broke in the Stable of Mr. *John Roosevelt* over against the Fly-Market in this City, it burn'd the said Stable, his Bolting-house, Chockalet-Engine-house and part of his Linseed-Oyl Mill-house; the fire also took hold of three dwelling Houses." At first, it was unclear what might have caused it: "How the Fire came is uncertain as yet." But by January 1737, the *Gazette* reported that there was now "a strong Suspicion that some Negroes perpetrated so vile a piece of Wickedness." Two slave women were interrogated and arrested.[29] Later that month, the Common Council passed a law "that no Negro, Mullatto or Indian Slave, shall appear in the Streets of this City, above an hour after Sun-set without a Candle and Lanthorn, on Penalty of being Whipt at the Publick Whipping Post."

The body of legislation that constituted New York's "Negro Law" is a brutal testament to the difficulty of enslaving human beings, especially in cities. New York's slave codes were almost entirely concerned with curtailing the ability of enslaved people to move at will, and to gather, for fear that they might decide, especially when drunk, that slavery was not to be borne and one way to end it would be to burn the city down. A 1702 "Act for Regulateing of Slaves," the governor reported, had "become absolutely necessary through the great insolency that sort of people are grown to." So much anti-conspiracy legislation was passed under the first half century of English rule that in 1730 Governor John Montgomerie recommended that all such acts be repealed and replaced with a simpler law, on the grounds that it would be better if magistrates had "a plain rule to walk by." Under the terms of Montgomerie's act, which consolidated provincial slave codes passed in 1702, 1708, and 1712, it was not only illegal for slaves to have or use "any gun Pistoll sword Club or any other Kind of Weapon"; it was also illegal for more than three slaves to meet anywhere, at any time, unless it was "in some servile imployment for their Master or Mistress."

While the provincial Assembly attempted to legislate against the broad possibility of slave insurrection, the city's Common Council was more concerned with everyday opportunities for conspiring. The first New York City slave code adopted under English rule, "A Proclamation Prohibiteing ye Intertainment of Negers," was passed in 1680: it forbade whites from selling "Wine Rumm and other Strong Liquors" to slaves. Laws adopted by the city's Common Council between 1680 and 1740 made it illegal for slaves to "Absent themselves from their Masters Houses or Plantacions on the Lords Day" without a written pass; to gamble in the streets for money; to ride "their Masters Horses to Water . . . Swiftly, Hastily, Precipately or disorderly"; to buy or sell produce in city streets or markets; or to be in the streets after sunset without a lantern or lighted candle.[30] What was supposed to have happened at John Hughson's tavern just after Christmas in 1740—dozens of slaves walking to the outskirts of town, on a Sunday night, to drink rum punch served by whites—violated just about every law on the books.

New York's slave code was not necessarily an overreaction to the possibility of violent revolt. New Yorkers had good cause to worry about slave revolts; not only did they hold, in the back of their mind, the imperial wheel of fortune conjured by Savage ("Revolving Empire you and yours may doom"), they well remembered the revolt of 1712. Nor did they exercise restraint in punishing plotters. In 1712, more than seventy slaves and free blacks were eventually taken into custody, and forty-three brought to trial by jury. Eighteen were acquitted and discharged. Twenty-five were convicted, of whom twenty were hanged and three burned at the stake. One, a pregnant woman, had her execution postponed. But after giving birth, she, too, met her death.

Governor Robert Hunter, a skilled satirist and a friend of Jonathan Swift, was a contemplative man. He had been appalled by both the nature and the number of the 1712 executions. "I am informed that in the West Indies where their laws against their slaves are most severe, that in case of a conspiracy in which many are engaged a few only are executed for an example," he wrote to the Lords of Trade, complaining that "In this case" many were executed. Disgusted by the excess, Hunter fought hard against the remaining prosecutions and was able to reprieve five men, including two "Spanish Negroes" whom he considered not only unjustly convicted but unjustly enslaved. Yet, despite Hunter's objections to the severity of the prosecution, within months of the 1712 revolt the Assembly passed "An Act for preventing Suppressing and punishing the Conspiracy and Insurrection of Negroes and other Slaves." It allowed slaveowners "to punish their Slaves for their Crimes and Offences at Discretion, not extending to Life or Member," while mandating that any slave found guilty of murder, rape, arson, or assault would "suffer the pains of Death in such manner and with such circumstances as the aggravation or enormity of their Crimes . . . shall merit and require." The act also sought greatly to restrict the city's tiny population of free blacks ("an Idle slothfull people") by prohibiting them from owning "any Houses, Lands, Tenements or Hereditaments," and requiring any owner manumitting a slave to pay £200 security to the government and a £20 annuity to the freed slave.[31] (Such a sizable financial penalty made manumission effectively impossible.)

Writing again to the Lords of Trade, Governor Hunter apologized for the ferocity of the 1712 "Negro Act": even after the Governor's Council lessened the severity of some of its provisions, Hunter worried, "your Lordships will still think [it] too severe, but after the late barbarous attempt of some of their slaves nothing less could please the people." Hunter had cause to worry. As early as 1686, authorities in London had been astonished at the viciousness of New York's slave codes. That year, the Duke of York instructed the governor to pass "a Law for the Restraining of Inhuman Severitys which by all masters or overseers may bee used toward their Christian servants, or slaves, wherein provision is to be made that ye wilful killing of Indians & Negros may bee punished with death, And that a fit penalty bee imposed for the maiming of them." It was never passed. And Hunter, who served as the governor of both New York and New Jersey, was well aware that a 1704 New Jersey "Act for Regulating Negro Indians and Mulato Slaves," modeled after New York's 1702 "Act for Regulateing of Slaves," was so severe (among other things, it mandated castrating black men convicted of raping or fornicating with white women) that Queen Anne overruled it five years later, on the grounds that "the Punishment to be inflicted on Negroes &ca is such as never was allowed by or known in the Laws of this Kingdom."[32]

WHAT HAPPENED IN New York in 1712 cast a long shadow, especially for families caught up in the violence of both 1712 and 1741. Three of Rip Van Dam's slaves were sentenced to be hanged in 1712 (one was pardoned); in 1741, Van Dam's slave John was accused in the conspiracy, and his son, Isaac, served as a juror. Adolph Philipse had served as Third Supreme Court Justice in 1712, and his slave Amba stood accused; in 1741, his nephew Frederick held the second seat on the court, and both men owned slaves named in the trials, including Adolph's Cuffee, accused of setting fire to Frederick's warehouse. Gerardus Beekman, whose son Andries had been shot to death by Nicholas Roosevelt's slave Tom in 1712, served as a trial witness in 1741. Three other Beekmans served as jurors in 1741, as did Roosevelt's sons Jacobus and John.

There are also hints that whoever set the fires in 1741, if they were deliberately set, was commemorating 1712. Two of the days of the 1741 fires corresponded to the dates on which the 1712 plot was hatched: March 25 and April 6. At the 1741 trial of John Roosevelt's slave Quack and Adolph Philipse's Cuffee, William Smith suggested that the memory of 1712 ought to have deterred any future revolt: "That Justice that was provoked by former Fires and the innocent Blood that was spilt in your Streets, should have been a perpetual Terror to the Negroes that survived the Vengeance of that Day, and should have been a Warning to all that had come after them." In many families, that memory did indeed prove a perpetual terror, but it may also have inspired revolt. For killing Andries Beekman, Nicholas Roosevelt's slave Tom was burned over a slow fire in 1712. In 1741, John Roosevelt's slave Quack was burned at the stake. John was Nicholas's son. Was Quack Tom's son? That piece of genealogy is probably irretrievable. But generations of Roosevelts' slaves watched black men from their own household burn in torment. When John Roosevelt's warehouses went up in flames in 1736, his slaves were the first suspected. "Revolving Empire you and yours may doom."

As the ice melted in March and April 1741, England was at war, it seemed, with all the world. In their panic and despair, white New Yorkers contemplating the fires at Fort George, and Warren's house, and Van Zant's and Philipse's storehouses, and all around the city, recalled the fire in 1712 and the Caribbean rebellions and South Carolina of the 1730s, and began to cry, "The Negroes are rising!"

On April 6, after Jacobus Stoutenburgh's cry caused the crowd at Philipse's storehouse to chase Cuffee, the bucket brigadiers–turned–vigilantes swelled and swarmed across the city, taking up any black men unlucky enough to be out on the streets. As Horsmanden reported, "Many People had such terrible Apprehensions . . . and indeed there was Cause sufficient, that several Negroes (and many had been assisting at the Fire at the Storehouse, and many perhaps that only seemed to be so) who were met in the Streets, after the Alarm of their rising, were hurried away to Gaol; and when they were there, they were continued some Time in Confinement before the Magistrates could spare Time to examine into their several Cases, how and for what they came there."

From the second-story windows at City Hall, Clarke, meeting with his Council, could see the smoke and the flames and the mob, and could hear the commotion, two floors below, as two dozen slaves were thrown into the dungeon.[33] Magistrates, aided by Horsmanden, began their investigation, questioning first the "Spanish Negroes" and next any slaves who seemed suspicious. There was, as yet, precious little to connect the February 18 robbery at Rebecca Hogg's shop with the fires. But even two days after the fort fire, the mayor, John Cruger, had ordered Prince, earlier released on bail, recommitted. And on April 6, John and Sarah Hughson were arrested again, charged "as Accessories to divers Felonies and Misdemeanours." Sarah was jailed with her nursing baby. That night, Clarke ordered the militia to keep the city under watch: every night for the next three months crews of twenty-five men would patrol from dusk till dawn.

All week, city magistrates conducted interrogations. Quack, owned by the Englishman John Walter, was asked what he meant by what he had been overheard to shout while walking up Broadway: "*Fire, Fire, Scorch, Scorch,* A LITTLE, *Damn it,* BY-AND-BY." He said he was "*talking of Admiral Vernon's taking* Porto Bello," a recent English naval victory in the War of Jenkins's Ear, and "*that he thought that was but a small Feat to what this brave Officer would do* by-and-by, *to annoy the Spaniards.*" Quack was released.

But Daniel Horsmanden didn't believe a word of it. Perhaps his suspicions were fueled by the observation that four of the fires had attacked property owned by the most prominent members of the Court Party: the Governor's Mansion; stables owned by Attorney Joseph Murray, who had married Cosby's daughter; a storehouse owned by Frederick Philipse; and a house belonging to Captain Peter Warren, James DeLancey's brother-in-law.

Whatever unspoken fear of "latent Enemies" motivated Horsmanden, he placed his suspicions on the city's slaves. He was certain Quack's words meant "that the Fires which we had seen already, were nothing to what we should have *by-and-by,* for that then we should have all the City in Flames, and he would rejoice at it." Horsmanden was especially persuaded by the report of Quack's behavior: "for it was said, he lifted up his Hands, and spread them with a circular Sweep over his Head, after he had pronounced the Words (*by-and-by*) *and then concluded with a loud Laugh.*" The laughter. It was the laughter Horsmanden hated.

Whatever variety of opinions there might have been initially about the cause of the rash of fires, Horsmanden's view soon became the governor's official interpretation. On Saturday, April 11, the Common Council convened. Horsmanden attended in his capacity as City Recorder. He began the meeting by representing his interpretation of recent events as the conclusion any reasonable man must draw from the evidence:

> The Recorder taking Notice of the several Fires which had lately happened in this City, and the Manner of them, which had put the Inhabitants into the utmost Consternation; that every one that

reflected on the Circumstances attending them, the Frequency of them, and the Causes yet undiscovered; must necessarily conclude, that they were occasioned and set on Foot by some villainous Confederacy of latent Enemies amongst us; but with what Intent or Purpose, Time must discover.

At Horsmanden's recommendation, the Common Council voted to offer a reward of £100, and a pardon, to anyone who would reveal those "latent Enemies":

> Order'd that this board Request his honour the Lieut. Governor to Issue a Proclamation Offering a Reward to any white person. that Shall Discover any person or persons lately Concern'd in Setting fire to any Dwelling House. or Store House in this City. (So that Such person or persons As be Convicted thereof) the Sum of One hundred pounds. Current Money of this Province. and that Such person Shall be pardon'd if Concern'd therein. And any Slave that Shall Make Such Discovery to be Manumitted or made free. And the Master of Such Slave to Receive Twenty five pounds. therefor. And the Slave to Receive besides his ffredom the Sum of Twenty pounds. and to be pardon'd. And if a free Negro. Mulatto or Indian. to Receive forty five pounds. And also to be pardon'd if Concern'd therein.[34]

The proclamation was posted across the city. Meanwhile, the Council decided to scour the city for evidence, and to try to halt the looting of abandoned homes that had begun after fearful whites fled. "A Scheme was proposed, that there should be a general Search of all Houses throughout the Town, whereby it was thought probable Discoveries might be made, not only of stolen Goods, but likewise of Lodgers, that were Strangers, and suspicious Persons." The scheme was kept secret over the weekend. On Monday, April 13, each alderman led a search party through his ward while militiamen stationed themselves at street corners, stopping everyone "carrying Baggs or Bundles, or removing Goods from House to House." Every building in the city was searched, and every person found identified. That *not a single stranger* was detected in all of Manhattan is perhaps the best testament to the intimacy of this eighteenth-century city. Nor were any stolen goods discovered. "But some Things were found in the Custody of *Robin,* Mr. *Chambers's* Negro, and *Cuba* his Wife, which the Alderman thought improper for, and unbecoming the Condition of Slaves." Robin and Cuba were arrested.

For the rest of that week, magistrates continued questioning jailed slaves. From the general search, the interrogations, and the posting of the reward, nothing much about a plot emerged, and precious little evidence of conspiracy. Days passed with no alarms. And then, on April 21, the Supreme Court opened its regular session, and Daniel Horsmanden donned his robe.

CHAPTER THREE

Stone

A T NINE-THIRTY on Tuesday, April 21, 1741, the bell ringer, paid ninepence for his pains, pulled the rope that rang the bell in the cupola atop a two-and-a-half-story stone building on the corner of Wall and Broad streets, to announce the sitting of the Supreme Court of Judicature of the Province of New York. The court, established in 1691, was only slightly older than the building, whose foundation was laid in 1699. It took four years, a herd of horses, and hundreds of men, slave and free, to build City Hall, out of stones that had once formed a barricade built by slaves generations before, at Wall Street. In 1703, City Hall opened to house meetings of the Supreme Court, as well as the city's mayor and Common Council and the province's General Assembly, although the assemblymen had cause for complaint: the Assembly Room, on the east wing of the second floor, wasn't furnished for another year. While politicians and lawyers argued in chambers, plumbers and plasterers trudged along the hallways, trailing their ladders behind them. And still the work continued. "A Cage Whipping post pillory and Stocks" were soon erected in front of the triple-arched arcade, opening onto Wall Street.

In 1707, wainscot was nailed to the walls. Three years later, seats for grand and petit jurymen were finally installed in the elegantly appointed Supreme Court Room, on the second floor. In 1711, masons working in the cellar's "Great Gaol," an open space that ran the length of the building, walled off corner cells. City Hall's bell and cupola, faced with a magnificent clock of four dials, a gift of Stephen DeLancey, James DeLancey's father, topped the roof. A decade later, a jailer's apartment was built in the garret over the east wing, and in 1727 a "prison for small crimes" was added to the garret opposite. Two debtor's apartments occupied the corners of the west wing garret, separating them from the decidedly squalid ("neither cieled nor plastered") debtor's prison that ran under the roof. In 1730, when the Society for the Propagation of the Gospel donated 1,642 books to the city, carpenters built shelves and desks in the west wing jury room, which then became a library. Two years later, the imported Newsham fire engines arrived and were stored in a small room on the ground floor's east wing

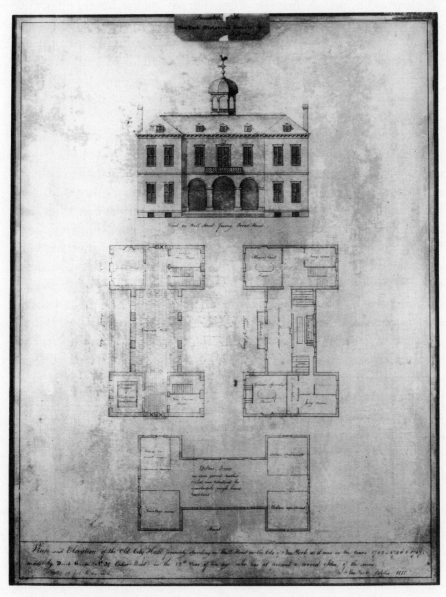

Plan of City Hall, c. 1740, by David Grim, 1776. Collection of
The New-York Historical Society.

until a house for them was built on Broad Street in 1736. Beginning in 1733, the Assembly Room was graced with a large mahogany table. And in 1741, after the fire at Fort George, all of the books and papers rescued from the Secretary's Office were moved, at Daniel Horsmanden's request, to City Hall's Common Council Room, until a better place could be found.[1]

Courtroom, prison, mayor's office, library, engine house, pillory, archive. New York's City Hall stood at the center of the metropolis, a monument to government, order, and retribution. Authority, wealth, and status descended along its stairwells, from the windowed and wainscoted Supreme Court on the second floor to the open walk of the ground floor's Common Hall to the dank, cramped cellar dungeon, an enduring display of rank in a world of daily deference.

At the sound of the bell on that Tuesday in April 1741, marking a half-hour warning, birds fluttered, scattering from their perches on the cupola, and flew over the city, and those officers of the court who had not already arrived entered through the Wall Street arcade, a gentle breeze at their backs, walked across the Common Hall, climbed up the east wing stairs and under an arched entryway, and assembled in the Supreme Court Room, where they were bathed in the early spring's slight morning light. Admitted by the doorkeeper, in came the clerk, the sheriff and his deputies, the crier, the bailiffs and constables. Spectators settled themselves on benches and on the balcony. In the dungeon below, thieves and alleged conspirators—Caesar, Prince, Cuffee, Peggy Kerry, John and Sarah Hughson, and the more than two dozen city slaves and "Spanish Negroes" rounded up in the first weeks of April—listened to the peal of the bell and the clatter of footsteps.

Last came the judges. Chief Justice James DeLancey was noticeably absent; he, along with New York's surveyor-general, Cadwallader Colden, had been called to Providence to serve on a committee arbitrating a boundary dispute between Massachusetts and Rhode Island. DeLancey had left New York the first week of April and would not return to City Hall until July 2. In his absence, Second Justice Frederick Philipse officially headed the court, but Third Justice Daniel Horsmanden, with his English legal education, wielded overarching influence on the bench. (Even when DeLancey was present, Horsmanden "often held the pen" for him.)[2]

The room hushed as the judges entered. Despite his penury, Horsmanden probably insisted on hiring a coach-and-six, a wild extravagance, to travel through town. Perhaps just such a coach stopped in front of City

Hall that morning, its spry coachman opening the door and escorting the Third Justice down from the carriage and across the paving stones, past the cage, the whipping post, the pillory, the stocks. In New York, William Smith, Jr., reported in his *History*, "judges and practisers in the Supreme, and all other courts, wear no particular habits as they do at Westminster." But Daniel Horsmanden had made a splash in 1732 when, as a young lawyer and new arrival, he insisted on wearing his "barr gown" at court. (James Alexander had mocked him for his foppery.) According to Smith, Horsmanden's "chief Merit consisted in a Gentlemanlike Exterior, a strict Attention to the Formality and Decorum of the Court & a Defence of the Profession agt. the vulgar and parcimonious Prejudices of an uncultivated Populace." Much later in his career, in 1764, Horsmanden would mandate Westminster pomp in the courtroom: "considering that it has been the Usage of most of the civilized Nations in Europe to distinguish the different Orders of Men in the learned Professions by their Dress" and convinced that such dress would "advance the Dignity Authority Solemnity and Decorum of the Court," Horsmanden ruled that New York Supreme Court judges must appear "in Robes and Bands" and attorneys "in the Bar Gown and Band."[3]

On Tuesday, April 21, as on every other day the Supreme Court sat in session, Daniel Horsmanden, with his "Gentlemanlike Exterior," arrived at City Hall in a wig and robe finer than he could well afford. He was, at age forty-seven, a decidedly portly man, whose rolling jowls were girdled by a stiff white collar just visible above his black robe. His wig, more gray than white, was parted at the middle and bulged out over his ears, like two cottony rabbit tails. He had a high, wide forehead; a long straight nose; thin, expressive brows, quick to arch; and a stare that was at once wounded and meant to intimidate.

At ten o'clock, the bell tolled once more, and the crier called out: "Oyes! Our sovereign lord the king does strictly charge and command all manner of persons to keep silence upon pain of imprisonment." The Second Justice brought the court to order and began the process of impaneling a grand jury to investigate the fires. A year older than Horsmanden, Frederick Philipse looked younger; his almond-shaped eyes, half-lidded, peered out from a baby face, with flushed cheeks and full lips. Philipse cleared his throat and handed a writ to Sheriff William Jamison: "We Command you that you Cause to come before our Justices of our Supreme Court of Judicature . . . twenty four principal Freeholders of your Bailiwick to serve us and our Said City and County as Grand Jurors."

Daniel Horsmanden, *by Matthew Pratt. Oil on canvas. Courtesy of
Art & Visual Materials, Special Collections Department,
Harvard Law School Library.*

Spectators eagerly watched Jamison, a man with "a homely carbuncle
kind of a countenance with a hideous knob of a nose," which he
"screwd . . . into a hundred different forms while he spoke and gave such a
strong emphasis to his words that he merely spit in one's face att three or
four foot's distance, his mouth being plentifully bedewed with salival juice,
by the force of the liquor which he drank and the fumes of the tobacco
which he smoaked."[4] The sheriff apologized that he was only able to present seventeen men, not twenty-four. Although he had ordered citizens to
serve—"answer to your names every Man at the first Call and save your

Fines"—a few invariably failed to obey his summons, electing, instead, to pay a penalty of 13 shillings. The seventeen grand jurors stood up.

Next, the crier commanded silence on pain of imprisonment as the foreman, a merchant named Robert Watts, was sworn:

> You as foreman of the Grand Inquest for the body of the City and County of New York, Shall Well and truly Enquire, and true presentment make, of all such matters and things, as Shall be Given you in Charge, his Majesty's Counsel, your fellows, and your own, you Shall keep Secret, you Shall present no man for Envy, hatred, or malice, neither Shall you Leave anyone, unpresented, for Love, fear, favour Affection, or hope of Reward, but you Shall present things truly, as they Come to your knowledge, according to the best of your understanding, So Help You God.[5]

Any freeman over twenty-one with an estate valued at more than £30 was eligible to serve on a jury, but most of the men who took their oaths following Watts were prominent merchants who served on grand and petit juries again and again, like the Dutch trader Abraham Keteltass, who had served as a juror at John Peter Zenger's trial in 1735.[6] Nor were obvious conflicts of interest a bar to service; Winant Van Zant, whose dockside warehouse had burned to the ground on April Fool's Day, was sworn, too. Even greater bias, after all, could be found on the bench: Philipse's warehouse had been destroyed by a fire that his uncle's slave, Cuffee, had been jailed on suspicion of setting.

The grand jury sworn, Philipse cleared his throat again and delivered his charge. "*Gentlemen* of the Grand Jury," he began. "The many Frights and Terrors which the good People of this City have of late been put into, by repeated and unusual Fires, and burning of Houses, give us too much Room to suspect, that some of them at least did not proceed from mere Chance." The court's obligation was "to use our utmost Dilgence by all lawful Ways and Means to discover the Contrivers and Perpetrators of such daring and flagitious Undertakings." Arson, Philipse reminded the grand jurors, "is Felony at Common Law," and these particular fires were especially atrocious. "The Crime is of so shocking a Nature, that if we have any in this City, who, having been guilty thereof, should escape, who can say he is safe, or tell where it will end?"

Philipse could not have known it, but there would be no more warehouses burned, no more haystacks torched. The fires were over. But the

investigation was just beginning. "*My Charge, Gentlemen,*" Philipse concluded, is "to present all Conspiracies, Combinations, and other Offences,
from Treasons down to Trespasses." It would take not days or weeks but
months.[7] And before it was over, the dungeon underneath City Hall would
become as crowded, and as fouled, as the hull of a slave ship.

CITY HALL STOOD solid, stone upon stone, but the court that met
inside its walls rested on a shaky foundation. In 1689, when the colony had
been briefly without a government because of the Glorious Revolution in
England, a German merchant and militia captain named Jacob Leisler had
taken control of New York City and its fort and claimed the governorship
by royal authority. In March 1691, when the real royally appointed governor, Henry Sloughter, finally arrived, Leisler and his son-in-law Jacob
Milborne were tried for treason and sentenced to be hanged "by the Neck
and being Alive their bodys be Cutt downe to the Earth and Their Bow-
ells be taken out and they being Alive, burnt before their faces; that their
heads shall be struck off and their Bodys Cutt in four parts." But even as he
oversaw the beheading of his gutted predecessor, Sloughter faced a judicial
crisis: his royal commission gave him and his Council exclusive authority
to constitute courts, while a set of supplementary instructions commanded
him not to establish any courts "not before erected." But since every court
established under Leisler had been voided, there *were* no preexisting courts
in New York. Lacking the authority to erect new courts himself, Sloughter
turned to the General Assembly, which, in May 1691, passed the Judiciary
Act, establishing a system headed by a Supreme Court, the highest civil
and criminal court in the colony.[8]

But of course this, too, violated Sloughter's instructions, which had
given only the governor and his Council, not the Assembly, the power to
erect courts. At a time when the colony was still reeling from the bloody
end of Jacob Leisler, no one bothered to complain. But just eight years
later, the Assembly refused to renew the Judiciary Act, forcing a new governor to sign an ordinance authorizing the judiciary, which turned out to
be a poor patch over what one legal historian has called the colony's "constitutional abyss": the 1691 Judiciary Act placed every successive governor
and Assembly in a stalemate, with each insisting that it had the right to
establish courts but neither willing to challenge the other.[9]

That stalemate survived until 1732, when reckless William Cosby
arrived in New York. Determined to sue his predecessor, Rip Van Dam, for

the salary he had received as interim governor, Cosby retained Joseph Murray and Daniel Horsmanden as his personal attorneys. It was by no means clear what court should hear his suit. If Cosby sued Van Dam in the Supreme Court, he would face a jury, and Cosby knew that no New York jury would find in his favor.[10] Nor could Cosby file his suit in the Court of Chancery, since the governor, as chancellor, presided over that court, and he could hardly hear his own case.[11] Instead, Murray and Horsmanden recommended that Cosby take the unusual step of ordering the Supreme Court to sit as a Court of Exchequer, a juryless equity court with jurisdiction over royal revenues.

When Cosby's case came before the Supreme Court in April 1733, James Alexander and William Smith, serving as Van Dam's attorneys, filed exceptions objecting to the authority of the court to sit in exchequer. Sixty-two-year-old Chief Justice Lewis Morris upheld the objection, but the young Second Justice James DeLancey dissented, supported by Philipse. Furious, Morris then delivered his "Opinion and Argument" to John Peter Zenger, who printed it as a pamphlet.[12] In August, Cosby summarily dismissed Morris from the court; two days later, he elevated James DeLancey to Chief Justice, and Philipse to the second justiceship.

Promoted on the bench, DeLancey and Philipse were damned on the street. "Young delancy & Fred Philps have Lost a great deall of good Will by being in the Gov[ernor]s Interest," Abigail Franks wrote to her son in London that fall. James Alexander complained that the "Chief Justice & Second Judge are both Young men of no Experience or practice in the Law & the Second Judge has no pretence to any kind of Learning." Cadwallader Colden believed that DeLancey had accepted the office only out of "his Vanity love of power & the profits," but that "his Ignorance" of the law meant that "every time he was under a necessity of speaking from the Bench he exposed himself to the Contempt of the Auditors So that through too great fondness of Honour he lost all respect & became pitifull to men of sense."[13]

Meanwhile, Morris only gained favor, inspiring Cosby's critics to consider further use of the power of print. One reason Morris had his *Opinion* published was that Cosby, otherwise, controlled the press. For most of the seventeenth century, New York lacked a printing press; royal instructions sent to the governor in 1686 had warned, "as great inconvenience may arise by the liberty of printing . . . you are to provide by all necessary Orders that noe person keep any press for printing, nor that any book, pamphlet or other matters whatever bee printed without your special leave & license."

That leave was first given in 1693, when thirty-year-old William Bradford was appointed "King's Printer," a position he held until 1742, earning £50 a year for printing the province's laws, its Assembly proceedings, and assorted English reprints. When a young runaway apprentice named Benjamin Franklin came to New York looking for work in 1723, he stopped at Bradford's printshop. Bradford, a "cunning old fox," refused to hire him; he was well served by his workers, who included not only his twenty-six-year-old German apprentice, John Peter Zenger, but also slaves. In 1735, when Bradford was sixty-one, he began printing the city's first newspaper, the *New York Gazette*. In it, he printed lists of ships in and out of port, foreign news extracted from other newspapers, speeches of the governor, and records of the votes of the Assembly. He wrote precious little of the newspaper's editorial content. And any politically sensitive news in the *Gazette* was contributed by the Recorder.[14]

It was for publishing his *Opinion*, as much as for having it, that William Cosby punished Morris.[15] But dismissing the Chief Justice did little to silence Cosby's opponents, who were deeply influenced by political theorists like John Trenchard and Thomas Gordon: in *Cato's Letters*, their set of essays published between 1720 and 1723, Trenchard and Gordon had argued that "freedom of speech . . . is inseparable from publick liberty."

To exert that freedom in New York, Cosby's critics turned to Zenger, who, after apprenticing with Bradford, had set up his own printing shop in 1726. In June 1732, two months before Cosby arrived in the colony, but after word of his appointment had reached New York, James Alexander had bought *The History of the Art of Printing* at Montgomerie's library auction. By the fall of 1733, Alexander arranged for Zenger to begin printing an opposition newspaper, the *New-York Weekly Journal*, for which Alexander would supply essays and political commentary.[16]

While Alexander employed the art of printing against the new governor, Cosby, after dismissing Morris, continued to pursue his case against Van Dam in the courts. In the spring of 1734, the question of whether the Supreme Court could sit in exchequer was put to the Assembly.[17] After hearing opposing arguments presented by Joseph Murray and William Smith, the Assembly, wisely, decided to do nothing, and Cosby was forced to drop his suit. Meanwhile, Recorder Francis Harison defended the governor in Bradford's *Gazette*, and Alexander attacked him in Zenger's *Weekly Journal*. Cosby ordered James DeLancey to secure grand jury indictments against Zenger for libel. In January 1734, DeLancey did as he was told, charging a grand jury: "If you, Gentlemen, do not interpose, consider whether the ill consequences that may arise from any disturbances of the public peace may not in part lie at your door?"[18]

Much to the dismay of Cosby and the frustration of DeLancey, the grand jury refused to return an indictment against Zenger. DeLancey waited until the October term, and tried again, charging another grand jury to return an indictment for libel, now specifically for two "scandalous" ballads printed by Zenger in September, whose excruciatingly bad verses included opinions on the constitutional crisis of the courts:

> Exchequer courts, as void by law,
> > great grievances we call;
> Though great men do assert no flaw
> > is in them; they shall fall.[19]

"Sometimes heavy, halfwitted men get a knack of rhyming," DeLancey complained, "but it is time to break them of it, when they grow abusive, insolent, and mischievious."

This time the grand jury returned the indictment but claimed that it was impossible to identify the author of the ballads, despite Cosby's offer of a £50 reward. (Alexander had never signed any of his contributions, except with pseudonyms such as "Jeremy Anonymous," and despite the Council's offer of a reward, he was never named.) Cosby then asked the Assembly to order the newspapers to be burned, but the Assembly refused. Enraged, Cosby turned to his Council. In meetings on October 17 and November 2, 1734—at which the Council's three Country Party members, Van Dam, Alexander, and Abraham Van Horne, were absent, Cosby having neglected to summon them—Clarke, Harison, DeLancey, and Horsmanden were appointed to a committee charged with pointing out "the particular seditious paragraphs" in Zenger's paper.

Cosby's Council, minus its opposition members, decided that Zenger should be arrested, that the governor should offer a reward for the discovery of the author of the essays in his newspaper, and that Zenger, as printer, and the author or authors, if they could be identified, should be prosecuted for sedition.[20] In November, Cosby's Council ordered the city's common hangman to burn four especially incendiary issues of the *Weekly Journal*.

But while Cosby had easily manipulated DeLancey, Philipse, and his Council, he had far less influence among municipal officers. In response to Cosby's order to burn Zenger's papers, the city's Cosby-hating Court of

Quarter Sessions issued its own order, forbidding the common hangman, the sheriff, or any other member of the Corporation of the City of New York to destroy the newspapers. Whereupon the sheriff, John Symes, a Cosby appointee, ingeniously found someone, a legal non-person, who *could* light the match: Symes delivered stacks of the *Weekly Journal* "unto the hands of his own Negro" and ordered him to burn them.

DeLancey signed a warrant for Zenger's arrest in January 1735. Since no grand jury was willing to indict the printer, Attorney General Richard Bradley filed charges against Zenger "on information," a high-handed means by which a man could be prosecuted without an indictment. Zenger's attorneys, James Alexander and William Smith, began preparing his defense. Now New Yorkers would discover whether the Supreme Court would protect their liberty, or make them slaves.

IN PREPARING FOR John Peter Zenger's trial, Alexander intended to argue that the passages in the *Weekly Journal* were not libels because they in no way specifically impugned Cosby; instead, they were an attack on the power of New York's governors, of *all* its governors, and on the rule of men and not of law. Notes Alexander prepared before the trial reveal that he intended to argue that even before Cosby's arrival in 1732, "Judges, justices, sheriffs and coroners, in whose hands are our laws, our liberties and properties, were . . . appointed by the govr. alone contrary to the royal instructions, and consequently our lives, liberties and properties were at the mere will of a govr." Turning, again, to the rhetoric of freedom and bondage, Alexander made notes to argue: "Before this Govr. came, I think no man will say but that this is a state of slavery, and so no libel on the present administration as charged."[21]

Alexander never had the chance to introduce his argument. When Zenger's trial opened on April 15, 1735, Smith and Alexander began by challenging the authority of DeLancey and Philipse on the grounds that the judges had been commissioned to serve "during pleasure" (meaning at the king's pleasure, or at the pleasure of his agent, the governor) when they should have been commissioned to serve "during good behavior," an argument that asserted the independence of the judicial from the executive branch. But coming after Cosby's dismissal of Morris and his promotion of DeLancey and Philipse, it was impossible for the judges not to see this move as a challenge to their qualifications for the bench and, even, as an assault on the integrity of the court itself. "The judges lost all temper at the tender of the exceptions," Smith, Jr., wrote in his *History*.[22] Stunned and outraged by this unexpected attack on his authority, a nervous DeLancey immediately adjourned the court.

The next morning, in a packed courtroom, DeLancey declared to Zenger's attorneys: "You thought to have gained a great deal of applause and popularity by opposing this Court, as you did the Court of Exchequer; but you have brought it to the point that either *we must go from the bench, or you from the bar*." In an act of astonishingly naive political miscalculation, the young Chief Justice ruled that Smith and Alexander be disbarred. (On hearing of this, Lewis Morris scoffed, "authority Shews the man.") DeLancey silenced two of the city's most learned and accomplished lawyers for their contempt in having denied "the legality of the judges their commissions . . . and the being of this Supreme Court."

Alexander, unwilling to be silenced, immediately protested that "the exceptions were *only to their commissions* and *not to the being of the Court*," and Smith pointed out that challenging the judges' commissions did not itself imply a challenge to the court: "the Court might well exist though the commissions of all the judges were void." Wary lest the wording of the disbarment be used against them, Zenger's attorneys "prayed that the order might be altered" to delete the phrase "and the being of this Supreme Court." DeLancey refused.[23]

In place of Alexander and Smith, DeLancey appointed John Chambers, a young Cosbyite, to serve as Zenger's attorney. So that Chambers might prepare a defense, the case was postponed until the next regularly scheduled court session, in August. Meanwhile, the lull did little to extinguish "Party flames." In June, Abigail Franks wrote to her son that "party rage has bin Carryed on with Such Violence that for my part I hate to hear it mentioned." (Franks took an equivocal view: "if the Governor has had his fault the other Side have not bin without theire failings.") That July, at the celebration of the building of the new battery, Sheriff John Symes was killed in a freak accident when a cannon exploded at George Augustus' Royal Battery during a dedication ceremony hosted by Cosby, which involved "several Barrels of Punch and Beer."[24]

IN 1735, John Chambers was only twenty-five years old, and "more distinguished for a knack at haranguing a jury than his erudition in the law." Alexander, despairing of the defense Chambers would offer, believed Zenger was better off with no lawyer at all. Supposing Zenger had best defend himself, Alexander drafted an opening and closing argument for the defendant to deliver to the jury. That he held out little hope for Zenger's acquittal under these circumstances is evident in the title he gave to the speeches: "Prologue and Epilogue to the Farce."[25] But Zenger never delivered the speeches Alexander had written for him. During the adjournment, Alexander secretly recruited the fifty-nine-year-old Philadelphia attorney Andrew Hamilton to come to Zenger's aid.

When the trial reconvened, in August, Bradley began by reading excerpts from the *Weekly Journal* that he said were intended "to traduce, scandalize and vilify" Cosby. Chambers delivered an opening statement in which he offered the standard defense against libel by questioning Bradley's ability to prove that the passages in question specifically referred to Cosby or to anyone else in his administration.

Just as young Chambers took his seat, Hamilton, with dazzling dramatic flourish, rose to his feet from the back of the courtroom, revealed himself as Zenger's chosen attorney, and proceeded, quite entirely, to take control of the trial. Hamilton, Smith, Jr., said, "had art, eloquence, vivacity, and humour, was ambitious of fame, negligent of nothing to ensure success, and possessed a confidence which no terrors could awe." Rather than denying Zenger's responsibility for the newspaper, or his intent in attacking Cosby in its editorials, Hamilton stipulated both and then argued two points before the jury (all but ignoring the stupefied justices on the bench): first, that Zenger was innocent because what he printed was true, and second, that freedom of the press was especially necessary in the colonies, where governors asserted more authority than did rulers in England (after all, Hamilton winked, they controlled this very court) and where other checks against their power were weakened by distance.

Before the day was over, the jury found Zenger not guilty, "upon which there were three Huzzas in the Hall" and "a mixture of amazement, terror, and wrath appeared in the bench." One of the judges threatened to arrest whoever had started the cheer, but Captain Matthew Norris, Lewis Morris's son-in-law, rose from his seat and "pertly declared that huzzas were common in Westminster Hall," whereupon the shouts were once again raised. Andrew Hamilton was carried from City Hall, one block east on Wall Street, and then south on Smith Street, to be fêted at the Black Horse Tavern across from Zenger's printshop. Zenger himself spent the night in jail—he was released the next day—after having spent eight months in the dungeon (during which time Francis Harison had visited him and threatened to beat him with a cane) because Alexander and Morris had decided that paying his bail would have dampened public sympathy for him.[26]

Zenger's acquittal was a tremendous victory for Cosby's political opponents. But, ironically, the battle had weakened Cosby's opposition. Alexander and Smith had been disbarred. Lewis Morris had left New York for London, to argue there for the removal from office of Cosby, Harison, and Horsmanden, and for his own restoration to the Supreme Court. But the Court Party sustained losses, too. Harison fled the province in disrepute in 1735, after which Cosby appointed Horsmanden to the office of Recorder. In November 1735, Cosby became "dangerously ill of a violent Pleurisie." At a meeting of his Council held in his bedroom, he suspended Van Dam. When the governor died of pneumonia in March 1736, Clarke was elected president of the Council assumed the governorship—a position Van Dam, as senior member of the Council, would have had if he had not been removed.

Alexander and his allies arranged for the Country Party's choice for governor, Rip Van Dam, to set up a rival government, in which William Smith, not Daniel Horsmanden, was to be Recorder. "We had all the appearance of a civil War," Cadwallader Colden wrote. Warned of a plot "to seize his person or kill him in the Attempt," Clarke retreated to Fort George "& put the place in a posture of Defence."

But the actual assault came by pen, not by sword, as Alexander continued to attack Clarke in the *Weekly Journal.* In September, Clarke wrote to England that he was "terrified by Zengers Journal." Only after confirmation of Clarke's role arrived from England on October 13, 1736, just a day before the rival governments were to be sworn, was Van Dam's government dismantled. (Clarke was named lieutenant governor, but the newly appointed royal governor, Baron Delawarr, never bothered to travel to New York, leaving Clarke in charge.) Finally, the opposition yielded. "Happy are we that we escaped the Ruin that *M—r-s,* an *A—x——r* and a *S—th* were hurrying the Province into," wrote Horsmanden in Bradford's *Gazette.* "Let us with Horror and Detestation look back upon them, who, under the pretence of Friendship, liberty, sought our Destruction, to gratifie their own Passions."[27]

Although party strife continued through 1739, the colony quieted. Lewis Morris failed to regain his position as Chief Justice but was handed a considerable concession prize: he accepted the governorship of New Jersey in 1738 and more or less disappeared from New York politics. James Alexander and William Smith were reinstated to the bar in 1737 and resumed their lucrative practice. Meanwhile, Clarke proceeded to reward party loyalists: in 1737, he appointed Daniel Horsmanden to the third place on the Supreme Court, which had been vacant since Morris's dismissal.

Whatever else the crisis of the 1730s resolved, or failed to resolve, it did not answer the problem of "the being of this Supreme Court."[28] The court's authority, vulnerable to partisan machinations from the beginning, was badly bruised in the legal and political battles of the 1730s. By 1741, the authority of its judges, and its independence from the governor, remained open questions.

ON TUESDAY, April 21, 1741, on the second floor of City Hall on the first day of the Supreme Court's spring session, Second Justice Frederick Philipse delivered his charge to the grand jury, and then he adjourned the court. The next morning, Clarke reported to the Lords of Trade in London that "many Negroes are imprisoned on suspicion, but as yet no proof appears against them."[29] At City Hall, the grand jury set to work, seeking that proof.

In its first act, the grand jury summoned John Hughson's sixteen-year-old servant, Mary Burton. She refused to come. The constable set out again to fetch her, this time with a warrant. Brought to the second-floor jury room, Burton refused to be sworn. Asked if she knew anything about the fires, she sat in silence. According to Horsmanden, "as it was thought a Matter of the utmost Concern, the Grand Jury was very importunate, and used many Arguments with her, in publick, and private, to persuade her to speak the Truth, and tell all she knew about it." The governor's proclamation was read to her, with its promise of her freedom and a £100 reward. *"She seemed to despise it."* All morning they pressed her. Finally, as "all was in vain," Burton was ordered arrested. On her way down the stairs to the dungeon, "she considered better of it," and headed back up.

After she was sworn, Mary Burton told the grand jury "she would acquaint them with what she knew relating to the Goods stolen from Mr. *Hogg's, but would say nothing about the Fires.*" The slip must have been deliberate; as Horsmanden observed, "it did by Construction amount to an Affirmative" that she knew who had set the fires. The grand jury proceeded to question her almost entirely on that subject. At the end of the day, Burton signed a detailed deposition, describing a vast plot. She named Prince, Caesar, Peggy Kerry, and the Hughsons as authors of the robbery at Hogg's. Of far greater interest to the grand jury, she described meetings at Hughson's in which they talked "of burning the Fort; and that they would go down to the Fly and burn the whole Town" and "*when as the white People came to extinguish it, they would kill and destroy them.*" Most shocking of all, "when all this was done, *Caesar* should be Governor, and *Hughson* her Master should be King." The wheel would turn, the empire would revolve.

Mary Burton's statement changed everything. On Thursday, April 23, quick on the heels of Burton's astonishing deposition (which "could not but be very amazing to every one that heard it"), Philipse and Horsmanden "summoned all the Gentlemen of the Law in Town, to meet them in the Afternoon, in order to consult with them, and determine upon such Measures as on the Result of their Deliberations should be judged most proper to be taken upon this Emergency." The aging Attorney General Richard Bradley was too ill to attend, but after lunch Philipse and Horsmanden held an extraordinary meeting with all of the city lawyers qualified to practice before the Supreme Court: Joseph Murray, James Alexander, William Smith, John Chambers, Richard Nichols, Abraham Lodge, and William Jamison.

New York's bar was one of the best educated in the colonies. Bradley was a Cambridge graduate, Smith a Yale alumnus. Alexander, Chambers, Murray, and Smith were, like Horsmanden and DeLancey, members of the London Inns of Court. Together, the members of the New York bar had hammered New York jurisprudence into considerable conformity with the law of England.[30] Inspired to promote their own professional interests, they had also managed, on more than one occasion, to rise above partisan loyalties. In 1725, Smith, Murray, Alexander and Chambers, Nichols and Lodge had signed an anti-competitive agreement.[31] Five years later, when Joseph Murray drafted a new charter for New York City, he granted a monopoly to himself and his closest legal colleagues—Alexander, Chambers, Smith, Nichols, Lodge, Jamison, and George Lurting—deeding them exclusive right to practice in the Mayor's Court.

In 1734, after the New Jersey Assembly passed a law regulating lawyers' fees, Alexander, Smith, Chambers, Murray, and Lodge (all of whom also practiced in New Jersey) successfully petitioned the Lords of Trade for the law's repeal. And when DeLancey appointed Chambers to serve as Zenger's attorney in 1735, Chambers, rather than toadying to Cosby's wishes, as Alexander and Smith expected he would, instead prepared notes for an able defense before being replaced by Andrew Hamilton. In 1737, Smith and Alexander were reinstated to the bar on a motion made by

Joseph Murray on their behalf.[32] Long before they gathered together in City Hall on April 23, 1741, New York's attorneys had joined forces to serve their clients and protect their practices and, in the process, had helped protect the courts from the machinations of governors, assemblymen, and partisan rancor.

Most if not all of these attorneys also owned slaves, several of whom would eventually be named in the conspiracy, along with Justice DeLancey's Othello and Justice Philipse's Frank. By April 23, two of Chambers's slaves, Robin and Cuba, had already been arrested. Another Cuffee, owned by William Jamison, would soon be implicated, as would two of Murray's slaves, Jack and Adam. Jamison, Smith, Murray, and Chambers had also frequently handled civil litigation involving slaves; so common were such cases that Murray, in his book of forms, kept several detailing the proper language to use in filing a complaint against a slave seller on behalf of a buyer who purchased slaves advertised as healthy but who fell ill or died soon after sale.[33]

Gathered at City Hall with the Supreme Court judges on April 23, the gentlemen of the law had a crucial decision to make: how to prosecute slaves accused of the plot Burton described, and in what court. After some discussion, they agreed that although by law slaves accused of conspiracy could be summarily tried without a jury, or in the municipal sessions court, in these circumstances the conspiracy ought to be "taken under the Care of the Supreme Court."

It was a very odd decision. Slaves accused of crimes in New York were rarely brought before any court, and almost never before the Supreme Court. Typically, slaveowners administered justice themselves. Under the terms of the 1730 "Act for the more effectual preventing and punishing the Conspiracy of Negro and other slaves," it was legal "for any Master or Mistress to Punish his her or their Slave or Slaves for their Crimes and offences at discretion not Extending to Life or Limb." Even those slaveowners whose discretion extended beyond life and limb were rarely charged. In 1736, a slave owned by the Dutch blockmaker John Van Zant ran away. When he was found and returned, Van Zant "corrected him with a Horse-Whip." The slave subsequently died, which "occasion'd a Report, that he was whipt to Death"; but a coroner's inquest convinced a jury that "the Correction given by the Master was not the Cause of his Death, but that it was by the Visitations of God." Van Zant went unpunished.[34]

Nor did owners too squeamish to do the whipping themselves suffer insolence. For the modest sum of 3 shillings and 6 pence per whipping, New Yorkers could send to the Poorhouse "all unruly and ungovernable

Servants and Slaves there to be kept at hard labour, and punished according to the Directions of any one Justice with the Consent of the Master or Mistress."[35]

Horsewhip in hand, the Poorhouse just blocks away, slaveowners had little need to bring errant slaves to City Hall. Criminal charges were filed against slaves at a rate much lower than their percentage in the population (slaves constituted less than 7 percent of those charged with crimes), undoubtedly because owners administered their own justice without recourse to the courts. On the rare occasions when city slaves were indicted, they were usually tried summarily by justices of the peace. "Slaves are the Property of Christians or Jews and cannot without great Loss or detriment to their Masters or Mistresses be Subjected in all Cases Criminal to the Strict Rules of the Laws of England," the 1730 code declared. In other words, since punishing slaves by fines, imprisonment, or execution deprived their owners of their property, other remedies were to be sought. In a summary criminal trial, the owner paid for any damages caused by a slave's trespass and the justices ordered the slave whipped, after which the slave could immediately return to service. Tried before justices of the peace or lower courts, slaves were, not surprisingly, very likely to be found guilty: nearly 70 percent of indicted slaves were convicted, compared to a slightly less than 50 percent conviction rate for English and Dutch.[36]

The 1730 slave code stipulated similar summary proceedings for slaves suspected of conspiracy, arson, or murder. Such suspects were to be brought "before three or more of his Majesties Justices of the Peace . . . in Conjunction with five of the Principle freeholders . . . without A Grand Jury seven of whome agreeing shall put their Judgement in Execution." Only if he was willing to pay the costs could an accused slave's owner insist on a jury trial.

In 1741, Caesar and Prince, charged only with burglary, and the other prisoners, suspected of conspiracy, might easily have been brought before a juryless panel of three magistrates. It would have been far quicker and much cheaper, and the desired outcome, conviction and execution, almost assured. In his *Journal,* Horsmanden insisted that the April 23 decision to bring these cases before the Supreme Court was made because Burton's grand jury testimony hinted that "there was reason to apprehend there was a Conspiracy of deeper Design and more dangerous Contrivance than the Slaves themselves were capable of." That is to say, whites were involved, too, and they could best be brought to justice in a jury trial following a grand jury inquiry.

Horsmanden's explanation was, at best, disingenuous. Conducting the trials in the Supreme Court, even if whites were involved, was by no means required by law. And Horsmanden and his colleagues must have understood the risk of staking their own and the court's reputations on the prosecution of rebellious slaves. In 1712, eighteen of the twenty-five slaves sentenced to death had been swiftly convicted in the city's Court of Quarter Sessions in trials held between April 12 and May 30, after which the remaining cases were transferred to the Supreme Court for its scheduled summer session, which began on June 3. And that was only because Attorney General May Bickley wanted to retry a slave named Mars, owned by attorney Jacob Regnier, a rival of Bickley's (Regnier had opposed Bickley's appointment to Attorney General. Mars had been acquitted, *twice*, in the Court of Quarter Sessions). Bickley called Regnier to testify against Mars in both trials, and Regnier twice refused to aid the prosecution; each time, he actually testified on Mars' behalf. Governor Robert Hunter wrote that Bickley had then determined to prosecute Mars to the death, and "had him by some fetch of law try'd again at the supream court, where he found a jury tractable to his purpose." But Bickley's machinations had not gone unpunished. Hunter pardoned Mars, complained that Bickley had turned the trials into a "party quarrel," and forced Bickley to resign from his lucrative post as City Recorder.[37]

In 1741, Daniel Horsmanden expected no such censure from George Clarke, who, in 1712, had been Secretary of the Province and a supporter of Bickley.[38] And in 1741, Clarke had watched his own house burn to the ground, at a personal loss of some £2,000–£3,000. He had given Horsmanden considerable latitude in pursuing the investigation.

But, in case there was any room for doubt, Horsmanden, with great dispatch, assembled the city's attorneys on Thursday, April 23, in order to further consolidate his, and the court's, authority and to establish its jurisdiction. At the judges' urging, Murray, Alexander, Smith, Chambers, Nichols, Lodge, and Jamison "generously and unanimously offered to give their Assistance on every Tryal in their Turns." "All the Gentlemen of the Law in Town" agreed to aid the prosecution. Horsmanden would not allow this investigation to turn into a "party quarrel." To the contrary. To Horsmanden it was an opportunity to assert not only the authority of the Supreme Court but also its transcendence over party loyalties, and to help restore the court's reputation after the debacle of Zenger's trial. Moreover, with DeLancey out of town, a high-profile prosecution rescuing white New Yorkers from nefarious black villains presented Daniel Horsmanden with the pleasing prospect of advancing his own career, and of making a point about political opposition itself—by exposing the perfidy of the slave plot to replace the governor.

A conspiracy uncovered, the Supreme Court's jurisdiction established, the bench and bar joined in common purpose, the full force of the law marshaled, it remained to fathom the plot's extent and to bring the conspirators to justice. In cases brought before the Supreme Court, it fell to the grand jury to conduct an inquiry, examine witnesses, and find bills of indictment: to charge specific individuals with specific crimes.[39] But in this case, the investigation was led by the judges, and, most of all, by Daniel Horsmanden himself.

THE GRAND JURY, Horsmanden said, "bore the Burthen of this Enquiry," but the *"Business by Degrees multipled so fast"* that *"the Judges . . . found it expedient to examine the Persons accused, upon their first taking into Custody, whereby it seemed most likely the Truth would bolt out, before they had Time to cool, or Opportunity of discoursing in the Jail with their Confederates."* In the *Journal,* Horsmanden referred, again and again, to "the Judges" to provide cover for activities that were largely his; DeLancey was out of town, and Philipse was rarely present except when court was in session (and not always then). Horsmanden, alone, interrogated nearly every suspect, before anyone else had a chance to. Only after he had interrogated suspects did he turn them over to the grand jury. "The Examinations thus taken by the Judges," he explained, "were soon after laid before the Grand Jury, who interrogated the Parties therefrom in such manner, as generally produced from them the Substance of the same Matter, and often something more."

That one of the judges headed the investigation was not, by the standards of the eighteenth century, wholly unusual. Nor was it strange that, with all the attorneys in town serving the prosecution, the defendants had no lawyers. Early English and colonial criminal courts worked quite differently from modern courts. Before the rise, late in the eighteenth century, of an adversarial system in which attorneys for the king and the prisoner took turns presenting evidence before a supposedly neutral judge, lawyers other than the Attorney General and his assistants were hardly ever present at criminal trials; instead, a "collegial trial bench," usually consisting of three justices, participated in conducting the investigation, informed by very few rules of evidence other than the unevenly applied exclusion of hearsay. In theory, the defendant did not require counsel because the judges were supposed to protect his interests, making sure that he understood the matters of law pertaining to his case. As to answering the charges against him, it was believed that the accused served his own interests best. According to William Hawkins's *Pleas of the Crown,* an influential legal manual, "Every one of Common Understanding may as properly speak to a Matter of Fact, as if he were the best Lawyer." Defense lawyers were not even allowed in English courts until 1696, and then only in cases of treason. By the 1730s, that prohibition was being slowly lifted—after all, Zenger had a defense attorney—but it remained a rare defendant who had a lawyer, especially because the whole point of a trial was to get the defendant to explain himself to the jury, so that jurors could tell whether or not he was lying. Allowing a defendant an attorney, or allowing him to call more than a few witnesses on his own behalf, thwarted that end. As Hawkins explained, "the very Speech, Gesture and Countenance, and Manner of Defense of those who are Guilty, when they speak for themselves, may often help to disclose the Truth, which probably would not so well be discovered from the artificial Defense of others speaking for them."[40] Horsmanden believed that, confronted by his accusers, a black man "betrayed his Guilt" with his face: "Those who are used to Negroes may have experienced, that some of them when charged with any Piece of Villany, they have been detected in, have an odd Knack or (it is hard to call or how to describe it) Way of turning their Eyes *inwards,* as it were, as if shocked at the Consciousness of their own Perfidy; their Looks at the same Time *discovering* all the Symptoms of the most inveterate Malice and Resentment."

The trial brought the defendant, alone, to face the jury. In theory, the judges served as the defendant's counsel, but in practice criminal trial procedure strongly favored prosecution. So did pretrial evidence gathering. Long before there existed anything like an investigative police force, courts relied overwhelmingly on two kinds of evidence: the pretrial interrogation of "crown witnesses," often members of criminal gangs who were paid for "turning king's evidence" (testifying against their accomplices); and pretrial, custodial confessions, often obtained by promises of pardon or reduction of charges. Not until the beginning of the trial did the defendant hear the charges and see the evidence against him. This evidence was then paraded before the defendant in a kind of pageant, designed to get him (or her) to speak and, ideally, to confess.[41]

Such were the procedures of criminal investigation available to magistrates in New York City. With Mary Burton's deposition on April 22, the grand jury secured its first crown witness, although Burton always insisted that she was merely an innocent bystander to, and not a member of, the crime ring she described. Better still would be to convince a member of Hughson's gang to turn king's evidence. Peggy Kerry seemed the best candidate. Kerry was painfully vulnerable: she had been named in Burton's deposition; she had been arrested (and jailed, probably with her nursing newborn); and her lover, Caesar, seemed doomed.

On Thursday, April 23, while Horsmanden and Philipse were meeting with all of the city's attorneys, the grand jury interrogated Kerry. Although she had little to lose by cooperating with the prosecution, and her life to gain, Kerry "positively denied knowing any Thing about the Fires." Philipse and Horsmanden decided to apply more pressure. That evening, after adjourning the meeting with the city's lawyers, the judges descended to the cellar of City Hall to conduct their own examination. In Kerry's cell, "they exhorted her to make an ingenuous Confession and Discovery of what she knew of it, and gave her Hopes of their Recommendation to the Governor for a Pardon." Kerry turned out to be more willful than they had expected: "she withstood it, and positively denied that she knew any Thing of the Matter; and said, *That if she should accuse any Body of any such Thing, she must accuse innocent Persons, and* WRONG HER OWN SOUL."

Kerry's intransigence was a considerable obstacle. The crown's case against the first five prisoners awaiting trial—Caesar, Prince, Peggy Kerry, John and Sarah Hughson—was uneven. The evidence supporting charges of burglary was unassailable: the stolen goods, after all, had been found in the prisoners' possession. But the case for conspiracy, the case Daniel Horsmanden cared about, rested almost entirely on the April 22 deposition of Mary Burton, a loose-lipped servant girl accused by one of the suspects of having once birthed a bastard. She was hardly an exemplary witness. On Friday, all five prisoners were indicted on the burglary charges, and pled not guilty. Their trial, originally scheduled for April 25, was postponed several times while Bradley and Murray built a case against them, and waited for someone to talk.

On May 1, Caesar and Prince were tried separately from their white accomplices, to give Kerry more time to ponder the prospect of pardon. In a crowded courtroom, Bradley opened the indictment and Murray examined witnesses, including Rebecca and Robert Hogg, Christopher Wilson ("Yorkshire"), and Mary Burton. Conducting their own defense, Caesar and Prince denied the charges against them and called three witnesses, including Prince's owner, John Auboyneau, whom they examined themselves. None of this trial testimony survives, although at the sentencing Philipse assured the prisoners: "you have been proceeded against in the same Manner as any white Man, guilty of your Crimes wou'd have been: You had not only the Liberty of sending for your Witnesses; asking them such Questions as you thought proper; but likewise making the best Defence you could." A twelve-man jury found them guilty.

Peggy Kerry and the Hughsons were scheduled to be tried for receiving stolen goods on the following Wednesday. Over the weekend, a more damning crown witness, one who could aid the conspiracy case, conveniently presented himself: Arthur Price, a white indentured servant in jail for petty theft, told jailkeeper James Mills that he "had had some Discourse in the Gaol with *Peggy*." Mills summoned one of the judges, probably Horsmanden, who examined Price in his cell on the evening of Sunday, May 3.

Price said Kerry had spoken to him through "the Hole of the Prison Door," which suggests that he, or she, was confined to a walled cell. Zenger had been imprisoned in just such a cell in 1734. He was allowed to speak only to his wife and servants, and only "through the Hole of the Door," through which food was probably also passed in, and waste, or "Ordure Tubbs," out.[42] Other prisoners may have been at liberty to wander around the open space of the "Great Gaol."

The sole surviving architectural drawing of City Hall includes no floor plan for the cellar; in his *History*, William Smith, Jr., described it only as a "dungeon." In the mid-eighteenth century, no one except debtors was ever sentenced to prison, and they were allowed to stay in the garret. Instead, the jail was a holding pen for those awaiting trial, execution, or corporal punishment. It was not particularly secure. In 1733, a convicted burglar named Martha Cash had escaped after setting the prison door on fire. In 1735, in an effort to better secure its prisoners, the dungeon was equipped with iron shackles which could be hitched to iron staples, fixed to the stone walls of the foundation.[43] After that, criminals considered dangerous were literally bolted to stone.

In the spring of 1741, more improvements were hastily made to the dungeon: wooden-framed plaster walls were erected to divide the open space into smaller cells. "*All proper Precautions were taken by the Judges,*" Horsmanden wrote, "*that the Criminals should be kept separate; and they were so as much as the scanty Room in the Jail would admit of; and new Apartments were accordingly fitted up for their Reception.*" Because of the privacy afforded by those "*new Apartments,*" Price's meeting with the judges was kept secret from the other prisoners.

In the first of three revealing depositions, Price told Horsmanden that Kerry had said, "*She was very much afraid of these Fellows* (meaning the Negroes, as he understood) *telling or discovering something of her; but,* said she, *if they do, by G-d, I will* HANG *them every one;* but that she would *not* FORSWEAR *herself, unless they brought her in.*" By Price's recollection, the conversation moved quickly from the robbery to the conspiracy:

PRICE: Peggy, *How* FORSWEAR *yourself?*
KERRY: *There is Fourteen* SWORN.
PRICE: *What, is it about* Mr. Hogg's *Goods?*
KERRY: *No, by G-d,* ABOUT THE FIRE.
PRICE: *What,* Peggy, *were you a going to set the Town on fire?*
KERRY: No, but *by G-d, since I knew of it, they made me swear.*
PRICE: *Was* John *and his Wife in it?*
KERRY: *Yes, by G-d, they were both sworn as well as the rest.*
PRICE: *Were you* not afraid that the Negroes would discover you?
KERRY: *No; for* Prince, Cuff *and* Caesar *and* Forck's [Vaarck's] Negro [Bastian] *were all true-hearted Fellows.*

To Price, Kerry damned Mary Burton: "that Bitch . . . has fetched me in, and made me as black as the Rest." And the last thing Peggy Kerry whispered to Arthur Price, through the hole in the prison door, before he ratted her out to Mills was: "*you Son of a B—h, don't speak a Word of what I have told you.*"

Three days after Arthur Price made his deposition, Kerry and the Hughsons were tried on the lesser burglary charges and found guilty. The Hughsons' daughter Sarah was arrested and sent to the cellar jail. The next day, May 7, Price told Philipse and Horsmanden that young Sarah had confided to him about the conspiracy in great detail, and had named Joe, owned by dancing master Henry Holt, and Dundee, owned by tavernkeeper Robert Todd, as conspirators.

Soon afterward, "*Arthur Price* having been found by Experience to be very adroit at pumping out the Secrets of the Conspirators," Philipse and Horsmanden ordered Mills to put Cuffee "into the same Cell with him, and to give them a Tankard of Punch now and then, in order to chear up their Spirits, and make them more sociable." Cuffee, apparently, drank more than he ought to have. The next night, Price offered a deposition providing all the details of Cuffee's involvement in the conspiracy and said that Cuffee had told him that Quack, owned by John Roosevelt, had set the fire at Fort George.

From the prosecutors' point of view, Price was priceless. But no one imagined he was blameless. As Horsmanden admitted in a footnote in his *Journal:* "*Upon the Supposition, that* Arthur *knew nothing of the Secrets of the Conspiracy before he came to Gaol, the Reader may be apt to judge, that he acted with more than ordinary Acuteness for one of his Station, in pumping so much out of* Peggy *and* Sarah (Hughson's *Daughter) and their Confidence in him, if he were a Stranger to them, was somewhat extraordinary.*" More than extraordinary. Horsmanden, and anyone else who was paying attention, knew that Price was a servant of Vincent Pearse, captain of the *Flamborough*, the same ship on which Christopher Wilson was a sailor. (As Pearse was the subject of an unrelated civil suit heard before the Supreme Court during these same months, it's hard to imagine that the justices failed to make the connection between Price and Wilson.)[44] Wilson, who had committed the robbery at Hogg's with Caesar, Cuffee, and Prince, and then betrayed them to the constables and later testified against Caesar and Prince at their trial, must have known Arthur Price. And Price just as surely knew Kerry, Cuffee, and the Hughsons long before any of them ever were arrested.

Because there were no police and no detectives to collect evidence, eighteenth-century criminal courts depended on crown witnesses, particularly on men like Arthur Price, members of criminal gangs willing to impeach their colleagues in exchange for pardon or reward. Not surprisingly, the system was rife with abuses. Gang members seeking cash or clemency all too frequently offered false testimony and, in some cases, accused their compatriots of crimes that never even happened. Just such an abuse occurred in 1732, when a petty London criminal named John Waller was convicted of lying to collect a reward. The case became the talk of the town when Waller, on the pillory for perjury, was beaten to death by the brother of one of his victims. This kind of corruption came under increasing scrutiny over the course of the century, as English courts attempted to compensate for the all too obvious flaws of pretrial evidence gathering by weaning prosecutors of their reliance on crown witnesses. Indeed, it was in an effort to reform this system that the first modern detective agency, and the progenitor of the Criminal Investigation Division of Scotland Yard, was created by the novelist and magistrate Henry Fielding, in the late 1740s, at his offices in Bow Street. Fielding, a justice of the peace from 1748 until his death in 1754, provided the courts with his services as an amateur detective, primarily in the investigation of gang crimes, and with his brother John innovated procedures for collecting evidence and conducting interrogations.[45]

But in New York in 1741, the best pretrial evidence was still a crown witness, however corrupt. Nonetheless, Arthur Price's usefulness came to an end on the night of May 12 when Quack was arrested. That arrest, combined with Price's "being often sent for," made the miserable prisoners in the cellar of City Hall finally wise to his ways. When Quack was arrested after Cuffee had spent the night in Price's cell sharing a tankard of punch, Cuffee never spoke to Price again. Instead, he "read sometimes, and cried much."

ARTHUR PRICE'S MAY 3 deposition doomed Peggy Kerry. On May 7, the day after the "*Newfoundland Irish Beauty*" was found guilty of receiving stolen goods, she began to talk not just to Price but to the magistrates. Her confession was partial; she knew about the plot, she said, but it had been hatched not at John Hughson's but at the house of a shoemaker named John Romme, who lived by the Battery. (Romme was nowhere to be found; he had skipped town. His wife, Elizabeth, interrogated on May 9, admitted that she and her husband had served liquor to slaves, but denied any knowledge of a plot.) Kerry did name seven slaves who had conspired at Romme's—Cuffee, Brash, Curacoa Dick, Caesar (Pintard), Patrick, Jack (Breasted), and Cato (Moore)—who proposed "*to burn the Fort first, and afterwards the City; and then steal, rob and carry away all the Money and Goods they could procure . . . and that they were to murder* every one that had Money."

On May 8, Caesar and Prince, convicted of burglary, were sentenced to death by hanging. The next day, knowing that the father of her child was headed to the gallows, Kerry elaborated on the plot during an intensive examination by Philipse and Horsmanden, naming still more slaves as conspirators but claiming of others that their "Names, or the Names of their Masters, she does not now remember; but believes she should remember their Faces again if she should see them." That night, the men Kerry named (not including Cuffee, who was already in jail) were "passed in Review before her" and she "distinguished them every one, called them by their Names," and declared that they had sworn to the plot.

On Monday, May 11, Caesar and Prince were taken from their cells to a cart, waiting on the street. "It was thought proper to execute them for the Robbery, and not wait the Bringing them to a Trial for the Conspiracy," Horsmanden explained, "though the Proof against them was strong and clear concerning their Guilt." He hoped that the execution of Caesar, in particular, might break Kerry or, better still, that the two men might them-selves confess on the gallows. A crowd, eager to find out, gathered outside City Hall and followed the horse-drawn cart one block west, to Broadway, where it headed straight out of town. Past Broadway Market, past the Common, past the line marking the edge of the city, where the cart rolled noisily down a small hill to a specially erected gallows "in the valley between Windmil-hill and Potbakers-hill," a natural amphitheater for the public spectacle and just a stone's throw from the Negroes Burial Ground.[46] Even as the hangman approached, Caesar and Prince refused to confess. They "died very stubbornly," Horsmanden complained, "without confessing any Thing about the Conspiracy; and denied they knew any Thing of it to the last."

But death was not the end of it, at least for Caesar. His corpse was gib-beted, hung from chains, and displayed "on the Island near the Powder-House" in the Little Collect Pond, where it could be easily seen but not as easily smelled. The court, and Daniel Horsmanden most of all, hoped that this "Example and Punishment might break the Rest, and induce some of them to unfold this Mystery of Iniquity."

JOHN AND SARAH HUGHSON were arraigned on charges of conspir-acy on the morning of Tuesday, May 12; Kerry's arraignment was post-poned until the following Friday. On May 13, and again on May 14, Mary Burton offered new details in depositions taken before Horsmanden and Philipse, naming several more slaves in the conspiracy. Kerry was exam-ined again, too, but what she said "was not altogether satisfactory," in large part because she continued to insist that the plotting had taken place at Romme's tavern, rather than at Hughson's.

Frustrated by Kerry's intractability, the court found a black man or, really, a boy, willing to turn king's evidence. Sandy, ordered arrested and fetched from Albany (where he had recently been sold), arrived in New York on May 14. In the dungeon, he was jailed near to Francis, a "Spanish Negro" owned by a Dutch sea captain named Jasper Bosch. Francis had been in jail since that fateful Monday, April 6, when vigilantes rounded up every "Spanish Negro" they could find. Francis told Sandy "he would kill him if he told any Thing." Eight days after Sandy was arrested, jailkeeper James Mills fetched him from the cellar. As Mills escorted Sandy to be brought up for questioning, "several Negroes winked" at him.

Upstairs, the grand jury "for a long Time argued with him, to persuade him to speak the Truth." Sandy refused to speak, saying that he had heard that during the 1712 inquiry, after "*the Negroes told all they knew, then the white People hanged them.*" But "the Grand Jury assured him, *that it was false;* for that the Negroes which confessed the Truth and made a Discovery, were certainly pardoned, and shipped off." Promised his life, Sandy began to talk, naming fifteen slaves (including Francis and three more "Spanish Negroes") who had planned to burn the city.

Confessions by people in Sandy's circumstances, like the testimony of crown witnesses who were criminals, became increasingly suspect over the course of the eighteenth century. In 1756, a landmark treatise, *Law of Evidence,* would declare: "Confession must be voluntary and without Compulsion." Still, the courts were slow to change, and it wasn't until the 1783 case *Rex v. Warwickshall* that English courts disallowed rewards and threats, finally decreeing: "A confession forced from the mind by the flattery of hope, or by the torture of fear, comes in so questionable a shape . . . that no credit ought to be given to it."[47]

Although this reform of English criminal courts took place long after New York's Supreme Court of Judicature met in the spring and summer of 1741, stricter rules of evidence were already emerging in colonial courts, on the force of public sentiment. But such sentiment was rarely animated against the use of force or torment on jailed slaves. In Antigua in 1736, slaves charged with conspiracy were tortured: broken on the wheel, gibbeted alive. Even before men convicted in Antigua were brought to the gallows and the stake, many were already dead, from suffocation, blood loss, or massive internal injuries. In grim anticipation of the fate that awaited him, one black Antiguan tried to commit suicide in jail, stabbing himself nineteen times, but his outraged captors revived him and put him to death on the wheel, where his bones were slowly bent and then finally broken until he died of his wounds. As the Antigua prosecutors explained: "Of so great Concern was the Matter under our Consideration to the Island, that to enable us to make a full Discovery, an Act was pass'd for inflicting Torture on Persons suspected of the Plot."

In 1741, New York did not pass a law authorizing torture. Nor, in his *Journal,* did Horsmanden record a single instance of torture, or offer the slightest hint of physical abuse. Still, it would be preposterous to conclude from these silences that jailed black men in New York in 1741 were treated well. Jailkeeper Mills, who lived in a small garret apartment in City Hall, was both vicious and corrupt. Before he turned jailkeeper, he made his living pulling teeth. He was responsible for emptying prisoners' "Ordure Tubbs" and supplying them with food, water, and the occasional bowl of rum punch; but as he himself had to pay the cost of "Victualling" prisoners and later present to the Common Council an account for reimbursement, he must have been sorely tempted to provide less food than he promised and pocket the difference in cash. Although he served as the city's jail-keeper for all but three years between his appointment in 1738 and his death in 1771, Mills was, at one point, charged before the Supreme Court with mistreating prisoners, and, at another point, indicted by a grand jury for extortion. He weathered both scandals, if only because no one else could be found to do his job.[48]

If not Horsmanden and Philipse themselves, Mills and the parade of magistrates who escorted prisoners and conducted interrogations may have beaten black suspects, even though no documents survive to count the blows. Court-sanctioned torture was amply and unabashedly docu-mented in New York in 1712, when black men were broken on the wheel and roasted over a slow fire, and in Antigua in 1736, when they were starved to death and gibbeted alive. If court-sanctioned torture had been employed in 1741, it is hard to imagine that Horsmanden would have both-ered to suppress the evidence of it, especially given that there seems to have been little public censure of Antigua's exertions. On the other hand, the occasional bashing, beating, and whipping may have struck him as hardly worth noting, especially if it were conducted by the slaves' own masters, either before or during their imprisonment. In short, there is every reason to believe but no way to prove that at least some slaves in that dungeon below City Hall were beaten, maybe very badly; just as there is every reason to believe but no way to prove that the court never ordered it.

Sandy confessed on May 22. Before the day was through, one of the few black men named by Sandy who was not already in jail, Fortune, owned by the Englishman John Wilkins, was arrested and brought before the grand jury. Fortune fingered Quack, owned by John Roosevelt. Two days before the fire at the fort, he said, Quack told him *"That the Fort would be burnt"*; and when he met him the day after the fire, Quack had boasted, *"The Business is done."* During a second day of grand jury interro-gation, on May 23, Fortune implicated Cuffee in the fire at Philipse's storehouse.

On May 28, Quack and Cuffee pled not guilty to "two Indictments, for a Conspiracy to burn the Town, and murder the Inhabitants; and for two actual Burnings, the House in the Fort, and Mr. *Philipse's* Storehouse." The next day, they left the dungeon and headed upstairs to the Supreme Court, where light filled the room, for the first conspiracy trial of 1741, "a Cause of very great Expectation."

CHAPTER FOUR

Paper

A T TEN O'CLOCK in the morning on Friday, May 29, at the peal of the bell in the cupola of City Hall, spectators stopped fidgeting, the crier called out "Oyes!," Frederick Philipse raised his gavel, and Daniel Horsmanden picked up his quill. *King v. Quack and Cuffee* was about to begin.

What happened next? Did Quack's wife, Barbara, weep from the balcony? Did Cuffee wink at Mary Burton, who was waiting to be called as a witness?

The trial of Quack and Cuffee, like nearly everything else that happened in City Hall, upstairs and down, between the opening of the Supreme Court on April 21 and its closing on August 31, 1741, is both richly documented and maddeningly unknowable. Of 133 days of arrests, interrogations, accusations, confessions, retractions, testimony, cross-examinations, judgments, verdicts, executions, pardons, threats, promises, whispers, cries of despair, and shrieks of pain, almost the sole surviving record is what Daniel Horsmanden included in his *Journal of the Proceedings in The Detection of the Conspiracy.*

The Supreme Court minutes disappeared during the American Revolution. Documents filed by the court were badly damaged in a devastating fire in 1911. James Alexander wrote to his stepson David Provost on April 22, and Elizabeth DeLancey, wife of the Chief Justice's brother, Peter, wrote a revealing letter to her father, Cadwallader Colden, on June 1; but very few other letters survive. No slave left even a single scrap of paper describing what happened, at least not that has ever been found. Nor are the city's newspapers any help. Almost the entire 1741 run of Bradford's *Gazette* is missing. And Zenger's *Weekly Journal* offered only scant reports, hampered by Horsmanden and Philipse, who kept the printer at arm's length. "We are in Hopes that we have discovered the Foundation of this Plot," Zenger reported on May 31, promising that "the Particulars shall be published as soon as they may be obtain'd of the Magistrates." Soon afterwards, Zenger printed a column and a half summarizing the "horrible and wicked Conspiracy" uncovered by the grand jury; more details were emerging every day, "some of them so horrid that we may not publish them as yet." On June 15, Zenger again pledged, "As soon as we can obtain a full Account of this Plot and Leave from the Magistrates we shall publish the same." But no full account ever came; the judges never gave Zenger leave to print one.[1]

Still, notwithstanding the chilling silences, Horsmanden's *Journal* stands as one of the most complete trial records in early American history, even if, as Horsmanden admitted on the first page, his sources, too, were incomplete, and he himself had left much out:

> THE *Reader must not expect in the following Sheets, a particular and minute Relation of every Formality, Question and Answer that pass'd upon the Trials, it may suffice, if he be assured he has the Substance; for indeed more cannot be expected, when it is considered, that we have no One here, as in our Mother Country, who make it a Business to take Notes upon such Occasions; or any others, that we know of, who are so dexterous at Short-Hand, as to be sufficiently qualified for such a Purpose; but he will be sure to have all that could be collected from the Notes that were taken by the Court, and Gentlemen at the Bar; with all which the Compiler has been furnished.*

Horsmanden began gathering papers relating to the conspiracy sometime after November 1741, when the Assembly paid him £250 to digest and prepare for printing all the laws of the colony. Instead of completing the assignment for which he had been paid, Horsmanden turned to the conspiracy. Smith, Jr., wrote in his *History,* "Of the digesting act, Mr. Horsmanden took no advantage, hoping greater gain by compiling the proceedings against the late conspirators." He began with the minutes hurriedly taken down in the courtroom by a subordinate clerk, untrained in shorthand, probably George Joseph Moore. Frustrated by the incompleteness of the court minutes—and they were notoriously skimpy—Horsmanden interleaved them with documents filed by the grand jury and the officers of the court and whatever other notes and comments he could collect from anyone willing to share them. When Horsmanden wrote to Cadwallader Colden, begging for his recollections of events, Colden sent along some remarks, offering, "if you think this account of any use in what you design to publish in relation to the Negro Conspiracy you may freely do it in what shape you please."[2]

Horsmanden worked quickly. In July 1742, a New York printer, James Parker, distributed a broadside soliciting advanced subscriptions for the *Journal,* at 7 shillings each, promising that the work "is now almost ready for the Press."[3] Parker advertised "the whole Evidence and Proceedings, by Way of Journal," and it was a journal, not a history, that Horsmanden intended. Although he had decided to arrange the documents "in the Order of Time," he insisted that his chronological account was most decidedly not a history. Had he been writing a history, he would have considered himself at greater "Liberty to abstract the several Originals"—to summarize, condense, and interpret them. Instead, Horsmanden titled the work a *Journal of the Proceedings,* the standard label for official transcriptions of legislative, committee, and council meetings (like the annually printed *Journal of the Votes and Proceedings of the General Assembly*).

Horsmanden's *Journal of the Proceedings in The Detection of the Conspiracy* was a daily record whose documentary purpose, he said, compelled him to reproduce the originals in unaltered form, with only the slightest editorial interventions: *"lopping off from them, what, in print, he thought would be a superfluous Formality, such as* The Deponent further saith, *and such like, which he thought would have been a needless Incumbrance to the Book."* Indeed, Horsmanden had every reason to remain faithful to the originals: during his lifetime, they were stored at City Hall and at the Secretary's Office in Fort George (rebuilt by November 1741), where they could be easily compared with the *Journal.*[4] That almost all of these originals have since been lost or virtually destroyed is hardly Daniel Horsmanden's fault.

Fortunately, a handful of the original documents, however badly burned, are still partially legible, and in June 1741, Governor Clarke had copies made of some of the earliest confessions and trial minutes, which he sent to the Lords of Trade. Today, they are stored in the National Archives at Kew, outside London. Of a badly damaged set of originals, then, there are two sets of reproductions: Horsmanden's printed *Journal* and Clarke's manuscript copies. Written as the events they describe were unfolding, Clarke's copies are a better source than Horsmanden's *Journal,* even though they are less complete. More important, they serve as yardstick by which to measure Horsmanden's credibility as an editor. On the whole, they vindicate Horsmanden, whose *Journal* turns out to be exactly what he said it was: a lightly edited collection of rather conventional legal documents, or, as Clarke himself put it, "very little more than a Copy of the Court Entries."[5] Because Horsmanden shaped the proceedings *as they were happening,* he had little need to doctor the written record. But he did doctor it some, and that doctoring matters.

AFTER PHILIPSE LOWERED his gavel, the trial of Quack and Cuffee began with the swearing of the jurors. Clarke's transcript failed to list their names, and Horsmanden could remember only eight of the twelve: Samuel Weaver, an English tanner; John Shurmur; John Lashier; Charles Arding, an English tailor; George Witts; Thomas Bohenna; Daniel Bonett, a French cordwainer; and John Robins, an English currier. All whose occupations can be identified were artisans. Two, Weaver and Shurmur, owned slaves who would later be accused of conspiracy.

Attorney General Richard Bradley then delivered an opening statement, which Horsmanden reproduced. Bradley had no affection for the men he was to prosecute. Years before, when his wife needed a servant, Bradley had written to a friend that he and his wife preferred German servants to slaves: "wee don't like negroes."[6]

Bradley called Quack and Cuffee "Monsters in Iniquity," and promised the jury that he would prove "CRIMES, *Gentlemen,* so astonishingly cruel and detestable; that one would think they could never have entered into the Minds, much less the Resolution, of any *but a Conclave of Devils* to execute." Clarke's transcript omits Bradley's speech, indicating only that Bradley "enlarged on the heinousness of the offense," a remark that, however clipped, is entirely consistent with Horsmanden's account. At the trial, the court amanuensis was forced to summarize what he heard, but in 1742 Horsmanden must have copied Bradley's own notes.

After Bradley returned to his seat, Joseph Murray and William Smith, Council for the King, took turns examining nine white and two black witnesses, beginning with Mary Burton. Murray, at age forty-seven, was the senior member of the city bar. Smith was only three years younger, and almost Murray's equal in experience. Both had ably prepared their witnesses. Burton repeated what she had said at her earlier depositions, that Cuffee had been to meetings at Hughson's, where a plot was hatched, adding that one night at Hughson's, Cuffee had said to her (according to the Clarke transcript) "that if all the white men were killed & she kept their Counsel he would have her for his wife." Horsmanden included much the same testimony ("he intended to have her for a Wife"), but in the *Journal* Burton's testimony continues: "she had a Dishclout in her Hand, which she dabbed in his Face, and he ran away," a detail entirely lacking in the Clarke transcript. The dishcloth slap matters. With it, Burton both polished her own virtue and distinguished herself from Peggy Kerry, prostitute to slaves, mother of a child "of a motley Complexion." Maybe Horsmanden remembered the slap. Maybe he found it mentioned in Bradley's notes. But by the time Horsmanden compiled his *Journal,* Burton had lost much of her credibility as a witness. Maybe Horsmanden invented that slap.

In his *Journal,* Horsmanden separated the trials of Quack and Cuffee, presenting the testimony as though all of the witnesses against Cuffee were questioned first, and then brought back to the stand a second time to testify against Quack. Clarke's transcript proves that, on the contrary, the two men were tried together, with each witness testifying just once.

Horsmanden reproduced all of the whites' testimony first, so that Mary Burton is followed by Arthur Price and seven other whites before the two black witnesses, Fortune and Sandy, take the stand. In the Clarke transcript, Sandy and Fortune directly follow Burton. Possibly Horsmanden altered the sequence in the interest of coherence, but the change had the effect of making "Negro Evidence" seem less important to the trial than it actually was. If the order of witnesses was Burton, Sandy, Fortune, Price (followed by the seven relatively insignificant white witnesses), then the prosecutors must have believed that what Sandy and Fortune could establish was crucial to the case. By placing Sandy and Fortune's testimony last, Horsmanden made it appear ancillary.

Horsmanden had good reason to make this change: admitting Sandy and Fortune's evidence had been controversial. In colonial courts, which were otherwise rather lax about rules of evidence, quite particular evidentiary rules applied to slaves: "Negro Evidence" was generally not allowed. Slaves could not be deposed or serve as witnesses because oaths could only be administered to Christians. In most criminal cases, including the burglary trial of Caesar and Prince, that slaves could not swear oaths was no bar to their conviction because the testimony of whites was usually sufficiently damning. But the prohibition on slave testimony did affect the courts' ability to prosecute slaves for conspiracy, where slave witnesses were indispensable.

Frustrated by this obstacle, some colonial legislatures had mandated exceptions to the exclusion of "Negro Evidence." In Maryland after 1717, slaves could testify in criminal courts, but only against Indians or blacks.

Virginia altered its laws in the 1720s to make it possible to punish slaves for perjury by administering a special, godless oath, backed by biblical punishments: "You are brought hither as a witness; and, by the direction of the law, I am to tell you, before you give your evidence, that you must tell the truth, the whole truth, and nothing but the truth; and that if it be found hereafter, that you tell a lie, and give false testimony in this matter, you must, for so doing, have both your ears nailed to the pillory, and cut off, and receive thirty-nine lashes on your bare back, well laid on, at the common whipping-post." No such fearful oaths were required in South Carolina, where, after 1740, non-whites could testify, but, again, only against other non-whites. In the conspiracy trials held in Antigua in 1736, slave testimony was allowed because, as the prosecutors reported, "it is expressly left by any Act of our Island, to the Discretion of the Justices, to examine any Slave, as Witness against another Slave, and give what Credit to his Testimony he thinks it in Conscience deserves."[7]

In New York, "Negro Evidence" was strictly circumscribed: not only was it only allowed against other slaves, it was only admissible in cases of conspiracy, arson, and murder, according to the province's 1730 law "for the more effectual preventing and punishing the conspiracy and insurrection of negroes and other slaves." It was this law that was brought to bear in the courtroom in New York on May 29, 1741. Both Horsmanden's *Journal* and the Clarke manuscript agree that before calling his "Negro Evidence" to the stand at the trial of Quack and Cuffee, Joseph Murray addressed the court and read aloud the portions of the 1730 New York law decreeing that

Negroes Evidence is good against each other . . . no Slave or Slaves shall be allowed as Evidence or Evidences in any Matter Cause or thing whatsoever excepting in Cases of Plotting or Confederacy among themselves, either to run away Kill or distroy their Master Mistress or any other Person, or burning of houses Barns, barracks or Stacks of hay or of Corne or the Killing of their Master or Mistresses Cattle or Horses and that only against one another, in which Case the evidence of one Slave Shall be allowed good against an other Slave.[8]

When Sandy and Fortune took the stand on that spring day, neither took an oath. Instead, the justices "put them under the most solemn Caution that their small Knowledge of Religion can render them capable of." Each repeated what he had said in his earlier depositions. Sandy testified that he had heard Cuffee say, "hang him or burn him, he would set fire to the Town." Fortune said that after the fort fire, Quack told him, "*The Business is done.*" According to Horsmanden's *Journal,* Fortune said that Caesar, Prince, and Cuffee had asked him "to go with them to *Hughson's;* but that he never did, but was told they had a Dance there every other Night." And there his testimony ends. But according to Clarke's minutes, Fortune said something else, which Horsmanden left out: "that the Prisoners had asked him to go to Husons house where they frolick'd often, but remembering the free Masons Club who were punished for meeting he declined it and did not go there."[9]

In 1742, when he set about compiling his *Journal,* Horsmanden copied the same minutes of Quack and Cuffee's trial that Clarke's copyist had transcribed in June 1741. He made only very slight alterations: reordering witnesses, adding a detail to Burton's testimony, and deleting Fortune's reference to Freemasonry. The first two changes were an attempt to silence his critics. By the time Horsmanden was writing, the court had been condemned, even ridiculed, for its reliance, first, on the testimony of Mary Burton, a glib young girl; and second, on "Negro Evidence," which had long been controversial. But why bother lopping off Fortune's testimony?

Fortune said that he declined Quack and Cuffee's invitation to go to Hughson's because he remembered "the free Masons Club who were punished for meeting." In deleting this remark, Daniel Horsmanden buried a story crucial for any understanding of what happened in New York in 1741: the story of the black Freemasons, who were caught and punished in 1738.

On the night of January 27, 1738, Cuffee, along with Caesar and Prince, had broken into Richard Baker's tavern, on the corner of Wall and Water streets, just opposite the slave market. From Baker's cellar, they stole several barrels of Geneva liquor, better known as "gin." As a badge of their success, they christened themselves the "Geneva Club." They may have hidden their takings in John Hughson's house; in 1738, he lived on Dock Street, just a few blocks away from Baker, and was already notorious for "entertaining Slaves."[10] It was, in any event, a robbery much like the one they would later perpetrate at Rebecca Hogg's shop.

The next night, Saturday, January 28, Caesar, Prince, and Cuffee were arrested. They confessed to robbing Baker's tavern. No trial was necessary. The following Thursday the men of the Geneva Club were paraded through the city on a cart, stripped to the waist, and whipped at every street corner. Three days later, William Bradford printed an account of their crime and punishment in his *New York Gazette.* It was probably written by Daniel Horsmanden, who, like Recorder Francis Harison before him, wrote the *Gazette*'s politically sensitive news. In a deeply satirical essay, the *Gazette* reported that the Geneva Club was actually a lodge of black Freemasons:

> Last Saturday Night was Discovered here a New Club, Lodge or Society of *Free Masons* (as they called themselves) being a Company of Blacks or Generation of Vipers assembled together to carry on their private and obscure Works of Darkness. At a Meeting of a Lodge of Black Masons, held the 28th Day of January last, an elegant Entertainment being provided, some of the Fraternity having the Night before broke open a Cellar and stole a large Quanitty of strong Liquor in order to make themselves merry. When at this Meeting or Lodge, Mr. *Don Dago,* Master of this Lodge and Dishonourable Society of *Black Masons,* being about to depart this Province, had the Honour to Resign his Office in Form.

The *Gazette*'s account of the "Dishonourable Society of *Black Masons*" was aimed at the city's white Masons. A New York lodge of the Ancient and Honourable Society of Free and Accepted Masons first formed in New York City in early 1737, just after the near–civil war over Clarke's assumption of the governorship after Cosby's death. Although Masons were supposed to rise above party divisions, the New York lodge was a vehicle for the Country Party. The *Gazette*'s account of the Geneva Club quite closely mimicked an account that had been published in Zenger's *Weekly Journal* the week before, of a *white* Masonic meeting. On the night of Saturday, January 21, 1738, New York's grand lodge of Masons held a dinner at the Black Horse Tavern in honor of lodge master David Provost, Jr., James Alexander's nephew, who was about to leave the colony to open up an import business in Savannah, Georgia (where he would also found a Masonic lodge).[11] In Provost's place, the lodge elected Captain Matthew Norris, Lewis Morris's son-in-law (the man who had raised the huzzas in City Hall at the announcement of Zenger's acquittal in 1735). The Masons, in white aprons, marched down the street to Norris's house to mark his ascension. In a celebratory notice in the *Weekly Journal* on January 24, Alexander reported on the festivities: "Last *Saturday,* Mr. *David Provoost* jur. Master of the Lodge of the Ancient and Honourable Society of Free and Accepted Masons in this Place, gave an Elegant Entertainment to the Fraternity at the Black Horse."

In its account of the "Dishonourable Society of *Black Masons,*" Bradford's *Gazette* mocked what Alexander had described as the white Masons' "further Mark of their Unanimity and Concord" in a "well regulated and decent Procession" to Norris's house. The *Gazette*'s satire (again in the guise of a report on the whipping of Caesar, Prince, and Cuffee), continued:

> As a further Mark of Honour and Respect due to this Fraternity or black Guard, their two Masters were waited upon the Thursday following by two Carts one after another, in a well regulated and suitable Procession round the Town, attended by a Number of Spectators of all Degrees Ages and Sizes, and were continually complimented with Snow Balls and Dirt, and at every Corner had five Lashes with a Cowskin well laid on each of their naked black Backs, and then carried home to Gaol. Sundry others of the Brother-hood were lashed at the Publick Whipping-Post, according to the Antient and Honourable Practices of this Place, for punishing the Members of such a vile and wicked Society of Hell-Cats.

James Alexander took considerable offense at the *Gazette*'s conflation of black thieves and white Masons and the parallels drawn between slaves' public whipping and a Masonic parade. In Zenger's *Weekly Journal* on February 13, Alexander—writing, as always, anonymously—chided his "Brother Scribler" for having gone too far: "IT has always been laid down as a constant Rule among the Polite Authors, That even in the severest Satyrs there is a certain Limitation or Standard for *Good Manners*, from which no one can depart without rendring his Writings not only less poignant but disagreeable to the Reader." Alexander called the *Gazette*'s satire not only witless but "downright Bawdy" and complained at the paper's continued abuse of Freemasons. "Not to mention the Encouragement this elaborate Performance gives to the pampered Insolence of the Slaves, I must confess my self at a Loss to find a Cause for the many groundless and idle Reflections often cast upon a Fraternity, to whom I could never learn any other Objection, but that valuable Quality *of Knowing how to keep a Secret.*"

The day after Alexander called the satire "downright Bawdy," his "Brother Scribler" pointed out that the general tone of Zenger's *Weekly Journal* in the turbulent years of its publication had been just as vicious:

> I was extreamly surprized that Mr. *Zenger* (or his Correspondents) above all others, should censure so hard, as to call out *Bawdy, Billingsgate,* &c. at some harsh Expressions made use of in Mr. *Bradford's Gazette* . . . relating to a piece of Wickedness carried on by a Company of black Slaves. I would recommend Mr. *Zenger* to

look back but a few Months into his past Journals, and there see and compare whether his recommending of *Politeness*, and advice of using *good Manners*, proceeds from any inclination he has for either? or whether it is only to Reproach Brother Scribler?

Still more ardently, the *Gazette*'s correspondent (probably Horsmanden) attacked Zenger "or his Correspondents" (Alexander) for defending, of all people, criminally convicted black slaves: "I must indeed confess my self at a loss, in what sence he ascribes the Encouragement given to the pamper'd Insolence of the Wicked Slaves, when, on the contrary, their Punishment was just, and justly due, and the infliction highly approved and commended, and their Wickedness highly censured, on which occasion some harsh Expressions have slipt out of the Pen." More important, "Brother Scribler" pointed out that his essay was only partly satire since what he reported was essentially true—Caesar, Prince, and Cuffee and their friends actually *had* formed a Masonic lodge—"for it is sufficiently known in this City, that as one of this black Guard was brought down to receive his Punishment, he was so impudent as to cry out, *Make Room for a Free MASON*."[12]

And there the exchange ended, and the case of the 1738 "Confederacy of Negroes" came to a close. The incident failed to touch off fears of slave insurrection; it didn't even generate an investigation. Instead, the Geneva Club was put to use fanning the flames of continued political tensions among whites, between the *Gazette* and the *Weekly Journal*, between Bradford and Zenger, between Horsmanden and Alexander, between Court and Country Party. In 1738, the city was still "in the midst of Party flames." When Caesar, Prince, and Cuffee robbed Baker's tavern, whites were too distracted with their own factiousness, now inflamed by Freemasonry, to worry that the robbery was part of a vast slave conspiracy. But in the winter of 1741, when Quack and Cuffee invited Fortune to John Hughson's tavern, he, "remembering the free Masons Club," kept away. And on May 29, when Fortune took the stand at their trial as "Negro Evidence," he reminded the court and the jury of the black Masons. But in 1742, when Horsmanden prepared Fortune's testimony for publication, he made sure the "Dishonourable Society of *Black Masons*" would be forgotten.

QUACK AND CUFFEE conducted their own defense. Together they called ten witnesses, in an unsuccessful attempt to establish alibis for the time of the fires. Next, according to Horsmanden, "The Prisoners being asked, what they had to offer in their Defence; they offered Nothing but peremptory Denials of what had been testified against them, and Protestations of their Innocency." The defense was hopeless; the most interesting thing about it is that Quack and Cuffee, who were legally not even *people*, were given the opportunity to conduct it, as the prosecution was keen to point out. "The Prisoners have been indulged with the same Kind of Trial as is due to *Freemen*," William Smith reminded the jury, "though they might have been proceeded against in a more summary and less favourable Way."

According to the Clarke transcript, Bradley then "summ'd up," but Horsmanden attributed the closing statement to the jury to William Smith. Smith was said by his son to have had "the natural advantages of figure, voice, vivacity, memory, imagination, promptness, strong passions, volubility, invention, and a taste for ornament." He was a captivating speaker.[13]

"*Gentlemen*," Smith began, "No Scheme more monstrous could have been invented; nor can any Thing be thought of more foolish, than the Motives that induced these Wretches to enter into it! What more ridiculous, than that *Hughson*, in Consequence of this Scheme, should become a *King!* Caesar . . . a *Governor!* That the White Men should be all killed, and the Women become a Prey to the rapacious Lust of these Villains! That these Slaves should thereby establish themselves in Peace and Freedom in the plunder'd Wealth of their slaughter'd Masters!" Smith proceeded to review the question of "Negro Evidence," reminding jurors that although it was impossible to administer an oath to "Pagan Negroes," the testimony of Fortune and Sandy was damning. The witnesses, he argued, had offered "FULL PROOF" that Cuffee had set fire to Frederick Philipse's storehouse and Quack had burned Fort George.

The jury withdrew to deliberate, attended by a constable, sworn to "suffer no person whatever to speak to them" and to keep them "without Meat, Drink, Fire or Candle light" until "they are agreed on their verdict."[14] It didn't take long. The jury returned and declared Quack and Cuffee guilty as charged. Before adjourning, Philipse deferred to Horsmanden to deliver the frightful sentence: "you shall be chained to a Stake, and burnt to Death." When Mills brought the two men back to the dungeon, Cuffee, passing John Hughson in his cell, seethed at him, "*I may thank you for this.*"

. . .

BURNING AT THE STAKE was a punishment reserved for those who committed "petty treason" by defying the relationship between ruler and ruled, in this case, slaveowner and slave. It was an atrocious way to die, but, by contemporary standards, it was a grisly kind of restraint. Compared to the men and women convicted of conspiracy in New York in 1712 and in Antigua in 1736, Quack and Cuffee were objects of mercy. In 1712, Robin, who had killed his owner, Adrian Hoghlandt, was hung by chains until he starved to death; Claus, convicted as accessory to Hoghlandt's murder, was broken upon the wheel, to languish until dying of his wounds; and Tom, owned by the bolter Nicholas Roosevelt, was, for shooting Andries Beekman with a pistol, sentenced to be roasted to death *slowly*, over a closely tended fire, to be tormented for eight to ten hours, until his body was consumed to ashes. In Antigua in 1736, the punishments were just as fierce: hanged in chains, some men convicted in Antigua lived for days before dying of hunger and thirst; one man fell out of his irons "by his Body being wasted," and was hoisted back up "into his old Birth" to suffer still. Court, the king of the slaves, was "broke on the Wheel, his Head cut off, and put on a Pole at the Gaol Door, his Body burnt."[15]

In Clarke's transcript of Quack and Cuffee's trial, the sentencing is omitted, but Horsmanden, in his *Journal*, having deleted Fortune's mention of the Freemasons, added Burton's dishcloth slap, and downplayed the importance of "Negro Evidence," concluded his record of the trial by reproducing his own speech in its entirety. The Third Justice addressed the prisoners in rhetoric more florid even than Smith's, stressing both the fiendishness and the futility of the plot:

> YOU both now stand convicted of one of the most horrid and detestable Pieces of Villainy, that ever Satan instilled into the Heart of human Creatures to put in Practice. . . . I know not which is the more astonishing, the extreme *Folly*, or *Wickedness*, of so base and shocking a Conspiracy; for as to any View of Liberty or Government you could propose to yourselves, upon the Success of burning the City, robbing, butchering and destroying the Inhabitants; what could it be expected to end in . . . but your own Destruction?

On Saturday morning, May 30, a minister visited Quack and Cuffee in the dungeon and urged them to confess. They protested their innocence.[16] At three o'clock, Sheriff William Jamison came for them, placed them in shackles, carried them upstairs and outside, loaded them onto a cart. A parade of New Yorkers followed to a site at the edge of the Negroes Burial Ground, just south of the Little Collect. There, Jamison chained the two condemned men to tall wooden stakes, rising like ship's masts from a sea of faggots. The crowd was huge. Jamison called it a mob. It was near to rioting. New Yorkers flocked to see Quack and Cuffee "surrounded with Piles of Wood ready for setting Fire to, which the People were very impatient to have done, their Resentment raised to the utmost Pitch against them."

Eighteenth-century executions were public spectacles, attended by men, women, and children of all ages. (In Philadelphia in 1738, a five-year-old boy died after he accidentally hanged himself while imitating a recent "Execution of Negroes.") As a very young boy, New Yorker David Grim attended the executions in New York, and he never forgot the sight: "I have a perfect idea of seing the Negroes chained to a stake, and there burned to death."[17]

Swarms of Antiguans had watched all eighty-eight executions in 1736, out of hatred, out of obligation, out of fascination. "The Burning of the Negroes, hanging them on Gibbets alive, Racking them upon the wheel, &c. takes up almost all our Time," one weary white Antiguan complained. "I am almost dead with watching."[18]

White New Yorkers attended with the same dedication. "The chief talk now in Town is about the Negroes conspiracy," wrote Elizabeth DeLancey to her father. Standing in the crowd, Prince, owned by the English bolter Gabriel Crooke, was amazed by "the great Numbers of white People present." Next to him, his friend York, owned by the Dutch baker Peter Marschalk, whispered that the gathering itself looked like a good place "*to rise*" and kill whites. But Prince said it wasn't worth it; "they might only kill one or two, and then they should be taken, and hanged for it."

Like imprisonment, interrogation, and trial, an execution was a pageant, intended to produce a confession. After Quack and Cuffee were chained to their stakes, George Joseph Moore, the Supreme Court clerk, and John Roosevelt, Quack's owner, questioned them, "endeavouring to persuade them to confess their Guilt." Moore, lying, told Cuffee that Quack had already confessed; Roosevelt told Quack that Cuffee had. Betrayed, and desperate to be spared the flames, the two men blurted out hasty confessions and together named nearly thirty other men as co-conspirators. Cuffee admitted to burning Philipse's storehouse, setting the fire with lighted charcoal he had carried "in his Pocket between two Oyster Shells." Quack admitted to setting fire to the fort, having carried a "lighted Stick" from the servants' hall, through the room of his wife, Barbara, who was Clarke's cook, and placing it "*near the Gutter, betwixt the Shingles, and the Roof of the House.*" His wife, he insisted, "was no Ways concerned," and his young son, Denby, "knew nothing of the Matter." Both men obligingly agreed that John Hughson "*was the first Contriver of the whole Plot*" and "that they should never have thought of it, if he had not put it into their Heads." With "*the Mob pressing forard and interrupting,*" Quack could barely finish his confession. "In the Midst of great Noise and Confusion," the confessions "were minuted down," endorsed, "As told to me at the Stake," and signed by Moore. Clarke sent a copy of both confessions to England.

The written confessions were incomplete, and riddled with errors. Elizabeth DeLancey, who attended the executions, reported to her father that Quack and Cuffee had confessed "that the Spaniards are concern'd & that ours in particular design'd to have sat fire to the house & to have distroy'd us. He is still in prison."[19] But according to the original confession, Clarke's transcript, and Horsmanden's *Journal,* neither Quack nor Cuffee ever mentioned a "Spanish Negro" owned by Elizabeth or Peter DeLancey, and the only one of their slaves that Horsmanden ever reported as having been arrested, Pompey, was not Spanish, and was not jailed until June 20.

In spite of the conditions under which such confessions were taken, Horsmanden and many of his contemporaries did not consider them suspicious; rather, they were all the more valuable because they were "particularly and expressly confirmed in the Midst of Flames, which is the highest Attestation." Relying on a more medieval, inquisitorial view of justice than that which would lead, decades later, to the exclusion of involuntary confessions, Horsmanden considered the threat of death a badge of truth.

By law and custom, the confessions of Quack and Cuffee ought to have secured, at the very least, a reduction of their sentence from burning to hanging. But Quack and Cuffee found no mercy in New York. The mob grew restless, and Jamison decided that the spectators, who had come to watch a burning, would not be denied. If anything, the confessions only further inflamed the crowd. The sheriff "declared his Opinion, that the carrying the Negroes back" to City Hall while a gallows was built "would be impracticable" and would have required "a strong Guard," which was not on hand. The piles were lit, and Quack and Cuffee shortly longed for death.

BEFORE NIGHTFALL, the men accused by Quack and Cuffee were rounded up and thrown in jail. On Sunday, a day of rest and prayer, from pulpits at Trinity Church, at the New Dutch Church, at the Old Dutch Church, and everywhere across the city, ministers preached about the lessons to be learned from these "Monsters of Iniquity" while the charred remains of Quack and Cuffee still smoked in a valley of dew-covered spring grass and wildflowers. Maybe Quack's wife, Barbara, tried to take his body down, to bury it. Maybe Cuffee's father and brother tried to bury his. More likely, the sheriff insisted that no one touch them, that they should serve, instead, as a monument. That night, "a Negro of [Benjamin] Pecks cut his throat." Elizabeth DeLancey wrote to her father, "I suppose he knew himself guilty & did it to prevent a harder death."[20] (In his *Journal,* Horsmanden did not report this man's death, nor did he record his name.)

On Monday morning, June 1, the investigation resumed. Mills fetched Sarah, "*Mrs. Burk's Negro Wench,*" from her cell. She was, said Horsmanden, "one of the oddest Animals amongst the black Confederates, and gave the most Trouble in her Examinations; a Creature of an outragious Spirit." Sarah had been arrested on May 25, after Sandy said that she and another man named Fortune, owned by John Vanderspiegle, "were to have set Fire to the Meal Market." (The Meal—grain—Market, at the base of Wall Street, also served as the slave market.) On the day of her arrest, Sarah said "she knew Nothing of the Matter." As Horsmanden described it, her denial was passionate: she "threw herself into most violent Agitations; foamed at the Mouth, and uttered the bitterest Imprecations." But after it was made clear "that she could entertain no Hopes of escaping with Life" except by confessing, Sarah began to speak, and, according to Horsmanden, she "*seemed abundantly easier after disburthening Part of the Secret.*"

She confessed that although she had never been to John Hughson's tavern, she had been to a meeting of twenty or thirty black men at the house of Dutch cooper Gerardus Comfort, "about five Weeks before the Fort was fired." Sarah proceeded to reel off a long list of names, and to paint a vivid scene of villainy—black men, and a handful of black women, at Gerardus Comfort's house who "whetted their Knives on a Stone, some complaining, that their Knives were rusty and blunt; and some said, that their Knives were sharp enough to cut off a white Man's Head."

But Sarah's "outragious Spirit" soon returned. When her statement was read over to her, "she retracted, and excused many Persons; saying, such a One and such a One went away *before the Bargain was made.*" Sarah was sent back down to the dungeon.

Later that afternoon, John Hughson, who, like everyone in that cellar, must have thought a good deal about Quack and Cuffee's final minutes, told Mills that he wanted to "*open his Heart*" to one of the judges. Horsmanden, still vexed by Sarah's retraction, summoned Hughson for an interview in chambers. Hughson asked for a Bible to offer a sworn statement, but Horsmanden refused to give him one and instead hotly "reproached him with his wicked Life and Practices." Hughson changed his mind about confessing, "Whereupon the Recorder remanded him to Jail."

THREE DAYS LATER, on Thursday, June 4, Hughson, his wife and daughter, and Peggy Kerry were tried on three new charges, all of which stemmed from Quack and Cuffee's confessions: they were indicted for entering into a conspiracy with Caesar, Prince, and Cuffee to burn the city; for aiding Quack in burning the fort; and for aiding Cuffee in burning Philipse's storehouse. At City Hall, spectators filled the benches on the floor, crowded, standing, in the aisles, and burdened the balcony.

Only Horsmanden's account of this trial survives; Clarke did not send a copy of the trial minutes to England. Sixteen jurors were sworn, at least two of whom, Lashier and Arding, had served in the trial of Quack and Cuffee. Hughson successfully challenged one juror, "a young Gentleman, Merchant of the Town," at which Kerry "seemed out of Humour, and intimated, *That he had challenged one of the best of them all;* which occasioned some Mirth to those within the Hearing of it." Kerry, Horsmanden intimated, had provided her sexual services not only to slaves but also to white men wealthy enough to serve on a jury.

After the indictments were read, Attorney General Bradley delivered an opening statement naming Hughson the "author" of the conspiracy:

> *Gentlemen,* It will appear to you in the Course of the Evidence for the King upon this Trial, That *John Hughson* was the chief Contriver, Abettor, and Encourager of all this Mystery of Iniquity:— *That* it was *He,* who advised and procured secret and frequent Meetings of the Negroes, and the Rest of the Conspirators, at his House, there to form and carry on these horrible Conspiracies.— That it was *he* that swore the Negroes *Quack* and *Cuffee,* with many others, and himself too, into this direful Plot.—*That* it was *He* who devised Firebrands, Death, and Destruction to be sent among you. . . . *He—Murderous* and *Remorseless He!* . . . *Infamous Hughson!—* . . . *Gentlemen, This is that Hughson!* whose Name, and most

detestable Conspiracies will no doubt be had in everlasting Remembrance, to his eternal Reproach; and stand recorded to latest Posterity,—*This* is the Man!—*This,* that Grand Incendiary!—*That* Arch Rebel against God, his King, and his Country! . . . *Gentlemen, Behold* the Author, and Abettor of all the late Conflagrations, Terrors, and Devastation that have befallen this City.

Fortune and Sandy were not allowed to testify at this trial, since "Negro Evidence" was not allowed against whites, which made the dying confessions of Quack and Cuffee all the more important: the prosecution called George Joseph Moore and John Roosevelt to "prove the Confessions of those two Negroes, taken in Writing at the Stake." (In fact, it was necessary for Quack and Cuffee to die before the Hughsons and Kerry could be convicted; only their dying confessions, and not their living testimony, was admissible.) Arthur Price and Mary Burton also took the stand. When Burton testified, the defendants rolled their eyes "as if astonished, and said, she was a very wicked Creature, and protested all she said was false." Meanwhile, Sarah Hughson had her nursing child brought to her, but even as it sucked, it "was ordered to be taken away."

John Hughson conducted the defense for all four prisoners. He called four rather weak witnesses, including a soldier's wife named Eleanor Ryan, who had lodged at Hughson's all winter, lying "sick in Bed in the Kitchen almost Day and Night." She had seen "no Negroes there" except for Cuffee and Caesar, and "never saw any Entertainments there for Negroes." One of Hughson's witnesses, Adam King, proved more valuable to the prosecution. King testified "That of late he took *Hughson's* House to be disorderly; for he saw whole Companies of Negroes playing at Dice there," after which a smirking Attorney General Bradley turned to Hughson and asked, "Have you any more such Witnesses as this?"

William Smith delivered the closing statement, echoing Bradley's argument that in Hughson the "Ringleader" had been found. Then, lest the jury hesitate to convict, Horsmanden delivered an unambiguous charge: "I make no doubt, but you will discharge a good Conscience, and find them Guilty." After brief deliberation, the jury returned with the desired verdict. Four days later, Philipse delivered the sentence of death by hanging, regretting only that no more severe punishment was allowable by law since the whites, unlike the blacks, had not committed "petty treason" and could not be burned at the stake (something that Elizabeth DeLancey also regretted: "I think no death can be too bad for him," she wrote of

Hughson, "he is prov'd to be a most vile wicked Wretch").[21] Philipse took the occasion to express his disgust at what had taken place at Hughson's tavern: "For People who have been brought up, and always lived in a Christian Country, and also called themselves Christians, to be guilty not only of making Negro Slaves their Equals, but even their Superiors, by waiting upon, keeping with, and entertaining them, with Meat, Drink, and Lodging; and what is much more amazing, to plot, conspire, consult, abet and encourage these black *Seed of Cain,* to burn the City, and to kill and destroy us all.—GOOD GOD!"

ON MONDAY, June 8, six black men were tried for conspiracy: John Chambers's Robin; Thomas Ellison's Jamaica; another Caesar, owned by an English glover, Benjamin Peck (whose fellow slave had cut his throat in jail the night after Quack and Cuffee were burned); another Cuffee, a slave of a wealthy Portuguese Jewish merchant, Lewis Gomez; and Cook and Jack, owned by Gerardus Comfort, at whose house the slave Sarah, that "Creature of an outragious Spirit," had said she had attended a meeting of twenty or thirty black men and women. All six men were sentenced to die. Five, including Jack, were to be burned at the stake the next day.

That night, eyeing death, Jack sent a desperate message to the judges: "if his Life might be spared, he would discover all that he knew of the Conspiracy."

Daniel Horsmanden and Frederick Philipse rushed to City Hall and began their interrogation. Jack had been arrested on May 26. He had been in jail for two weeks; he had heard Cuffee weep, and had seen him and Quack taken from their cells to be burned at the stake. He knew that he, and everyone convicted alongside him, had been mentioned in Quack and Cuffee's dying confessions. Jack was ready to confess, and he didn't want to risk waiting until the flames licked his feet. But when the judges arrived, they encountered an obstacle: Jack's "Dialect was so perfectly Negro and unintelligible, 'twas thought, that 'twould be impossible to make any Thing of him without the Help of an Interpreter."

It is difficult to know what language Jack spoke. Many city slaves spoke more than one language, having acquired over their lifetimes as many tongues as masters: English, Dutch, French, German, Welsh, and more. Adolph Philipse's Cuffee spoke English and understood Spanish: "*Venez a qui Seignior,*" a "Spanish Negro" once called to him. Jacobus Vaarck's slave Bastian spoke both English and fluent French. Only that 30 percent of the newest arrivals who came directly from Africa could "scarce speak a Word of English," speaking, instead, one of their native tongues: Kikongo, Akan, Gã, Mandinga, Soninke, Temne, Fulbe, Sere, or any of the many other African languages heard on the streets of New York. Two of Comfort's slaves, Cook and Jenny, spoke Akan, and Jack might have, too. Akan was, in fact, a lingua franca in West Africa. Cook, who was also called "Acco," probably came from Accra (now the capital city of Ghana) and may have spoken Gã, a language known in the eighteenth century as Accra. Gã is closely related to Akan, and in the eighteenth century most Gã speakers could also speak Akan.[22] Jack may have spoken Akan as well, and may have been born in Africa. Maybe he was once called Quack, before his name was anglicized.

Most black New Yorkers also spoke languages that mixed Old World and New: whatever other languages Jack spoke when he talked to Acco or other black men and women, to whites he apparently talked in a "perfectly Negro" dialect, probably a creole. To whites, creolized black speech was worthy of ridicule. When Dr. Alexander Hamilton was on the road to New York City in 1744, his slave Dromo asked directions from a black woman on Coney Island. She spoke with such a strong Dutch inflection that Dromo, a Marylander who spoke an eighteenth-century black English, could barely understand her. Hamilton found their conversation so amusing that he recorded it in his journal:

> "Dis de way to York?" says Dromo. "Yaw, dat is Yarikee," said the wench, pointing to the steeples. "What devil you say?" replys Dromo. "Yaw, mynheer," said the wench. "Damme you, what you say?" said Dromo again. "Yaw, yaw," said the girl. "You a damn black bitch," said Dromo, and so rid on.[23]

Horsmanden included a similar sample of dialect in his *Journal*, evidently for his readers' amusement. The first slave Jack accused was Ben, owned by Captain Marshall. In Jack's confession in the *Journal*, he refers to Ben as "*Ben* (Capt. *Marshall's* Negro)." But Horsmanden, in a footnote, reported that Jack had actually identified Ben differently: *"His Master live in Tall House Broadway. Ben ride de fat Horse."* This was what Horsmanden meant by "*unintelligible* Jargon": a Caribbean creole, quite possibly the speech of an Akan-speaking man born in Africa who had spent time in Jamaica. It was all of Jack's speech that Horsmanden left intact.

Confronted with Jack's "unintelligible" speech, Philipse and Horsmanden sought the aid of two of Gerardus Comfort's sons-in-law, who said "they could make a shift to understand his Language." Slowly, Jack's confession took shape: his speech was translated, transcribed, and transformed. By nightfall, the work was unfinished, and "there was not Time to commit his Confession to Writing." Only after questioning Jack for "three successive Days, Morning and Afternoon" did Horsmanden draft a document entitled "The Confession of Jack," on June 10. Ten days later, Clarke had it copied and sent it off to the Lords of Trade. After the trials ended, the document was filed in the Secretary's Office as "June 8, 9, 10. Confession. Jack, giving account of a large meeting of the negro conspirators, at Comfort's house, naming each negro, and what each agreed to do."[24] A year later, Horsmanden copied it, and in 1744 he included it in his *Journal* as "*Examination & Confession of* Jack (Comfort's) *Before One of the Judges.*"

The differences between Clarke's manuscript "Confession" and Horsmanden's printed "*Examination & Confession*" are more typographical than textual. A line from the "Confession,"

Scipio Vanbersens Negro said he would Sett his Mistresse house on fire before he would Go out to fight

becomes paragraph six from the "*Examination & Confession,*"

6. "*Scipio* (Van Borsom's Negro) said, He would set "his Mistress's House on fire before *he would go out* "*to fight.*

Horsmanden probably directed the use of italics for emphasis, but his printer, James Parker, was responsible for introducing the two other typographical changes: italicizing people's names and using quotation marks in the margin of every line of a quoted passage to indicate that the enclosed text was spoken by another.

Quotation marks were by no means universally employed in the eighteenth century, and not until the very end of the century did grammar books describe and require their use in marking off another person's words or text. Earlier in the century quotation marks were most often used to enclose quoted passages from the published writings of celebrated authors—Cicero, Milton, Pope—for readers to copy into their commonplace books. Parker's enclosing the speech of slaves in quotation marks seems, at first glance, to lend them a certain weight and authority. But it serves another purpose: over the course of the eighteenth century quotation marks also evolved as a print equivalent of the criminal courts' growing preference for voluntary confession. By certifying a confession's authenticity, quotation marks effectively *replaced* torture as the "highest Attestation" of truth.[25] In Jack's *"Examination & Confession,"* the double quotation marks along the margins of the page both credit the confession as genuine and shackle Jack in typographical handcuffs.

Both Horsmanden and Philipse probably took notes as Jack spoke, but none of those notes survive and, in any event, what they contained was different from what Jack said. The original confession, titled "June 8, 9, 10. Confession. Jack, giving account of a large meeting of the negro conspirators, at Comfort's house, naming each negro, and what each agreed to do," was not a record of the interrogation; it was a summary of legally significant statements made during that interrogation, digested and abbreviated for the purposes of the prosecution. As Horsmanden admitted in the Preface to his *Journal,* none of the confessions were uttered in *"precisely in the same Words"* in which they were recorded. Instead, *"Abstracts were taken of those Evidences, and Briefs prepared for the Council concern'd in each Trial"* so that the prosecuting lawyers could direct questions to witnesses that would allow them to keep *"close to the Text"* on the witness stand, and deliver *"in Court the Substance of the Evidence they had before given in their Depositions, Examinations, and Confessions."*

Who wielded the pen was rarely recorded. When Peggy Kerry confessed on May 7, someone else, possibly James Mills, wrote it down and she signed with an "X." Horsmanden added a footnote in his *Journal: "This Confession was penn'd by a Jail Secretary."* Mills brought Kerry's confession to Daniel Horsmanden in the middle of the night, and the next day Philipse and Horsmanden signed it, probably after having read it back to Kerry. Arthur Price signed his depositions with an "A," which Horsmanden and Philipse witnessed. Mary Burton signed with a sort of "S." Not only was her signature witnessed by Horsmanden, but some of her depositions were written in what appears to be his handwriting.

But, so far as it is possible to tell from the badly burned original documents, confessing slaves did not sign their confessions at all, not even with an "X." Some of their confessions are in the handwriting of their owners, some in Horsmanden's handwriting. Arrest warrants, too, were signed by Horsmanden, and apparently written in his hand.[26]

Jack's confession was taken in Horsmanden's presence, and was wit-

The Confession of Jack Comfort's Negro taken
the 9th 10th(?) of June 1741

Says That a little after New Year on a Monday about 4 of the
Clock in the afternoon Coen Capt. Marshall's Negroe came to Comforts
house to fetch Tea Water where he left his Cagg in the Shop &
went to Husons house (Huson & his Wife being then Gone in the
Country) Ben staid about two hours there and then returned to
Comforts And told Jack that he had there met 6 Spaniards
among whom were Anthony & Warin (now in Goal) and said
to him Countryman I have heard some Good News. What News
said Jack, Ben said there were Spanish Negroes at Husons who
told him they had Designs of taking this Country against the
Warr come to which Jack said what would they do with this
Country, Ben answered O You Fool these Spaniards know better
than York Negroes & could better help to take it then they because
they were more used to Warr, But they must begin first to set
their houses on fire ———— That the Sunday following Huson &
his Wife came home and brought with them a Goose a Quarter
of Mutton & a Fowl home; That Ben came a little after Church
out in the afternoon to Comforts & told him Brother Go to Husons
all our Company is come down, he went with Ben thither Ben went
round the house & went in at the Back door when he came there they
sat all round the Table & had a Goose a Quarter of Mutton & a
Fowle & 2 loaves of Bread — Huson took a Flask of Rum out of
a Case & sett it on the Table & Cloth was laid & 2 bowls of
Punch were made Quash Hermanus Rutgers Negroe, Fortright's
Cæsar, Pedro a Spanish Negro, John Roosevelt's Toby, Shurmurs(?)
Cato, Comfort's Cook, Vaarick's John, Marshall's York & London
Carpenters Dirk & others, Beschi, Francis, Bastian als Tom well(?)
Mr. Vanburens Scipio, Captain Marshall's Ben were all present
and also six Spanish Negroes among them were Sarin & Anthony

nessed by him.[27] During those three days of interrogation, Horsmanden turned Jack's speech into text. Comfort's sons-in-law translated the words that came out of Jack's mouth, and Horsmanden fixed meaning to them.

The Recorder found this process tedious. He complained, at great length, about the "*Drudgery*" of interrogating slave suspects and determining what, of all that they said and didn't say, was worth writing down:

> *The Trouble of examining Criminals in general, may be easily gues'd at; but the Fatigue in that of Negroes, is not to be conceived, but by those that have undergone the Drudgery: The Difficulty of bringing, and holding them to the Truth, if by Chance it starts from them, is not to be surmounted but by the closest Attention; many of them have a great deal of Craft; their unintelligible Jargon stands them in great Stead, to conceal their Meaning; so that an Examiner must expect to encounter with much Perplexity; grope through a Maze of Obscurity; be obliged to lay hold of broken Hints, lay them carefully together, and thoroughly weigh and compare them with each other, before he can be able to see the Light, or fix those Creatures to any certain determinate Meaning.*

How that meaning became "fixed," out of "*broken Hints*" and "*unintelligible Jargon,*" and how Horsmanden found his way through such "*a Maze of Obscurity,*" can best be discovered in the events of the 1730s, when Horsmanden employed much the same skills, with less success, in attempting to prosecute John Peter Zenger.

DANIEL HORSMANDEN was something of an expert at interpreting sedition, at "fixing meaning" to words. In October 1734, Cosby had appointed him to a committee whose charge was to "point out . . . the particular Seditious paragraphs" in Zenger's *Weekly Journal*. Horsmanden's frustrations were considerable, as Alexander had gone to some lengths to write ambiguously. Of his close reading of Alexander's essays in the *Weekly Journal*, Horsmanden might well have made much the same complaint he would make about interrogating slaves in 1741: "*an Examiner must expect to encounter with much Perplexity; grope through a Maze of Obscurity; be obliged to lay hold of broken Hints, lay them carefully together, and thoroughly weigh and compare them with each other, before he can be able to see the Light, or fix those Creatures to any certain determinate Meaning.*"

In the Zenger case, fixing meaning was exactly the task at hand. But James Alexander argued that it was in this very act, of attaching signifi-

64   *JOURNAL of the Proceedings against*

" *Marshall's* Negro) came to *Comfort's* House to fetch Tea
" Water, where he left his Cag in the Shop, and went to
" *Hughson's* House (*Hughson* and *his Wife* then gone into
" the Country) *Ben* staid about two Hours there, and then
" returned to *Comfort's*, and told *Jack*, that he had met
" there *Six Spaniards*, among whom were *Anthony*, and
" *Wan (q)* (now in Goal) and said to him, Countryman,
" I have heard some good News: What News, said *Jack* ?
" *Ben* said, *there were Spanish Negroes at Hughson's*, who
" told him, they had Designs of taking this Country against
" the Wars came : What would they do with this Coun-
" try, said *Jack* ? To which *Ben* answered, Oh ! you
" Fool, *those Spaniards know better than York Negroes*,
" and could help better to take it than they ; because they
" were more used to War ; but they must begin first to set
" the House [i. e. the Houses] on fire.

  2. " That the Sunday following, *Hughson* and *his Wife*
" came home, and brought a Goose, a Quarter of Mutton,
" and a Fowl home. That *Ben* came a little after Church
" out, in the Afternoon, to *Comfort's*, and told him, *Bro-*
" *ther go to Hughson's*, all our Company is come down :
" He went with *Ben* thither, and went round the House,
" and went in at the back Door ; when he came there,
" they sat all round the Table, and had a Goose, a Quar-
" ter of Mutton, and a Fowl, two Loaves of Bread :
" *Hughson* took a Flask of Rum out of a Case, and set it on
" the Table, and two Bowls of Punch were made ; some
" drink Dram ; a Cloth was laid :

Quash,	H. Rutgers's Negro.
Cæsar,	Koertrecht's.
Pawlus,	*A Spanish Negro*.
Toby, or *Cato*,	Provoost's.
Cato,	Shurmur's.
Cook,	Comfort'e.
John,	Vaarck's.
York, }	
London, }	Marschalk's.
Ticklepitcher,	Carpenter's.
Francis,	Bosch's.
Bastian alias *Tom Peal*	
Scipio,	Mrs. Van Borsom's.
Ben.	Capt. Marshall's.

" were all present, and also *six* Spanish *Negroes*, among whom
" were *Wan* and *Anthony*, and a Negro lately belonging to
" *John Marschalk*, the Three others he should know if he
" saw them : *Hughson*, and *his Wife*, and *Daughter* sat
" down on one Side of the Table, and the Negroes on the
" other : Two or Three Tables were put together to make
" it long ; *Hughson's Daughter* brought in the Victuals,

(q) Mr. Peter De Lancey's (*See* § 29) *and Capt.* Sarly's.

" and just as he came in, *Sarah* brought the Cloth and laid
" it ; *Mary Burton* did not come into the Room ; but
" *Hughson* said, she was above making a Bed : *Peggy* came
" down Stairs, and sat down by *Hughson's* Wife at the
" Table, and eat with them ; when they were eating, *they*
" *began all to talk about setting the Houses on fire* ; and *Hugh-*
" *son* asked *Ben*, who would be the Head Man or Captain
" for to rise ? *Ben* said, *Yes*, he would stand for that ; and
" said, *he could find a Gun*; *Shot and Powder*, at his
" Master's House : That his Master did not watch him,
" he could go into every Room : *Ben* asked *Quash*, What
" will you stand for ? He said, he did not care what he
" stood for, or should be, but he could kill Three, Four,
" Five White Men before Night.

  3. " That *Quash* said, he could get two half Dozen of
" Knives in Papers, three or four Swords ; and that he
" would set his Master's House on fire, and when he had
" done that, he would *come abroad to fight.*

  4. " That Marschalk's *York* said, That his Mistress
" had scolded at him, and he would kill her before *he*
" *went out to fight.*

  5. " *London* (Marschalk's other Negro) said, That before
" he went out *to fight*, he would set his Master's House on
" fire.

  6. " *Scipio* (Van Borsom's Negro) said, He would set
" his Mistress's House on fire before *he would go out to*
" *to fight.*

  7. " *Cato* (Shurmur's Negro) said, He would set his
" Mistress's House on fire ; and that as the Houses stand
" all together, the Fire would go more far.

  8. " *Cato* alias *Toby* (John Provoost's Negro) said, He
" would get his Master's Sword, and then set the House
" on fire, and *go out to fight.*

  9. " The *Spanish Negroes* he could not understand.

  10. " *Cæsar* (Kortrecht's Negro) said, He would set
" his Master's Bakehouse on fire.

  11. " *Ben* said (when it was proposed to burn his Master's
" House) *No, if they conquer'd the Place, he would keep that*
" *to live in himself.*

  12. " That *Curacoa Dick* came in just as they had done
" eating, but Victuals enough were left for him, and he
" sat down and eat : When *Dick* had done eating, he said,
" Every one must stand to his Word ; and that he would
" get his Master's Gun, and after that would set his Stable
" on fire.

                                    13. " He

Jack's confession, in Horsmanden's Journal. *Collection of
The New-York Historical Society.*

cance to another man's words, that the freedom of speech was most vulnerable to abuse. Alexander complained of the work Horsmanden's committee conducted that

If they will fix determinate Meanings to Sentences and even
Blanks, which the Authors have not fixt, and to which other Mean-

ings can with equal Justice be applyed; I would be glad to know wherein this Liberty of Writing consists?[28]

In spite of Alexander's argument, the text Horsmanden's committee selected was brought to bear at Zenger's trial, where Bradley used it as evidence. Bradley charged that Zenger "*did falsely, seditiously and scandalously* print and publish, and cause to be printed and published, a certain *false, malicious, seditious scandalous* Libel, entituled *The New York Weekly Journal* . . . in which Libel . . . among other Things therein contained are these Words." Bradley then read brief passages from Zenger's newspaper, inserting, parenthetically, as verbal asides, their seditious meaning:

They (the People of the City and Province of New-York meaning) *think as Matters now stand that their* LIBERTIES *and* PROPERTIES *are precarious, and that* SLAVERY *is like to be intailed on them and their Posterity if some past Things be not amended, and this they collect from many past Proceedings,* (Meaning many of the past Proceedings of His Excellency the said Governor, and of the Ministers and Officers of our said Lord the King, of and for the said Province.)

With Horsmanden's aid, Bradley had prepared an able case. But then the ambitious young lawyer from Purleigh sat in dismay in the Supreme Court in August 1735 as Zenger's attorney Andrew Hamilton poked fun at Bradley for fixing meaning even to punctuation—"I had not the Art to find out (without the Help of Mr. Attorney's *Inuendo's*) that the Governor was the Person meant in every Period of that News Paper"—and argued that the only legal question at hand was not what the text meant, but whether or not it was true. "To save the Court's Time and Mr. Attorney's Trouble," Hamilton said, "I will agree, that if he can prove the Facts charged upon us, to be *false*, I'll own them to be *scandalous, seditious* and *a Libel.*"

Hamilton was ahead of the law here; there was little precedent that truth was a defense against libel. And he was on even shakier legal ground when he insisted that a jury could decide the question, which was a matter of law, not a matter of fact. With this unprecedented assertion, DeLancey had adamantly disagreed.

Mr. Chief Justice. No, Mr. *Hamilton;* the Jury may find that *Zenger* printed and published those Papers, and leave it to the Court to judge whether they are libellous. . . .

Mr. Hamilton. I know, may it please Your Honor, the Jury may do so; but I do likewise know, they may do otherwise. I know they have the Right beyond all Dispute, to determine both the Law and the Fact. . . . This of leaving it to the Judgment of the Court, *whether the Words are libellous or not*, in Effect renders Juries useless.

While DeLancey refused to grant Hamilton this point, the jury did, especially after Hamilton delivered a stirring closing statement that it-self echoed the very words Zenger was charged with having published seditiously:

The Question before the Court and you Gentlemen of the Jury, is not of small nor private Concern, it is not the Cause of a poor Printer, nor of *New-York* alone, which you are now trying: No! It may in it's Consequence, affect every Freeman that lives under a British Government on the main of *America*. It is the best Cause. It is the Cause of Liberty; and I make no Doubt but your upright Conduct this Day, will not only entitle you to the Love and Esteem of your Fellow-Citizens, but every Man who prefers Freedom to a Life of Slavery will bless and honour you, as Men who have baffled the Attempt of Tyranny.[29]

For DeLancey and Philipse, who sat on the bench, and whose instruc-tions to the jury were entirely ignored, Zenger's acquittal in 1735 was a stunning defeat. For Bradley and for Horsmanden, who had helped pre-pare Bradley's case, it was a gross humiliation. Six years later, in 1741, Daniel Horsmanden and Frederick Philipse controlled the courtroom. Richard Bradley again led the prosecution. And their old adversaries, Zenger's lawyers William Smith and James Alexander, had sworn to serve on the prosecution. For Horsmanden, it was an unrivaled opportunity to consolidate the court's power. He could make a name for himself. He could ferret out sedition, for the slave plot to overthrow the government was nothing if not seditious, and he could fix whatever meanings he liked to the words spoken by the "Creatures" who stood before him. He could write whatever "Confession" he liked for Jack, and for all the rest, and no one would oppose him. Daniel Horsmanden may not have succeeded in fixing seditious meaning to words Zenger printed in the *New-York Weekly Journal*—"*SLAVERY is like to be intailed on them and their Posterity*"—but he could fix it to Jack's "perfectly Negro and unintelligible" speech.

. . .

AT THE END of the first night of his three-day interrogation, Jack "desired he might be removed from the Cell where his fellow Criminals, condemn'd with him, were lodged." As well he might. Jack's request was granted. On the afternoon of June 9, Robin, Caesar (Peck), Cook, and Cuffee (Gomez) were taken together from City Hall, cursing Jack. Even as Jack was listing new names to his interrogators, these four men were burned at the stake. All died without confessing.

Meanwhile, seven of the men Jack implicated were arrested. Three more, Bastian, Francis, and Curacoa Dick, had already been scheduled to be tried on June 10, along with Albany, owned by the English butcher Elizabeth Carpenter. In order that Jack might testify at that trial, he was pardoned just before the court opened its session.

Albany, Bastian, Francis, and Curacoa Dick were tried for participating in what Bradley called "the most horrible and destructive Plot that ever was yet known in these Northern Parts of *America*." For Francis, a "Spanish Negro," an interpreter was provided. As the trial began, the prisoners successfully challenged the impaneling of Ben Thomas, on the grounds that his house was among those buildings set on fire. It was a wise move, and a good start. The challenge was allowed. But then the prisoners faced Jack's damning testimony. Curacoa Dick, Jack said, had pledged to torch a stable owned by his master, the Dutch carpenter Cornelius Tiebout. Bastian, when asked if he would help burn the city, said he would. Sandy then testified that he had heard Francis, outside Captain Lush's house, "talking of burning the Town and killing the People." Albany was accused of little more than having been a friend of Cuffee (Philipse): he had stood next to him in the bucket brigade fighting the fire at Fort George. After hearing the evidence, the jury, acting swiftly, found the prisoners guilty.

The next day, all four men were called to the courtroom and sentenced to be burned. Before he was escorted back to his cell, Bastian broke down and confessed. Because he, like Jack, was likely to prove "a Witness worthy of Credit," Bastian was recommended for pardon.

Cheered by the pattern of eleventh-hour confessions, the prosecutors had high hopes the next morning, Friday, June 12, when John and Sarah Hughson and Peggy Kerry were to be carried to the gallows. The execution of Sarah Hughson, the daughter, was postponed, as Horsmanden expected her to be easily broken after her parents were hanged. When the Hughsons and Kerry were taken out of jail, they, too, were urged again to confess but refused. During the slow ride out of the city, Hughson "stood up in the Cart all the Way, looking round about him as if expecting to be rescued." With the noose around her neck, Sarah "stood like a lifeless Trunk" and "said not a Word." Peggy "was going to say something, but the Old Woman, who hung next to her, gave her a Shove with her Hand." All three "seem'd unconcerned at dying, and one of them curs'd the Executioner."[30] None confessed. After he was hanged, John Hughson's lifeless body was hung in chains, next to Caesar's rotting corpse, on the island in the midst of the Little Collect.

But the executioner's work was far from done. Before the sun went down, Albany, Curacoa Dick, and Francis were burned to death, denying their guilt to the last. Smoke and the smell of burning flesh wafted over the city. Back at City Hall, two prisoners awaiting trial confessed, and named names. Nine more men were arrested. The cascade of confessions had begun.

On June 11, the judges were astonished to hear that when Bastian swore to the plot, Caesar had called to Hughson, "*set his Name down.*" Hughson, apparently, kept "*a List of the Names of those who were to rise.*" Who kept this list? the grand jury asked Tickle, a fellow slave of Albany, also owned by Elizabeth Carpenter. "*Ben* had it," Tickle admitted. But Ben, arrested on June 9, denied it.

Ben was tried and found guilty on June 13. Two days later, Horsmanden sentenced him to be burned: "You, *Ben*, by the Course of the Evidence appear to have been a principal Ringleader in this most horrid and devilish Conspiracy, this Master-piece of Villainy. . . . And so exact a Man were you in your Business and Trust, that, it seems, *you kept a List:* You say you cannot read; but so active and forward have you appeared in this Villainy, that a List of this black Band was committed to your Care." For this, "Thou vile Wretch!," Horsmanden warned Ben that he would be "thrown into the infernal Lake of fire and Brimstone, together with the Devil and his accursed Spirits, where the Worm never dyeth, that is, the biting, gnawing Worm of Conscience will forever be upbraiding you, and the Fire will never be quenched; but in this Torment you must remain under the most bitter Weeping, Wailing, and Gnashing of Teeth, Time without End." (A contemporary once wrote of Horsmanden, "He was most disliked for his Asperities to the unhappy Criminals who received sentence from his Mouth.")[31] On Tuesday, June 16, Ben was burned at the stake. No list was ever found.

It would have made Horsmanden's work easier. Instead, on June 19, at the urging of the grand jury, and considering the crowdedness of the prison, Clarke published a proclamation promising "His Majesty's most gracious Pardon to any and every Person and Persons, whether white People, free Negroes, Slaves, or others, who had been or were concerned in the said Conspiracy, who should on or before the *first* Day of *July* then next, *voluntarily, freely and fully discover, and Confession* make, of his, her or their Confederates, Accomplices, or others concerned in the said Conspiracy, and his, her, and their Part or Share, Actings and Doings therein."

"Now many Negroes began to squeak," Horsmanden noted with satisfaction. Confess, and be saved. But since every confession included still more accusations, every confession led to more arrests. Horsmanden reported: "we were apprehensive, that the Criminals would be daily multiplying on our Hands; nor could we see any Likelihood of a Stop to Impeachments; for it seemed very probable that most of the Negroes in Town were corrupted." By June 27, there were more than a hundred slaves in the Great Gaol, which "began to be so thronged, 'twas difficult to find Room for them." Horsmanden and Philipse resolved to expedite the extraction of confessions and the trying of criminals, and convened another meeting of the city's Gentlemen of the Law, to divide up their work more efficiently. William Jamison had "sufficient Business upon his Hands" in his capacity as sheriff, and was spared further duties. Joseph Murray, William Smith, James Alexander, and John Chambers were "to assist in their Turns, as Council upon the several Trials." Richard Nichols and Abraham Lodge, the most junior attorneys in the group, were assigned "to take the Negroes Confessions, and abstract them and the other Evidence into Briefs."

Those confessions were then recorded in a table of several columns. Having failed to find Ben's list, the prosecution made a list of its own. Nichols and Lodge extracted fourteen confessions in a single day, another twenty-one by the end of the week. They had so many confessions to write down that they recorded them not individually, but in a ledger.

Some suspects confessed more than once. And still the jail filled. Interrogated before a grand jury, before the Supreme Court, before Nichols and Lodge, and, in many cases, simply by their owners, who transcribed and often translated their confessions for the court, slaves sought to save their lives by confessing.

"Could these be dreams?" Horsmanden asked of the confessions, anticipating his critics, "or is it more rational to conclude, from what has happen'd amongst us, that they were founded on Realities?" The question turns, in part, on the matter of authorship. Was Daniel Horsmanden the author of the confessions? Or is it possible that the condemned men who confessed were, by some measure, *any* measure, the authors of their own words?

Horsmanden called himself "the Compiler" of his *Journal,* never its author. He also put only his title—"*the Recorder of the City of* New-York"—not his name, on the book's cover. Nor did he ever alert readers that the Recorder happened to be the Third Justice of the Supreme Court. The veil Horsmanden placed over his identity didn't fool anyone in New York, but it did hide his role on the bench from readers outside the city. (And it later confused library cataloguers, who frequently misidentified the anonymous "Compiler" of the *Journal* as Simon Johnson, who held the role of Recorder from 1748 to 1766.)[32]

But of course Horsmanden was more than a compiler or recorder. He issued the arrest warrants. He was the first interrogator of nearly every suspect. And he himself questioned Mary Burton, again and again, from the beginning. He also drafted crucial confessions in his own hand, made dozens of speeches from the bench, and wrote a Preface, Introduction, and Conclusion to the *Journal* that framed the entire proceedings for posterity. In 1741, and in the published record, the prosecution's story—at least the story of the feast at Hughson's—was a story of Horsmanden's making.

Faced with the question of who set the fires and why, Horsmanden led the investigation. In a post-providential, pre-Enlightenment world, he detected the work of criminals, not God, not nature. In an anxious empire, he found monstrous black creatures. In a rebellious province, he spotted political plotters. He traced their motives, limned their characters, and followed their fates. In the *Journal,* Horsmanden produced something that resembles an early English novel.

The boundary between history and fiction at the time was decidedly blurred. Histories could be fancifully elaborated, and the first English novels, Defoe's *Robinson Crusoe* (1719) and Swift's *Gulliver's Travels* (1726), adapted the trappings of histories. But unlike most histories, novels had, at their heart, ordinary people trying to make sense of an extraordinary world. The novel emerged when the world looked most inexplicable—caught between the medieval and the modern—and placed, at its center, an individual plotting a course through life, making sense of the mysteries around him.

That new techniques of criminal investigation emerged at the same time was hardly a coincidence, as the career of Henry Fielding shows.

During the very years that he ran a criminal investigation agency in London, Fielding not only wrote social tracts closely related to his detective work, including *An Enquiry into the Cause of the late Increase of Robbers* (1751), but also novels, including *Tom Jones* (1749) and *Amelia* (1751). Horsmanden, if he had had literary merit rather than political ambition, might have been an American Fielding.[33]

But Horsmanden did not place himself at the center of his *Journal,* doggedly interrogating suspects, sifting through the evidence, putting together the pieces of the puzzle. His *Journal* lacks a protagonist. Because Horsmanden erased the evidence of his own role in the investigation whenever possible, the *Journal* tells the story not of an individual searching for truth but of truth revealed. Horsmanden's role in the investigation can be uncovered, by careful reading and by placing the *Journal* alongside other evidence, like Horsmanden's letters and the surviving court manuscripts. But Horsmanden himself did his best to bury it.

He had every reason to hide. If, as critics charged as early as July 1741, New Yorkers had suffered "in the merciless Flames of an Imaginary Plot," then Mary Burton, Arthur Price, Sandy, Fortune, and Jack had lied, innocent black men had died, and their owners had lost a rather vast investment in property. For Horsmanden to draw attention to his role in interrogating suspects would have made their testimony more dubious. In 1742, when he set about compiling documents, Horsmanden deleted himself from his own investigation. And, if only by reproducing each slave confession in its entirety, he attempted to stress slaves' authorship not only of the plot but of their confessions.

But that authorship was difficult to establish, not least because no slave actually wrote down his own confession. In the dungeon, Cuffee (Philipse) "read sometimes, and cried much." When Scipio was interrogated by Nichols and Lodge, he held "his Bible in his Bosom, which he said he read in Gaol as often as he could." Even those men who could read did not necessarily know how to write, since writing was a separate skill, much less frequently taught. From a slaveowner's point of view, a slave who could write was dangerous. By writing, slaves could name and disguise themselves: one New Yorker liked to call her slave "Johnsey," but he "writes his Name *Jonathan Stow,*" she warned in an ad for his return after he ran away.[34] By writing, slaves could free themselves, forging passes. A man named Cesar ran away from John Moore in 1728: "He Reads and Writes English, and its believed, has got a sham Pass."[35] By writing, slaves could revolt. They allegedly signed Hughson's book, which pledged them to

*The Ledger of Confessions. Courtesy of the New York State Archives, series
A1894, New York Colony Council Papers, 74–99.*

secrecy. And Hughson's list, to which some slaves allegedly signed their
own names, was crucial to the conspiracy, at least from the point of view of
the investigation. Horsmanden suspected that more slaves than would
admit to it were literate. "You say you cannot read," Horsmanden said to
Ben, sentencing him to death, "but so active and forward have you
appeared in this Villainy, that a List of this black Band was committed to
your Care."

To write was to defy bondage, so much so that, beginning with the earliest slave narratives, the quest for literacy proved central to an emerging
African-American literary tradition. In a world in which literacy marked a
kind of dividing line between "savagery" and "civilization," writing and,
more, *authorship* became crucial to blacks' insistence on their own humanity.[36] Later in the century, a handful of black writers became published
authors: Olaudah Equiano, Phillis Wheatley, Ignatius Sancho. Each of
these writers served, for Enlightenment philosophers, as "specimens of
ingenuity," empirical evidence, positive or negative, of the intellectual and
artistic potential of blacks. As one eighteenth-century anti-slavery activist
observed, "no literary performance would be better received by the humane
and liberal people of England, than a vindication of African capacity by
the pen of an African."[37]

The black author, the "specimen of ingenuity" best known to early eighteenth-century New Yorkers, was the black poet and mathematician Francis Williams. Williams was born to free parents in Jamaica in 1697. "Being a boy of unusual lively parts," he "was pitched upon to be the subject of an experiment, which, it is said, the Duke of Montague was curious to make, in order to discover, whether, by proper cultivation, and a regular course of tuition at school and the university, a Negroe might not be found as capable of literature as a white person." The duke had the boy sent to England, where he attended grammar school, then studied mathematics at the University of Cambridge, and in 1721 was admitted to study law at the Inns of Court in London (while Daniel Horsmanden was studying there). Williams wrote poetry in Latin, including verses in which he drew his own conclusions from Montague's experiment:

> To all of human kind, benignant heaven
> (Since nought forbids) one common soul has given.
> This rule was 'stablished by th'Eternal Mind;
> Nor virtue's self, nor prudence are confin'd
> To *colour;* none imbues the honest heart;
> To science none belongs, and none to art

Despite Williams's accomplishments, David Hume, in his 1741 essay on "National Characters," concluded:

> I am apt to suspect the negroes to be naturally inferior to the whites. There scarcely ever was a civilized nation of that complexion, nor even any individual eminent either in action or speculation. No ingenious manufactures amongst them, no arts, no sciences. . . . Not to mention our colonies, there are NEGROE slaves dispersed all over EUROPE, of whom none ever discovered any symptoms of ingenuity. . . . In JAMAICA, indeed, they talk of one negroe as a man of parts and learning; but it is likely he is admired for slender accomplishments, like a parrot, who speaks a few words plainly.[38]

Those who chose to found in Williams's work evidence of blacks' intellectual equality; those who didn't want to acknowledge that equality found his work deficient.

In Jamaica, Williams's capacity for reason, which turned on his ability to speak and write, to be the author of his own life, determined whether "Negro Evidence" could be admitted against him in court. In 1708,

Williams's wealthy and prominent free black father, John Williams, had successfully petitioned the Jamaican Assembly to pass "An act to prevent slaves being evidence against John Williams, a free negro"—a law that essentially defined Williams and his family as whites, against whom "Negro Evidence" was inadmissible.[39] Hume may have considered Francis Williams a mere parrot, but in the Jamaican court of law he was a white man.

Whether Francis Williams's accomplishments were "slender" and whether he was, in effect, a "parrot" were hotly debated topics in England and its colonies, and not just at universities. When Dr. Alexander Hamilton stayed in New York in 1744, he found Williams the topic of conversation among the gentlemen drinking at Robert Todd's tavern: "There, talking of a certain free negroe in Jamaica who was a man of estate, good sense, and education," a visiting gentleman from that colony "gravely asked if that negroe's parents were not whites, for he was sure that nothing good could come of the whole generation of blacks." (Following this conversation, Hamilton returned to his room at Robert Hogg's house and, "to pass away time," picked up a book hot off the press and "read some of the Journal of Proceedings against the conspirators att New York.")

There was no African "man of letters" in eighteenth-century New York City. Not Jack, with his "perfectly Negro" speech. Not Cuffee, reading sometimes and crying much in his prison cell. Not Scipio, pressing his Bible to his breast. Not Ben, who kept the list but couldn't read it. When these men spoke, they spoke on pain of death. They left not an inkblot behind.

REMEMBERING THAT whites did not believe Africans could be authors helps explain why Daniel Horsmanden so desperately needed John Hughson, and why it was so crucial for Quack and Cuffee, in their dying confessions, to agree that Hughson was "the first Contriver and Promoter of the whole Plot" and "that they should never have thought of it, if he had not put it into their Heads." From the court's perspective, slaves who confessed *were* parrots; but they weren't parroting Daniel Horsmanden, they were parroting John Hughson. As Attorney General Bradley told a jury during one slave trial: "*Gentlemen,* It cannot be imagined that these silly unthinking Creatures (*Hughson's black Guard*) could of themselves have contrived and carried on so deep, so direful and destructive a Scheme." Bradley and Horsmanden, again and again, called Hughson the "author" of the con-

Francis Williams, the Jamaican Scholar, *by anonymous Jamaican,
British, or American painter, c. 1745. Courtesy of V&A Images /
Victoria and Albert Museum.*

spiracy; "wherefore," the Attorney General declared, "it may justly be called HUGHSON'S PLOT." Hughson was a thief and a smuggler, and he kept a "disorderly House." But the court needed him to be more. As Bradley put it to the jury at Hughson's trial: "*Behold, the Author*"!

Unfortunately, John Hughson was a particularly implausible leader of a vast slave conspiracy. As for Hughson supplying hundreds of men with feasts and free drinks, even Horsmanden allowed, "*'Tis somewhat amazing! how* Hughson, *a poor Cobler, with a Wife and House full of Children, and scarce any visible Business, or Means of Subsistence, should be able to support such extraordinary Generosity.*" By July, Horsmanden would be forced to cast about for another main character, a white man who would make a better, more plausible "Author, and Abettor of all the late Conflagrations, Terrors, and Devastation that have befallen this City."

It was a "*Maze of Obscurity,*" to be sure. Burdened by the drudgery of fixing meaning, busy finding a main character to replace himself, Horsmanden lost control of the story. Those confessions have more tales to tell, and there were more plots being hatched than the one to burn the city, kill the white men, marry the white women, make Hughson king and Caesar governor. Meanwhile, the condemned men had every reason to collude with Horsmanden in agreeing that John Hughson was the author of their crimes. Even Horsmanden admitted that while Jack had committed the darkest of deeds, he "had more Wit than to be hanged for them."

CHAPTER FIVE

Water

O N   T H E   E V E   of the trial of Quack and Cuffee, a contradiction in
the evidence had threatened to weaken the prosecution. Mary
Burton stood by her story that dozens of black men met in the
warmth of John Hughson's tavern just after Christmas, where they ate and
drank and plotted to burn down the city and name Caesar governor, and
three slaves had confessed to knowing about a plot. But none of the three,
Sandy, Fortune, and Sarah, had admitted to attending the meeting Mary
Burton described. More troubling still, all three insisted, as Fortune put it,
that they had "never heard of a House where they met; nor knew *Hughson.*"

If Sandy, Fortune, and Sarah had never met John Hughson, the supposed "author" of the plot, nor seen his house, how and where had they
conspired, in the bitter cold of that hardest of winters? They learned of the
plot, they said, not from a poor white cobbler at his house at the edge of
town but from other slaves, all over the city: down by the docks in the
chilled stillness of sunrise; in darkened alleys at dusk; on snow-covered
cobbled streets in the bleakness of day, slivers of sunlight low in the sky; at
corner markets where hogs and oxen snorted steam and sacks of grain
froze to the ground; and at icy wells and pumps, where they went, morning, noon, and night, balancing kegs on their heads, to fetch water for their
masters' tea.

Fortune heard about the plot from Cuffee when he ran into him on
New Street; and from Quack when he saw him "near Mrs. *Carpenter's*" and
again "near Mrs. *Richets's.*" Once, he had taken a walk with Quack on the
Common, shoulders stiffened against the wind, and had snuck with him
into the fort. Another time, he met him "at the Pump near the great Slip."
Sandy first learned of the conspiracy on an errand to Coenties Market, and
he, too, had bumped into Quack and Cuffee on the street. Sandy told

Sarah about the plot when they met "at the Pump in the Neighbourhood," filling their kegs and casks, where Sandy cursed, his breath like a cloud, "*G-d d—m all the white People,*" promising, "*if he had it in his Power, he would set them all on Fire.*"

That the prosecution's "Negro Evidence" of whispering by water pumps did not altogether support Mary Burton's story of feasting by Hughson's fireside by no means derailed the conviction of Quack and Cuffee; the jury proved quite willing to overlook this baffling contradiction between white and black testimony. The discrepancy, in any event, was nicely addressed at Quack and Cuffee's execution, when both condemned men obligingly agreed that Hughson "was the first Contriver and Promoter of the whole Plot" and "that they should never have thought of it, if he had not put it into their Heads."

While prosecutors prepared for John Hughson's trial, the grand jury wisely turned its attention away from the scene at his tavern. Ignoring leads in earlier testimony about a conspiracy hatched out of doors, at docks, markets, wells, and street corners, investigators searched for another house where conspirators who had never met Hughson might have gathered. They found it on May 25, when Sandy told the grand jury that, while he had never been to Hughson's, he often walked to Gerardus Comfort's, next door, to pump water from Comfort's well, stepping inside the house to warm himself before beginning the bracing walk back to the Dock Ward. Once, passing Comfort's house on a Sunday in February, "*Jack* called him in, where were about Twenty Negroes"; "upon his coming into the Room, they gave him Drink, and then asked him to burn Houses." The grand jury, considerably relieved at having extracted from Sandy a story at least somewhat consistent with Mary Burton's—a Sunday indoor assembly of slaves, drinking and talking about burning houses—had ordered the arrest of Jack, and another of Comfort's slaves, the old African-born man named Cook. On May 30, at the stake, Quack lent support to Sandy's testimony by naming Jack "*a leading Man*" in the plot. Two days later, Sandy added a compelling detail: at Comfort's, Jack had once held up a glistening, sharpened knife and boasted "if it came a-cross a white Man's Head, it would cut it off."

At his trial on June 4, John Hughson, unaware of how deeply his neighbor's slaves had by now been implicated, called Gerardus Comfort as a defense witness. Comfort had little to say except that "he saw nothing amiss" at Hughson's. Philipse and Horsmanden found this answer incredible, even contemptuous, and addressed Comfort directly in a heated exchange:

COURT. Mr *Comfort,* you are a next door Neighbour to *Hughson;* you live opposite to him, and surely you must have seen Negroes go in and out there often, as the Witnesses have testified, that there were frequent Caballings with the Negroes there; pray what have you observed of the House since *Hughson* came to live there?

COMFORT. I have seen nothing amiss; I have seen no Harm there.

Sheepishly, Comfort volunteered that "he was often abroad, and went very seldom to his House." But this, too, galled the judges, who found his extended absence—leaving his slaves unsupervised—appalling. Not surprisingly, Comfort's testimony failed to loosen the noose around John Hughson's neck.

On June 8, the day Hughson was sentenced to death, Jack and Cook were tried for conspiracy, along with Robin, Jamaica, Caesar (Peck), and Cuffee (Gomez). With this trial, Attorney General Bradley launched a strategy he would successfully pursue for weeks to come: try as many slaves together as possible, to compensate for the uneven quality of evidence against any one of them; present witnesses, white or black, willing to place the accused at a meeting at either Hughson's *or* Comfort's, or better still, at both; and, in drawing out courtroom testimony, elide any distinctions between those witnesses and those meetings.

Joseph Murray examined witnesses against Jamaica, Caesar, and Cuffee; John Chambers examined those against Jack and Cook and against his own slave, Robin. Mary Burton, who had never seen fit to mention either Comfort or his slaves in any of her previous statements, was happy to swear that "*Jack* and *Cook* used to be at the Meetings at *Hughson's.*" Sandy, Sarah, and Fortune, who had never been to Hughson's, could only place the defendants at meetings at Comfort's. Still, the combined evidence was damning enough. "'Twas agreed among them that *Jack* should be a Captain," Sarah said; Sandy testified that "*Cook* was to be an Officer" and said he'd heard Caesar say that "he would kill the white Men, and drink their Blood to their good Healths." The dying confessions of Quack and Cuffee were read aloud by a court clerk: Quack had accused Caesar and Cuffee of setting fire to Van Zant's storehouse. Mary Burton had once heard Jamaica, a fiddler, delight in the plot to kill whites, saying "he would dance over them while they were roasting in the Flames; and said, he had been Slave long enough."

Robin, who had been in jail since April 13 when a search of the city revealed some (unspecified) items in his possession "improper for, and unbecoming the Condition of Slaves," was accused of little more than this, and of having been at a meeting at Comfort's. But Chambers, apparently, was determined to see his slave convicted, and sentenced to death, if only to avoid appearing partial in protecting his own property from destruction. Conducting their own defense, the prisoners "asked the Witnesses now & then a few trifling Questions; and denied all that was alledged against them." Jamaica probably reminded the court that, in Quack's dying confession, he had insisted that the fiddler was "not concern'd," which gave the judges pause. Murray delivered a closing statement, and the jury, "after a short Stay," found all six men guilty as charged. Jamaica was sentenced to be hanged; Jack, Cook, Robin, Caesar, and Cuffee were to be burned.

That night, Jack began his three-day confession, eventually admitting to everything of which he stood accused. Yes, he had hosted the February meeting at Comfort's, exactly as Sandy had said; and yes, he had been to John Hughson's house; and yes, he had sworn to the plot, just as Mary Burton testified. Despite his "perfectly Negro and unintelligible" speech, Jack became the first black New Yorker to corroborate Burton's story of the "Great Feast" at Hughson's.

Between April 21, when she told the grand jury of the plot, and June 8, when Jack confessed, Mary Burton had been the only eyewitness to describe what happened at Hughson's feast, that humiliating night when she was forced to wait on slaves, even on Cuffee, who flirted with her.[1] (Peggy Kerry had described a conspiracy, but had placed it in John Romme's house.) Only after Jack corroborated Burton's story and received a governor's pardon did other jailed men begin to supply similar, indeed nearly identical, confessions. But into those formulaic confessions discrepancies continued to creep. Many men who confessed continued to tell tales of the kind of conspiring Sandy, Sarah, and Fortune had first described: chance, hushed encounters on street corners, out of whites' earshot, and larger meetings at Jack's, where whites almost never crossed the threshold.

Prosecutors paid attention to what happened at Comfort's. When Nichols and Lodge began collecting confessions, they made a table of "several Columns, viz. One for the Name of each Negro; another for his respective Owner; another for the Matter or Substance of the Confession; another for the Negroes they accused; and two others for the Place where sworn at, viz. *Hughson's* or *Comfort's*." But then they simply put the differences between what happened at Hughson's and at Comfort's aside, except to conclude that these all-black meetings must have been directed, however remotely, by John Hughson himself, "that Grand Incendiary! *That Arch Rebel against God, his King, and his Country!—That Devil Incar-*

nate!" The two columns of that table, "At Hughson's" and "At Comfort's," were merged. Clinging to their conviction that blacks were incapable of authoring a plot, Bradley, with the complicity of the grand jury and, especially, of the justices on the bench, carefully wove into one what were really two different kinds of meetings. It remains to disentangle them, to unravel strands of fiction, from strands of truth.

JACK KNEW EXACTLY when he had first heard of the conspiracy: at four in the afternoon on the first Monday in January. Ben (Marshall) "came to *Comfort's* House to fetch Tea Water, where he left his Cag in the Shop, and went to *Hughson's* House"; returning two hours later to pick up his keg, Ben said to Jack, "Countryman, I have heard some good News." "What News?" asked Jack. "*There were Spanish Negroes at Hughson's,*" Ben said, and "they had Designs of taking this Country." The following Sunday, Ben came back, and called, "*Brother go to Hughson's,* all our Company is come down." Jack "went with *Ben* thither, and went round the House, and went in at the back Door," to Hughson's "Great Feast": "they sat all round the Table," before "a Goose, a Quarter of Mutton, and a Fowl, two Loaves of Bread"; a tablecloth was laid and two bowls of punch were served. Hughson declared he would "*be their* KING"; and, when the meal was done, Mary Burton, servant to slaves, "took away the Dishes and Plates."

To Horsmanden and Philipse, who interrogated Jack, his confession's value must have been immediately apparent: it served remarkably well as a bridge between "Hughson's Plot" and what the prosecution called the "Negro Plot." From Comfort's pump, it seemed, it was but a short walk, and a slippery slope, to Hughson's tavern. And, as the judges well knew, few black men in the city could plausibly deny that they had ever been to Comfort's pump.

Gerardus Comfort had settled in a remote part of the West Ward sometime in the 1720s ("Comfort's Dock" first appears on a map dated 1730). With the help of his wife and children, and his slaves Cook, Jenny, and Jack, Comfort built a house, workshop, and barn; sank a well; and erected a dock, to which he rolled his newly made wooden barrels, smelling of pine forests after a hard rain, to sell to ship's captains steering their vessels up and down the Hudson. In 1733, the shop and stable were destroyed in a fire that "burnt with great violence" and nearly destroyed the house, too, along with a ship being built in the yard.[2] By that time, Comfort was already living in another house he owned on New Street, in the

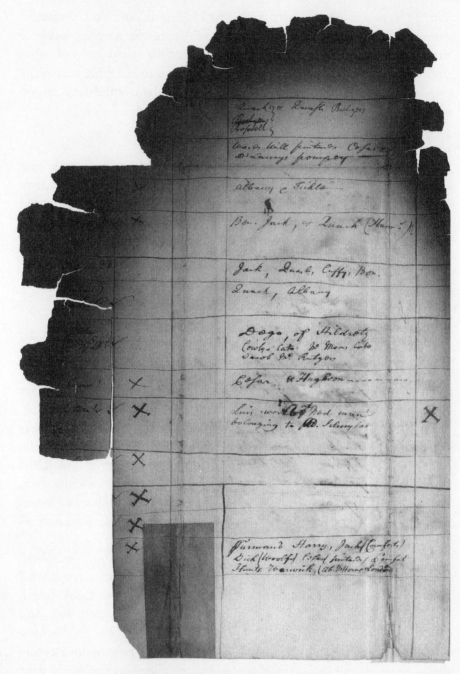

Columns in the Ledger of Confessions.
Courtesy of the New York State Archives, series A1894,
New York Colony Council Papers, 74–88.

center of town. Nonetheless he rebuilt the house and shop on the river, and, perhaps frustrated by his inability to fight the fire, decided to dig a bigger well and to engineer a pump.

As it happened, Comfort tapped into an underground spring that provided some of the best fresh water to be found on Manhattan Island, an act of hydrological serendipity that had at least one entirely unintended consequence: for years to come, all day and often into the night, slaves tied small boats to Comfort's dock, or walked through the city to and from his house, carrying kegs, empty and full, in their arms, on their heads, on their backs, or pulling them in carts or sleighs. In a city with precious little water and no water pipes at all, New York's slaves formed a kind of human aqueduct, ferrying tea water from Comfort's pump to their owners' kitchens, and into their kettles.

What made New York a prosperous port—its deep saltwater rivers— made its drinking water lousy. By the middle of the eighteenth century, Manhattan's water was already infamous: there was too little of it and what little there was tasted terrible. It made even visiting horses sick. Flowing under a granite island surrounded by saltwater rivers, much of the city's groundwater was brackish; contaminated by a city populated by pigs, cows, and people, New York's well water was so filthy that it stank.

As the first European settlers on the island noted, the best drinking water was to be found at a place the Dutch named the Kolck and the English called the Collect, or the Fresh Water: a seventy-acre spring-fed pond some seventy feet deep. To the north of the Collect lay wooded, rocky hills, with plentiful fresh water; to the south, a low-lying flatland of brine-wet loam, swamps, and salt marshes. But it was to the south that the Dutch settled, far from the Kolck and the well-watered land beyond it. At the island's swampy tip, they began building dikes, to make a strange place look like home. The Heere Gracht, the ditch that became Broad Street, was so deep that unmasted ships could sail all the way up to the wall, and so "almost through ye towne." For water to use in their kitchens, the Dutch built rain cisterns and dug shallow wells in their yards, on their farms, and in the middle of their little city's streets. Meanwhile, they threw their waste into the ditches, where hogs wallowed, and the groundwater worsened. When an English fleet arrived in 1664, Dutch soldiers garrisoning themselves in the fort found that they had not nearly enough water to survive a siege, especially since the fort lacked "either well or cistern." Governor Stuyvesant had no choice but to surrender, for lack of water.

By 1677, under English rule, the Common Council ordered the digging of the first public wells, lined with stone and sunk at well-traveled street corners; in 1696, these were placed under the supervision of city aldermen, charged with keeping the wells "Sweet Usefull and in Good repair." But as the city's population grew larger, its water grew filthier. The swamps bred mosquitoes, and these, along with the accreted muck on the streets, bred disease. In 1731, the Common Council ruled that all "Tubs of Dung, Close Stools or Pots of Ordure or Nastiness" were to be dumped in the river, but more than a few citizens still dumped them—or carelessly spilled them— in the streets. Yellow fever, cholera, and smallpox plagued the city with heartbreaking regularity (6 percent of the population died of smallpox in 1731) as contaminated street runoff seeped into cellars, since, as Cadwallader Colden observed, nearly every house stood on "moist slimy ground."[3]

What saved early eighteenth-century New Yorkers from still more sickness was that very few of them drank water straight from wells. Instead, they drank beer and they drank tea, both made from water that had been boiled. Unfortunately, however much healthier it became by heating, water from wells in the densely settled part of the city still tasted horrible. The poor drank it anyway, of course, while people living in the rural Outward, rich and poor, simply got their water from the Collect. But for wealthy city dwellers, the pump at Gerardus Comfort's house offered the best and most convenient alternative, especially since they could afford to delegate to their slaves the backbreaking task of carrying kegs, morning and night.

JOHN HUGHSON BECAME Gerardus Comfort's next-door neighbor in 1738. Before then, Hughson lived along the docks in the South Ward, where he was a near neighbor of Daniel Horsmanden; they lived just a dozen buildings from each other. In May 1738, Hughson packed up his large family and his small belongings and moved well away from the densely settled part of the city. Perhaps he fled because a neighbor, a cooper named Francis Silvester, had complained that Hughson "kept a very disorderly House, and sold Liquor to, and entertained Negroes," who had been seen dancing with Hughson's wife and daughter. (Silvester's own slaves may have been among Hughson's guests.)[4] Hughson told Silvester that "*his Wife was the chief Cause of having the Negroes at his House*," and that it was she who liked to live in town; he preferred to live in the country.

Maybe Hughson, overcoming his wife's objections, simply wanted to lead a quieter life. Maybe he found Silvester a nosy, annoying neighbor.

Hughson himself appears to have had an abusive manner. In 1737, he insulted a man from the East Ward named Lancaster Symes. What Hughson said about Symes is not recorded, but Symes retained John Chambers as his lawyer and sued Hughson for defamation. The case was heard in the Supreme Court in January 1738. (Horsmanden, just recently appointed to the court, was absent on the day of the trial.) After hearing the evidence, James DeLancey and Frederick Philipse required Hughson to state "in open Court that the words spoken by him of the plaintiff were false Malicious & Scandalous and without any Just Grounds." Hughson obliged, and Symes dropped his suit.[5]

Maybe that spring, life in the city was getting too close, with men like Silvester and Symes nearby. But Daniel Horsmanden believed Hughson moved because his new house in the West Ward, next to Gerardus Comfort's, was a better place to be a smuggler: "*This House was more out of the Way, private and fit for* Hughson's *Purposes on all Accounts, for caballing and Entertainment of Negroes, and with respect to receiving stolen Goods; it was said to be built with such Privacies in the several Rooms and Cellars as might conceal run Goods.*"

Hughson's move also coincided with a significant change in the neighborhood that was his destination. In April 1738, the inhabitants of the West Ward had petitioned the Common Council "praying leave to Erect a Market House in the Broadway" where corn, grain, and meal could be sold. They pled hardship over the distance they had to walk to get to the Meal Market at the base of Wall Street, the only other place in the city where grain could be sold. They proposed building a 25- by 42-foot market "in the Publick Street of the Broadway in the Middle of the same fronting the Street in which his Honour the Chief Justice lives and Opposite to Crown Street." The Common Council approved the request on April 13, and construction of the Broadway Market House, just across from James DeLancey's mansion, began immediately.[6] Anyone considering moving to a less densely populated part of the city in the spring of 1738 had good reason to consider the West Ward, since the Broadway Market would make that neighborhood newly convenient.

But John Hughson had another reason to move. In January 1738, the principal members of the lodge of black Freemasons or the Geneva Club—Caesar, Cuffee, and Prince—were arrested and publicly whipped for robbing Richard Baker's tavern. Three months later, Hughson packed his bags.

John Hughson may well have been involved in the Baker robbery; he may have fenced the goods the black Masons stole in 1738; he played the same role in the burglary of Hogg's shop in 1741. At the very least, he knew the men of the Geneva Club, and had hosted them at his house. (And Hughson also knew Baker; the two men served in the same militia company.)[7] Just after New Year's 1738, days before the January robbery of Baker's tavern, Joseph Murray's slave Adam went to a cockfight at the city house of Adolph Philipse, where he met Hughson, Cuffee, Caesar, Prince, Othello, and several other black men. (Philipse was not at home.) As they were leaving by Philipse's gate, Hughson asked Adam back to his house, and revealed to him the plot, telling him that Caesar, Prince, Cuffee, "and a great many more" were already involved.

Daniel Horsmanden found this story, told by Adam in his 1741 confession, difficult to believe: "If what this Negro says is true, this hellish Plot was some Years a brooding before they attempted the Execution of it." But Adam wasn't the only slave to date the plot to 1738. Robert Todd's slave Dundee talked about events "three Summers past," the summer of 1738, when Dundee first began fetching water at Comfort's well, the first summer that Hughson was Comfort's neighbor. Something happened then, something important.

What is more difficult to credit about Adam's story is Hughson's indiscretion. "If what this Negro says is true," Horsmanden wrote, Hughson met Adam for the first time at a cockfight, where not a soul was sober, and, before the night was through, told him about a conspiracy "*to set Fire to the Houses of the Town, and to kill the white People.*" This is the author of a *secret* plot?

There are three possible explanations for Hughson's indiscretion: (1) Adam was lying; (2) Hughson was drunk; or (3) Hughson was joking. Adam might well have lied in his confession, but this particular anecdote served no good purpose in securing his pardon; it was, if anything, a distraction from the matter at hand, confessing to conspiring in 1741, and it only diminished his credibility. Hughson may have had loose lips, but it strains credulity to believe that, even while drunk, he spoke sincerely about a plot to destroy the city to every black man he met for three years running without being betrayed or discovered. The evidence that he was joking, on the other hand, is promising. But getting the joke requires piecing together what can be known about the strange events of 1737 and early 1738, and the political context in which black and white Masons met in New York.

. . .

EARLY IN 1737, James Alexander and other gentlemen of the Country Party established a Manhattan lodge of Freemasons. They met at the Black Horse Tavern, opposite Zenger's printshop. Leadership in founding the lodge may have been provided by Henry Holt, the dancing master, who had recently come to New York from Charleston, South Carolina, where he was a member of that city's first Masonic lodge.

Although Masons were supposed to be "resolv'd against all *Politicks*," the rise of the Masons coincided with a new political era in New York. When Clarke became lieutenant governor in 1736, he called for the first legislative elections since 1728. In elections held in May 1737, the Country Party gained a majority in the General Assembly. James Alexander was elected from New York City; Lewis Morris, Jr., won a seat from Westchester and became Speaker of the Assembly. When Clarke addressed the newly elected Assembly in April 1737, he declared, "We have the pleasure to see peace restored to this once divided Province."[8]

In June 1737, Morris, Jr., in his capacity as Speaker, appointed Zenger to print the Assembly's proceedings. With this appointment, Zenger, who had been tried for seditious libel just two years before, became the official printer of the province, displacing William Bradford. In Zenger's newspaper for June 27, he printed a dialogue between two New Yorkers. "*Hy ho, this is a strange World we live in!*" cries one. "Ay, replies another, I think so too; for here I see *John Peter Zenger* appointed to print the Votes of the Assembly, and if any Body had told me that, less than three Months since, I should have wanted Faith to believe it."[9]

But the Country Party's victory was by no means complete, and despite Clarke's optimistic address to the Assembly, the province, or at least the city, remained divided. In the May Assembly elections, the race between Adolph Philipse, of the Court Party, and Cornelius Van Horne, of the Country Party, had been too close to call. A by-election was held at City Hall on September 10. Philipse, with 413 votes, beat Van Horne, with 399. But Sheriff William Cosby, Jr., son of the former governor, was widely suspected of manipulating the returns. Describing the by-election, Cadwallader Colden wrote to his wife, "The sick the lame and the blind were all carried to vote they were carried out of Prison and out of the poor house to vote such a strugle I never saw and such a hurraing that above one half of the men in town are so hoarse that they cannot speak." Four hundred and fifty people signed a petition sent to Clarke, maintaining "That wee have this day seen or heard of the most Barefaced Villany Committed by Willm Cosby Esqr present high Sheriff of this Citty & County . . . in the Face of

the world in Declareing Adolphe Philipse to be chosen Representative."
On September 16, the Assembly voted to investigate the election. After a
lengthy inquiry, Philipse was declared the legitimate victor on October 10.[10]

Meanwhile, party politics continued to be waged at the city's two principal taverns, as committees of the Country Party assemblymen met at the
Black Horse Tavern and committees of Clarke's Court Party Council
retired to Todd's tavern. But now the Black Horse was newly associated
with Masonry, which quickly became a target of partisan warfare. In his
New York Gazette in August 1737, William Bradford reprinted an essay
from the *London Magazine* arguing that Englishmen should not tolerate
Masonic lodges, "dark and clandestine Assemblies where Plots against the
State may be carried on under the Pretence of *Brotherly Love* and *Good-
Fellowship.*"[11]

On November 14, 1737, Alexander retaliated, printing a bizarre classified ad in Zenger's *New-York Weekly Journal:*

> TAKEN Out of the House of Mr. *Todd,* a small Silver Square, a
> Level, a Plumb-Rule, and Silver Pen, and other Utensils belonging
> to the Lodge of Free Masons in New-York, Whoever brings them
> to the Printer hereof shall be handsomely rewarded, and no Ques-
> tions ask'd.[12]

The Square, the Level, and the Plumb are the "three Immovable Jew-
els" of a Masonic lodge, and also the "working tools" given to Masons of
the second degree of Masonry, Fellow of the Craft. What were they doing
at Robert Todd's tavern, if the Masons met at the Black Horse? Most
likely, the ad was itself a joke. (When a Masonic lodge was established in
Charleston, South Carolina, the city's newspaper reported the event as the
arrival of the ship *Freemason* from Providence.)[13] Maybe Alexander, whose
political party had risen to prominence in the Assembly, taunted his Court
Party adversaries by implying that the mantle of Masonry had been stolen
from them.

Bradford responded by publishing an anti-Masonic letter, which complained: "All other Societies that have appeared in the World have published their Principles and Practices, and when they meet set open their
Meeting-house Doors for all that will come in and see and hear them, but
this Society called Free Masons, meet with their Doors shut, and a Guard
at the outside to prevent any to approach to hear and see what they are
doing." In an attempt to undermine Masonry, Bradford went so far as to
print the Masons' sacred secret oath in his November 28 *Gazette:*

I, A.B., Hereby solemnly Vow and Swear in the Presence of Almighty God and this Right Worshipful Assembly, That I will Hail and Conceal, and never Reveal the Secrets or Secrecy of Masons or Masonry, that shall be revealed unto me; unless to a True and Lawful Brother, after due Examination, or in a just and Worshipful Lodge of Brothers and Fellows well met. I further more Promise and Vow, That I will not Write them, Print them, Carve them, or Engrave them, or cause them to be Written, Printed, Marked, Carved, or Engraved on Wood or Stone, so as the Visible Character or Impression of a letter may appear, whereby it may be unlawfully obtained. All this under no less Penalty than to have my Throat cut, my Tongue taken from the Roof of my Mouth, my Heart pluck'd from under my Left Breast, them to be buried in the Sands of the Sea, the Length of a Cable Rope from Shore, where the Tide ebbs and flows twice in 24 Hours, my Body to be burnt to Ashes and to be scatter'd upon the Face of the Earth, so that there shall be no more Remembrance of me among Masons. So help me God.[14]

At just about this time, in the late fall of 1737, Caesar, Prince, Cuffee, and others met together and hatched a plan to rob Richard Baker's tavern, and allegedly formed a black Freemasons lodge. Just after New Year's, they gathered, with John Hughson, for a cockfight at Adolph Philipse's house. Hughson asked Adam to swear by his book to a plot *"to set Fire to the Houses of the Town, and to kill the white People,"* and told him that Caesar, Prince, and Cuffee were already involved. On January 21, 1738, the white Masons held a procession, which Alexander reported in Zenger's *Weekly Journal.* One week later, Caesar, Prince, and Cuffee robbed Baker of his gin, after which they took to calling themselves the Geneva Club. Within days, they were arrested and confessed. As one of them, probably Cuffee, was being carried to the whipping post, he cried: *"Make Room for a Free MASON."* In Bradford's *Gazette* in January and February 1738, a Court Party writer, probably Horsmanden, used the Geneva Club to satirize Masonry, at which Alexander took considerable offense. Three months later, John Hughson moved to the edge of town.

ALTHOUGH FREEMASONS trace their ancestry to medieval stonecutters' guilds, the society's known history began in London around 1720, and Masonry first became popular in the colonies in 1736. Mockery swiftly followed. In the 1730s and 1740s, a group calling itself "The Scald Society of Miserable Masons" took to the streets in both London and Boston, riding backward on asses, while prose and poem satires of Masonry filled page after page of British and colonial newspapers and almanacs. Benjamin Franklin, himself a Mason, liked to point out that the Masons' "Grand Secret is, That they have no Secret at all." Alexander Hamilton, also a Mason, mocked his own brothers in his "History of the Ancient and Honorable Tuesday Club." Peppered with bawdy jokes about the club's "longstanding members," Hamilton's "History" was essentially an affectionate farce of Freemasonry.[15]

But mocking Masons could be dangerous. In January 1738, while Bradford's *New York Gazette* mocked New York's "Dishonourable Society of *Black Masons*," Philadelphians were reckoning with the repercussions of a fatal prank played on a young man named Daniel Rees, a would-be Mason. One evening in June 1737, Evan Jones, a Philadelphia apothecary, and several of his friends conducted a mock Masonic initiation on Rees, Jones's apprentice. Jones, who was not a Mason (although Rees thought he was), required his apprentice to read a blasphemous oath and, while Rees was blindfolded, bid him "kiss the book," presenting him not with a Bible but with the naked backside of one of Jones's friends. Soon afterward, Jones met Benjamin Franklin in a tavern and told him about the prank. Franklin was so amused that he took a copy of the oath home with him and read it to friends. That night, young Rees, still unaware that he was being played with, attended another mock initiation, where, in a dark room, Jones and his friends held pans of flaming brandy under their chins to make their faces appear gruesome. Jones spilled his pan's contents on Rees, badly burning him. Rees died within days. In January 1738, while in New York Cuffee at the whipping post cried out, "*Make Room for a Free MASON*," Evan Jones was tried for manslaughter in Philadelphia, and found guilty.

Rees's death caused a stir in Philadelphia, not least because Franklin's rival, Andrew Bradford, the printer of the *American Weekly Mercury* (and the son of New York's William Bradford), called Franklin complicit in the boy's death, a charge Franklin nervously denied.[16] William Bradford's reprinting, in August 1737, of an anti-Masonic essay was, no doubt, partly inspired by the events surrounding Rees's death in June: by printing it, Bradford supported his son's assault on Franklin. And when William Bradford printed the Masons' oath in his *Gazette* in November 1737, he did so largely to expose and demystify Masonry, so that gullible men like

Daniel Rees might not be so gullible in future. The *Gazette*'s scalding satire of the New York black Masons, which William Bradford printed in January 1738, just at the time of Jones's trial, was as much an attack on Benjamin Franklin as on James Alexander. Back in Philadelphia, meanwhile, Andrew Bradford reprinted the story of New York's black Masons in the *American Weekly Mercury* on February 14, the same day he attacked Franklin. In this, Bradford *fils* did his father a good turn, supporting him in his rivalry with Zenger.

Into this highly charged debate involving rival printers and playful, dangerous, even fatal pranks about politics and Masonry stepped John Hughson. Just after the ad for the stolen Masons' tools ran in Zenger's *Weekly Journal,* just after William Bradford printed the Masons' secret oath in the *New York Gazette,* just at the time of the Evan Jones trial, John Hughson shared the secret of a plot with black men he had only just met, took them to his house, and initiated them. It can hardly have been a coincidence.

John Hughson was a cobbler, tavernkeeper, and petty criminal who fenced stolen goods. Maybe Hughson found Masonry ridiculous, fancy gentlemen in ruffles wearing artisans' aprons and swearing oaths of spooky secrecy, and mocked it mercilessly, parodying Masonic rituals and pledges. But he was probably just as ignorant of Masonry as Daniel Rees had been: all that he knew was what he learned from the newspaper, for Hughson, like Cuffee, could read. Maybe Cuffee and Hughson thought Evan Jones's prank funny, and when they met gullible young recruits like Adam, eagerly swore them into a fake fraternity. When Cuffee, Caesar, and Prince were arrested for robbing Baker's tavern, they spilled the story about the mock Masonry, which allowed Horsmanden, in the *Gazette,* to put their story to his own political ends.

The plot the prosecution labeled "Hughson's Plot," then, began in 1737 and was, essentially, a prank that grew out of proportion. At meetings at Cuffee's and at Hughson's, Hughson, Cuffee, Caesar, and Prince parodied gentlemen's clubs and conducted mock Masonic initiations. This plot was real—it happened—but it was also fake; it was meant as mockery. But what Hughson could not have realized was that what may have been, for him, playing at plotting had tapped into his companions' much deeper well of hatred of whites, of traditions of rebellion, and of grievances against slavery. Consider one final detail about the goings-on in New York in the fall of 1737: that September, a black girl was tending a white infant in a yard in front of a house when a white boy, about fourteen or fifteen years old, playing with a gun, leaned out the window and in a jesting manner said, "*I'll shoot ye.*" And then he shot her brains out.

WHEN JOHN HUGHSON moved in May 1738, he settled in a house just down the hill from Gerardus Comfort's house; and in June 1741, after Hughson was convicted and Comfort's slave Jack confessed, the proximity of their two houses preoccupied the prosecution. As soon as Jack said that Ben "came to *Comfort's* House to fetch Tea Water, where he left his Cag in the Shop, and went to *Hughson's* House," Comfort's tea water seeped into nearly every confession. London, owned by Captain Roger French, said he "was sent ashore for Water" at Comfort's when his ship docked on the river. Dundee had been getting water at Comfort's well for three summers (he must have hauled enormous quantities, since his owner, Robert Todd, was also a vintner and used Comfort's water to make wine). Under interrogation, the city's slaves found it difficult to deny knowing Jack. And, as interrogators might well argue, if they knew Jack, they must have known Hughson. Harry (Kipp), Pedro (DePeyster), Jack (Sleydall), Cato (Cowley), and Fortune (Clarkson) all confessed that they went "to *Comfort's* for Tea Water," and ended up calling "for a Dram at *Hughson's.*"

Meanwhile, the judges, prosecutors, and grand jurors now recalled that Sandy, Sarah, and Fortune, in their earliest confessions, had all also mentioned fetching water. By June 12, tea water flooded the investigation so thoroughly that the grand jury asked the Assembly to pass three laws. The first two targeted men like John Hughson: one was "to limit the Number of Publick Houses within the City of *New-York* . . . and to prohibit them to sell any sort of strong Liquors to Negroes"; and the second aimed "to prohibit the receiving any goods from Negroes, upon any pretence whatsoever, unless by express leave or License from their Masters in Writing." But a third law targeted slaves: the grand jury asked the Assembly to pass "a Law to restrain Negroes from fetching Tea-Water on Sundays."[17]

In the years following the conspiracy trials, it would prove nearly impossible to stop tavernkeepers from serving liquor to slaves, or smugglers from trading with them, but New York's tea-water supply system was wholly restructured in the wake of the investigation. In November 1741, the Assembly passed "An Act for mending & keeping in Repair the Publick Wells and Pumps in the City of New York," under which aldermen were required to appoint overseers and inspect every well or pump in their wards. In 1742, the city's Common Council passed a law dictating that "no Negro Molatto or Indian Slave: within this City . . . Shall on any Lords Day or Sunday Presume to fetch any water: other than from the Next well or pump: to the place of their Abode."[18] Lest wealthy New Yorkers in fashionable districts be forced to drink tea brewed with the brackish, slimy water found in their neighborhood wells, "Tea-Water Men," *white* men, began carrying and selling water from remote pumps like the one at Comfort's. By the time Dr. Hamilton visited the city in 1744, white "Tea-Water Men" walked the streets, hawking water by the keg and cupful. "Ever since the negroe conspiracy," Hamilton explained, "certain people have been appointed to sell water in the streets, which they carry on a sledge in great casks and bring it from the best springs about the city, for it was when the negroes went for tea water that they held their caballs and consultations."[19]

What happened at Comfort's—what the prosecution called the "Negro Plot"—was both like and unlike what happened at Hughson's. At Comfort's, Tickle said, "the Talk there was the same as at *Hughson's.*" And it was just as crowded—"*There were two Rooms full of 'em, some were in the Kitchen and some in the Shop.*" The house itself was small, according to Jack: "the Kitchen and Shop join to each other; the Doors into each went out into the Street, or into the Yard; so that to go from one to the other, you must go either into the Yard, or on the Dock." In either room, or spilling out into the yard or dock, men plotted—"Quack was pitched upon to set fire to the Fort"—and they drank—Jack offered them drams. But Jack was not as generous a host as John Hughson: there was no table, no bread, no meat. Instead of feasting, the conspirators in Comfort's well-stocked workshop sharpened their knives. "Every one in the Shop had Knives," York said, "and they were sharpening of them; and they were to cut white Men's Heads off." Some men went outside, to sharpen their blades on "a brown Stone that lay in the Yard."

At Hughson's, plotters swore among whites—the Hughsons, Mary Burton, Peggy Kerry. At the meetings at Comfort's, only blacks were allowed. Gerardus Comfort "was often abroad, and went very seldom to his House"; most likely, he spent much of his time at his house on New Street.[20] Nor was John Hughson to be found among the guests at Jack's. Nor Mary Burton, nor Peggy Kerry, nor the two Sarah Hughsons. At Gerardus Comfort's house on the Hudson, there were almost never any whites at all, with the infrequent exception of Comfort's sons-in-law, and when they were there, Jack and the black men and women who visited him kept silent. Once, Dundee arrived at Comfort's to find "That *Jack* was at work in the Shop, but his young Master was there; and so they could not speak together."

Jack not only supplied water for slaves who came to fetch it, he sold them the casks in which they carried it. Comfort, after all, was a cooper, and Jack ran a cooper's shop. There is strong evidence that he managed a considerable business. In September 1737, "sundry Coopers of the City of *New-York*" presented a petition to the Assembly "complaining that several considerable Merchants of the same City, employ great Numbers of Negroes in that Occupation, not only to supply their own Occasions of Casks, but sell and dispose thereof to other Merchants." In November of that year, the Assembly recommended "that Negroes may be supprest of having the Benefit of poor Labourers and Tradesmen."[21]

Perhaps because weaving, metalworking, and woodworking were important African crafts, black artisans in New York clustered in two types of trade: tailoring (including weaving) and carpentry (including coopering). As white artisans saw it, black tradesmen threatened their livelihood. And the city was full of them, like the "Two very good Negro Men Slaves Taylors, and one Negro Man Slave, a Butcher and Sawyer" or the "Negro Man named Scipio, a Cooper, about 22 years old," advertised in 1730. In 1733, "a Negro Man Slave, named Andrew Saxon, a very black tall Fellow," ran away from Jacobus Van Cortlandt. He "speaks very good English," Van Cortlandt wrote in the ad for his return, and "is a Carpenter and Cooper by Trade, and has Tools for both Trades with him."[22] New York merchants who traded with the Caribbean profited by their unwanted cargo by hiring them out for day labor, and skilled slaves brought better wages home to their masters. But what profited white merchants threatened white artisans.

The city's white coopers were clustered in the North Ward, and were also among the least wealthy taxpayers in the city; their average wealth assessment in 1730 was £20, compared to £35 for a silversmith, £46 for a gentleman, £24 for a baker. But Gerardus Comfort's assessment in 1730 and again in 1734 was £91, quite possibly because he managed to keep his labor costs very low by relying almost exclusively on slaves.[23]

Popular outcry and even legislation against the use of black tradesmen, and especially the employment of slaves by coopers, had not stopped Comfort from leaving Jack to manage his cooper's shop. Comfort left Jack so entirely in charge that Jack "looked upon the House as his own, and himself as his own Master." Jack was "*a leading Man*" in the conspiracy; he ran the meetings, going "backwards and forwards from the Shop to the

Kitchen," swearing black men into the plot, keeping a list of their names, making threats, making promises. He looked *"like a Gentleman."* He was fierce. When Sandy cried in front of him, Jack said, "D—m you, do you cry? I'll cut your Head off in a Hurry." When Dundee pledged to "cut his Mistress's Throat in the Night," Jack said he'd kill Robert Todd himself, because he "once followed *Dundee* to *Comfort's* House, when he went for Tea-Water, and made a Noise at him for staying."

Black men and women who came to Jack's house called him "Captain," and "Uncle, and Brother, and Cousin." And they called him "Country-man." Because what Horsmanden recorded of Jack's literal speech—*"Ben ride da fat Horse"*—sounds Jamaican, it's likely that Jack, who may have been an Akan-speaking Coromantee, had lived for a time in Jamaica. At Hughson's, plotters swore an oath that sounded like a Masonic pledge. But at Comfort's, Jack made them swear "that the first Thunder that came, might strike them dead, if they did not stand to their Words," an oath much like the Akan oaths sworn by a supernatural power that would kill those who violated it.[24] Not only the oaths but much of the plotting to which slaves confessed in 1741 bears considerable resemblance to cere-monies known to have taken place among other Akan-influenced commu-nities in the New World. The coronation of a king, like that of Court in Antigua in 1736, was an Akan rite, which raised a respected and worthy member of the community, even a commoner, to the status of nobility. In New York, Mary Burton set the precedent for testifying that Hughson was to be king, and Caesar merely governor, but at least one slave had it the other way: Bastian said that "Hughson was to be the Governor" and "Cae-sar was to be King."[25]

Coromantee rituals had played a similar role in the 1712 revolt: 19 per-cent of those accused in 1712 bore Akan names. In 1741, 8 percent of the accused—and 38 percent of those burned at the stake—had Akan names. Given that the incidence of Akan names in the general slave population was about 4 percent, these numbers are significant. (People with Akan names also made up a disproportionately high number, 14 percent, of the city's runaways.)[26] At Jack's, men born in New York, in the Caribbean, and in Africa—and perhaps especially men like Jack and Cook, born in Africa and "seasoned" in the Caribbean—forged bonds of fictive kinship and par-ticipated in Akan-influenced rituals that named leaders and established a new political order. A "king" was often chosen on the basis of his wealth, something that Caesar, who was wealthy enough to pay for Peggy Kerry's lodging, could easily have boasted. And the naming of "captains" like Jack drew on. Coromantees, long military tradition; some of the men who ended up in New York might once have been soldiers, experienced with the guns they so frequently described in their confessions.[27]

Horsmanden grudgingly acknowledged Jack's crucial role in the slave community. "To his Well every Morning and Evening resorted Negroes from all Quarters of the Town for Tea-Water," he wrote, "which therefore afforded him convenient Seasons for gaining Parties, which he made Use of to the Utmost; and hereat *Jack* was so dexterous, that he became the very Counter-part of his Master *Hughson*." But what if Horsmanden had it backward: What if Hughson was merely the counterpart of Jack? What if Hughson practiced a Masonic prank but Jack commanded a brotherhood whose best English translation was "Freemasonry"?[28]

To Horsmanden, what happened at those black gatherings in New York was a slave conspiracy that could be put to use in suppressing white political opposition. To Hughson, it was a mockery of Masonry. To Jack, it was a brotherhood of countrymen. Like Hughson's Plot, the "Negro Plot" was real—it happened—but it was no prank.

"WHAT NEWS?" Jack asked Ben, hauling his keg to the tea-water pump. "What News?" he asked Cato on "the Night that *Hilton's* House burnt . . . for he had heard that there had been a Fire at that End of the Town." Jack was, above all, a collector and a reporter of news. Zenger and Bradford printed their newspapers weekly, and filled their pages with slow-traveling letters from foreign correspondents. White New Yorkers who wanted to find out what happened in Amsterdam two months ago could read the *Weekly Journal* at the end of the week. Or they could meet in coffeehouses and taverns, to read newspapers from other cities.[29] Black New Yorkers who wanted to find out what happened in the city all day, and overnight, could find out at Jack's before the sun rose.

In a small, crowded, bustling metropolis, then as now, most people spend a good deal of time walking the streets, conducting errands, picking up bits of news. But in eighteenth-century New York, people who were enslaved walked greater distances, conducted more errands, and picked up news earlier in the morning and later at night. Unlike the conditions in large rural slave plantations, where slaves lived with their families in slave quarters, well apart from whites, city slaves slept in the attics and cellars of their owners' houses, or in "Negro kitchens," and worked all day alongside whites—servants, artisans, laborers. In New York, whites and blacks lived, literally, on top of one another. If slaves lacked separate quarters, they did have different hours: slaves woke up earlier than anyone else (servants woke up next), and stayed up later (servants went to bed just before them). And, since the very first and the very last chore slaves did every day was fetching water, which meant meeting friends and neighbors at pumps, they heard the news first.[30]

If there were nothing else to be learned from the confessions extracted in New York City in the spring and summer of 1741, there would be this: while slaves in Manhattan lived and worked alongside whites, they sought out other slaves, for news, for companionship, for love, and they found it, all over the city. Forever conducting errands, fetching water, visiting friends and family scattered across the city, slaves *circulated*, even more than free whites, who lived in the same houses as their husbands, wives, and children. Most enslaved New Yorkers lived in households where there were only one or two other slaves. A lucky few found mates in the same household, like Robin and Cuba, the married couple owned by attorney John Chambers; but even then, they were likely to be separated, eventually, by sale. James Alexander and Cadwallader Colden congratulated themselves on their own happy marriages ("I agree with you in the Commendations of the married State & believe where it hits right it yields the greatest Satisfaction in this Life," Alexander wrote to Colden in 1730) even as they attempted to sever romantic attachments among their slaves: Colden wrote to a North Carolina man who had purchased his slave, Gabriel, in 1726, "Since you went my Negro Wench tells me that Gabrield designs to return if he do not like the place but as one reason of my selling him was to keep him from that Wench that I value You must not allow him to return."[31]

In New York, slave families most often lived apart. Running away usually meant running to visit a wife, a child, a parent. Nearly two thirds of runaway slaves in colonial New York were suspected of having fled to family members.[32] But running away wasn't always necessary. Since the city was so small, a man might live just doors away from his wife, or a mother just blocks away from her grown children; most family members must have lived less than a mile apart. In these circumstances, some spouses belonging to different owners managed to sleep together. Quack (Roosevelt) usually went to the fort to "stay there a-Nights with his Wife," Barbara. On Sundays, while most whites went to church or stayed at home with their families, slaves spent their day of rest walking across the city to see family and friends. One Sunday, Ben (Marshall) and his wife together visited Jeffrey, owned by Captain Brown, and his wife, greeting them, "*How d'ye do, how d'ye do, my Friends?*" Quack, a slave of an East Ward English butcher named John Walter, saw his wife, Maria, often, since her owner, Paul Richards, lived in the same ward. Adam had been friends with Quack since childhood, when they played marbles together, but Quack preferred his wife's company; when Adam sent for Quack to come to a plotting meeting, Quack, "being at Mr. *Richard's* with his Wife, refused to go."

In the geography of the city, neighborhoods—or wards—mattered more to whites, especially property-owning white men, who elected ward aldermen, paid taxes to ward tax collectors, and, in general, organized their political, economic, and social lives around ward divisions.[33] Slaves mapped the city differently. Daniel Horsmanden concluded that "*the Conspirators had divided the City . . . into two* Districts": one at the east end of town, near the Fly Market, run by a gang called "the Fly-Boys"; and one at the west end, run by the "Long-Bridge Boys." He may have been right. In any case, the slaves' web of social connections stretched across the map, a pattern grimly, if persuasively, illustrated in their confessions: forced to name names, men jailed in the basement of City Hall almost never accused slaves only from their own wards; the men they named came from all across the city.

Consider Caesar, owned by John Pintard, an alderman from the Dock Ward. Peggy Kerry named Caesar on May 7; he was arrested two days later. On June 1, Sandy told the grand jury that Caesar had attended the great meeting at Comfort's; Sarah (Burk) agreed. On June 12, Jack (Sleydall) said Caesar was at Hughson's "Great Feast." Ten days later, Peter DeLancey's slave Pompey told one of the judges that Caesar had initiated him into the conspiracy. Caesar confessed later that same day, availing himself, as Pompey had, of Clarke's June 19 proclamation of amnesty. Before the ink was dry on Caesar's confession, Cato (Moore) confessed too, and said that he had walked with Caesar to the feast at Hughson's.

How did Caesar's accusers know him? Kerry had definitely met him somewhere: she correctly identified him in a lineup on May 9. Sandy probably knew Caesar as a neighbor; before Sandy was sold and sent to Albany, he, too, had lived in the Dock Ward. Sarah and Jack may not have known Caesar at all; maybe they offered his name because they had met him in jail. Pompey and Cato knew Caesar better; they were his friends, not his neighbors: Pompey lived in the East Ward and Cato in the South Ward. In accusing Caesar, Cato and Pompey by no means sent him to the gallows or the stake. They named him on the day that he himself confessed and they knew that in doing so they did little to worsen his situation; he, like them, was sure to be granted a pardon. Quite possibly, the three friends coordinated their confessions.

In his own confession, Caesar accused twenty-three black men of involvement in the conspiracy. Nine of these men had already been executed, as Caesar well knew: Quack (Roosevelt), Caesar (Peck), Curacoa Dick (Tiebout), Cato (Provost), Fortune (Vanderspiegle), Cato (Cowley), Albany (Carpenter), Caesar (Vaarck), and Ben (Marshall). Eight had already been arrested as, again, Caesar well knew: Jack (Breasted), Tickle (Carpenter), Will (Ten Eyck), Prince (Crooke), Jack (Comfort), London (Wyncoop), Primus (DeBrosses), and Harry (Kipp). Six men were new to the inquiry, and were arrested following Caesar's confession: Mars (Benson), York (Peck), London (French), Will (Vaarck), Tony (Brazier), and Bridgewater (Van Horne). These were the men Caesar betrayed.

These last six names mattered most, not least because it was only by supplying *new* names that Caesar secured for himself a pardon. (As it would turn out, none of the six was executed; all were, like Caesar, ultimately pardoned and transported.) How did Caesar know these six men? Will and London lived in the Dock Ward and were, like Sandy, Caesar's neighbors, at least in the limited sense of residing in the same ward. But Mars and York lived in the Montgomerie Ward, and Tony and Bridgewater in the East Ward. Their owners were neither all French, like Pintard, nor all Dutch, nor all English; nor were they all bakers, or all merchants or aldermen. In short, Caesar's social network does not seem in any way to have followed his owner's pattern of association.

Caesar was accused nine more times after he confessed. But none of the people he named ever accused him, just as he did not accuse any of the people who had accused him. How Caesar knew Mars, York, Tony, and Bridgewater, and how Pompey and Cato knew him, is in all likelihood entirely unrecoverable. But that these men knew one another is indisputable. Their range of acquaintance spanned the city.

Indeed, it seems altogether possible that every black man in New York knew every other black man in the city. Two hundred and fourteen black men and women were mentioned in the investigation of the conspiracy. Eighteen of these were women (of whom only one, Burk's Sarah, was convicted). Of the remaining 196, 5 were described as "boys": Sandy, Denby, Hereford, Cato (Richards), and Patrick. Sandy, age sixteen or seventeen, and Denby, Quack's son, were not adults; but calling Hereford, Cato, and Patrick "boys" may have been more a reflection of status than age.

(Whites, including John Hughson, commonly called grown black men "boys.") The conspiracy was, above all, a fraternity. In 1741, there were probably about 450 black men over age sixteen living in New York.[34] When Daniel Horsmanden said, "it seemed very probable that most of the Negroes in Town were corrupted," he meant the men. Out of a possible adult black male population of about 450, nearly 200 were bound up in the conspiracy in one way or another. All 200, and even all 450, may well have known one another, at least in passing.

Black women in New York spent much of the working day indoors, or near the house, cooking and doing domestic work. A 1734 classified ad enumerated the skills and virtues of "a Young Negro Woman, about 20 Year old, she dos all sorts of House work; she can Brew, Bake, boyle soaft Soap, Wash, Iron & Starch; and is a good darey Women she can Card and Spin at the great Wheel, Cotten, Lennen and Wollen, she has another good Property she neither drinks Rum nor smoaks Tobacco, and she is a strong hale healthy Wench, she can Cook pretty well for Rost and Boyld." But black men spent much more of their time outdoors, working for day wages for their owners, doing skilled or unskilled work, hauling crates and barrels on the docks, building and repairing boats, carrying goods to and from markets and warehouses, walking across the city fetching tea water. John Roosevelt hired out Quack all the time: alongside dozens of black men from across the city, Quack helped build George Augustus' Royal Battery, stone by stone. In 1731, when the city needed a new Watch House, the Common Council paid substantial wages to white bricklayers and carpenters but also smaller sums to a long list of slaveowners, no doubt the daily fee for hiring their slaves. Slaves owned by Elizabeth Carpenter, Peter Lowe, and John Roosevelt helped build the Watch House, working together for days.[35] Carpenter's Tickle and Albany; Lowe's Juan and Sam; Roosevelt's Jack and Quack—all probably worked together building that Watch House.

Even if their trades and their unskilled labor and their errands didn't take them across the city, black men circulated on Sundays, when they visited friends, wives, and children. All day and into the night, black men walked the streets of the city.

Consider this walk described by Pedro, in a confession he made on June 29: "last Fall he went out one Sunday Morning with Mrs. *Carpenter*'s Negro *Albany;* that as they went along the Broad-Way, they met with Mr. Slydall's *Jack,* who was going to *Comfort*'s for Tea-Water; that at the Market near Mr. *DeLancey*'s House they met two other Negroes; and that

Albany asked them all to go down to *Hughson's* and drink with them." Pedro lived in the East Ward with his owner, the Dutch merchant Peter DePeyster. Albany probably lived near the Old Slip Market, a meat market at the bottom of Smith Street, because his owner, the butcher Elizabeth Carpenter, rented a stall there (the Old Slip was once known as the "Great Flesh Market").[36]

The DeLancey house, on Broadway between Little Queen and Little Stone streets, was just south of the Broadway Market, in the middle of Broadway, at Crown Street. If Pedro began his trip in the East Ward, he would have had to walk south down Queen Street or Little Dock Street, to meet Albany near Carpenter's house; north up Smith Street to Wall Street, which he would have followed for three blocks, past the Sugar Refinery, past City Hall, to Broadway, and from there northeast to the Broadway Market to meet "two other Negroes"; and west to the river, down Crown or Cortlandt Street, which would put him and his three friends at Comfort's pump—and that's without accounting for where they picked up Jack, owned by Joshua Sleydall. Even if Pedro made up everything he said about what happened at Hughson's (which he might have; he later recanted his confession), his walk there was so utterly ordinary a description of a slave's Sunday morning as to be entirely plausible, both to him and to his interrogators.

Nonetheless, ordinary as Pedro's walk was, it violated several laws, including a 1730 act stipulating that "it shall not hereafter be lawful for above three Slaves to meet together att any other time, nor att any other place, than when it shall happen they meet in some servile Imploym't for their Master's or Mistress's proffitt, and by their Master or Mistress consent, upon penalty of being whipt upon the naked back, at discretion of any Justice of the peace, not exceeding fforty Lashes." Of Pedro and his four companions, only Jack (Sleydall) was "in some servile Implym't": fetching water. If the sun wasn't yet up when Pedro left his house, and if he wasn't carrying "A Lanthorn and lighted Candle in itt so as the light thereof may be plainly seen," he was guilty of violating a municipal law prohibiting slaves from being in the streets in the dark without express permission. If, along the way, Pedro and his friends laughed too loudly, or hollered, or gambled for money, they would have violated another municipal law, passed in 1731, charging that "No Negro, Mulatto or Indian slaves, above the Number of three, do Assemble or meet together on the Lords Day Called Sunday, and Sport, Play or make any Noise or Disturbance, or at any Other time at any place from their Masters service, within this

City." If any of them was riding a horse, and rode it "Swiftly, Hastily, Pre-cipately or disorderly, and Otherwise than softly Orderly Patiently without Pasing Swiftly, Trotting fast or Galloping," he would have been guilty of breaking a city law "for Punishing Slaves who Shall Ride Disorderly through the Streets." And if Pedro had met his friends on a market day and had tried to buy or sell fruit, they would have broken a law, passed in August 1740, "to Prohibit Negroes and Other Slaves Vending Indian Corn Peaches or any other Fruit with this City."[37]

The city's Common Council passed all these laws, of course, because slaves did walk through the city at night, even without lanterns or candles; just as they met together and gambled and sold fruit and galloped on horseback. On weekdays, markets were the best place for black men to meet, especially the Meal Market, at the base of Wall Street, where newly arriving slaves were auctioned and black New Yorkers were hired out by the day. Powlus met Jack at the Meal Market at dusk. York and Jack took a walk there. Quack met Caesar there, the constables be damned. And damn the constables they did. When Fortune went to the fort with Quack (Roosevelt) after dark, he told him "he must be going; for that the Watch would take him up." Quack laughed; "there was no Danger of that." Visit-ing his wife, Barbara, at the fort every night, Quack knew how to avoid the watchmen.

On Sundays, the only day of the week when markets were closed, black men and women went "frolicking in the Fields," especially in summer. The Fields, a wide swath of land, north of the Negroes Burial Ground, thinly populated by scattered farms, stretched from the Bowery, on the east, all the way to the road to Greenwich, on the west. There were very few free blacks in New York, especially as manumission was all but impossible. But almost all of that handful of freed men and women lived in the Fields.

"Mate, we wanted you very much last Night at a Frolick out of Town," Curacoa Dick said to a friend, when they met "at a Well by the New Dutch Church" on a Sunday in the summer of 1740. "They had a free Dance and were very merry." When Braveboy, owned by the widow Elizabeth Kier-sted, confessed, he admitted that he "was at a Free Negroes (the Negro Man and his Wife *Isabella* present) at a House between Mr. *Bayard*'s Land and Greenwich Lane."

When Braveboy visited the house of Isabella and her husband, he was not alone. "Frolicks" were parties, where men and women danced together. In his confession, Braveboy supplied a list of those in attendance, both men and "wenches":

PRESENT,

Men,	Wenches,
Robin, }	Lucena, Mr. Franks's
Sussex, } Mrs. Bickley's	Mr. Richard's, *Quack's Wife*
Fortune, Cruger's	Maria }
Both Mr. Haines's Slaves,	Sarah, }
one a Mulatto the other	and Three free Negroes
a Negro.	Hannah,}
Othello	

Quack, Walter's

Curacoa Dick, who play'd on *Braveboy's* Fiddle.

Mr. Henry Cruger's *Neptune* came there late about eleven at Night, but the Wenches turned him away.

These summer Sunday frolicks, where husbands and wives and courting couples danced to fiddle music, never became a focal point of the investigation. They were utterly unlike the indoor all-male gatherings at Hughson's and Comfort's, and no one, not the grand jury, not Horsmanden, considered them particularly dangerous. Still, they were yet another example of exactly the "Excess of Liberty" Horsmanden condemned when he sentenced Quack and Cuffee to burn at the stake: "*Ye* abject Wretches, the Outcasts of the Nations of the Earth, are treated here with Tenderness and Humanity; and, I wish I could not say, with too great Indulgence also; for *You* have grown wanton with Excess of Liberty, and your Idleness has proved your Ruin; having given you the Opportunities of forming this villainous and detestable Conspiracy." In this, Horsmanden took his lead from the 1736 Antigua report, in which investigators concluded that the plot there was "carried on by the very top Negroes of this Island, and such as were indulged in such liberty that they kept one or two Horses a piece."[38]

Yet, however much "liberty" some enslaved New Yorkers might have enjoyed, it was always fragile and nearly always illicit. Constables could catch, report, and punish slaves who were found out on the streets at night without their master's permission. The most intimate of human relationships were vulnerable to that authority. Will, from Antigua, used to walk across the city to spend the night with his wife until the captain of the watch, Cornelius ("Major Drum") Van Horne, decided to stop him. "Mr. *Van Horn* would not allow him to come to his Wife," Will complained, and "would not allow a Candle." (Instead, Will made a makeshift torch to find his way through the city at night, ducking behind buildings when the watch approached.) In the summer of 1740, "the Governor had forbid *Quack* coming to the Fort" to spend the night with his wife, and it was this, and nothing John Hughson ever said, that committed Quack to decide "*that he would burn the Fort.*" Of the thirteen black men burned at the stake in 1741, at least five—Will, Quack, Ben, Robin, and Cook—had wives who were also slaves, and probably children, too. To be married was a liberty that made slavery more painful still.

Black men and women sought out one another's company, on street corners and at frolicks and other gatherings. Some married, although slaveowners discouraged that. In any event, slave marriages were not legal, or legally binding; they were simply acknowledged, or not. Some black men, like Caesar, had sex with white women, like Peggy Kerry. But when friendship, sex, and love crossed racial lines, as they did for Caesar and Peggy Kerry, it was not without censure: Kerry was dubbed "Negro Peg." In 1737, a New York bricklayer named William Carr divorced his wife, Anne, on the grounds that she had "behaved herself in an undecent and Wicked manner, by being to familiar with a Negro Man," Carr's slave Jonneau. Jonneau, charged with rape, was acquitted: the sex was voluntary. Anne was put to hard labor in the Poorhouse.[39]

In New York, as in every slaveowning society, white men who owned female slaves could exploit them sexually and were never held accountable. When white women had sex with black men, the consequences were more dire. Horsmanden, who had spent his wayward youth visiting prostitutes in London, was sickened by the thought of Peggy Kerry and Caesar together. And Mary Burton refused to care for their baby; indeed, nothing incensed Burton more than when Cuffee flirted with her, telling her he would have her for his wife. In a world where slaveowners labored to keep black men and women separated and where white men preyed on black women, they worried, lusted, and fantasized, endlessly, about the reverse. In 1734, New York taxpayers paid an additional tax to cover a one-time sum of £28 used "for the prosecution Execution & Payment for a Negro Man Slave lately Convicted and Executed for attempting to Committ a Rape." The alleged rapist, a slave of the French merchant Peter Vallet, was convicted of attempting to ravish a "pretty virtuous young Woman," fourteen or fifteen years old, and sentenced to death after other evidence appeared "That said Negro had endeavoured to make the like Attempt on another Woman some Time before." (There was some debate about whether the rape was attempted or completed—a consideration that mattered more to the girl's reputation than to the man's fate, since blacks, unlike whites, could be executed even for attempted rape—and it was claimed that Vallet's slave had given up and fled after the girl cried out, "*That she knew him and who was his Master.*") Vallet's slave was burned at the stake, "in the Presence of a numerous Company of spectators, great part of which were of the Black Tribe," where "he shew'd not the least sign of Repentance, but died like a Wretch harden'd in iniquity, for was hardly heard to Complain, only call'd for Water."[40]

Nor were public punishments for illicit interracial sex or for any challenge to the racial order limited to men. In February 1737, Rose, a "Malatto Slave," was arrested "for damning the white Peoples Throats." She was ordered taken "to the Common Whipping Post & there be striped from the middle upwards & receive upon the Naked back thirty nine lashes by the Common Whipper," after which she was sold and shipped out of the colony. But before leaving the city she was to be "tied & Carried round some of the Wards of this City & receive on the Naked Back thirty Nine lashes more by the Common Whipper."[41]

In the face of this vulnerability, the talk at Comfort's, damning white people's throats, encouraged solidarity. At the great meeting at Comfort's, when Cato's friends told him "*the Negroes were going to rise against the white People;* and asked him whether he would join with them?" Cato replied, "he was not willing; he had no Occasion for it; for he lived well," to which "*Quash* made answer, that he himself lived as well or better than he; and *Ben* said so did he; but 'twas a hard Case upon the poor Negroes, that they could not so much as take a Walk after Church-out, but the Constables took them up; therefore in order to be free, they must *set the Houses on fire, and kill the white People.*"

If "Hughson's Plot" was a Masonic prank translated by Daniel Horsmanden into a conspiracy that could be put to use attacking political parties, the "Negro Plot," hatched at Jack's, on street corners, and in markets, was the forging of an Akan-influenced brotherhood and a political order that encouraged individual and collective acts of vengeance, of cursing whites and setting fires, skirmishes in the daily, unwinnable war of slavery. At Comfort's, to the extent that men like Cato and Ben and Quash talked about freedom, this was the freedom many meant: the freedom to "take a Walk after Church-out," to dance at a frolick, to spend the night with one's wife, to play dice with one's mates. Dutch merchant Abraham Leffert's slave Pompey said his fellow conspirators promised him that if they set their masters' houses on fire, "they would be all *Free,* and be free from Trouble."

. . .

HUGHSON'S PLOT and the "Negro Plot" overlapped: many of the same people met at both Hughson's and Comfort's, especially at two crucial holidays, Christmastime and Whitsuntide. "Whitsuntide" is the English name for what the Dutch called "Pinkster," the seventh Sunday after Easter. In their confessions, a host of slaves dated their first knowledge of the conspiracy to Whitsuntide 1740. Sterling, owned by the English mariner Samuel Lawrence, said that he and Scipio, owned by a Dutchman named Abraham Abrahamse, had first gone to Hughson's at Whitsuntide. London, a Spanish Indian whose master, Benjamin Wyncoop, was a Dutch silversmith, said he met several men on the street, who "asked him to go and drink Beer" at Hughson's for Whitsuntide. Tom, owned by an English ship's captain, Henry Rowe, admitted that he was there then, too. All of these confessions confirmed testimony that emerged at John Hughson's trial, when Constables Joseph North, Peter Lynch, and John Dunscomb gave evidence that they had been tipped off about a Whitsuntide gathering at Hughson's, and "when they came there, they went into the Room where the Negroes were round a Table, eating and drinking, for there was Meat on the Table, and Knives and Forks; and the Negroes were calling for what they wanted." Constable North had "laid his Cane about them, and soon cleared the Room of them."[42]

What happened at Hughson's at Whitsuntide happened again the following Christmas. In their confessions, dozens of New York slaves described their "Christmas Hollidays" as a feast and revel, a world turned upside down, where young white women served a lavish, bountiful meal to black men who were seated around a fine table—with a tablecloth—listening to music, as if they were gentlemen; pledging themselves to a secret society, in imitation of Masons; plotting to overthrow the government, like politicians. Mary Burton, who had only just come into Hughson's service, was appalled by the role she was expected to play in this charade. As Horsmanden wrote, admiringly, Burton had a temper that could "ill brook the Ceremony of attending and serving upon Slaves."

But this topsy-turvy was exactly the point. Christmastime had long been celebrated in New York as a pagan carnival of turning the world upside down, of men dressing like women, and of wassailing, in which the rich gave gifts of money to the poor who wandered the streets and knocked at their doors. By the turn of the century, New Yorkers' wassailing Christmases would become so notoriously riotous and, finally, so threatening to public order and to the sensibilities of an emerging white middle class that the whole holiday would be domesticated and moved indoors, along with the evergreen. New Yorkers like Clement Moore, who wrote "'Twas the Night Before Christmas" in 1823, invented a fireside tradition of family gift-gifting, under the grandfatherly eye of Santa Claus, to put an end to the street carnival of poor and working-class whites and blacks.[43] Whitsuntide, meanwhile, moved to the streets.

By the second half of the eighteenth century, black Pinkster, and a similar celebration in New England known as "Nigger 'Lection Day," would become regular, publicly celebrated holidays. On both, crowds of slaves and free blacks met in town commons and city parks to drink and dance and elect a black man king. "The blacks their forces summon. / Tables & benches, chairs & stools / Rum-bottles, Gingerbread & bowls / Are lug'd into the common," one white versifier wrote in Boston in 1760. Whites found these public celebrations farcical, hugely entertaining, and above all greatly reassuring, not unlike later minstrel shows, by convincing them that blacks were, finally, so childishly comic as to be entirely harmless. But for the men and women who took part in Negro Election Day and Pinkster (called by one historian "one of the most important and revealing cultural phenomena in the history of the black experience in America"), these ceremonies meant something much different: in their elections, they chose important, prominent men, often African-born, who in many cases actually ruled, serving as respected leaders within the black community.[44]

Long before Pinkster and Negro Election Day were observed and recorded by whites, black elections, both mock and real, must have taken place privately, at places like John Hughson's tavern. A tradition like Pinkster does not simply sprout from the earth in a day. When Joseph North and his fellow constables testified at Hughson's trial, they drew for the court an alarming picture of role reversal at Hughson's during Pinkster the previous spring. What Constable North, barging in, saw was only the most immediately obvious of these reversals: young white women waiting on black men, "The Negroes . . . calling for what they wanted." It certainly irked the court. Philipse accused Hughson and his wife "not only of making Negro Slaves their Equals, but even their Superiors, by waiting upon, keeping with, and entertaining them, with Meat, Drink, and Lodging."

The black men who met at Hughson's tavern called on Dutch and English holiday traditions; even more, they called on the tradition of Caribbean Christmas, or black saturnalia. In the British West Indies, the source of 65 percent of New York's slave population, the holiday between

Christmas and New Year's when slaves were spared hard labor—the time of Hughson's "Great Feast"—was celebrated by revels in which slaves were allowed into white men's houses for feasts and entertainment and gifts. The carousing easily turned violent. And easily slipped into rebellion. Thirty-five percent of all slave rebellions in the British Caribbean took place at Christmastime.

Not surprisingly, Caribbean slaveowners hated the holiday. But by the early eighteenth century, blacks had come so entirely to expect and demand it that Caribbean planters considered it more dangerous to abandon the practice than to continue it. And planters understood that the Christmas feasts and role reversals acted as a safety valve of sorts, allowing slaves to play at freedom rather than to fight for it. In mainland colonies, there was less experience with, and less tolerance for, Christmas revels, traditions imported by creole slaves. In South Carolina in 1739, just after the Stono Rebellion, the Assembly asked the lieutenant governor to order the military "to draw out of their respective Companies a Number of Men sufficient to patrol in the Christmas Holy Days," for fear that slaves would stage another rebellion over the holidays, "a Time of general Liberty to the Slaves throughout the Province."[45] Most white New Yorkers had even less familiarity with holiday role reversals, and little ability to measure their degree of frivolity or seriousness. Horsmanden, for one, complained about blacks' *fictitious hypocritical Grins.* He couldn't tell when he was being played. Maybe John Hughson couldn't either.

BLACK NEW YORKERS brought Caribbean traditions to bear on Dutch and English holidays, which nicely mixed, at Hughson's, with mock Masonry and, at Jack's, with Akan ritual. The city's "Spanish Negroes" may have attended gatherings at both places—they were certainly accused of being there, and of being part of a "Spanish Plot." But while they undoubtedly complained about the injustice of their enslavement (as they would at their trial), there is very little evidence that they plotted to destroy the city. The "Spanish Plot" was invented, as much by black as by white New Yorkers, the latter fearing what the former wished for: that the "Spanish and York Negroes" were joined in common cause.

On April 6, 1741, after the houses on either side of Jacob Sarly's had been set on fire, panicked citizens cried: *The Spanish Negroes; Take up the Spanish Negroes.* Constables arrested Sarly's slave, Juan de la Silva, and as many more Spanish slaves as they could find, including Antonio de St. Bendito, owned by Peter DeLancey, the Chief Justice's brother; Antonio de la Cruz, owned by a widow named Sarah Mesnard; Pablo Ventura Angel, owned by the English brewer Frederick Becker; and Augustine Gutierrez, owned by the Scotsman John Macmullen. In court, all of these men, "lately imported into this City as Prize Slaves," claimed to be free men, a claim that cast questions of slavery and freedom into sharp relief.

Many of the Spanish slaves in New York City had been captured by John Lush, captain of the twenty-gun sloop *Stephen and Elizabeth,* the first privateer to sail from New York in the War of Jenkins's Ear. Lush had sailed from New York in the fall of 1739, just weeks after England declared war against Spain. He captured two Spanish schooners off the coast of Cuba and a Spanish sloop off Port-au-Prince. All but one of the sailors on these three vessels jumped ship and swam to shore, or drowned trying. Near Mexico, Lush sighted "a large *French* Ship who hoisted *Spanish* Colours, and answered the Capt. in *Spanish.*" After a fierce battle, Lush captured this ship and its treasure of 22,000 pieces-of-eight, and then "sent to *Jamaica,* to know if there was War with *France*"—to learn whether he had any right to take this prize.

Only after a month of waiting did word come that there was, as yet, no war with France. Lush had no choice but to release the ship and relinquish the prize. "But the Crew not liking of this, 30 of his Men mutiny'd." The rest of the crew managed to suppress the mutineers and the *Stephen and Elizabeth* sailed to Jamaica, where Lush left the mutineers, replaced them with new men, and sailed to Porto Bello, off Panama. This time, he had better success in finding Spanish ships, and in taking their crews prisoner, as they were too far from shore to swim. By April 1740, the *New York Gazette* was able to report that Lush "has taken two extraordinary Rich Prizes, and is coming home with them." With a crew of only thirty-five men, Lush had by now one hundred Spanish prisoners in his hold, and commanded not only the *Stephen and Elizabeth* but the two prizes, the *Nuestra Señora de la Vittoria* and the *Solidad,* with all their cargo. He landed in New York on April 26, and, for his extraordinary triumph, was greeted by the deafening salute of all the guns on all the ships in the harbor.[46]

Among Lush's one hundred Spanish prisoners were "Nineteen Negroes and Molattoes." In presenting his prize to the New York Admiralty Court in May, Lush said that these nineteen men were slaves, and, as they could present no evidence to the contrary, the court declared them to be so. Eighteen were subsequently sold at auction. Lush kept one man, William, for himself.[47]

Inspired by Lush's success, Captain Benjamin Kiersted sailed his sloop, the *Humming Bird*, for Curaçao in July 1740. That October, he captured at least two vessels, and at least two "Spanish Negroes," including Pablo Ventura Angel. But on his return to New York, Kiersted's prize became the subject of dispute.[48]

Meanwhile, Lush's reputation had suffered as well. He had been accused of gross misconduct by one Lieutenant Wimbleton, a British naval officer. By February 1741, Lush had been arrested on an Admiralty warrant. Although bail was set at £2,000, Lush convinced the Admiralty judge, Lewis Morris, Jr., to reduce it to £40. On May 12, Lush's case came before the Vice Admiralty Court, and Morris again ruled in Lush's favor, charging a commission to inquire into the credibility of Wimbleton as a witness.[49]

New York's Vice Admiralty Court met at City Hall, in the same courtroom used by the Supreme Court. William Smith, Richard Bradley, and James Alexander practiced before that court. In the spring of 1741, Alexander acted as attorney in at least two cases before the Admiralty Court, involving Vincent Pearse, captain of the *Flamborough*, and Benjamin Kiersted, master of the *Humming Bird*. Daniel Horsmanden had served as justice on the Admiralty Court beginning in 1736, but Morris had replaced him in 1738. In his *Journal*, Horsmanden made no mention of the meetings of the Admiralty Court, but the two courts often met on the same day, and in the same room, and it's impossible that Horsmanden was unaware of the proceedings in Admiralty, which were, in any event, very much related to his own criminal investigation. On May 12, 1741, both courts were in session: in the morning, the Supreme Court heard indictments in *King v. John Hughson and Sarah his Wife*, and Horsmanden ordered Mills to put Cuffee in the same cell with Arthur Price; in the afternoon, after the Supreme Court had adjourned, John Lush's case came before the Admiralty Court. Not long afterward, "Spanish Negroes" became a focus of Horsmanden's investigation.

On May 22, Sandy told the grand jury that he had heard Lush's slave Will say that "if they did not send him over to his own Country, he would ruin the City." In this and subsequent interrogations, Sandy impeached several other "Spanish Negroes," too, saying that he had heard them talk on the street, and at Comfort's, about a plot to burn the city down. Jack placed them at Hughson's: "*There were Spanish Negroes at Hughson's,*" Ben had told Jack, and "they had Designs of taking this Country." Hughson promised to unify the (New) York and Spanish slaves, Jack said: "he would go before, *and be their* KING, and would mix them one amongst another *when they came to fight."* A conspiracy of slaves across the city now seemed to stretch across the Atlantic: Jack's confession transformed the plot into an international conspiracy. At Hughson's, he said, the city's slaves, New Yorkers and Spaniards, *"agreed to wait a Month and half for the* Spaniards *and* French *to come,"* before setting the city on fire. The fire at Fort George, Patrick said, was to serve as a signal to the Spanish that the rebellion had begun.

Bastian's was the first in a long procession of confessions to corroborate this; he said, *"they expected that War would be proclaimed in a little time against the* French; *and that the* French *and* Spaniards *would come here."* *"By-and by this will be put in the News,"* Cato (Moore) told Dundee, as they watched the fort burn, "and then the *Spaniards* will come and take us all."

It was not implausible. The Spanish could very well have hoped to incite rebellion among New York's slaves, in preparation for an attack on the city. And news of the war could easily have informed or even directed, the actions of some of New York's slaves, Spanish or no. Spain had earlier published a proclamation "declaring Freedom to all Negroes, and other slaves, that shall Desert from the English Colonies." A handful of slaves in South Carolina had fled to Spanish St. Augustine, and the Spanish governor there had refused to return them. South Carolina's 1739 Stono Rebellion took place the very weekend that official word reached Charleston that England and Spain were at war.[50] Two years later, New York's Fort George was set on fire just as word was arriving in the city that England was now also, if only unofficially, at war with France. When asked to raise more troops to fight against the Spanish, Clarke reported to the Lords of Trade, in late June, that no men in New York would be willing to leave the city, because the slave conspiracy "has begat a general opinion that no man ought to leave his habitation to go out of the Province and the apprehension of a French warr as this is a frontier Province will make every one, who has any thing at stake industrious to discourage men from inlisting themselves for this expedition."[51] What Spain promised led New York slaves to seek alliance with "Spanish Negroes," and, later, to betray them in their confessions, but there is little evidence that Spanish slaves joined either "Hughson's Plot" or the "Negro Plot."

THE FIRST SPANISH slave tried for conspiracy was Francis, on June 10. He spoke barely any English, and an interpreter was called to serve at his trial. Still, Jack (Comfort) and Mary Burton, neither of whom spoke

Spanish, were able to testify against him. Francis was burned at the stake on June 12. The next day, five more Spanish slaves were indicted: Juan de la Silva, Pablo Ventura Angel, Augustine Gutierrez, Antonio de la Cruz, and Antonio de St. Bendito. They pled not guilty and their trial was scheduled for June 15.

In the basement of City Hall, the five men arrived at a strategy for their defense. The next morning, Philipse and Hormanden called the "Spanish Negroes" to the bar to be tried. "But they complained," Horsmanden said, "that they had great Injustice done them by being sold here as Slaves; for that, as they pretended, they were Freemen in their own Country." They also "gave in their several Sir-names," asserting, by this too, that they were free men. While the court considered the question, their trial was postponed until Wednesday, June 17.

Horsmanden suspected that someone had given the prisoners legal advice. He believed this because their protestation of freedom had an important legal consequence: if the Spanish slaves were free men, the testimony of slaves could not be allowed against them, leaving only Mary Burton, who did not understand Spanish and was therefore a weak witness against them, to testify for the prosecution. "Should it be credited that they could speak only in a Tongue which she did not understand," Horsmanden believed "their Advisers" had suggested, "how could she tell what passed between them in Conversation at *Hughson's*?"

On Tuesday, as scheduled, "three Negroes were hang'd, and two burnt alive," as Zenger reported in the *Weekly Journal*. All five had been tried on June 13: Fortune, owned by John Vanderspiegle; Cato, owned by Joseph Cowley; a second Cato, owned by the Dutch cooper John Provost; Quash, owned by the Dutch brewer Hermanus Rutgers, Jr.; and Ben, who had kept the list. At their sentencing on June 15, Horsmanden told Fortune and "you two *Catoes*" that they were but "inferior Agents," yet he called Ben "a deep Politician" and damned him for his "hypocritical, canting Behaviour" during his trial—although what Ben had done, besides protest his innocence, was unrecorded. Horsmanden warned, "unless you acknowledge every one his Guilt, and bewail it with hearty Sorrow, and sincere Tears of Repentance; and beseech his Forgiveness; laying open the whole wicked Scheme, and discovering your several Confederates and Accomplices, all the Parties concerned. . . . Upon these Conditions only can you expect Mercy at the Hands of God Almighty." At the end of his lengthy speech, the Third Justice concluded: "It is a very tiresome Task to pronounce that Sentence which the Law requires of us; for we delight not in any Man's Blood; but the Law adjudges you unfit to live." On the morning of June 16, both Catos and Fortune were hanged, before a large crowd. After a break for lunch, New Yorkers headed once again to the outskirts of town. In the afternoon, Ben and Quash were burned. Zenger reported, "they all of them died hardned, professing innocency to the last."[52]

In between attending the executions, Philipse and Horsmanden spent the day considering the Spanish slaves' complaint. They arrived at a rather astonishing solution: they would try the "Spanish Negroes" on two separate indictments; on one, as slaves, and on the other, as free men. On Wednesday, De la Silva, Ventura Angel, Gutierrez, De la Cruz, and De St. Bendito were arraigned on a second indictment, "for counselling and advising the Negro *Quack,* to burn the Fort." In this indictment, their surnames were included. In the trial that followed, the five Spaniards were tried on both charges; on the first charge, of conspiracy, they were tried as slaves, against whom "Negro Evidence" was admissible; on the second charge, of counseling Quack, they were tried as free men, and only Mary Burton's testimony was allowed.

The "Spanish Negroes" had gained but a partial victory; Philipse and Horsmanden had refused to rule on whether they were slave or free and instead determined to prosecute them, whatever their status. Still, Juan de la Silva and his comrades had argued effectively. And when the trial began, the defendants also conducted what was by far the most elaborate and effective defense of any enslaved men accused in the conspiracy. Did they arrive at their strategy by themselves, or were they advised by someone else, someone with intimate knowledge of the law?

One possibility is that James Alexander advised them. On April 23, Alexander had agreed with "all the Gentlemen of the Law" to aid the prosecution, and to take turns in trying prisoners. He had served at the trial of John and Sarah Hughson and Peggy Kerry, but, even there, it's not at all clear what service he really offered. He neither opened nor closed to the jury; nor was he identified as examining specific witnesses; his name was simply listed as one of the "COUNCIL for the KING." Alexander appears to have been equally inactive at the trial of the five Spaniards on June 17. Chambers opened the indictment and summed up against De la Cruz and De St. Bendito; Murray summed up against Gutierrez and De la Silva. (Richard Bradley, who was ill, was unable to attend.) And after Alexander's brief and silent appearance at City Hall on June 17, he did not return to the courtroom for the duration of the proceedings against the city's slaves. Alexander, it seems, boycotted the trials.[53]

It is possible, but impossible to prove, that Alexander believed the Spanish slaves were innocent or even that they were free; or he may, by now, have become alarmed by the direction of the proceedings and the pace of the executions. He was, in any event, well aware of the proceedings in the Admiralty Court against Kiersted and Lush, and the fate of the "Spanish Negroes" may have had some bearing on his clients' cause in that court (although, since those records are lost, this is impossible to determine). Alexander could easily have met with the defendants either before their original trial date, June 15, or on June 16.

In any event, in the courtroom on June 17, Alexander sat, passively, as a member of the prosecution. Mordecai Gomez served as an interpreter. Murray and Chambers trotted out the evidence against the defendants: the confessions of Quack and Cuffee were read aloud; Mary Burton, Sandy, Jack, Tickle, and Bastian appeared on the witness stand. Burton testified that she had seen the defendants at Hughson's, where, even if she couldn't understand what the Spaniards had said, the plot was the "common talk." She had also heard Hughson say that the Spanish slaves "would burn *Lush*'s House, and tie *Lush* to a Beam, and roast him like a Piece of Beef." On the street in front of Lush's house, Sandy had seen De St. Bendito and other Spaniards point to the house and pledge, "D—m that Son of a B—h, if he did not carry them to their own Country, *they would ruin the City*." He and Jack, Tickle and Bastian dutifully reported seeing the defendants at Comfort's, or Hughson's, or both. To answer the defendants' complaint that they were free men, the prosecution called Richard Nichols, who served as Deputy Register of the Admiralty, to testify that all of the defendants had been properly and legally claimed as prizes.

The defendants proceeded to call no fewer than twelve witnesses. All five of their owners took the stand, and four offered testimony supporting the defendants' alibis, which rested on the wretched state of their health during their first winter in New York. Peter DeLancey said De St. Bendito had been at DeLancey's farm in the country from before Christmas until after the fort fire, and had been made lame with frostbite "after the first great Snow." Sarah Mesnard said De La Cruz had been similarly crippled, and hadn't been able to come downstairs all winter. Neither man had decent boots. Frederick Becker agreed that Ventura Angel had been sick in bed, too, and John Macmullen said Gutierrez "had an Ague" and "kept his Bed most of the Time." Nor were these defenses frivolous; De la Cruz presented two doctors, Francis DuPuy and Francis DuPuy, Jr., who had treated him for feet so injured "that he could not walk." The other defendants produced more witnesses to their incapacity. Of the five men accused, only Juan de la Silva was well enough to have walked to Comfort's or Hughson's in January or February. But he offered a defense more powerful than an alibi: when De la Silva examined his own owner on the witness stand, Jacob Sarly was forced to admit that "he had heard *that his Negro was free.*"

In separate statements to the court, each defendant also asserted his status as a free man by telling the court that he "had not kept Company with any Negroes since he came to [this] Country" because he "*had not been used to keep Company with Negroes*" at home. This point was taken up by the judges in their instructions to the jury, in which Philipse and Horsmanden asked jurors to put aside the question of whether the defendants were free: "be they Freemen, or be they Slaves, the main Question before you is, whether they, or any, or which of them are guilty of the Charge against them." Arguing that there had been "no sufficient or proper Evidence" that the defendants were actually free, the judges instructed the jury that "all the Negro Evidence which has been given upon this Trial against them, is legal Evidence."

But even if the jurors were persuaded that the defendants were free, there remained the charge of abetting Quack's crime, and the testimony of Mary Burton, who neither spoke nor could understand Spanish. Here, the judges admitted the weakness of that case: "To prove the Charge in this Indictment, there was the Testimony of *Mary Burton;* I must observe to you, that her Testimony, as to the Charge in this Indictment, is single; there is no other Witness; but nevertheless, *Gentlemen,* one Witness is sufficient; and if you give Credit to her Testimony, you will, no doubt, discharge a good Conscience, and find them Guilty; If you should have sufficient Reason in your own Minds to discredit her Testimony, if you can think so, you must then acquit them."

These were the most balanced jury instructions given in the entire course of the conspiracy proceedings, undoubtedly because the case rested on very weak evidence. But the jury found the defendants guilty on both counts after half an hour of deliberation. Sentencing all four to be hanged, Horsmanden put it to them that if "they were Free-men, they ought in all Reason to have waited the Event of the War, and suffr'd patiently under their Misfortune; and when Peace should have been concluded, they might have made the Truth of their Pretensions appear, and then Justice would have been done to them."

AT JUST THIS POINT, in mid-June, Joseph Murray's slave Adam began behaving strangely: "he appeared very uneasy and disturbed in his Mind." Murray owned five slaves: Adam, Jack, Caesar, Congo, and Dido. As Murray trudged to City Hall day after day, prosecuting black conspirators, he became more and more suspicious of the black men who lived in his attic, and in his cellar. And, as Murray's slaves saw Quack, Cuffee, Ben, and Quash burned, and more men hanged, they too grew edgy. Murray was busy in his study, preparing his cases: on June 17, he prosecuted the "Spanish Negroes"; on June 19, he prosecuted York and London, both owned by the Dutch baker Peter Marschalk; Harry, owned by the widow Katherine Kipp; and yet another Cato, this man the property of John Shurmur.

On June 25, Murray's slave Jack was accused. Brash, owned by the French merchant Peter Jay, who lived not far from Murray's house in the West Ward, told one of the judges that once "He and Mr. Murray's *Jack* went for Tea-Water to *Comfort's*," and from there they walked to John Hughson's house, where "*Hughson* carried *Jack* up Stairs, and *swore him* of this Plot . . . ; and *Jack agreed to burn his Master's Stable, his House, and to murder his Master and Mistress.*" Philipse and Horsmanden recommended Brash for pardon and ordered Jack arrested. Murray must have been horrified, though hardly surprised, to learn that his own slave had placed live coals under a haystack in his coachhouse in April.

On the night of June 25, constables arrested Jack at Murray's house on Broadway. The next morning, while Murray was at City Hall conducting the prosecution of Prince, owned by Anthony Duane, and Tony, owned by the English ship's carpenter John Latham, Adam, at home, "came several Times into the Clerk's Office, with a seeming Intention to disclose some Secret; the young Gentleman at last took Notice of it, and shutting the Door too, asked him, Whether he knew any Thing of the Plot?" Adam said no, but added, "*he was afraid some Dog or another would owe him a Spite, and bring him in.*"

In the afternoon, Murray and Horsmanden together interrogated Jack at City Hall. Just as Adam had suspected, Jack betrayed him. Murray's Jack confessed that he had been to Comfort's for tea water and, from there, went to Hughson's for the "Great Feast" in January. "As he was going home with the Tea-Water," he said, "he met *Adam*, his Fellow-Servant, by old Mr. *DeLancey's* House, and he told *Adam* where he had been and what had been talked of, and what Company was at *Hughson's* . . . *Adam* thereupon ordered him to set his Cag down; which he did, and gave it in Charge to one of Mr. *DeLancey's* Negro Wenches, and said they would go down there and drink some Punch." He added that he and Adam had sworn to the plot and "expected the *French* and *Spaniards* here, and then they would fire and plunder the Houses and carry all to *Hughson's,* who was to carry them off into another Country, and make them a free People." Both men had also attended the great meeting at Comfort's. There, Adam had agreed to kill Joseph and Grace Murray and their housekeeper Mrs. Dimmock and her daughter, while Jack had agreed to kill Murray's three other slaves: Caesar, Congo, and Dido.

When Murray returned home later that afternoon, he found Adam "running backwards and forwards like a distracted Creature." Murray called Adam to his study "and charged him as one concerned in the Conspiracy." Adam denied it. Murray attempted to persuade him to confess and "used many Arguments, to prevail with him." When Adam continued to protest his innocence, Murray "delivered him to the Constable."

That night, two of Murray's law clerks went to City Hall to see Adam in jail. They, too, tried to convince him to confess. He told them he was innocent and that "*it was Nothing but damn'd Lies that brought him there; that he knew who was the Author of them, and would be revenged if he died for it.*" He asked them to name his accuser, and they said Jack. Adam banged his head against a beam and declared, "*then I am a dead Man.*"

Before the two clerks left, Adam gave them his silver "Shoe- and Knee-Buckles" and asked them to give them to Caesar. They urged him again to confess. "What they would have him to say?" he asked. "They would have him *speak sincerely,* whether he was *guilty or not.*" "Why then," Adam said, "*to speak sincerely, I am guilty.*"

The next morning, Saturday, June 27, Adam's formal interrogation began. It lasted several days: "the Information that he gave came from him slowly and by piece-meals, which was very tiresome," Horsmanden complained, "and gave so much Trouble, that he was several Times remanded to Jail, and told that what he said would do him little Service; but as the Constable was taking him away, he would beg to stay, and say he would tell of all he could recollect."

In the end, Adam finally admitted that at Hughson's he had seen "*a little short Man,*" the newest, and final, villain: the priest.

CHAPTER SIX

Blood

S UMMER CAME and with it, mosquitoes, sucking blood. "These little animals can disfigure a person's face during a single night," one
itchy visitor to the city complained. Against a hazy sky, the harbor
filled with ships while boys jumped from rocks into the East River, keeping clear of lines cast by lazy fishermen from the sun-warmed pebble
beaches of its banks. The wind blew hot. In the streets, hogs sweated and
dogs panted, seeking the shade of doorways and market awnings and the
smooth coolness of the marble steps of fashionable houses, only to be
shooed away by broom-wielding servants and house slaves. At dusk, couples strolled on the Bowling Green and dined on lobsters and watermel-
ons. In the evening, with its unbearable humidity, well-heeled New
Yorkers sought relief on their rooftop balconies, cursing the city's teeming
population of tree toads, whose clamorous croaking drowned out the songs
of birds.[1]

Meanwhile, on a small island in the still waters of the Collect, the rotting corpses of John Hughson and Caesar hung from chains, stinking and
oozing in the sun. Caesar's body had been gibbeted on May 11, Hughson's
on June 12. The air was heavy, and the ground wet, with their decay. The
cobbler who would be king and the slave who would be governor fer-
mented and dripped, long since found by birds, beetles, flies, and worms,
pecking, sapping, gnawing. By the end of June a rumor had spread that the
two corpses had changed, had *exchanged* color: Hughson had turned black
and Caesar white. Curious New Yorkers flocked to find out. Those who
could bear the smell discovered, on rowing or wading out to the island,
that Hughson's "Face, Neck, Hands and Feet, were of a deep shining
Black, rather blacker than the Negro placed by him." Not only his skin but
his hair and nose and even his lips had changed: "the Hair of *Hughson's*

Beard and Neck (his Head could not be seen, for he had a Cap on) was curling like the Wool of a Negro's Beard and Head; and the Features of his Face were of the Symmetry of a Negro Beauty; the Nose broad and flat, the Nostrils open and extended, the Mouth wide, Lips full and thick." Caesar, at his side, a man who before his death "was one of the darkest Hue of his Kind," had "turned whitish," "bleach'd" by the sun.

The spectacle "drew Numbers of all Ranks, who had Curiosity, to the Gibbets, for several Days running, in order to be convinced by their own Eyes." Some considered it miraculous proof of both men's guilt, of the perversity of their transgression, of their devilish allegiance. More moderate people attributed the change to the natural course of decay, the blood pooling, purplish black, in Hughson's hands and face while Caesar's features took on the ghastly pallor of putrefaction. But all "Beholders were amazed at these Appearances." All summer long, Hughson and Caesar provided "Matter for much Speculation." And more matter for maggots.

Like the mercury, the number of jailed slaves climbed. "The Season began to grow warm, as usual," Horsmanden observed, "and 'twas to be expected that the Heat would be increasing upon us daily." From their chambers on the second story of City Hall, Horsmanden and Philipse worried about the poorly vented cellar dungeon below them, which housed more than a hundred prisoners. James Mills, responsible for "Emptying the Ordure Tubbs," must have cursed his job, and perhaps he didn't do it as often as he ought. The overcrowded dungeon clearly constituted a public health emergency. As Horsmanden explained, "'Twas feared such Numbers of them closely confined together, might breed an Infection." The judges worried less about the prisoners' welfare than about the possibility that an epidemic might spread beyond the walls of the dungeon and "breed a Sickness in this City."[2] Philipse and Horsmanden called a meeting of the city's lawyers for Saturday, June 27, to hasten the collection of confessions, hoping to empty the jail, one way or another, as swiftly as possible.

Just before they were to meet, Othello, James DeLancey's most valued slave, entered the city in irons. He had accompanied DeLancey to New England in March, when the Chief Justice led a delegation mediating a boundary dispute between Massachusetts and Rhode Island. In mid-June, while still in Providence, DeLancey questioned Othello about the conspiracy, the news of which he had followed closely, and urged Othello to confess, promising that "he would use his Interest with the Governor to save his Life," but warning that if Othello returned to New York without confessing, "he would leave him to Justice without Mercy." Othello denied everything. On June 22, Horsmanden sent word to DeLancey that Pompey, owned by the Chief Justice's brother Peter, had accused Othello of having sworn to the plot. DeLancey had Othello shackled, and boarded him on a ship heading for New York. When Othello's vessel docked, on June 27, he was carried through the city streets and thrown into the dungeon.

Horsmanden began his day, Saturday, June 27, questioning Joseph Murray's slave Adam, at City Hall. He told him that Othello had been arrested, and Adam, "hearing that, he immediately said, *Othello was concerned in the Plot*; as if naturally concluding that some Body else had impeached him; for till this Accident, he had not mentioned his Name." Adam said that Othello had known about the plot since it was first hatched in 1738, and had agreed to kill the DeLanceys. When Adam and Jack were finished butchering Murray's family, Adam said, they were to help Othello "in murdering the Chief Justice's."

In pointing out the suddenness of Adam's impeachment of Othello, Horsmanden, for once discriminating, cast doubt on Adam's confession. He was not pleased at the prospect of prosecuting Othello on the eve of DeLancey's return. Horsmanden knew Othello well. He "had more Sense than the common Rank of Negroes," Horsmanden allowed, "and great Influence amongst the inferiour Sort." Othello was a common name among slaves, but DeLancey's Othello may have been the boy that his brother-in-law, Peter Warren, had bought at the auction of John Montgomerie's estate in 1732; if so, Horsmanden had known Othello for almost a decade, as the liveried slave of the colony's most eminent men. As a boy, he served the governor himself. At Montgomerie's auction, Warren won the bidding on Othello, at £36. Sometime afterward, Othello may have come into DeLancey's hands; DeLancey managed a £6,000 trust for his sister, Susannah DeLancey Warren.[3] Perhaps, as Warren was often at sea—from 1735 to 1742 he commanded the *Squirrel*, and from September 1740 to August 1741 he patrolled the Caribbean—his wife found she had little employment for Othello, and gave or sold him to her brother.[4] Whether or not Warren's Othello was the same man as DeLancey's Othello, Daniel Horsmanden had known DeLancey's Othello for years, having "had frequent Opportunities of seeing this Negro at his House" when he visited the Chief Justice.

After interrogating Adam on the morning of June 27, Horsmanden attended his scheduled meeting with the city's attorneys, to better divide the labor of conducting interrogations and expedite the emptying of the dungeon. At the end of that meeting, Horsmanden rushed to question Othello. Othello insisted that he had never heard of the conspiracy. On Monday and Tuesday, Horsmanden returned to City Hall, repeated his inquiries, and reminded Othello that Clarke's promise of pardon required slaves to confess "on or before the *first* Day of *July*"—the following Wednesday.

Finally, on Tuesday, June 30, Othello was ready to talk: he had been at the feast at Hughson's at Whitsuntide, 1740, he told Horsmanden; he had been at the "Frolick in the Bowry last Summer," dancing to fiddle music with free black women; he had talked about the plot with Adam, Cuffee, Prince, Pompey, and Albany at Coenties Market; "and he agreed to join to *burn and kill, &c.*" It wasn't much. Othello would not admit to attending the "Great Feast" at Hughson's at Christmas. And everyone he named was either dead or had already confessed, except for Hanover, the mayor's coachman, who was apparently beyond reproach and was never arrested. What's more, it seemed to Horsmanden as if Othello had bided his time in jail. When the Third Justice asked him why he hadn't confessed on Saturday, "He answered with a Smile, 'Why, Sir, *I was but just then come to Town.*'" Horsmanden scoffed, "*He was willing to spy the Land first, to see how it lay, to inform himself of how Matters stood, what he had been doing, and to consider whether there could be Room for his Escape.*"

But there was little room for escape, unless it came with the return of his master, who was even then on his way back to New York. On Wednesday morning, Horsmanden sentenced ten convicted men to be hanged. That afternoon, DeLancey finally arrived. On Thursday, July 2, DeLancey entered the courtroom for the first time since the Supreme Court opened its session in April.

With a long face and delicate features framed by a tumbling, curled wig, DeLancey had a bearing more elegant than either of the two lower judges. In court, he first faced Will, the watchmaker's slave, who had confessed and been pardoned in St. Kitt's and Antigua, had pled guilty on June 25. The justices ruled that "it was thought high Time to put it out of his Power to do any further Mischief": without ever having been tried, Will was sentenced to burn.

On Friday, DeLancey did not attend court; perhaps he met with Clarke, to report on his travels. That morning, he probably attended the hanging of Prince (Duane), Tony (Latham), Cato (Shurmur), Harry (Kipp), and York (Marschalk). "At the Gallows, two of them died seem-

James DeLancey, *by Gerardus Duyckinck, 1728. Collection of
The New-York Historical Society.*

ingly very Penitent, but none of them acknolwedg'd any Guilt," Zenger
reported. "One of them (to the greatest Surprise of the Spectators) after he
had hang [*sic*] the common Time, or rather longer, when he was cut down,
shew'd Symptoms of Life, on which he was tied up again."[5] Even less fortunate was York, whose body was brought to the island near the Powder-
house, and hung next to those of Hughson and Caesar.

The next day, Saturday, DeLancey and half the city went to watch
Will's execution. Chained to a stake, Will confessed. He said that Othello's friend Quack, owned by the butcher John Walter, had plotted with
two Irish soldiers from the fort, William Kane and Edward Kelly. Com-

fort's Jack "*was a true Evidence,*" Will said—the "Negro Plot" was real—but Cato, owned by alderman John Moore, was not to be believed. Cato had confessed on June 22; he had corroborated Jack's testimony about the meetings at Comfort's but had also said that he had attended "a Supper at *Hughson's*" with forty or fifty other black men, including Will. In all, Cato had accused twenty-six men. For this, he had been pardoned. In jail, Cato had advised Will "that he would be certainly burnt or hanged if he did not confess; but that if he brought in a good many, it would save his Life; for he had found it so himself; and must say, he was to set his Master's House on fire, which would make the Judges believe him."

Will, who was "expert at Plots," knew that whatever he said at the stake, his life was beyond saving. His confession brought him no reprieve, not even a reduction of his sentence to hanging. "The Pile being kindled," Will "set his Back to the Stake, and raising up one of his Legs, laid it upon the Fire."

When James DeLancey arrived in New York, he found Othello in chains in the crowded and fouled dungeon, having admitted to plotting to burn the Chief Justice's house and murder his family. Within four days of his return, DeLancey saw five men hanged, one man gibbeted, and another man burned at the stake who, with his dying breath, insisted that while what Jack had said about what happened at Comfort's was true, everything else was a lie. Maybe DeLancey had seen enough. And maybe he wondered whether Horsmanden and Philipse, in his absence, had really followed Clarke's orders. "I desired the Judges to single out only a few of the most notorious for execution, and that I would pardon the rest," Clarke had reported to the Lords of Trade in June.[6] That few, it seemed, had become too many, at considerable cost to the city's slaveowners, who had lost a good deal of money watching their property go up in flames.

Just after Will's execution, DeLancey called a meeting with Philipse and Horsmanden, to examine the list of slaves who had confessed and "to mark out such as should be thought proper to recommend to his Honour the Lieutenant-Governor, to be pardoned." It was natural that this should be done at precisely that moment; Clarke's offer of amnesty had just expired. But it seems important that DeLancey's first major act in the proceedings was processing pardons. On July 4, forty-two men were recommended for pardon and transportation, their owners to pocket the proceeds of their sale in faraway colonies. Five days later, the first of these men were marched from City Hall to the docks and boarded a ship, the *Mayflower,* headed for Madeira.[7]

James DeLancey's return marked the beginning of the end. There would be only one more day of trials, on July 15, and only eight more men executed. Of these eight, one, Juan de la Silva, had been convicted in DeLancey's absence, and another, Othello, was essentially unpardonable, as it would have been more than unseemly for DeLancey to spare his own slave. After DeLancey's return, the court steered its attention away from the city's slaves and toward a different threat: papists. On Sunday, July 5, DeLancey began participating in the investigation in earnest, and steered it on a different course. He and Horsmanden together interrogated William Kane, the soldier, who had been named by Will at the stake, and who told a story altogether different from any other testimony that had come before.

Now the end was near, for now was discovered the final plot. In just a month's time, Othello would be dead, the last of the slave executions would be over, and Daniel Horsmanden would happily conclude, "the Old proverb has herein . . . been verifyed That there is Scarce a plot but a priest is at the Bottom of it."[8]

IN THE SECOND WEEK of June, Lieutenant Governor Clarke received a letter from General James Oglethorpe, from South Carolina, warning of "a villainous Design of a very extraordinary Nature, and, if true, very important, *viz.* That the *Spaniards* had *imployed* Emissaries *to burn all the Magazines and considerable Towns in the* English North-America, *thereby to prevent the Subsisting of the great Expedition and Fleet in the* West-Indies," that is, to deny provisions to British vessels fighting a sea war with Spain. "And that for this Purpose," Oglethorpe warned, "many *Priests* were employed, who pretended to be *Physicians, Dancing-Masters, and other such Kinds of Occupations; and under that Pretence to get Admittance and Confidence in Families.*" Oglethorpe had not been able to confirm this "intelligence" and could not give credit to it, "since the thing was too horrid for any prince to order," but he was sufficiently alarmed to issue the warning.

On June 20, Clarke forwarded Oglethorpe's letter to the Lords of Trade and reported, "Whether or how far the hand of popery has been in this hellish conspiracy I cannot yet discover, but there is room to suspect it, by what two of the Negroes have confest." On June 18, Tom, owned by the English sailmaker Benjamin Moore, had confessed that when he told Cuffee (Philipse) he wouldn't go to Hughson's any more because "what they were going about was a very great Sin . . . *Cuffee* then called him a Fool, and told him, *that if he thought it a wrong Thing, or a Sin, there was a Man that he knew, that could forgive him.*" Only a priest would promise such a thing, and it was a thing Protestants abhorred; absolution gave priests license to encourage depravity. "There was in Town some time ago a man who is said to be a Romish Priest, who used to be at Huson's," Clarke reported, "but [he] has disappeared ever since the discovery of the conspiracy and is not now to be found."9

The suspected priest did not elude capture for long. On June 24, constables arrested a man the court, and especially James DeLancey, would come to consider far more dangerous, *blacker,* than even John Hughson: John Ury, "alias JURY, who had lately come into this City, and entered into Partnership with *Campbell,* a School Master, pretending to teach *Greek* and *Latin.*" Mary Burton was summoned to City Hall to identify him and describe his role in the plot, despite her insistence, in her very first deposition before the grand jury on April 22, that "*she never saw any white Person in Company when they talk'd of burning the Town, but her Master, her Mistress, and Peggy.*"

But before Daniel Horsmanden, Burton swore that "the Person . . . shewn to her in Prison, lately taken into Custody on Suspicion of being a *Roman Catholick Priest,* is the same Person she has often seen at the House of *John Hughson.*" She was not certain of his name ("whether by the Name of JURY or URY, or DOYLE, she cannot now depose positively; but to the best of her Remembrance, some of his Names consisted only of one Syllable, and believes she has heard him called by all the said three Names").10 But she knew this much: he had come to Hughson's almost every night since Christmas, and, although he slept there, he was always gone by the time she woke up. Careful not to contradict her earlier deposition—that she had not seen any other whites but the Hughsons and Kerry talk of the conspiracy—Burton made clear that while she had never heard Ury *speak* of the conspiracy, "she esteemed his Actions and Behaviour to signify his Approbation and Consent." And although she had no real evidence that he was actually a priest, she offered an anecdote: once, "when the Negroes had provoked her, she wished those black Toads at the Devil," to which Ury replied, "*let them be black, or what they will, the Devil has nothing to do with them; I can forgive them their Sins, and you yours too.*"

Two days later, Joseph Murray's slave Adam said that Hughson had told him "*there was a Man that he knew that could forgive him all his Sins.*" What Tom and Adam had to say about Ury was useless, since it was "Negro Evidence" and inadmissible against a white man. Added to Burton's comically corrupt testimony about Ury, it hardly amounted to damning evidence. But when James DeLancey returned to the city and assessed the suspects in jail, he quickly came to consider John Ury the most suspicious among them, and determined to collect evidence against him.

On July 5, DeLancey and Horsmanden met at City Hall and together interrogated William Kane, the soldier who had been implicated by Will at the stake. Kane's great vulnerability to prosecution was that he had been born in Ireland (he had moved to the colonies at the age of six). DeLancey and Horsmanden accused him of being a Catholic. Kane denied it and "Professed himself a Protestant of the *Church of England;* and said, that he never was at any *Roman Catholick* Congregation in his Life." Nor would he admit to knowing John Ury, "nor had he any Acquaintance with him; nor was he ever at any Congregation or Meeting where the said *Jury,* alias *Ury,* either preached or pray'd." At this point in Kane's interrogation, James Mills, the jailkeeper, entered the room and told Kane "that *Mary Burton* had declared, that she had often seen him at *Hughson's.*" Burton, who had been waiting outside the door, was ordered into the room, where she identified Kane and declared her eagerness to offer another deposition, one in which she again risked perjuring herself.

Burton's zeal, apparently, gave DeLancey pause. "The Chief Justice, who was a Stranger to the Transactions concerning the Detection of the Conspiracy," found Burton's eagerness to accuse Kane alarming. He admonished her "in an awful and solemn Manner, concerning the Nature of an Oath, and the Consequences of taking a false one, more especially as it affected a Man's Life." Burton was not to be intimidated. "She was acquainted with the Nature of an Oath very well," she said, and "would not take a false one upon any Account." Burton was sworn, and deposed that Kane, whom she had never mentioned before, had talked with Hughson and his confederates about the plot. She had now directly contradicted her April 22 deposition.

Kane looked as if he might faint, and was given a glass of water. Told that, given Burton's deposition, he "must not flatter himself with the least Hopes of Mercy," he decided to confess. After two hours of questioning, his statement was read aloud to him, and "(not knowing how to write) he put his Mark to it."

William Kane was the first white New Yorker to confess to participating in a plot hatched at John Hughson's house. Parts of his confession followed the formula of earlier slave confessions: "he was at *two Meetings* at Hughson's *about the Plot;* the First was the second Day of Christmas, and

the Second the last Sunday in *February*, before the Fire at the Fort."
(Before Will named Kane, however, not a single slave had mentioned him
in their confessions.) Hughson had sworn him into a plot to burn the city:
"Their Design was *to wait for the* French *and* Spaniards, *whom they
expected; and if they did not come in six Weeks, then they were to try what they
could do for themselves.*" Hughson would be king and Caesar "the *Chief*
among the Negroes." Here was a slight departure: in Kane's new colonial
order, Caesar was noticeably *not* to become the governor of all New Yorkers, white and black, but only chief of the blacks.

Most of Kane's account, however, was at even greater variance with the
slave confessions—it had nothing to do with the "Negro Plot," but was,
instead, a new spin on Hughson's Plot. For one thing, "he, *Kane,* never was
at *Comfort's.*" He had no grievance against slavery, he made no complaints
about his inability to move freely about the town, and he mentioned
nothing about meetings at markets or frolics at the Bowery. Kane also
described a bizarre initiation rite that had never been mentioned in any
earlier interrogation or confession: "there was a *black Ring* made on the
Floor about two Foot and a half Diameter; and *Hughson* bid every one pull
off the left Shoe and put their Toes within the Ring, and Mrs. *Hughson*
held a Bowl of Punch over their Heads as the Negroes stood round the
Circle, and *Hughson pronounced the Oath*"—the slaves swore by thunder
and lightning that "*G-d's Curse and Hell Fire fall on them that first discovered
the Plot*"—"and then *Hughson's Wife* fed them with a Draught out of the
Bowl."

This mystical ceremony was only for blacks, Kane said. Whites separately swore a piratical pledge: "*he first who discovered it was to be hanged at
Low-Water Mark; his Privy-Parts were to be cut out and thrown in his Face;
his Belly ript open, and his Body eaten by the Birds of the Air.*" It was a saltier
version of the Masonic pledge to maintain secrecy on pain of "no less
Penalty than to have my Throat cut, my Tongue taken from the Roof of
my Mouth, my Heart pluck'd from under my Left Breast, them to be
buried in the Sands of the Sea . . . my Body to be burnt to Ashes and be
scatter'd upon the Face of the Earth." It sounded like nothing so much as
the hazing that hapless Daniel Rees had suffered in Philadelphia, at the
hands of the mock Mason Evan Jones. Since Masonry was spread,
throughout the British Empire, largely by lodges attached to regiments of
the British Army, Kane may well have had firsthand experience of it.[11]

The Priest's Plot to which William Kane confessed was not actually a
slave conspiracy at all; it was a conspiracy of clandestine Catholics, with

allegiances to France and Spain. "Most of the Negroes he believed would join them," Kane said, but this was a white conspiracy, a papist plot. It was also a conspiracy of the poor against the rich. "We were to kill the principal people," Kane said. Sworn to this plot, he said, was a crew of white men, two of them soldiers—Peter Connolly and Edward Kelly—and most of them poor—Jerry Corker, John Coffin, David Fagan, Henry Holt, and John Ury, "a little Man" in the city "who acted as Priest" and whose part in the plot was "*to burn the* English Church." Added to these were not only Hughson and his wife but Hughson's father and brothers and his mother-in-law, Elizabeth Luckstead.

By far the oddest element in William Kane's confession, which must have both troubled and thrilled James DeLancey and Daniel Horsmanden, was his description of what would happen in New York after the victory: the conspirators "were to burn what they could of the City, and get what Money and Goods they could and carry them to *Mr. Alexander's* House, which was to be reserved for *Hughson.*" James Alexander, who had quite successfully kept himself and his slaves at arm's length from the investigation during DeLancey's absence, had now become ensnared, and within just days of DeLancey's return. Alexander's opulent, elegant house had been intended, Kane said, as King Hughson's castle, the seat of iniquity, the papist palace.

WILLIAM KANE CONFESSED on July 4. John Hughson's four brothers, Nathaniel, Richard, Walter, and William, along with his father, Thomas—all farmers from outside the city—had been arrested on June 12, although there was no evidence against them until Kane's confession. Jerry Corker and Daniel Fagan eluded arrest. Of the other new white conspirators Kane named, only the two soldiers, Peter Connolly and Edward Kelly, were already in jail; they had been arrested during the last week of June, as suspected papists. Three more white men Kane accused were arrested in the days following his confession: John Coffin, a peddler; David Johnson, a hatmaker; and another soldier, Edward Murphy. These men, like Kane himself, came from the city's vast population of poor whites, unskilled or semi-skilled servants, soldiers, sailors, and apprentices. Most worked alongside slaves, in their masters' houses, along the docks, at the market, in shops. They also drank in the same taverns. Crime was interracial, too. The Geneva Club, that gang of thieves who first banded together in 1738, included not only Caesar, Prince, and Cuffee, but also John Hughson;

Christopher ("Yorkshire") Wilson, the sailor on the *Flamborough;* and probably Arthur Price, servant of that ship's captain. Fagan, Corker, Connolly, Kelly, Coffin, Johnson, and Murphy may have been perfectly innocent of anything but an acquaintance with William Kane; it is just as likely they were petty smugglers who drank at Hughson's and sometimes traded with him.

Whether or not these particular men were a part of it, a loose network of black and poor white thieves and smugglers apparently brought their takings to Hughson in exchange for the occasional feast and the more reliable dram of rum or bowl of punch. Just such an assortment of men— Caesar, Prince, Cuffee, Wilson, and Hughson—was behind the theft of Rebecca Hogg's silver and linen. One of Hogg's servants may also have been involved in the robbery. Just after Kane confessed and began naming his mates, Francis Jones, "a Welchman born," ran away from his master, Robert Hogg. Hogg took out an ad in the *Weekly Journal* offering 20 shillings for his return, describing Jones as "a Tall thin Man of a sickly Couler, about six foot three Inches high or there about, by Trade a Tanner, and Stiles himself a Prize fighter." After Jones ran away on July 11, he disappeared.[12]

Many of the city's working poor were Welsh. But Kane and most of the men he named were Irish, like Mary Burton and Peggy Kerry, and formed the overwhelming number of the city's poor, many of them recent arrivals. Soldiers like Kane and Kelly had probably been driven into the British Army by the Irish famine of 1740–41, the *bliadhain an air* ("year of the slaughter").[13]

Beginning with Kane's confession, Horsmanden and DeLancey made much of the Gaelic origins of their suspects. The fire at the fort, it was now recalled, took place on March 18, the day after St. Patrick's Day. Evidence was quickly discovered that the fire was *intended* for the night of St. Patrick's Day itself, but was delayed. The conspirators, Horsmanden said, "could not have pitch'd upon a fitter Season for perpetrating their bloody Purposes; for on this Night, according to Custom, their Commemoration of their Saint, might be most likely to excite in those of the infernal League, Boldness and Resolution."

That Kane named poor Irishmen to the conspiracy was new, and especially gratifying to prosecutors. But parts of Kane's confession followed accusations made by Adam on June 27. Adam said that he had met "*a little short man four or five Times at* Hughson's, *who used to teach school* at Campbell's." John Ury had been brought to Adam's interrogation room, and

Adam had said that yes, this was the man. Like Kane, Adam had also named Henry Holt, stating that "he saw *Holt,* the Dancing-Master, at *Hughson's* about New-Year Hollidays, at a Meeting of the Negroes, and another white Man belonging to him, whom they called *Doctor,*" whom Horsmanden identified as "Hamilton, *a pretended Doctor who lodged at* Holt's." At the heart of Adam and Kane's confessions, then, were four skilled white men: a Dr. Hamilton (whose first name was never mentioned); John Ury, a Latin instructor; John Campbell, a schoolmaster who had leased John Hughson's house after he was arrested; and Henry Holt, a dancing master.

Hamilton, Holt, Campbell, and Ury fit Oglethorpe's description perfectly. Hamilton, the "pretended Doctor," was never found, or any better identified. Holt, who had probably brought Freemasonry to New York with him from Charleston, had served as a live-in tutor for James DeLancey's children (Kane talked about Holt badly whipping his slave Joe "the Year he left Mr. DeLancey's House"), but he had, rather suspiciously, left the city in March, just after the fire at Fort George. Taking Joe with him, Holt moved to Jamaica. Campbell had opened a school just that spring; beginning on March 30 he advertised in Zenger's *Weekly Journal:* "ENGLISH, Latin, Greek, *Writing, Arithmetick and Merchant's Accompts, carefully Taught at the House of John Campbell's, School Master, living in Bridge Street, New York. N.B. And Youth boarded reasonably.*"[14] But by early June, Campbell's school had failed and he had been confined to the debtor's prison, in the garret of City Hall.

On June 18, just after Oglethorpe's letter arrived in New York, Tom told the grand jury that Cuffee had said that if he thought the plot was "*a wrong Thing, or a Sin, there was a Man that he knew, that could forgive him.*" Constables must have scoured the city for possible priests disguised as teachers and doctors. Holt was gone, Hamilton nowhere to be found, Campbell hapless. John Ury was the best they could find. He had only recently arrived in the city, he had lodged at Campbell's, and had tutored in private homes. He was arrested on June 24. First Mary Burton identified him, then Adam, and then William Kane. John Ury was doomed.

To BE A Roman Catholic priest was illegal in New York in 1741, a crime punishable by death. To be a priest disguised as something else—and, since being a priest was illegal, all priests were disguised—was to be a conjuror, a traitor, a liar, a seducer of women, a confidence man, a spy, a corrupter of children, an agent of the devil, a tyrant, a regicide in the making. This followed a long English tradition. In the conclusion to Horsmanden's *Journal,* he quoted at length from a great wealth of English anti-Catholic literature, "treating of the Intrigues of the Popes and Papists" through the reigns of several English monarchs.[15] In Farquhar's *Beaux' Stratagem,* "the mother of all this mischief is a priest," whom Scrub is able to see through his disguise "Because he speaks English as if he had lived here all his life, and tells lies as if he had been a traveler from his cradle."[16] To be a priest was to be false, cruel, wanton, lecherous, deceitful, treacherous, ruthless, and bloodthirsty.

To be a priest was to forgive sins, and thereby to exonerate the evilest of deeds among the basest of peoples. A New York Act against Jesuits and Popish Priests, passed in 1691, accused "Jesuits *and* Popish Missionaries" of laboring "*to debauch, seduce, and withdraw the Indians from their due Obedience to his sacred Majesty, and to excite and stir them up to* Sedition, Rebellion, *and open* Hostility *against his Majesty's Government.*" Priests might call Indians to war, and slaves to rebellion. They might stand the empire on its head.

But while it was true that New Yorkers' fear of religiously inspired rebellion flowed from Catholicism, and from England's war with Spain and France, it also flowed from Christianity more generally. Protestantism could incite slaves to rebellion, too, and was widely suspected of having played a part in the slave revolt in the city in 1712, which cast a long shadow over the events of 1741.

In the eyes of white New Yorkers, blacks had no religion at all, except for the "Spanish Negroes," who were professed Catholics. But many Africans imported to the city from Central Africa, even if by way of the Caribbean, had already been baptized. The Kongolese King Afonso I had established a Catholic Church in the kingdom of Kongo in the first half of the sixteenth century, and Portuguese colonists in Angola had spread Catholicism there. But if the black men and women they enslaved were Christian, New Yorkers didn't want to know about it. And they had little interest in converting others to Christianity, for fear that it would either set them free or encourage them to revolt. A law in force from the time of English possession in 1664 stipulated that "No Christian shall be kept in Bondslavery villenage or Captivity." It made slaveowners nervous enough that in 1674 a clarification was added: "This law shall not set at liberty any Negro or Indian Slave, who shall have turned Christian after they had been bought by a person." In 1699, King William III urged the passage of

"A Bill for facilitating the conversion of Indians and Negros," but it failed to win the necessary votes in the New York Assembly, "they having a notion that the Negros being converted to Christianity would emancipate them from their slavery." An "Act to Incourage the Baptizing of Negro, Indian and Mulatto Slaves" wasn't passed until 1706, and then only to remedy the "groundless opinion . . . spread itself throughout the colony" that baptizing slaves meant that "they would become free and ought to be set at liberty."[17] Despite repeated assurances that Christ would not put their investments at risk, very few owners encouraged their slaves to become Christian, and few slaves converted, at least until 1704, when a pious French merchant named Elias Neau opened "a Catechising School for the Slaves at *New-York.*"

Neau, a Huguenot, had settled in New York City in 1690, after fleeing violent persecution in Catholic France in 1679. On a business trip to London in 1692, he was captured by French privateers and sentenced to serve as a galley slave; later he was jailed on the infamous island of If off the coast of Marseilles. He was released in 1698, by which time he was a well-known Protestant martyr; in the 1690s, his letters from prison—mystical writings and hymns embracing the utility of despair—were published in Boston, New York, London, and Rotterdam.

Neau knew bondage. Upon his return to New York in 1699, he turned his attention to the spiritual condition of the city's slaves. Although a member of the city's French Huguenot church, Neau began corresponding with Anglican evangelical societies, developing a plan to convert New York's slaves. In 1703, the London-based Society for the Propagation of the Gospel offered Neau an annual salary of £50 to teach slaves, if he would affiliate with the city's Anglican church, Trinity. Neau agreed, and founded the school the following year.[18]

It was, at first, more plan than place. For years Neau simply went door-to-door, offering instruction. After that, a small group of slaves met at night in the attic of his house. "They were dull and sleepy, and remembered they must rise early the next Day, to their Labour." Yet Neau had some success, and eventually boasted a handful of acolytes who had learned to read the Bible, recite catechisms and creeds from memory, and sing from psalm books. The number of his students varied, between fifteen and twenty-five a year, and some, Neau admitted, "came only for the books," showing up to pick up tracts he was distributing and staying away when his bookshelf was empty.

Then came the 1712 slave revolt. Several of the rebels were Neau's converts, including a free black man, Peter the Porter; Mingo, owned by merchant John Barberie; and Caesar, owned by Peter Morin, a brazier. One New Yorker warned the Society for the Propagation of the Gospel that "the Persons whose Negroes have been found guilty are such as are declared opposers of Christianizing Negroes," and hinted that this, and not their "hard usage," formed the motivation for the slave rebellion.

Neau had more credibly reported that the "Horrid Plott" had led New Yorkers to impute "the Rebellion of their Slaves to the Instructing of them." On hearing the news, Neau's funders replied, "It is to be hoped people will conceive better things than be led to believe Christianity makes men worse." At every opportunity, Neau adamantly denied that the Gospel could incite slaves to question slavery, "as if the Christian Religion should not command Obedience to all Inferiors." Still, New Yorkers seemed to think otherwise: "his School was blaimed as the main Occasion" of the plot, and for days, Neau could "hardly appear abroad." When the Common Council issued its response to the revolt—an order forbidding slaves "to go about the Streets after Sun-set, without Lanthorns and Candles"—it was, "in Effect, forbidding them to go to Mr. *Neau's* School, for none of them could get Lanthorns, or come to him before Sunset."

Neau's school would have been closed were it not for the intervention of Governor Robert Hunter, who visited and, as Neau reported, "confirmed by himself that my Scholers have had no share in the Conspiracy of the Negroes." Hunter publicly defended Neau, sent four of his own slaves to his school, and, in a printed proclamation, urged New Yorkers to send to his school "their Children and Servants, Negro and Indian Slaves."

Neau's school survived, and even grew. Between 1704 and 1714, Neau instructed 134 blacks; 85 men and 49 women. In that time he baptized 54 of his pupils. In the year 1719 alone, he catechized 37 black men, 28 women, 12 boys, and 8 girls; of these, 85, 31 were baptized.[19]

After Neau died in 1722, he was succeeded, intermittently, by a series of lackluster schoolmasters. Their work, however, was undoubtedly aided, in 1727, by the publication of the Bishop of London's *Letter to the Masters and Mistresses of Families in the English Plantations abroad; Exhorting them to encourage and promote the Instruction of their Negroes in the Christian Faith*. This pamphlet, widely distributed in New York and throughout the colonies, testified both to slaveowners' considerable and continued unwillingness to convert their slaves and to "how small a Progress has been made . . . towards the delivering of those poor Creatures from the Pagan Darkness." Consider slaves "not barely as Slaves, and upon the same Level with labouring Beasts," the bishop urged his readers, "but as *Men*-Slaves and *Women*-Slaves, who have the same Frame and Faculties as your selves, and have Souls capable of being made eternally happy, and Reason and Understanding to receive Instruction." The bishop also sought, like New York's legislators, to reassure jittery slaveowners that baptism was no liberator: "Christianity and the embracing of the Gospel, does not make the least Alteration in Civil Property," he proclaimed. "The Freedom which Christianity gives, is a Freedom from the Bondage of Sin and Satan, and from the Dominion of Mens Lusts and Passions and inordinate Desires; but as to their *outward* Condition, whatever that was before, whether bond or free, their being baptized, and becoming Christians, makes no manner of Change in it." Nor was baptism likely to make slaves "more ungovernable"; to the contrary, "the Gospel every where enjoins, not only Diligence and Fidelity, but also *Obedience*, for Conscience Sake." Christianity, the bishop insisted, in no way undermines slavery, first, because the brutality of enslaving human beings "is not to be compared to the Cruelty of keeping them in the State of Heathenism"; and second, because a Christian slave will require fewer, and less vicious, corrections, since "one great Reason why Severity is at all necessary to maintain Government, is the *Want* of Religion in those who are to be governed."[20]

But as New Yorkers understood very well, Scripture can counsel obedience, and it can counsel rebellion. In 1730, the *New York Gazette* reported news of "an Insurrection of the Negroes" in Virginia, occasioned by a report that the new governor "had Direction from his Majesty to free all baptized Negroes." This inspired baptized slaves to claim their freedom, which, since their owners denied it, meant staging a rebellion. One enslaved Virginian apparently hid himself in a ship sailing from Williamsburg, "and being examin'd how he came on Board, said he was going Embassador from the Negroes to his Majesty King George."[21]

Beginning in the 1730s, New Yorkers grudgingly agreed to send a handful of their slaves to be educated by the Society for the Propagation of the Gospel minister Richard Charlton. By November 1740, Charlton boasted "that the number of his Catechusans increases, and that the Spiritual Knowledge of some Negroes who attend him, is such as might make many White People Blush."[22]

Charlton had his successes and his failures. Meanwhile, the city was gripped by a religious revival that Charlton found loathsome, as the eighteenth century's most popular evangelical, the Englishman George Whitefield, visited New York. In both England and America, the charismatic Whitefield preached to vast audiences—Samuel Johnson quipped that Whitefield "would be followed by crowds were he to wear a nightcap in the pulpit, or were he to preach from a tree." In Boston, Whitefield's revival meetings were so popular that four people were crushed to death when a meetinghouse balcony collapsed under the weight of the crowd. In New York in April and May 1740, and again in October and November of that year, he preached at the Commons "from a Scaffold, erected for that Purpose," to five or six thousand of "all sorts of People."[23]

Whitefield preached salvation through rebirth and challenged the authority of clergy who had not been born again. His message, with its emphasis on individuals' control over their own salvation, was notoriously appealing to black men and women, as the author of an anonymous poem noted:

> The *Negroes* too he'll not forget,
>> But tells them all to come;
> Invites the *Black* as well as *White*,
>> And says for them there's Room.[24]

In 1740, just before Whitefield visited New York, Benjamin Franklin printed in Philadelphia an essay by Whitefield addressed to "Inhabitants of Maryland, Virginia, North and South Carolina concerning the treatment of their Negroes," in which he meditated on the subject of slavery. Whitefield, like the Bishop of London before him, sought to reassure slaveowners that conversion was no bar to bondage: "I challenge the whole World to produce a single Instance of a Negroe's being made a thorough Christian, and thereby made a worse Servant. It cannot be." Whitefield condemned slaveowners for treating their dogs better than their slaves, but he also deemed slavery potentially useful: "Your present and past bad Usage of them, however ill-designed, may thus far do them good, as to break their Wills, increase the Sense of their natural Misery, and consequently better dispose their Minds to accept the Redemption wrought out for them, by the Death and Obedience of Jesus Christ."

Despite its embrace of slavery as a piety-promoting kind of misery, Whitefield's essay contained a more radical proposition, one that many slaveowners read as a defense of slave rebellion: "considering what Usage they commonly meet with, I have wondered, that we have not more Instances of Self-Murder among the Negroes, or that they have not more frequently rose up in Arms against their Owners. . . . And tho' I heartily pray God they may never be permitted to get the upper Hand; yet should such a Thing be permitted by Providence, all good Men must acknowledge the Judgment would be just."[25]

Throughout the colonies, men blamed Whitefield for their rebellious slaves. Writing from Rhode Island, one minister catalogued "Distractions, occasioned by the Doctrines and Strange Doings of Mr. Whitefield's Disciplines," including "one negro Slave formerly whipt for fornicating with a white woman" who had devised a "new method of preaching to the Blacks, but in the Quaker way," a performance he deemed "an open Burlesq upon that Religion." In New York, Richard Charlton came to blame Whitefield for inspiring the 1741 conspiracy: "Whence it had its rise I will not presume to say; but this I can't help declaring, that Mr. Whitefields letter to the people of Maryland etc gave great countenance to it, and I am Satisfied, that whoever carefully reads it will join in opinion with me; not that I sho'd think Mr Whitefield to be so extreamly wicked as to promote the destruction of this City, with its inhabitants; but the misfortune was that imprudence and indiscretion directed his pen, when he wrote that letter."[26]

Like Neau three decades earlier, Charlton reported with relief that only one of the city slaves he had baptized had been convicted in the conspiracy. This was probably Scipio, who "had had a better Education than most of his Colour." During interrogation, Scipio held "his Bible in his Bosom, which he said he read in Gaol as often as he could." He said that as a child, his owner, attorney Richard Nichols, had sent him to school and taught him to read. Unlike nearly all his fellow inmates, Scipio "appear'd very penitent and sorry for what he had done," Daniel Horsmanden wrote.

Here was a perfect illustration of the bishop's point: "the Gospel every where enjoins, not only Diligence and Fidelity, but also *Obedience,* for Conscience Sake." Horsmanden considered Scipio one of the few men of conscience to be found among the men and women interrogated in 1741. But his piety, even if it was genuine, did little to calm white fears about what Christianity meant for slavery, and nothing to assuage their fears of Catholicism.

THE WEEK THAT James DeLancey returned to New York and William Kane confessed, and that the court's attention began to turn, quite entirely, to a Catholic conspiracy, black men started to recant their confessions. On Wednesday, July 1, Pedro, owned by the Dutch merchant Peter DePeyster, told Constable John Schultz that his confession, which he had made two days before, "was not true." Will, that "expert at Plots," had told him in prison "That he understood these Affairs very well, and that unless he the said *Pedro* did confess and bring in two or three, he would be either hanged or burnt." The same day, a man named Jack, owned by the Dutch felt-maker Henry Breasted, told Schultz that he had falsely accused Hereford, a young boy, although Jack only offered this denial after Hereford's owner, Samuel Myers Cohen, insisted on questioning Jack himself, and urged Schultz to warn him "that *he should Care not to accuse any one unjustly.*"

The next day, London, owned by a butcher named Edward Kelly, con-fessed, and accused three men who had not already been arrested: Jack, owned by the Jewish merchant Judah Hayes; Quash, owned by the French silversmith Charles LeRoux; and York, owned by someone named Lud-low. But the day after that, Friday, July 3, William Nail, the English servant of a butcher named Thomas Cox, came to City Hall and deposed that before London was arrested on June 27, he had talked with him about the many "Negroes that were taken up on Account of the Plot," during which conversation London swore, "By G-d, that if he . . . should be taken up on Account of the Plot, he would hang or burn all the Negroes in *York*, *whether they were concerned or not.*"

The doubts cast over the confessions' truthfulness did not end there. The next day, July 4, when Will was chained to the stake, he said it was Moore's Cato, not him, who had told Pedro to lie, advising him to "say, he was to set his Master's House on fire, which would make the Judges believe him." On July 6, the two men arrested after London (Kelly) impeached them were "discharged by the Third Justice, pursuant to the Recommen-dation of the Grand Jury, who did not credit the Evidence" given by Lon-don. Three days later, a black man named Cambridge, who had confessed the same day as Pedro, and only after spending a month in jail, told Schultz, that he, too, had lied: "he had heard some Negroes talking together in the Jail, that if they did not confess, they should be hanged." Cambridge said "*That the Confession he had made before Messrs.* Lodge *and* Nicholls, *was intirely false.*" Moreover, Cambridge said, "he did not know in what Part of the Town *Hughson* did live, nor did not remember to have heard of the Man 'til it was a common Talk over the Town and Country, that *Hughson* was concerned in a Plot with the Negroes."[27]

"Negro Evidence" was fast losing its credibility. At just this stage in the investigation, on Friday, July 10, Othello was sentenced to be burned, never having been tried. Two days later, Othello, "*under Sentence of Death,*" met with Daniel Horsmanden and offered another confession.[28] He had been to Hughson's, he now admitted, but he had refused to swear to the plot. Othello now supported the prevailing interpretation of a predominantly white, Catholic conspiracy: "He has seen *many Soldiers* at *Hughson's*," he said, although he could not "tell whether they knew or were concerned in the Plot." Hughson told him that if he took part in the plot, "*he would commit no Sin thereby: Othello* understood, it would not hinder him from going to Heaven." (This last remark sounded more like Whitefield, who said slave rebellion was justified and no sin, than like a priest, who could *forgive* the sin of rebellion.) But Othello added that since he had been in jail, Adam had "advised" him to confess "that he was to have killed his Master and Mistress, that that would be a Means of getting him off," but that he had never agreed to do it.

The growing evidence that black men in the dungeon had advised one another to lie failed to halt the proceedings. "*A Criminal confesses himself guilty at his own Peril*," Horsmanden remarked, voicing English legal thought on the matter; "*once he confesses his Guilt, it will be standing Evidence against him.*" A confession could never be unsaid. But there was more than common law behind the court's decision to ignore the recantations. The accused might "*flatter themselves*" that they deserve pardon, "*as if for their Sakes, vile Wretches, the whole Town must run the Risque of their Houses being fired about their Ears, and having the Inhabitants butchered.*" But the accused, "*having once confessed their Guilt, a Recantation and Denial of it afterwards, will scarce be thought an Argument of sufficient Force to prove their Innocence.*" Citing precedent in the trials of slaves accused of conspiracy in Antigua in 1736, Horsmanden concluded: "*The Remark upon Negro Recantations once for all, is, That one can scarce be thoroughly satisfied when it is that they do speak Truth.*"

Yet the recanted confessions were not without effect. They began on Wednesday, July 1, just as James DeLancey made his return. With DeLancey in charge, investigators began processing slaves' pardons and looking on slave confessions with a more critical eye, even starting to discharge men falsely accused and failing to arrest men charged in dubious confessions. Moving away from slaves, they turned their attention more squarely on whites, especially Irish soldiers and suspected priests. Othello himself told DeLancey that he had been urged to lie, to say that he had planned to kill him. But Othello's story also raised the possibility that the entire plot had been a joke. When Adam first "asked him to be concerned; he (*Othello*) said, he would, and laughed." Horsmanden paid this no heed.

THE LAST SLAVE TRIAL, and the only one at which DeLancey presided, was held on Wednesday, July 15, a hot summer's day. In the morning, the court processed the pardons of thirteen black men and one black woman Sarah. All were pardoned on condition of transportation.

In the afternoon of July 15, a new jury was impaneled and eight black men—the only men left in prison who refused to plead guilty—were brought to trial. Mary Burton, William Kane, and six black men testified that they had seen the prisoners at Hughson's. Murray, Smith, and Chambers conducted the prosecution. The jury found all eight men guilty.

The next day, Philipse and Horsmanden sent a letter to Clarke stating their opinion that Othello was not entitled to the benefit of the proclamation of amnesty.[29] That same day, at a meeting of Clarke's Council, Clarke ruled that Othello could not be pardoned. DeLancey asked that Othello's sentence be reduced, from burning to hanging, and Clarke granted the request. It must have given Othello some hope that his life might yet be spared. On Friday afternoon, Othello told Constable Schultz that "he could make very considerable Discoveries relating to the Conspiracy, which he had a Desire to communicate to" the Recorder. Schultz sent a message to Horsmanden later that night. Horsmanden went to City Hall the next morning, Saturday, July 18, and met with Othello. Othello added the names of two more Irish soldiers, Thomas Evans and James O'Brien, and said that "*there were as many white People concerned as Negroes.*" And he insisted, again, that "*Adam* persuaded him, since he came in Jail, to say, that he had agreed to kill his Master and Mistress; and that by saying so, he would get clear: But this was all false, he never engaged to do any such Thing, nor was it ever proposed to him by *Hughson,* or any one else; *only* Hughson told him, he must rise with the Mob, and *kill the People in general,* as the rest were to do." Othello walked a thin line. To save his life, he had to corroborate the story of the plot at Hughson's; but if he hoped to regain DeLancey's favor and his continued intervention on behalf of his slave, he had to deny that he had ever agreed to actually murder the DeLanceys.

Horsmanden later wrote that Othello "behaved upon this Occasion with a great deal of Composure and Decency; with an Air of Sincerity, which very much affected the Recorder." But neither Othello nor his friend Quack, who was to die with him, could be pardoned. "The Judges could by no Means think them proper Objects of Mercy; and had they recommended them to the Governor as such, and his Honour had pardoned them, such Lenity towards them, might have been deemed Cruelty to the People." DeLancey could hardly spare himself the financial loss his court had imposed on so many other slaveowners. Still, it was unnecessary for Othello to burn, when hanging would do just as well.

At noon on Saturday, five of the eight men convicted on July 15 were hanged, one was burned at the stake, and two were reprieved and later transported. One of the men carried to the stake was "Doctor Harry," a "Negro Doctor" from Long Island who had previously been prosecuted for practicing medicine, and who had been accused of providing the plotters with poison, both to be used in poisoning whites and for committing suicide "if they were taken." If he ever had any poison, Harry had not used it in time to spare himself a wretched death. At the stake, Harry was questioned but said, "*it signified nothing to confess.*"[30] Othello, "asked some Questions at the Gallows about the Plot, answered, he had Nothing more to say than what he had this Morning declared to one of the Judges." He was the last "York Negro" to die.

ON JULY 25, a week after Othello's execution, the Supreme Court adjourned. Its spring term, begun April 21, had been extended so many times that it had almost run into the summer term, set to begin July 28. DeLancey closed the court for a brief recess. On July 27, Zenger's *Weekly Journal* reported, "We seem to be easier as to the Thoughts of the Negroes."[31] On July 28, the summer session began, and a new grand jury was called, to conclude the investigation of the Priest's Plot. The next day, John Ury was brought to trial, on a charge that he "of his Malice afore-thought, wickedly, maliciously, voluntarily, willfully and feloniously did counsel, abet, procure and encourage" Quack in setting the fort on fire.

Attorney General Bradley, who had been ill and had not attended court since June 13, opened the indictment, promising to prove that "the Prisoner was actually concerned in the Plot," that "he has frequently been at *Hugh-son's* House," that he swore the black men at Hughson's into the plot, and that he swore them to secrecy by making "a round Ring on the Floor with Chalk," standing in the middle of it "*with a Cross in his Hand,*" and promising to forgive them their sins. In a long aside, Bradley explained that Catholics like Ury "hold it not only lawful but meritorious to kill and destroy all that differ in Opinion from them, if it may any ways serve the Interest of their detestable Religion," which was, in any event, a "*Hocus Pocus,* bloody Religion."

Next, George Joseph Moore, the clerk, read aloud Quack's dying confession, after which Mary Burton was called to the stand, and John Chambers proceeded to question her. "Give the Court and Jury an Account of what you know concerning this Conspiracy," he asked her, "but speak slow, not so hastily as you usually do." Burton said she had often seen Ury at Hughson's "about Christmass and New-Year." He had sworn black men to the plot to burn the city. "I heard *Ury* tell them, they need not fear doing of it, *for that he could forgive them their Sins as well as God Almighty.*" Once, when they were all in a room upstairs, Mary looked under the door and saw "a black Ring upon the Floor, and Things in it, that seemed to look like Rats." Another time, she said, "I was listening at the Door of the Room upon the Stairs . . . and I looked through the Door, and saw upon the Table a black Thing like a Child, and *Ury* had a Book in his Hand, and was reading, but I did not understand the Language; and having a Spoon in my Hand, I happened to let it drop upon the Floor, and *Ury* came out of the Room, running after me down Stairs, and he fell into a Tub of Water, which stood at the Foot of the Stairs, and I ran away." The rats in the circle were supposed to have been black men's toes, as they swore an oath. The "black Thing like a Child," it was hinted, was a baby being baptized; the strange language, Latin.

Ury, conducting his own defense, cross-examined. He asked Burton what clothes he usually wore at Hughson's. Burton replied, "I cannot tell what Cloaths you wore particularly." To which Ury responded, "That is strange, and know me so well."

Next, Chambers called William Kane. Kane said two nights after Christmas he had gone to Coffin's house, where "they had a Child, and *Ury christened it,* and read Latin." Ury had tried to convince Kane to become a Catholic, he said, and was at Hughson's when Hughson swore Kane into the plot.

Again, Ury, on cross-examination, asked Kane what clothes he wore. Kane had a better answer: "I have seen you in black, I have seen you in a yellowish great Coat, and sometimes in a straight bodied Coat, of much the same Colour."

Chambers next called to the stand Sarah Hughson, John Hughson's seventeen-year-old daughter. Ury immediately objected, "for she has been convicted, and received Sentence of Death for being concerned in this Conspiracy, and therefore cannot be a Witness."

Ury was wise to object to Sarah Hughson's evidence against him. Sarah had been arrested on May 6 and tried with her parents on June 4. She was found guilty and, on June 8, sentenced to hang. But on June 11, the day before she and her parents were to die, her execution was postponed "in Hopes, that after her Father and Mother had suffered, she might be mollified to a Confession of her own Guilt, and raise some Merit by making a further Discovery." Sarah proved willful, however, and refused to confess. On July 1, she was again ordered executed, "THIS Criminal continuing inflexible." On July 8, the day of her hanging, she talked with her cellmate, Burk's "Negro Wench," another Sarah, who was to be hanged along with her. Sarah Hughson, according to her cellmate, "at last owned to her, that she had been sworn into the Plot." Sarah (Burk) then called for Mills, and "told what had pass'd between them." (It was this that saved black Sarah's life: instead of being hanged on July 8, she was shipped to Hispaniola one week later.)

Mills called DeLancey and Horsmanden, who came to interrogate Sarah Hughson. She confessed "with great Reluctance," and principally named William Kane and John Ury. But the judges deemed her confession "scanty," and two days later again ordered Sarah's execution. Once again, she confessed on the day she was to be hanged, and her execution was postponed. In her July 10 confession, taken before DeLancey and Horsmanden, young Sarah Hughson described a vast Catholic conspiracy, headed by "*John Ury the Priest,*" who, she said, had "christen'd *Caesar*" and other slaves and had "made her Father and Mother Papists." Peggy Kerry "*was a Roman,*" too.

But the next day, when Sarah was brought before DeLancey, Philipse, and John Chambers for further questioning, "she denied all she had confessed." (Like everyone else who recanted, Sarah recanted when Horsmanden wasn't there.) "Exhorted by those Gentlemen to speak the Truth," she changed her mind again, and said that her confession was true. Her execution was postponed yet again, but because of her recanting, she was not pardoned. In his *Journal,* Horsmanden saw fit to remark, "*From the untoward Behaviour of this Wretch upon her Examinations, the Reader will be apt to conclude, there could be little or no Dependance upon her Veracity . . . and indeed the Case would have been so, if her Testimony had stood single, and not corroborated by many other Witnesses.*" But, however weak a witness, Sarah Hughson was kept alive because she could prove useful at Ury's trial, when witnesses were in scarce supply, since only whites were allowed. Moreover, Sarah's testimony was the crucial link between Hughson's Plot and the Priest's Plot. On July 27, the judges decided that "if she could be affected with a Sense of Gratitude for saving her Life . . . and kept to her History concerning *John Ury . . .* they thought she would be a very material Evidence against him."

When Ury objected that a condemned criminal like Sarah Hughson could not take the stand, Bradley interrupted him: "But Mr. *Ury,* she has received His Majesty's most Gracious Pardon, which she has pleaded in

Court this Morning." Just moments before Ury's trial began—but before Ury had entered the courtroom—Sarah Hughson had finally been pardoned.

Chambers again called Hughson to the stand and asked her to give the court an account of Ury's involvement in the conspiracy. She repeated much of what she had confessed on July 10, that Ury had christened slaves, and had directed them to burn the city, promising that he would forgive their sins. Ury, in cross-examination, asked her who he had baptized, and she answered, "*Caesar, Prince, Bastian, Quack, Cuffee, and several other Negroes.*" Horsmanden said that Sarah, who, during previous interrogations was nearly hysterical, appeared in court "*composed and decent; she seemed to be touch'd with Remorse and Compunction: what came from her, was delivered with all the visible Marks and Semblance of Sincerity and Truth, insomuch, that the Court, Jury, and many of the Audience, looked upon her at this Instant, to be under* real Conviction *of Mind for her past Offences.*"

After Sarah Hughson stepped down, Joseph Murray entered as evidence the letter Lieutenant Governor Clarke had received from General Oglethorpe, warning of priests disguised as schoolmasters and dancing masters. Ury then began his defense, calling several witnesses to establish that he was, in fact, merely a schoolmaster from Philadelphia, and a "Non Jurying Minister," that is, an Anglican minister who refused to recognize the British monarch as the leader of the Anglican Church. Ury was a dissenter, he admitted, but no papist. When Ury called Joseph Webb, an English carpenter who had hired him to teach one of his children Latin, Bradley, on cross-examination, asked Webb, "in your Conversations together, what have you heard him say about Negroes?" Webb answered,

> We were one Day talking about Negroes, and I said, I thought they had Souls to be saved or lost as well as other People; *Ury said, he thought they were not proper Objects of Salvation;* I replied, what would you do with them then, *what would you damn them all?* No, says he, leave them to that Great Being that has made them, he knows best what to do with them; says he, *They are of a Slavish Nature, it is the Nature of them to be Slaves, give them Learning, do them all the Good you can, and put them beyond the Condition of Slaves, and in return, they will cut your Throats.*

Joseph Murray and William Smith then offered further evidence against Ury, reading passages describing priestly sacraments and Catholic doctrine. Ury read a long statement he had prepared for his defense. He asked the jury whether he could be so "Lunatick" as to have organized the plot and then remain in the city for weeks and months after the investigation began. He pointed out that Quack, in his dying confession, never mentioned him, and that "neither *Huson* his Wife nor the Creature that was hanged with them [Peggy Kerry] and all that have been put to Death since did not once name me." With rising passion, Ury addressed the court: "Gentlemen if I am a Priest as you take me to be I could not be so foolish as to engage myself in so absurd a Contrivance as to bind myself with a Cord for Negroes or what is worse profligate Whites the Scum of this Earth."

William Smith "summ'd up the Evidence for the King," conflating Hughson's Plot, the Spanish Plot, and the Priest's Plot, by arguing that the "horrible Plot, to burn and destroy this City" had at last been explained as the result of "a *Foreign Influence*": "a *Spanish* and *Popish Plot*," for "What can be expected from those that profess a *Religion*, that is at War with God and Man?" Ury "*tells you that he must have been a Lunatick to have staid in Town . . . if he had been guilty*," Smith reminded the jury. But "*all Wickedness* is in some sort *Madness*."

DeLancey delivered the charge to the jury, which then withdrew. The trial itself had lasted nine hours. The jury returned after only fifteen minutes, having found John Ury guilty.

URY'S CONVICTION had the effect of somewhat rehabilitating John Hughson. Once an arch rebel against God and country, Hughson was now demoted to "an indigent fellow of a vile character," a mere tool of Ury, little better than the credulous slaves he had also duped. In a letter to the Lords of Trade after Ury's trial, Clarke now summarized the conspiracy differently: Hughson, "casting in his thoughts how to mend his circumstances inticed some Negroes to rob their masters and to bring the stolen to him on promise of reward . . . but seeing that by this pilfering trade riches did not flow into him fast enough and finding the Negroes fit instruments for any villany he then fell upon the scheme of burning the fort and town and murdering the people as the speediest way to enrich himself and them, and to gain the freedom, for that was the Negroes main inducement." Enter John Ury, who converted Hughson to Catholicism, christened slaves, and planned to deliver the city to the Spanish.[32]

On August 4, James DeLancey sentenced Ury to death by hanging. He was to die on Saturday, August 15, along with Juan de la Silva. De la Silva had been convicted on June 17, together with the rest of Lush's "Spanish Negroes." All but he had apparently been pardoned, and were transported out of the colony, although Horsmanden never recorded their pardon or explained why they were made objects of mercy. That Saturday, De la Silva was hanged, "neatly dressed in a white Shirt, Jacket, Drawers and Stockings." He "behaved decently," Horsmanden said, and "prayed in Spanish, kiss'd a Crucifix, insisting on his Innocence to the last." Zenger's newspaper reported that De la Silva "died stedfastly in the Roman Catholick Profession."[33]

Meanwhile, Ury's execution was postponed; he had petitioned Clarke for a delay in order to better prepare his affairs, and to write his dying speech, a long sermon. Two weeks later, Saturday, August 29, Ury was carried to the gallows. He tried to read his speech, protesting his innocence, but "was turn'd off." Zenger reported that Ury "died intrepid and without showing the least Concern at Death." Death "is the Cup that my Heavenly Father has put into my Hand," said Ury, "and I drink it with Pleasure."[34]

CHAPTER SEVEN

Ink

D ANIEL HORSMANDEN did not watch John Ury die. The day
after Ury's sentencing, Horsmanden left for Albany, to preside
at a circuit court, glad to be away from New York, glad for a
break. En route, on August 7, he wrote to Cadwallader Colden. "After a
long cessation of Correspondence I take the Liberty of resuming the pen,"
he began. "Ever since the fire at the Fort," he explained, "I've been engag'd
in perpetual hurry, insomuch that I've been forced to dedicate part of my
resting time to the publick Service." The investigation into the conspiracy
had been grueling, Horsmanden complained, "but I think the Labour
bestowed has not been in Vain; for tho' the Mystery of Iniquity has been
unfolding by very Smal & Slow Degrees, it has at length been discovered
that popery was at the Bottom."

As Horsmanden told it in his *Journal,* he had groped through a "Maze
of Obscurity" to reach "the Bottom," the truth: the Priest's Plot. By the
time the investigation came to a close, Horsmanden had little choice but
to follow DeLancey's lead in asserting that the Catholic conspiracy contained within it all of the plots his investigation had earlier focused on:
Hughson's Plot of thieving mock Masons and Christmas revelers, the
"Negro Plot" of aggrieved black men planning arson and murder, and the
Spanish Plot of war and liberation. All of these, Horsmanden now maintained, were simply elements of the Priest's Plot. Hughson, Quack, Cuffee, the "Spanish Negroes," Jack, William Kane—all were mere tools of
John Ury.

"The Mystery of Iniquity has been unfolding," Horsmanden wrote
Colden. With these words, he boasted that his tireless inquiry had solved
nothing less than the problem of evil, the *Mysterium iniquitatis* of 2 Thes-
salonians (2:7–8): "For the mystery of iniquity doth already work. . . . And

then shall that Wicked be revealed, whom the Lord shall consume with the spirit of his mouth, and shall destroy with the brightness of his coming." In this, as in much of what Horsmanden wrote about the conspiracy, he employed language more often used to describe witchcraft. "This most horrible & Detestable piece of Villainy," Horsmanden told Colden, "must have been brooded in a Conclave of Devils, & hatcht in the Cabinet of Hell." And still New Yorkers refused to see the peril they had only very nearly escaped. Already Horsmanden was filled with resentment that New Yorkers were ungrateful for his work. Worse, they had begun to condemn the proceedings as unjust. "Tho' we have been So Successfull in prying into this Scene of Darkness & horror As to bring to Light near 90 Negroes & I think about a Dozen Whites Engaged to be actors in this black Tragedy," he wrote. "And tho' the Town were well pleas'd with the first fruits of Our Labours & inflicting the deserved punishment on the Offenders. Yet when it comes home to their own houses, & is like to affect their own propertys in Negroes & Cosinship in others; then they are alarm'd & they cry out the Witness must needs be perjured."

"Some among us," Horsmanden told Colden (but he did not say who) had made two complaints. First, they doubted the slave confessions, to which Horsmanden replied in exasperation, "How can a Discovery of Such works of Darkness be expected but from some of the Confederates themselves; & if the witnesses are kept apart & Examined apart as most of them have been in both Instances upon most if not all the Trials, & their respective Testimonys Tally & agree, what better Evidence can be desired or expected?" Second, they had taken "great pains . . . to bring a discredit upon Mary Burton," a girl Horsmanden considered "the happy Instrument of all this Discovery."

Horsmanden had a good deal to say about these doubters, "*wanton, wrong-headed Persons amongst us, who took the Liberty to arraign the Justice of the Proceedings, and set up their private Opinions in Superiority to the Court and Grand Jury. . . . God knows,*" he complained, "*they could not be Judges of such Matters; but nevertheless, they declared with no small Assurance (notwithstanding what we* saw *with our Eyes, and* heard *with our Ears, and everyone might have judg'd of by his Intellects, that had any*) That there was no Plot at all!*"

Horsmanden never named his critics, but in this letter to Colden he suggested that they had only begun to call the proceedings into question "when it comes home to their own houses, & is like to affect their own propertys in Negroes." This seems to have happened in July, and there is good reason to believe that among those critics was James Alexander, whose name was first mentioned in the proceedings on July 4, when William Kane told DeLancey and Horsmanden that, after the city was burnt, Hughson was to make Alexander's house his palace. That Alexander's slaves were not all hauled to City Hall for questioning after that remark is extraordinary, although it is easily explained if Alexander had begun to urge DeLancey to halt the trials.

Although Alexander, along with all the other Gentlemen of the Law, had been enlisted to serve the prosecution, he had all but boycotted the proceedings. He did not participate in the prosecution of even a single "York Negro." He was listed among the "Council for the King" in only three trials: the June 4 trial of the Hughsons and Peggy Kerry; the June 17 trial of the "Spanish Negroes"; and the July 29 trial of John Ury. But, even in these three trials, he never delivered a speech, addressed the jury, or examined a witness. (In each of these cases, every other lawyer listed specifically participated.) Nor did Alexander ever minute a confession, conduct an interrogation, or contribute to the prosecution in any other way, as is both established in Horsmanden's *Journal* and confirmed in surviving manuscript records. And although Alexander owned several slaves and lived in the very heart of the city, next door to where the first robbery had taken place, none of his slaves were ever accused. Moreover, Alexander's papers, which are unusually abundant and well preserved, include almost no mention of the proceedings after April 22, the day after the Supreme Court opened its session.

If James Alexander criticized the trials, his criticism has not survived. But whoever called the proceedings into question had good cause. As a category of testimony, "Negro Evidence" had been dubious from the start. And Burton's evidence, too, had long since strained credibility. The minute he met her, James DeLancey warned Burton not to perjure herself. But so long as Burton stuck to the same story, of black plotters at Hughson's "Great Feast," she was safe, no matter how many more black men she "remembered" having been there.

Publicly voiced doubts about Burton began in earnest when she accused John Ury in late June, but her credibility was much more grievously damaged "when the first Grand Jury drew near their Discharge," that is, just before July 25, when she began hinting that prominent whites were involved in the plot: "about this time she had suggested to some, that there were white People of more than ordinary Rank above the vulgar, that were concerned, whom if she told of they would not believe her."

The grand jury pressed Burton "to discover all she knew, whoever they were; but the Girl stood mute; nor could the Grand Jury prevail with her to name any, not with Threatenings of Imprisonment." Eventually, they handed her over to "Two of the Judges," probably DeLancey and Horsmanden.

At first, Burton would only complain of her lot. She told them "she had been very ill used; that . . . her Life had been threatened by Conspirators of both Complexions . . . and frequently insulted by People of the Town for bringing their Negroes in question." Petulant, Burton cried, "People did not believe what she said, and what signified speaking?" Prevailed upon, she eventually told the judges "that there were some People *in Ruffles* (a Phrase as was understood to mean Persons of better Fashion than ordinary) that were concerned." (Kane, too, had hinted that men of refinement were involved in the plot. On July 17, he said that he had often seen "a *young Gentleman with a Pigtail Wig*" at Hughson's, although he refused to identify him.) Burton said she was not willing to name names. But after being told that "she must expect to be imprisoned in the Dungeon," she "named several Persons which she said she had seen at *Hughson's* amongst the Conspirators, talking of the Conspiracy, who were engaged in it; amongst whom she mentioned several of known Credits, Fortunes, and Reputations, and of Religious Principles superior to a Suspicion of being concerned in such detestable Practices." (And here again, it's easy to suppose that Burton named James Alexander himself, especially if he had been publicly calling her credibility into question. Kane had already mentioned him by name.)

At this, the judges "were very much astonished." In his letter to Colden, Horsmanden remarked, "We could not but be Shockt, the persons mentioned being beyond Suspition; & the Consequence followed, that great Clamor has thence been raised against her & now, by Some, She must be esteemed a person of no Credit."

Now Daniel Horsmanden faced a dilemma. If Mary Burton was a liar, she had likely lied from the start, in which case Peggy Kerry, Sarah Hughson, John Hughson, and seventeen black men had been hanged for nothing, and thirteen innocent black men had been burned at the stake. Horsmanden refused to believe it. He decided to suspend credit; he had always found Burton disarming, even captivating. He believed he had rescued her, a helpless girl, from depravity. He admired her. "The things She Says, cannot but Stagger ones belief," he wrote Colden, "but I must observe, this is not the First time her Examinations have had that Effect upon me, but Several times, from my first taking her in hand, yet til now, every thing that has come from her, has in the Event been confirmed; but here must be a Suspension of Credit for a while, & time only can clear the matter up."[1]

With the reputation of Mary Burton and the justice of the proceedings at stake, it didn't take Horsmanden long to conclude that Burton had indeed lied about the "People in *Ruffles*." But he chose to believe that she had done so only because as yet undetected conspirators had corrupted her, with the intention of destroying her credibility and halting the investigation.[2] It was not that Burton had made up the plot, but that, in July, she had been tricked, by the conspirators themselves, into naming certain eminent men.

> [T]he conspirators could not have devised a more effectual Means (if they could but prevail with her) to put a Stop to further Enquiry, to procure the Names of Persons to be called in question at last, concerning this Scene of Villainy, whose Fortunes and Characters set them above Suspicion: They very well knew . . . if they could but prevail in this, they would thereby not only put a Stop to further Discovery, but likewise have some Pretence, according to their usual Custom, to clamour loudly, *there was no Plot at all; 'twas a mere Dream!*

That Burton must have been prevailed upon to lie, Horsmanden argued, in no way called into question any of her earlier testimony. Instead, it only provided more evidence that key conspirators remained at large.

By the end of July, New Yorkers were insulting Mary Burton on the street and crying, "There was no plot!" According to Horsmanden, the outcry came from two kinds of people: the undetected conspirators who had "tampered" with Burton; and "Owners of Slaves, who happened to humour this Artifice" in order to put a stop to their loss of property. The detection of the conspiracy, after all, had come at considerable cost, not only to private individuals but also to the city and the province. The Common Council had paid a carpenter to build gallows and gibbets, and gave jailkeeper James Mills a bonus for his extra work. By August, owners whose slaves had been accused were encouraged to avoid trial altogether, and instead arrange to sell their suspected slaves, so as not to incur the costs of their trial and possible execution. Nor did the expenses end with the closing of the investigation. There was the cost of paying the new white "Tea-Water Men," the charge of the greatly expanded night watch, and the fees due to constables enforcing the law, passed in 1743, prohibiting "any Negro or other Slave" from buying "Victualls or provisions" at any market in the city. When the Assembly asked Clarke for crown money to pay for rebuilding Fort George, the lieutenant governor instead recommended "a Provincial Tax which would hardly be felt." And, if the Assembly sought relief from the crown, the city sought relief from the Assembly: in 1742, the Common Council presented the legislature with a petition "Praying that the Negroes: Executed. for the Late Conspiracy: may be paid for out of the Revenue."[3]

To execute slaves was to burn money. Mary Burton was cursed on every street corner.

THE SAME WEEK that Cadwallader Colden received Daniel Horsmanden's letter complaining that New Yorkers had come to question the proceedings, he received another letter whose author suggested that New Yorkers had suffered "in the merciless Flames of an Imaginary Plot."

Sometime between July 15 and August 6, someone delivered an envelope, addressed "To the Honourable Cadwallader Colden Esq at New York," to Colden's daughter, Elizabeth Colden DeLancey, who lived in the city. Elizabeth forwarded the letter to her father, who lived sixty miles away, at Coldengham, his country estate. "I inclose a letter which I receiv'd by the Boston Post," she explained. Colden received it on Saturday, August 8. It is the sole surviving criticism of the trials (as opposed to Horsmanden's representation of that criticism). It is eloquent, and startling, and worth reading closely:

> Sr
> I am a stranger to you & to New York, & so must beg pardon for the mistakes I may be guilty off in the subsequent attempt; The Design whereof is to endeavour the putting an end to the bloody Tragedy that has been, & I suppose still is acting amongst you in regard to the poor Negros & the Whites too. I observe in one of the Boston News letters dated July 13th that 5 Negros were executed in one day at the Gallows, a favour indeed, for one next day was burnt at the stake, where he impeached several others, & amongst them some whites. Which with the former horrible executions among you upon this occasion puts me in mind of our New England Witch-

craft in the year 1692 Which if I dont mistake New York justly reproached us for, & mockt at our Credulity about; but may it not now be justly retorted, *mutato nomine de te fabula narratur.* What grounds you proceed upon I must acknowledge my self not sufficiently informed of; but finding that these 5 who were put to Death in July denied any Guilt, It makes me suspect that your present case, & ours heretofore are much the same, and that Negro & Spectre evidence will turn out alike. We had near 50 Confessors, who accused multitudes of others, alledging Time & Place, & Various other circumstances to render their Confessions credible, that they had their meetings, form'd confederacies, sign'd the Devils book &c. But I am humbly of Opinion that such Confessions unless some certain Overt Act appear to confirm the same are not worth a Straw; for many times they are obtain'd by foul means, by force or torment, by Surprise, by flattery, by Distraction, by Discontent with their circumstances, through envy that they may bring others into the same condemnation, or in hopes of a longer time to live, or to dy an easier death &c. For any body would chuse rather to be hanged than to be burnt. It is true I have heard something of your Forts being burnt, but that might be by Lightning from Heaven, by Accedent, by some maliceous person or persons of our own colour. What other Feats have been performed to petrify your hearts against the poor blacks & some of your neighbours the whites, I cant tell; But 2 things seem impossible to me almost *in rerum natura,* That the whites should join with the Blacks, or that the Blacks (among whom there are no doubt some rational persons) should attempt the Destruction of a City when it is impossible they should escape the just & direfull Vengeance of the Countries round about, which would immediatly & unavoidably pour in upon them & destroy them

Possibly there have been some murmuring amongst the Negroes & a mad fellow or 2 has threatened & design'd Revenge, for the Cruelty & inhumanity they have met with, which is too rife in the English Plantations (& not long since occasioned such another tremendous & unreasonable Tragedy at Antego) And if that be all it is a pity there have been such severe animadversions. And if nothing will put an end hereto till some of higher degree & better circumstances & Characters are accused (which finished our Salem Witchcraft) the sooner the better, lest all the poor People of the Government perish in the merciless flames of an Imaginary Plot.

In the mean time excuse me & dont be offended, if out of Friendship to my poor Countrymen & compassion to the Negros (who are flesh & blood as well as we & ought to be treated with Humanity) I intreat you not to go on to Massacre & destroy your own Estates by making Bonfires of the Negros & perhaps thereby loading yourselves with greater Guilt than theirs. For we have too much reason to fear that the Divine Vengeance does & will pursue us for our ill treatment to the bodies & souls of our poor slaves and therefore

Let Justice be don to your own people, whatever Treatment the People of the Massachusets may meet with when you set in Judicature about their affairs. All which is humbly submitted by a Well wisher to all humane Beings & one that ever desires to be of the mercifull side &c.

The letter was unsigned and undated. It made Cadwallader Colden's blood boil. Two days after he received it, he made a copy, which he kept for himself, and sent the original to Clarke, in the city. Colden was certain the letter was written by "a feign'd hand." He suspected that it had not in fact come from Boston, but was written by someone in New York who wanted to disguise his identity. He hinted that Clarke would do well to consult with the postmaster, who, "upon viewing the Cover [might] perhaps recollect whether such a letter really came by the Post or whether it came in the Boston bag or only by the Post man for it may have been sent to my Daughter as from the Post house tho' otherwise."[4]

Clarke could have received Colden's letter, with its enclosure, as early as August 9, if it was sent express, by a fast rider. Soon after he received it, Clarke showed the letter to James DeLancey, and the two men tried to guess its author. Horsmanden was by now in Albany, and unavailable for consultation. On August 18, Clarke returned the letter to Colden. (The original has since been lost; all that survives is the copy in Colden's handwriting.) Clarke told Colden, "I fear it will be difficult to discover the author." But Clarke and DeLancey were unpersuaded that it had been written by a New Yorker pretending to be a Bostonian, "for it seemes to be wrote by an angry man, and it may be in your Examinations you may have wrung a Conscience too close."[5]

Those "Examinations" were the work of the committee on which Colden and DeLancey had served in Providence from April 1 to June 30, arbitrating a boundary dispute between Massachusetts and Rhode Island. Clarke hinted that the writer was a member of the commission, composed of delegates from Massachusetts and Rhode Island and members of the Governors' Councils of New York and Newfoundland. Both Massachusetts and Rhode Island claimed Bristol County, on the bay of Mount Hope, once the homeland of the Wampanoag grand sachem Massasoit, and later of his two sons, Alexander (alias Wamsutta) and Philip (alias Metacom). After the English defeated the Wampanoags in King Philip's War, in 1675–76, those lands became part of Plymouth Colony. But when Plymouth became part of Massachusetts, Rhode Island claimed Philip's homeland.

After weeks of examining deeds and conducting interrogations, the commissioners ruled in favor of Rhode Island, and Massachusetts lost Bristol County. The Massachusetts members blamed the decision on the New York delegates—"A gentleman of the council of New-York had great influence at the board of commissioners" when he argued that Massachusetts was already too big and Rhode Island too small. It was not lost on the Bay Colony commissioners that this argument also served New York in advancing its own boundary claims against Massachusetts, which, at the time, was the larger province, as it included all of what is now the state of Maine.

Five New York members of Clarke's Council served on the commission: Colden, DeLancey, Abraham Van Horne, Philip Livingston, and Archibald Kennedy. Any one of them could have been the "gentleman of the council of New-York" who dominated the discussion, basing his argument not on deeds and land claims but on the relative size of the two provinces. But Colden, who also served as New York's surveyor-general, was the most likely man to make this argument, especially as he was most intimately acquainted with the importance of this dispute for his own colony.[6]

"You may have wrung a Conscience too close," Clarke wrote to Colden. And he suggested that Colden, who was on the eve of a return voyage to New England to discuss an appeal of the commissioners' decision, might have better luck finding the anonymous letter writer there than Clarke and DeLancey had had in New York.

There is good reason to believe that Clarke was right. The letter's penultimate sentence strongly supports the idea that its author was one of the Massachusetts members of the commission: "Let Justice be don to your own people, whatever Treatment the People of Massachusets may meet with when you set in Judicature about their affairs." It reads as a double entendre, referring both to New Yorkers' redrawing of the Bay Colony's boundary with Rhode Island and to their condemnation of Massachusetts for the witchcraft trials. (In 1692, New Yorkers *had* condemned the trials; one New York minister wrote to Massachusetts governor Sir William Phips, "The minds of men, especially of the ignorant or depraved, can easily be and frequently are deceived by the devil.")[7]

Ten Massachusetts men served on the commission. Who wrote the letter? The best hint lies in the author's discussion of the 1692 trials: "We had near 50 Confessors, who accused multitudes of others, alledging Time & Place, & Various other circumstances to render their Confessions credible, that they had their meetings, form'd confederacies, sign'd the Devils book &c." Here was more than passing acquaintance with the story of Salem; this was specific knowledge. As it turns out, this description appears to be a paraphrase of a passage in Reverend John Hale's *Modest Enquiry into the Nature of Witchcraft,* printed in Boston in 1702: "the . . . confessors . . . amounted to near about Fifty. . . . And many of the confessors confirmed their confessions with very strong circumstances: As their exact agreement with the accusations of the afflicted; their punctual agreement with their fellow confessors; their relating the times . . . their Witch meetings . . . their signing the Devils book."[8]

John Hale was a minister from Beverly who had been involved in the witchcraft trials but had almost immediately regretted that involvement. He began writing his *Modest Enquiry* in 1697 in order "to prevent for the future such sufferings." He explained, "Among Satans Mysteries of iniquity, this of Witchcraft is one of the most difficult to be searched out by the Sons of men," but in their search in 1692, grievous errors had been committed, including the court's reliance on spectral evidence. "What grief of heart it brings to a tender conscience, to have been unwittingly encouraging of the Sufferings of the innocent." Hale completed his book in 1698 but was reluctant to publish it. He died in 1700. Two years later, his *Modest Enquiry* was finally printed.

By 1741, *Modest Enquiry* had been out of print for almost forty years. It was a rare book. But whoever wrote that anonymous letter to Cadwallader Colden had a copy handy. Whoever wrote to Colden not only owned Hale's *Modest Enquiry;* he also understood legal matters, knew Latin, read Boston newspapers, followed foreign news closely, and—the most difficult criterion to satisfy of all—believed in the essential humanity of Africans: "who are flesh & blood as well as we."

Such sentiments had long been voiced in Boston: in 1700, the Bostonian Samuel Sewall had argued that "Ethiopians, as black as they are," are "brethren and sisters of the last Adam, and the offspring of God." Elsewhere, such views were expressed most often by Quakers, as part of an emerging anti-slavery movement. The London Yearly Meeting condemned slave trading as early as 1727. Two years later, Benjamin Franklin printed a tract by a Philadelphia Quaker, Ralph Sandiford, entitled *A Brief Examination of the Practice of the Times,* in which he called slavery "the most arbitrary and tyrannical oppression that hell has invented on this globe." (Sandiford's book was reprinted the following year under the title *The Mystery of Iniquity;* for Sandiford, the problem of evil was slavery itself, not slave rebellion.) In 1738, Franklin printed a call by another Philadelphian, Benjamin Lay, addressed to *All Slave-Keepers, That keep the Innocent in Bondage.* Lay, an ascetic who lived in a cave, railed against slavery at Quaker meetings throughout the middle colonies. In New Jersey in 1738, he hid a bladder filled with pokeberry juice in a hollowed-out book and called out to the meeting, "Oh all you Negro masters who are contentedly holding your fellow creatures in a state of slavery. . . . It would be as justifiable in the sight of the Almighty . . . if you should thrust a sword through their hearts as I do through this book!" With that, he drew a sword and stabbed the book, which burst, splattering the crowd with pokeberry juice blood.

In 1741, John Bell in London warned Quaker slaveowners in the colonies that the "Vials" of God's "Wrath shall be poured forth upon the Unmerciful, the cruel Oppressors, and all the Workers of Iniquity." Five years later, the colonial Quaker John Woolman, in his essay "Some Considerations on the Keeping of Negroes," reminded readers "that all nations are of one blood." Like Bell and George Whitefield, Woolman also warned of God's vengeance: "Many slaves on this continent are oppressed, and their cries have reached the ears of the Most High! Such is the purity and certainty of his judgments that he cannot be partial in our favour. . . . Should we now . . . neglect to do our duty . . . it may be that terrible things in righteousness God may answer us."[9]

Whoever wrote that letter to Cadwallader Colden echoed all of these writings when he warned: "For we have too much reason to fear that the Divine vengeance does & will pursue us for our ill treatment to the bodies & souls of our poor slaves." But the writer also appears to have been a slaveowner himself.

MOST OF THE MASSACHUSETTS COMMISSIONERS understood the law, knew their history, and several had Salem connections.[10] But the person most likely to have written the letter to Colden is Benjamin Lynde, Chief Justice of the Massachusetts Superior Judicial Court and the father of one of the commissioners, Benjamin Lynde, Jr. Lynde the elder was born in Boston in 1666 and admitted to Harvard in 1682, where he quickly became a master of Latin and Greek. In 1692, while spectral evidence damned witches to their deaths in Salem, Lynde was in London, studying law at the Inns of Court. He returned to Massachusetts in 1697 and, two years later, married Mary Browne and settled in her hometown: Salem. (Lynde's wife's father, William Browne, was Judge of Common Pleas for Essex, and her uncle, Jonathan Corwin, had been a judge during the witchcraft trials.) In 1712, Lynde was appointed to the Superior Court. Three years later he began living in a house in Salem, given to his wife by her father, but previously owned by William Hathorne, ancestor of Nathaniel Hawthorne). In this house, Lynde discovered the manuscript confession of one of the afflicted girls, Abigail Hobbs, which he later shared with a historian compiling a history of Massachusetts.

In 1728, Benjamin Lynde, Sr., was promoted to Chief Justice of the Massachusetts Superior Judicial Court. In 1734, while New Yorkers burned a black man at the stake for *attempted* rape, Lynde presided over a similar case in Boston, where a black man named London was charged with rape. Lynde sentenced him to hang. Although Lynde headed a court more merciful to slaves than New York's bench, he was himself a slaveowner. In 1736 he purchased for his own use a "a negro boy about 12 years old," to whom he gave the name Scipio. But Lynde was also sympathetic to the idea that slavery was an evil. The same year that he bought Scipio, Lynde presided at the Admiralty Court trial of John Barns, a slave trader accused of murdering a black boy on board his ship. Lynde recounted the case at considerable length in his diary, reporting that Barns's lawyer had argued "that the negro boy was a slave, and, as master of the cargo, the said Barns might do what he would with him, even to the taking away his life." Lynde, presiding over a court without a jury, found Barns guilty of murder.

Lynde also prided himself on his generosity to his own two slaves, Scipio and William. On May 27, 1741, slaves in Salem celebrated Negro Election Day, which Lynde noted in his diary, recording gifts of cash: "Election; Negro's halloday here at Salem; gave Scip. 5s and Wm 2s. 6d." Lynde knew about role reversals and topsy-turvy rituals.

If Lynde wrote the letter to Colden, he could have posted it from Boston or Cambridge, where he was attending court from July 28 to August 1. On August 25 he was back in Boston, presiding at the trial of four white men accused of whipping a black man to death; all four were found guilty of "homicide by misadventure."[11] With Benjamin Lynde at the center seat on the Superior Court, justice in Massachusetts looked rather different than it did in New York.

Whether Benjamin Lynde wrote the letter is probably impossible to prove. Whoever its author, the letter sent to Colden quite remarkably illustrates the range of thinking about slavery and race in the northern colonies in 1741. In a world where it was possible to burn black men at the stake as monsters, it was also possible to see them as humans unjustly oppressed, whose rebellion would be just in the eyes of God.

Colden believed that the writer was a New Yorker disguising himself as a Bostonian.[12] This is difficult to credit. All the same, it seems strange that just after Burton began accusing "People *in Ruffles,*" a letter, supposedly from Boston, arrived in New York, pleading that "if nothing will put an end hereto till some of higher degree & better circumstances & Characters are accused (which finished our Salem Witchcraft) the sooner the better, lest all the poor People of the Government perish in the merciless flames of an Imaginary Plot"—when news of accusations of men "of higher degree & better circumstances & Characters" probably never reached Boston. Mary Burton's high-profile accusations were probably never printed in any newspaper, and the names of the men she accused were barely whispered in New York, except at City Hall.

"THE DESIGN" of the letter was "to endeavour the putting an end to the bloody Tragedy." By the time Colden received it, on August 8, that tragedy had run its course. But the letter did ensure that the trial proceedings would be published. As Colden wrote to Clarke, "I am of Opinion it may be Proper to publish the Priests Tryal & the other Material Evidences of the Plot to prevent the prevailing of such an Opinion."[13] Horsmanden himself had written on August 7, "We come under a Necessity of making a Sort of Stand."

In November 1741, the Assembly voted to pay Daniel Horsmanden £250 to research and digest the laws of the colony, in order that they might be printed. Horsmanden accepted the payment, but used it, instead, to collect and prepare the conspiracy proceedings for publication—and not just Ury's trial, as Colden had suggested, but the entire investigation. Out of loyalty to DeLancey, Horsmanden was willing to defend Ury's conviction, but if he were to bother to vindicate the proceedings, he was keen to detail Hughson's Plot, with its political message about the dangers of party. Still, he despaired of persuading those who said "That there was no Plot at all!" "(*for that would have been a vain Undertaking;* the Æthiopian might assoon [*sic*] change his Skin)." If Horsmanden was motivated largely by political concerns, he also wanted to rehabilitate his reputation, and he hoped to earn some money.[14] But Horsmanden also wrote to rescue Mary Burton's reputation, and to ensure that she would receive her reward.

After the trials ended, Horsmanden took a break before picking up his pen. "*It was some Time before the Compiler could submit himself to undergo a Drudgery of this kind,*" he explained to his reader, for "*the Task was not very inviting, and he had borne a sufficient Fatigue, under an ill State of Health, in the Share he had in the Proceedings themselves.*" (What ailed him was never mentioned.) In the days, weeks, and months immediately following Ury's execution, Horsmanden, Philipse, and DeLancey tied up the loose ends of the investigation. On August 31, the Irish soldiers and assorted poor whites named by William Kane—John Corry, Andrew Ryan, Edward Kelly, Edward Murphy, Peter Connolly, John Coffin, and David Johnson—were discharged. On September 24, under Clarke's order, the city marked a Day of Thanksgiving, to give thanks to God for "the Deliverance of his Majesty's Subjects here from the Destruction wherewith they were so generally threatned by the late Conspiracy." A month later, John Hughson's father and brothers were pardoned, "upon Condition of their leaving the Province."

Meanwhile, Mary Burton, who had been promised her freedom, remained a servant. She had left Hughson's house on March 3, 1741. For a few nights, she stayed with the jailkeeper James Mills in his garret apartment at City Hall. Sometime before the fire at the fort, on March 18, she had been placed in the house of a man named Thomas Wilson, and became his servant; Wilson must have paid Hughson for her indenture. On June 19, 1741, the Common Council paid Wilson £10 "for the time of his Servant Mary Burton: and for the Cloaths he has purchased for her." Why Wilson chose to sell Mary Burton is unclear. But, in buying Burton's "time"—the remaining years of her indenture—from Wilson, the Common Council did not free her. Instead, Burton became a servant of the Corporation of the City of New York.

Mary Burton believed she was due the reward that the Common Council had promised, in a proclamation of April 11, 1741, "to any white person. that Shall Discover any person or persons lately Concern'd in Setting fire to any Dwelling House. or Store House in this City. (So that Such person or persons As be Convicted thereof) the Sum of One hundred pounds." But it seems likely that the Common Council, which proved unresponsive to her request, believed she was not eligible for the reward since her most substantial discoveries—exposing the plot and naming Caesar, Prince, Cuffee, the Hughsons, and Kerry—had come before April 11. Over the summer, when Mary Burton was being damned in the streets, she knew better than to press her case. But she must have bridled at her continued servitude, as did Daniel Horsmanden.

By winter, Horsmanden had begun stirring up fears of slave rebellion once again. A January 1742 letter, signed by Clarke but undoubtedly written by Horsmanden, lamented that "the Insolence of the Negroes is as great, if not greater, than ever." "One would think our signal Preservation could never be forgot," Clarke remarked, warning that more conspirators were at large: "*though we have felled the Tree, I fear it is not entirely rooted up.*" Over the next two months, Horsmanden tried to generate interest in conducting more prosecutions, especially after a fire broke out at a house near the Old Dutch Church in February. A slave named Tom, owned by Mrs. Divertie Bradt, was arrested and tried in the municipal court. A jury of five freeholders, including James Alexander, found him guilty. On March 2, 1742, Horsmanden, in his capacity as Recorder, delivered the sentence before "a large Audience," taking the occasion to remind New Yorkers of the nature of their slaves and to "awaken the People to a Sense of their Danger."[15] His hatred of blacks was, if anything, even more zealous than it had been the year before. "You Negroes are treated here with great Humanity and Tenderness," Horsmanden said to Tom, but

Such worthless, detestable Wretches are many, it may be said most, of your Complexion, that no Kindness can oblige ye; there is such an Untowardness, as it should seem, in the very Nature and Temper of ye, that ye grow cruel by too much Indulgence: So much are ye degenerated and debased below the Dignity of Humane Species. . . . even the very Dogs . . . will, by *their Actions* express *their* Gratitude to the Hand that feeds them, their Thankfulness for Kindnesses; they will fawn and fondle upon their Masters; nay, if any one should attempt to assault them, they will defend them from Injury, to the utmost of their Power. Such is the *Fidelity* of these *dumb Beasts;* but ye, *the Beasts of the People,* though ye are cloath'd and fed, and provided with all Necessaries of Life, without Care; in Requital of your Benefactors, in *Return for Blessings ye give Curses, and would scatter Firebrands, Death and Destruction around them,* destroy their Estates and *butcher* their Persons. Thus monstrous is your Ingratitude!

It's hard not to suspect that Horsmanden's remarks about monstrous ingratitude were also aimed at those in the city who would doubt Burton's credibility, and withhold her reward. Four days after Horsmanden made this speech, on March 6, the Common Council "ORDERED that the Indentures of Mary Burton be Delivered up to her: and that She be Discharged from the Remainder of her Servitude: AND ORDERED the Mayor Issue his Warrant to the treasurer to pay to the said Mary Burton or Order the Sum of Three pounds Current money of this Colony: in Order to buy her Necessary Cloathing." Finally freed, Burton was handed only £3 in cash, not the £100 reward.

On the gallows on March 15, Tom confessed, and was hanged nonetheless. Horsmanden hoped that a fuller investigation would be made, especially after more fires erupted. When the Supreme Court opened its regular session on April 20, DeLancey ordered a grand jury to inquire into the fires; but the grand jury refused to return any indictments against anyone, and the matter of the slave conspiracy of 1742 was, rather quietly, entirely dropped. Meanwhile, Mary Burton, who could not read or write, filed a petition seeking her reward, probably drafted by Horsmanden himself.

It was at just this point that Daniel Horsmanden began collecting *new testimony* about the 1741 conspiracy. In April 1742 he busied himself collecting depositions that, while ostensibly gathered for his *Journal,* clearly served to support Burton's petition. That petition was referred to the Supreme Court on April 9, 1742. On April 13, Horsmanden took a deposition from Ann Kannady, to whom Burton had first talked of the plot; and the next day, he deposed Rebecca Hogg. Kannady's evidence highlighted Burton's crucial, early role in the investigation. Still the Common Council dragged its feet, reluctant to pay Mary Burton even a shilling. In May she applied to the mayor "for the payment of One hundred pounds to her: as being the person that made the first Discovery: of the persons formerly Concernd in Setting fire to Some houses." Meanwhile, the Common Council ordered "That if any person will Appear: before this Board and Make it Appear: to the Satisfaction thereof: That Such person is Entituled to Either of the Rewards: Mentioned in the said Request: and Proclamation: That they will thereupon Order a Warrant to Issue to the treasurer of this Corporation: for the payment of Such of the said Rewards: as Such person Shall Appear to be Entitled unto."

But still Burton did not receive her money. On July 15, Horsmanden secured another deposition, this one from Susannah Masters, a young woman who had befriended Burton when she lived at Wilson's house, just down the street from where Masters lived with her husband, Daniel. Kannady had depicted Burton as a helpless girl, terrified of John Hughson. Masters made her more vulnerable still. All through the summer of 1741, Masters said, Burton had been "crying and bemoaning herself." Far from the deceitful and avaricious young woman Burton's critics had complained about, Burton was merely a girl with "no Friends or Relations in this Country to advise with upon her Case, or to protect her." Susannah Masters was "very much affected, and could not but take great Compassion of her."

On September 2, with these depositions before them, and with Horsmanden, as Recorder, in the room, the Common Council finally handed Mary Burton £81, her £100 reward minus the £19 paid to Wilson to purchase her indenture and buy her clothes.[16]

And then, Mary Burton disappeared.

"I'm glad I've got an Opportunity of a little Relaxation from this intricate pursuit," Horsmanden had written to Colden in August 1741, just after Ury's trial, "tho' at the same time from the length of my Letter you may take occasion to imagine I'm not quite tired of it." In truth, Horsmanden wasn't tired of it at all. He spent much of 1742 stirring up renewed fears of slave conspiracy and securing new depositions about the 1741 conspiracy, both to vindicate the court—to prove that there really had been a plot— and to help Mary Burton gain her reward. At what point it occurred to him that better vindication could be achieved by making the proceedings public is unclear. There is no mention of the *Journal* before July 1742, when printer James Parker solicited advance subscriptions on the purchase price, 10 shillings, promising that the book "is now almost ready for the Press" (although, of course, it wasn't ready at all and wouldn't be published for two more years). Subscriptions were taken in New York, Boston, and Philadelphia.[17]

Parker had been apprenticed to William Bradford in 1727, when he was thirteen years old, just after Zenger left Bradford's printshop to set up his own. In 1733, Parker ran away from his master, but eventually returned to New York to complete his service. In 1741, Benjamin Franklin helped Parker set up his own shop in New York, serving as a silent partner.

(Franklin supplied a press and 400 pounds of type.) Parker specifically set up shop on the promise of printing the digest of the province's laws that Horsmanden had, in November 1741, been hired to compile, and he was disappointed—and financially imperiled—when "that Job dropt through." After Horsmanden abandoned the task to which he had been assigned in favor of compiling a journal of the proceedings in the detection of the conspiracy, Parker had no choice but to take on the job.

By the time the manuscript was finally ready for publication, in the spring of 1744, Parker had become the official government printer.[18] He apparently determined to produce a particularly stunning book. On May 14, 1744, Parker placed an ad in his newspaper, the *New York Weekly Post-Boy:* "Those Gentlemen that live in Town, who have subscribed for this Journal, are desired to send for their Books to the Printer thereof." Anyone who hadn't subscribed was out of luck: "As there are but few more printed than what are engaged for, any Person that intends to purchase them, must apply speedily."

In the *Journal,* Parker flaunted his skill and showcased his type. The books subscribers picked up were in large format, and rather spectacularly decorated with intricate, fanciful borders. Horsmanden's personal copy was bound with crimson morocco, its edges gilted, and its inside cover adorned with his armorial bookplate.[19]

Horsmanden was "expecting a large Sale." But he was to be sorely disappointed. Parker sold fewer than fifty copies before a London printer brought out a much smaller and cheaper edition in 1747, denying Parker the opportunity to export what he could not sell in the colonies. Still, it wasn't Parker who suffered the loss. His failure to move his inventory went "to the Damage of the Author several Hundred Pounds."[20] Horsmanden had paid for his *Journal* to be printed, out of the £250 paid him by the Assembly to compile a digest of the colony's laws, and its failure came at the cost of his reputation.

Not long after the *Journal's* publication, Daniel Horsmanden, who had struggled with debt his whole life, found himself in even more dire straits. In 1745 he asked the Assembly for more money to complete the work for which he had originally been paid; but the Assembly denied his request, perhaps because by now the new governor, George Clinton, had begun to complain of the Assembly's practice of "giving to Mr Horsmanden sums of money for extraordinary services, without that either he or the Assembly acquainted the Govr with any of the particulars of those services."[21]

Clinton's appointment in 1743 set about a realignment of New York's

Jan 2. 1895. 1742
3Y 1742

PROPOSALS

For Printing by Subscription,

A

JOURNAL

Of the PROCEEDINGS in the Detection of the Conspiracy, formed by some White People in Conjunction with several Negroe and other Slaves, for Burning the City of NEW-YORK, in *America*, and Murdering the Inhabitants thereof: Which Conspiracy was partly put in Execution by burning His Majesty's House in Fort GEORGE, within the said City, on Wednesday the *Eighteenth* Day of *March*, 1740-1, and setting Fire to several Dwelling and other Houses there, within a few Days succeeding. And by a further Attempt made in Prosecution of the same infernal Scheme, by putting Fire to two other Dwelling-Houses within the said City, on Monday the *Fifteenth* Day of *February* last, which was accidentally and timely discovered and prevented.

TOGETHER WITH

A

NARRATIVE

Of the Tryals, Condemnations, Executions, Behaviour of the several Criminals, (Whites and Blacks) at the Gallows, and Stake, with their Speeches and Confessions.

To which will be added,

Some additional Evidence concerning the said Conspiracy and Conspirators, which has come to Light since their Tryals and Executions; with Observations and Reflections, occasionally interspersed, for the better Illustration of the Whole.

WITH

A LIST of the several Criminals (Whites and Blacks) executed, and of those transported, with the Places whereto: And a Table referring to the several Tryals.

By One of the *Justices of the Supreme Court of the Province,* and Recorder of the City of New-York.

THE CONDITIONS.

First, ✱✱✱S the greatest Part of these Proceedings took up a ✱ A ✱ Course of about *Five Months* last Year, when ✱✱✱ the Term for sitting of the Supreme Court was found necessary by the Government to be continued, and was by several Ordinances from time to time enlarged, insomuch, that one Term was continued to the Foot of another, *April* to *July*, and *July* Term likewise continued further on, 'till the Business was come to a Stop: The Occasion whereof being, that so much Light as has been got into this Mystery of Iniquity (for that the Bottom has been fathomed, there is not sufficient Reason to imagine) was discovered by very slow Degrees: It is designed to print the whole Evidence and Proceedings, by Way of Journal, that by setting forth the Examinations and Tryals in the Order of Time they were taken and had, the Reader may be furnished with the most natural View of the Whole, and thereby be better enabled to conceive the Design and dangerous Depth of this hellish Project, and the Justice of the several Prosecutions.

Secondly, That the Work shall be printed in Quarto, on the same Paper, and in the same Character with these Conditions.

Thirdly, That the Work shall be published with all convenient Expedition, after a sufficient Number of Subscriptions are taken, in order to defray the immediate and necessary Expence of compiling and printing the same, which is now almost ready for the Press.

Fourthly, That the Book shall be delivered compleat to the Subscribers in Sheets, upon their paying at the Rate of *Four Pence* per Sheet.

Fifthly, That in regard it is computed the Price will amount to about *Seven Shillings New-York* Currency, at the Rate aforesaid; it is proposed, That every Subscriber do pay down the Sum of *Three Shillings and Six Pence* for every Book, at the Time of his Subscription, in Part of Payment for the Whole, in order to defray the necessary Charge of forwarding the Printing of the same.

Sixthly, That if, when the Work is printed, the Number of Sheets at the Rate aforesaid, should exceed the Price of *Seven Shillings* per Book, that the Subscribers do pay at the Rate of *Four Pence* per Sheet, for the Number of Sheets exceeding: And if the Number of Sheets according to the same Rate, should not bring the Price to *Seven Shillings*, that an Abatement shall be made to the Subscribers accordingly: But by the nearest Calculation that can be now made, it is thought the Price will amount to about *Seven Shillings.*

N.B. *Very few more Copies will be printed than what are subscribed for.*

SUBSCRIPTIONS *will be taken in at* Mr. NICHOLLS's, *the Post-Master in* NEW-YORK, Mr. HENCHMAN's *and* Mr. HANCOCK's, *Book-sellers in* BOSTON, Mr. FRANKLIN's, *Printer in* PHILADELPHIA, *and by several Others who will take Papers of Proposals for that Purpose:*

New-York, July 16, 1742.

At my Request,

politics. James DeLancey, long allied with the colonies' governors, feuded with Clinton and led a powerful opposition against him, with strong support in the Assembly. In the first years after Clinton's arrival, Horsmanden attempted to straddle the fence, boasting that he "had the Confidence of both Mr. Clinton and the Assembly & wrote the Speeches" of both sides. But in 1747, Horsmanden took DeLancey's side in a dispute with Clinton and became the mouthpiece of DeLancey's opposition. Clinton, accusing Horsmanden of being "the chief contriver and actor in that faction, and being likewise of no estate in the Country and much in debt, whereby he may be too much exposed to temptations," stripped Horsmanden of all of his political appointments, removing him from both the Supreme Court and the Governor's Council, and replacing him as Recorder.[22]

Horsmanden, left with no income, was "cast upon the private bounty of the party by whom he was employed, applauded, and ruined." Faced with the prospect of debtor's prison, he reinvented himself as a champion of political liberty and a defender of the freedom of the press. He became a political hack, writing essays in newspapers and pamphlets opposing Clinton's use of arbitrary authority, and viciously attacking Cadwallader Colden, the governor's defender. (Colden damned Horsmanden as an "infamous scribler" and, in 1748, warned the governor never to reappoint Horsmanden to any of his offices, to which Clinton replied that there was "no condition which ever shall induce me to restore Horsmanden.") So quickly did Horsmanden earn a reputation as a critic of executive power that, in January 1748, a newspaper reply to one of Horsmanden's essays took the form of a fake advertisement for a book in press, on "the whole Art and Mystery of abusing Governors":

> To publish by subscription,
> An *Abridgement of the learned* Don Daniel Scriblerus, who lately, with great Accuracy and Judgment, wrote himself out of Bread, into a beggarly Dependence upon his Friends and Assembly-Men. All that is necessary for the present Generation, or useful to Posterity, in the Representation, Remonstrance, the angry Answers to Messages, and the long tautological Letter to the Governor, will be comprised in a small Octavo, about the Size of a Child's Primmer; wherein will be illustrated the whole Art and Mystery of abusing Governors, in order to gain Popularity, and keep up the Spirit of Levelling; besides some other Arcana in Politics hitherto unknown.

This Book will be very useful for small Politicians, Boutefeus, and fractious Assembly Men, but more especially to such as may hereafter become Tutors, or Hackney-Writers to an Assembly.[23]

While Horsmanden became an expert in "the Spirit of Levelling," James DeLancey was appointed lieutenant governor by the king, much to Governor Clinton's dismay. Refusing to allow DeLancey to take office, Clinton simply pocketed his commission, and only handed it to him in 1753, when he was leaving New York to be replaced by a new governor, Sir Danvers Osborne. And, just as he was leaving the colony, Clinton reinstated Horsmanden to the third seat on the Supreme Court. When Osborne, grieving his wife's recent death, killed himself within a week of taking office, DeLancey assumed the governorship, and Horsmanden found himself once again in the favor of those in power. DeLancey restored him to the Governor's Council in 1755.[24]

The vicissitudes of Horsmanden's career in the 1740s and 1750s reveal the volatility of New York's factional politics at midcentury. That Horsmanden could join the opposition so easily, and return to power almost overnight, and that the city's political alignment could so dramatically shift with the appointment of a new governor, all testify to the tenuousness of political alliances. In 1747, when Governor Clinton stripped him of all his offices, Horsmanden came to understand the arbitrary power of colonial governors and became an expert at critiquing it. Far from England, where checks against such power were to be sought, Horsmanden, like DeLancey, found himself driven to political opposition through the power of print, and to the embrace of faction and party. But when they returned to power, both men proved willing and eager to exert that same arbitrary authority themselves, to enjoy all of its privileges, and to display, once again, an intolerance for opposition.

The shallow factionalism that characterized New York politics before the 1730s, and returned in the 1740s and 1750s, bore little resemblance to the far bolder embrace of party that had marked the years surrounding Zenger's trial, when even a writer for the Court Party *New York Gazette* had argued that "Parties . . . serve to maintain the public Liberty" and that "Opposition is the Life and Soul of public Zeal" which, "instead of clogging, regulates and keeps in their just and proper Motion the Wheels of Government."[25] Ideas such as those found little purchase in the 1740s and 1750s, when men like DeLancey and Horsmanden, keen to lead the opposition when they were out of power, were just as eager to silence it when they reclaimed the seat of government.

It is impossible to understand how faction and party worked in New York, and could have been embraced with both such passion and such shallowness, without considering slavery, and how real and imagined slave conspirators functioned as a phantom political party. A faction, Thomas Hobbes wrote in 1642 in *De Cive,* is "a multitude of subjects" who have made "Pacts, or Leagues of mutuall defence between themselves against all men, not excepting those who have the supreme power in the City": "A faction therefore is as it were a City in a City."[26] He might have been describing New York City's slaves in the hard winter of 1741, cursing whites at tea-water pumps, sharpening knives at Comfort's, talking about burning the city down and cutting the throats of their masters. Whether Quack and Cuffee, Jack and Othello ever actually planned to destroy New York or set a single fire, they were undoubtedly, by Hobbes's definition, a faction, a "City in a City."

In the 1730s, white New Yorkers, led by James Alexander, conducted an experiment in political liberty, and defended their right to constitute an oppositional party as a political form not only not destructive of but actually essential to good and just government, a form especially necessary in the colonies as protection against the abuse of unchecked governors who, by becoming tyrants, made their subjects political "slaves." In 1741, a phantom black political party—of real slaves—was discovered lurking in the shadows. Its discovery marked both the logical consequence of and an end to Alexander's experiment in political liberty. Having endured a white "City in a City" whose leaders had gone unpunished, New Yorkers reckoned with their black "City in a City" by banishing, burning, and hanging its most threatening subjects.

In eighteenth-century New York, slavery made liberty possible, one kind of liberty, when the threat of slave conspiracy rendered white political opposition palatable, when burning black men at the stake made what James Alexander had written and John Peter Zenger had printed seem harmless. But slavery also, paradoxically, worked to suppress political experimentation by extinguishing "Party flames," and helping to heal and therefore erase party divisions. Yet, however white New Yorkers understood their relationship to their governors and their king, their ideas about forming parties and waging revolutions were shaped by their fear of slave conspiracy, just as slave rebellions, and the emerging anti-slavery and later abolitionist movements themselves, were always shaped by colonial and American ideas about political opposition and political liberty. While they ebbed and flowed, fear of black rebellion and the embrace of opposition, like liberty and slavery, traveled with the same tide.

This was what had animated Horsmanden's investigation from the beginning. The conspiracy Mary Burton first described, in her astonishing deposition of April 22—Hughson's Plot, of men meeting in a tavern plotting to replace the governor—looked to him so much like a blacker version of the Country Party of the 1730s that he dedicated himself to the task of exposing these "latent Enemies." That lawyers and grand jurors and ordinary New Yorkers went along with him for so long, through the public executions of thirty black men, is a testament both to the credibility of the other plot the confessions ultimately described—the "Negro Plot"—and to the pervasiveness of the city's simmering racial and political tensions. Even as the evidence Horsmanden uncovered took him further from the plot described by Burton, he remained wedded to a story with implications for faction and party, sedition and insurrection. In July, he reluctantly yielded to James DeLancey in shifting the focus of the investigation to the all-encompassing Priest's Plot, but in his *Journal,* which gave center stage to Hughson's Plot, Horsmanden made his political point: a slave conspiracy is like a political party, only even more sinister.

AND WHAT OF Daniel Horsmanden and his *Journal?* For a time, both the man ("Don Daniel Scriblerus") and his book became objects of ridicule. In 1744, when Clarke was asked about "Mr. Horsmanden's History of the Negro Conspiracy," he joked, "I am sure the Author of the History had no Hand in the Plott."[27] In 1748, Horsmanden's printer cut by a third the price of those copies still left on his shelves, announcing that "as he has been a considerable Loser by printing that Book, he proposes to sell 'em very cheap."

Written as a "standing Memorial" to the danger of giving slaves an "Excess of Liberty," Daniel Horsmanden's *Journal of the Proceedings in The Detection of the Conspiracy* was remaindered, at 3 shillings a copy.

Dust

O N A MISERABLY COLD DAY in February 1777, Daniel Horsmanden, eighty-three years old, aching and brittle-boned, drafted his will. "I give my Soul to God," he began. His earthly estate he scattered; he had no children to inherit it. To Elizabeth Sherbrook, the wife of his American executor, he left his beloved "Chariot and Horses." To his sixteen-year-old Virginia goddaughter, Maria Horsmanden Byrd, daughter of William Byrd with whom he had caroused in his youth, Horsmanden left £500. The £2,500 of South Sea stock he had inherited from his unmarried sister Ursula, better known as "Nutty," he distributed among an English bishop's fund; the caretaker of a farm he owned in England; and his sister-in-law Lucretia, widow of his brother Samuel, who had been vicar of Purleigh, the place Horsmanden would have had if he had not decided to pursue a career in law.

The rest of the estate he left to charity. Horsmanden gave £500 to King's College (now Columbia University), founded in 1754. His largest bequest, £1,500, went to "the Rector and Inhabitants of New York in Communion with the Church of England," to be used to buy a pulpit and desk for Trinity Church and to help rebuild the Rector's House and the church's charity school.[1] It was as much a political statement as an act of generosity. In the chaos of the Revolution, Trinity was still the Church of England, and Horsmanden was a Loyalist to the awful end of his days.

American independence devastated Daniel Horsmanden. Like other New Yorkers loyal to the crown, Horsmanden was tempted to flee in June 1775, when Washington rode through the city en route to Boston and Cambridge to take command of the Continental Army. Loyalists left New York by the thousands—for England, for Nova Scotia, for the countryside, for the nearest British ship. Those who stayed behind risked being taunted and beaten by vigilantes or investigated and arrested by the patriots' Committee for the Detection of Conspiracies, established to track down Tories.

Horsmanden might have retreated to his country home in Flatbush; his presence was no longer needed in New York. He had been Chief Justice of the Supreme Court of the Province of New York since 1763, but he took his seat on that bench for the last time in October 1775. Once New York called itself a state, the provincial court was dismantled. Horsmanden's hard-won chief justiceship, the consuming ambition of his political career, became just another casualty of revolution.

No longer needed at City Hall, and with a country home waiting for him, Horsmanden was nevertheless trapped in the city; his second wife, Ann, was desperately ill, too ill to move, "dying under the excrutiating Tortures of a cancered Breast." In the spring of 1776, William Smith, son of Zenger's attorney, visited the Horsmandens in the city and pled with them "to retire from the Metropolis," to no avail. "I spent two Hours with him & his Wife," Smith recalled, "moved with Compassion for Persons whose Minds were sunk below their Adversities, supported neither by the Consolations of Religion nor Philosophy. Intent upon a Retrospect of what they were once, I could not elevate their Hopes by any Prospect of the Future. His Age & her Cancer presented Death to their View as at the Door and involved them in a Gloom, which Nothing I offered, could illuminate or dispel."[2]

In the spring of 1776, William Smith, Jr., may well have been Daniel Horsmanden's only visitor. He had no fondness for Horsmanden, who generally appeared to sensible men as a scheming opportunist, always eager for a loan. Only by marrying the wealthy and aged widow, Mary Reade Vesey, in 1748, had Horsmanden avoided debtor's prison. (Horsmanden was fifty-four when he married; Reade must have been in her seventies. She had married her first husband in 1698, when Horsmanden was only four years old.) "Until his marriage with Mrs. Vesey," Smith wrote, "Mr. Horsmanden was an object of pity; toasted, indeed, as the man who dared to be honest in the worst of times, but at a loss for his meals, and, by the importunity of his creditors, hourly exposed to the horrors of a jail." In 1753, Governor Clinton restored him to his position as Third Justice. Seven years later, Mary Horsmanden died, leaving Horsmanden the bulk of her estate.[3]

In 1763, Horsmanden, at age sixty-nine, was promoted to Chief Justice. That same year, he married Ann Jevon, this time for love. "Would you believe it Daddy Horsmanden has entered the Lists with Miss Jevon," one

New Yorker remarked, "& is as Juvinile a Bridegroom as you could desire to see of above three score and ten." In this, as in much that characterized his later years, Horsmanden had become an object of ridicule. "Mr Horsmanden has set all the Town a laughing at his intended Marriage with Miss Jevan," another New Yorker wrote, adding, "Many are the Jests this Occasions, it has made even the Dull witty."[4]

Horsmanden had also become physically frail and appeared, for years, to be nearing death. "Old Horsey's Life has been . . . despaired of," wrote William Smith, Jr., in 1769, when Horsmanden became ill. "Horsey" was no accidental nickname. Horsmanden was known for his equine enthusiasm; his ostentatious coach-and-six was one of only a handful in the city, and absurdly extravagant. In 1771, hooligans attacked it: "The coach was destroyed & the poor horses lost their tails." Horsmanden, who by now had great difficulty walking, was left to rely on his smaller chariot, pulled by mortifyingly tailless horses.[5]

By 1776, the Chief Justice had long since outlived his contemporaries, and he made few youthful friends in his later years. James Alexander died in 1756, Frederick Philipse in 1751, Richard Bradley in 1752, George Clarke and James DeLancey in 1760, John Chambers in 1765, William Smith, Sr., in 1769. Cadwallader Colden, who had served as lieutenant governor of the province during the 1760s and 1770s, died in September 1776. None of these men had met mortality as bereft of solace and companionship as Daniel Horsmanden. James Alexander had five children, DeLancey six, Clarke ten, Colden eleven, Smith fifteen. Horsmanden had none. Joseph Murray, too, never had children, but when he died in 1757 at the age of sixty-three, he enjoyed a wide acquaintance and the esteem of his colleagues; he was lauded in his obituary as "a Gentleman of the strictest Integrity, Fidelity and Honour." Daniel Horsmanden lived out his final days in a world that despised him.

Soon after visiting Horsmanden, William Smith, Jr., himself a Loyalist, was banished by the patriots' Committee for the Detection of Conspiracies. He fled to Canada. Horsmanden, alone but for his dying wife, watched with sadness as Washington returned from Boston and put James Alexander's fifty-year-old son William, a brigadier general, in command of the Continental Army's defense of the city. Washington commandeered "Frog Hall," Horsmanden's house on what is now West 44th Street (a house his second wife had brought to the marriage), for use as a hospital.[6] At the beginning of July, Horsmanden heard the shattering news that the Continental Congress had endorsed the Declaration of

Independence; New York delegate Lewis Morris, Jr., son of Horsmanden's old adversary, was among the signers. Horsmanden may have roused himself from his gloom to witness the shocking events of July 9: when the Declaration was read to William Alexander's troops assembled on the Common, they marched down Broadway to the Bowling Green, pulled down a massive equestrian statue of King George, and staked its head on a pole. It must have seemed to Horsmanden that the "unruly spirit of independency" manifest in New York in the tumultuous 1730s had grown monstrous. The Alexanders and the Morrises had won. Now had the world truly turned upside down.

Suffering in spirit, Horsmanden by no means escaped the physical indignities that befell those who resisted the Revolution. That summer, the Chief Justice was kidnapped "by a party of ruffians" and carried into the country to be jeered at, and possibly lynched, "but he proved so troublesome on the journey, that they chose to leave him on the side of the road." Somehow, Horsmanden made his way back to the city. He found no peace there. At the end of the summer, the patriots' Committee for the Detection of Conspiracies summoned him, feeble and friendless, to City Hall "to appear before them & deliver up his Arms." Miles Sherbrook, an English merchant who had business dealings with Horsmanden, took pity on him and, "compassionating his Desertion and Solitude, led him by the Hand out of the Capital." Sherbrook escorted Horsmanden and his wife safely to Flatbush. It was in payment for this kindness, undoubtedly, that Horsmanden made Sherbrook executor of his estate and left his chariot to Sherbrook's wife, Elizabeth, who may have helped care for Ann during the journey. Ann died the following spring.[7]

Meanwhile, the battle for New York began, as much a civil war as a fight for independence. James DeLancey's younger brother Oliver, brigadier general and the senior Loyalist officer in the British Army, fought with the redcoats in the Battle of Long Island. William Alexander helped his men escape the British after the Battle of Brooklyn in August (although Alexander was himself captured). In the end, Washington's troops failed to halt the invasion, and New York City fell to the British in September 1776. Before retreating, Washington considered burning the city, but held back. Someone else, apparently, did the job for him. On the night of September 21, 1776, after the British had gained the city, fires once again raged across Manhattan, and proved far more devastating than the blazes of 1741. Trinity Church, where James DeLancey's body had gone to its final rest in a vault beneath the center aisle, burned to the ground.

(Horsmanden's bequest, in his will written five months later, aimed to aid rebuilding efforts.) Five hundred buildings, more than a quarter of the city, were reduced to ashes. "The Number of Fires which appeared at the same Time at very distant Parts . . . afford too fatal a Proof of an Intention to destroy this City," a British commandant reported.[8] An investigation was begun. Two hundred patriots were arrested and questioned on suspicion of arson, and an American spy, Nathan Hale, was hanged, regretting that he had but one life to lose for his country.

In October, Daniel Horsmanden, now a widower, wearily returned to the charred city, seeking refuge under the British occupation; his name led the list of nine hundred signers of a pledge of allegiance delivered to the British commanders in City Hall. Along the road, Horsmanden's carriage passed hundreds of African-American slaves traveling to the city from all over the countryside, seeking the freedom promised to all those who volunteered to serve in the British Army.

In February 1777, from British-held New York, Horsmanden set about writing his will, and prepared for death. Yet one more humiliation awaited him. In April, Horsmanden learned that a committee led by Gouverneur Morris, another son of Lewis Morris, had drafted a state constitution, whose Article 24—"the judges of the Supreme Court . . . [shall] hold their offices . . . until they shall have respectively attained the age of sixty years"—was a thinly veiled indictment of Horsmanden's stubborn and widely criticized refusal to step down from the bench well into his eighties, even as senility weakened his judgment and infirmity interrupted his attendance.

Horsmanden lingered for a year and a half, in solitary despair. And then, one day, he went out "for his usual ride but was struck by a Palsy in the Evening and continued speechless from that Moment."[9] The victim of a stroke, Daniel Horsmanden died on September 23, 1778. Two days later, a small procession carried his coffin to the Trinity churchyard, a man-made hill of over 100,000 human remains piled layer upon layer, rising high above street level, and ever shifting. In the shadow of a church in ruins, Horsmanden's coffin was lowered into a shallow grave. His headstone has since sunk underground, in the unhurried quicksand of time.

DANIEL HORSMANDEN owned no slaves. If he had, he would have listed them in his will, along with his other personal property. New Yorkers preferred to keep their slaves, like their real estate and movables, in the family. Such, after all, is the chief purpose of writing a will: to hand on property from one generation to the next, to maintain and consolidate wealth across history. In his 1740 will, Abraham Van Horne, who was not only a slaveowner but an active slave trader, decreed: "All my Negro Slaves are to be sold to the highest Bidder among my Children, to prevent their falling into the Hand of Strangers." (Before Van Horne died in 1741, he lost two of those slaves in the conspiracy that year: London fled prosecution and was never found; Bridgewater pled guilty and was shipped out of the colonies.) The family auction was the most common means of distributing slaves, but Hermanus Rutgers, Jr., whose son's slaves Quash and Galloway were executed for conspiracy in 1741, wrote in his will in 1750: "My negro woman Isabel shall have the liberty of choosing her master," presumably from among Rutgers's children. Some men left the dispersal to their wives to decide. In August 1741, Samuel Myers Cohen left all of his slaves to his wife, including Hereford, who had been released from jail only weeks before. (Windsor, another of Cohen's slaves, pled guilty and had already been transported.) When the widow Jane Gilbert drafted her will in 1751, she bequeathed to her daughter "a negro wench and her two children," possibly the wife and children of Pompey, who had been shipped to Madeira in 1741 and never saw his family again.[10]

Only a handful of New Yorkers used their wills to free their slaves, but Joseph Murray, who had prosecuted so many black men to their deaths in 1741, was among them. In 1741, Murray's slaves Adam and Jack said that Caesar had refused to participate in the conspiracy. In his 1757 will, Murray ordered: "My negro Cesar and his mother are to be free, and to have £20 yearly for support." This, by any measure of its time, constituted an extraordinary act of generosity, and one that must have raised eyebrows. Perhaps Caesar was more than Murray's slave. Perhaps he was his only son.

Slaves appear everywhere in New York City wills, except as their authors, since enslaved human beings could not legally own property. Nor did they always know where their children were, or how to find them. With rare exception, enslaved men and women did not pass wealth from one generation to the next, to be maintained and consolidated across history. All that slaves could legally hand down to their children was their status. What slaves inherited was slavery.

When slaves died in eighteenth-century New York, they were buried in the Negroes Burial Ground, six desolate acres of marshy ravine just north of the Common, just south of the Collect, set aside for the purpose after Trinity Church banned blacks from its graveyard in 1697. The thirty black men hanged or burned to death in 1741 had but a short distance to travel to their graves, if they were allowed the dignity of a proper burial; the gallows and the stake were a stone's throw from the burial ground. When Othello was hanged on July 18, 1741, whatever family he left behind probably released him from the hangman's rope, wrapped him in linen, affixed the shroud with straight brass pins, and eased the body into a narrow wooden coffin. They may have tossed shells or beads into the coffin or delicately placed coins over his eyes to pay for his passage across the river of death.

With so many of the city's black men dead or gone or still in jail, Othello's friends and family would have been hard-pressed to find men to carry the coffin. Perhaps they managed to haul it onto a cart and drive it to the burial ground. Earlier in the century the Common Council, fearing that funerals might provide opportunities for plotting a rebellion, had passed a law requiring that slaves be buried by daylight. (Night funerals are common in West Africa.) Mourners, bearing no pall, might have carried Othello's coffin to the grave. The Common Council, believing that palls conferred too much dignity on the occasion, ruled: "if any Slave shall hereafter, presume to hold up A Pawl or be A Pawl Bearer at the Funeral of any Slave, such slave shall be Publickly whipped at the Publick Whipping Post."

At the grave, Othello's coffin might have been lowered into the dirt with his head pointing to the west so that when he awoke he would sit up to face the rising sun. Mourners gathered in a circle around the grave. Early in the century, large parties of men, women, and children gathered at funerals, which alarmed the Common Council: "Great Numbers of slaves Assembling & Meeting together at their Funerals, under pretext whereof they have great Opportunities of Plotting and Confederating together to do Mischief." By 1731, the Council ruled that there were to be no more than twelve mourners at a slave funeral; violators were to be whipped.[11]

At the graveside, the handful of mourners could have wailed for Othello, for the beauty of his life and the staggering sadness of his death. They might have beat drums and passed an infant over the grave, to remind them that life goes on. Before Othello's body was lowered into the ground, they may have danced or walked clockwise around the grave shaft, pacing the circle of life and death.

Death, for Othello and the people who mourned him, was not an end but another beginning, a journey to a different kind of life. Only a proper burial, however, could send Othello to a place where he could watch over future generations. Only a proper burial could transform the merely dead into exalted ancestors. In West Africa, secret societies, mortuary societies like the *Mmuo,* made sure that proper burial rites were followed. New York slaves' secret societies might have played the same role.[12] If so, one of the most profound tragedies to the black community in 1741 may have been the loss of the very men who ensured the proper burial of the dead.

Twenty thousand men, women, and children were buried in the Negroes Burial Ground before it was closed in 1795, when the land was sold for house lots. It was not that the burial ground was no longer needed: there were still thousands of enslaved and free blacks in New York at the end of the century (slavery was not completely abolished in New York until the very late date of 1827). But, as the city grew, the burial ground, once at the edge of the city, found itself at its center, and developers were unwilling to leave it alone. Early in the nineteenth century, the ravine was leveled with twenty feet of fill and the first of several generations of buildings was raised on top of the abandoned burial ground. Eventually, the graveyard's very existence was forgotten, along with most of the city's slave past. Twenty thousand bodies, twenty feet under the growing metropolis, rested, unremembered, for nearly two centuries.

IN THE SUMMER OF 1991, archeologists came to survey the site in preparation for the construction of a thirty-four-story federal office building. They found bones—many more bones than they had expected. They had consulted maps and knew about the burial ground, but they hadn't understood the topography: they didn't know how deep the ravine had been, and never guessed the bodies could have remained so wholly undisturbed. In the months following, 408 burials were excavated, catalogued, and preserved. As an archive of colonial African-American life, this was by far the most valuable set of remains and artifacts ever found. Among the coins and shells, shroud pins and bits of pottery, archeologists found identical cufflinks buried with several adult men—ornamented with a Freemasonry motif. Set into the lid of one coffin were ninety-two iron nails which looked, some said, like a heart or, said others, like the Sankofa symbol, used by the Akan people of Ghana to represent the idea of turning one's head to the past. These graves had stories to tell.

"Each individual burial can talk to us," said one city archeologist, Daniel Pagano. "The way the tendons grow tell us who was a carpenter, who rode horses, who was a butcher." The history of New York would have to be rewritten. "We have nothing else that speaks out of their mouths," said an anthropologist, Sherrill Wilson.[13]

Meanwhile, African-American activists, led by New York's black mayor, David Dinkins, protested that disinterring the remains constituted an unforgivable violation of the dignity of their ancestors. "If this was the Pilgrims' graves, this wouldn't have happened," said one protestor. In the winter and spring of 1992, activists made a series of demands: that the excavations stop; that only black archeologists serve on the project; and that the remains already disturbed be reburied as soon as possible. After a protracted struggle, those demands were met: the human remains were sent to Howard University, while the artifacts found in the burials remained in New York, for further study and in preparation for reburial. Dinkins, contemplating the importance of the site, compared the burial ground, now a National Historic Landmark, to Plymouth Rock and Ellis Island. "The African Burial Ground," he said, "is the irrefutable testimony to the contributions and suffering of our ancestors."

That testimony, unfortunately, was heard only behind closed doors. The research progressed slowly, and secretively. Researchers refused to grant access to the remains and artifacts to outside scholars and scientists and would not publish their own findings. The promised reburial was postponed again and again, as Howard University scientists locked heads with funding agencies. Then, on September 11, 2001, the artifacts, stored in the basement of 6 World Trade Center, were nearly destroyed when hijacked planes crashed into the twin towers. They were saved only when Ground Zero workers rescued one hundred boxes before 6 World Trade Center, crushed in the initial explosion, collapsed. Perhaps that brush with destruction lent new urgency to the calls for reburial, which was then accelerated, in advance of the publication of the research (which means that by the time the research is published, the remains and artifacts can no longer be consulted for verification).

On a clear, windy day in October 2003, 408 sets of remains and artifacts, boxed in tiny wooden coffins made in Africa, arrived by boat at the Wall Street pier, near where arriving Africans were once auctioned. Drummers and singers, including the Harlem Boys Choir, greeted them. David Dinkins, Jesse Jackson, and a litany of other public figures spoke from a soundstage, but for most spectators, corralled beyond a rope barrier, the speeches were utterly inaudible, distinguishable only as an angry rumble punctuated by muffled applause.

When the speeches stopped, the tiny coffins were loaded on horse-drawn wagons parked along South Street. Black New Yorkers—toddlers, grandmothers, businessmen—approached, tentatively, to touch the coffins, to caress them, reaching into their own past, mourning the dead and the horror of slavery. But those still moments of intimacy, of prayer and reckoning, were drowned in a sea of flickering flashbulbs, jostling camera crews, and the calculated chaos of what quickly became a political rally. Journalists and photographers prowled the street for subjects to interview, finding always the most vocal of the self-styled "Descendant Community," who spoke less about the people who were being laid to rest that day than about twenty-first-century African-American economic inequality. A mustached black man in a black wool turtleneck, leaning on a coffin-bearing wagon, told a bleached-blond television reporter in a fur coat, "If every black adult in the country died today, leaving everything to his or her children, the children would have nothing. Zero. Less than Zero. But if every white American adult died and left everything to his or her kids, they'd inherit $4 trillion. That's what we have lost. That's what we have lost."

Hired livery drivers in top hats mounted the wide-wheeled wagons, tugged at their horses' reins, and the procession began, up Wall Street toward Broadway to Chambers Street. (Lower Manhattan's street names are an index to the men of law who prosecuted thirty slaves to their deaths in 1741: Chambers Street, Murray Street, Delancey Street. There is no Horsmanden Street.) The mood was more furious than joyful, more suspicious than sacred. A woman in the crowd, following the wagons, complained to a friend, "And did the mayor give the kids the day off from school for this? Did he close the schools today? No, they won again." A man nearby interjected, "They don't *want* us to know this. They don't *want* us to know." Together they walked, complaining of the final conspiracy, the conspiracy of history.

At Chambers Street, across from a grassy quadrangle set aside for the reburial at 290 Broadway, the wagons came to a halt. The coffins were unloaded, one by one. The crowd grew restless. An older black woman wearing a purple headdress, who had perched silently on top of one of the wagons during the procession, suddenly shouted: "They will not rest, they will not rest, until we are repaid!" All eyes turned to her. "They owe us!" she called. "They owe us! They owe us!" And the crowd hollered back: "*Reparations!*" "They owe us!" The crowd: "*Reparations!*" "They owe us!" The crowd: "Reparations *NOW!*"

. . .

IN ONE SMALL wooden coffin buried at 290 Broadway are the remains of a middle-aged woman who died sometime before 1742. She was born in Africa. Two of her front teeth had been chiseled, one into the shape of an hourglass, one to a point. When her coffin was opened in 1992, her remains were marked "Burial 340." One hundred and eleven beads were found along her pelvic bone; they had once been strung and wrapped around her waist.[14]

Most of the beads found with Burial 340 were made of glass, blue and green and turquoise, the color of the ocean over which she had traveled and of the river she must cross. Glass beads like these were manufactured in Venice and Amsterdam and traded, for slaves, on the African coast. Two of the beads were cowrie shells, from Africa. One was amber. Another, a large black bead, was manufactured by the Iroquois, sometime between 1682 and 1750.

Waist beads were used in many parts of Africa in the eighteenth century, and carried different meanings in different cultures. They indicated status and wealth; they were thought to possess erotic power, and to encourage fertility. Beads were often heirloomed, passed from one generation to the next. In many African cultures, it was quite unusual to actually bury them.

And yet the woman named only Burial 340 was buried with her beads. Without a will, without a pen, without property, without paper, maybe this is how she handed down her history. She brought it with her, for safekeeping, across the river of death.

Bead scholars know much more about European beads than they do about African beads, just as it's much easier to find out what books Daniel Horsmanden owned than it is to discover what music African drummers drummed at John Hughson's tavern in 1741. Because beads, like ideas, are heirloomed, passed along from one generation to another, they aggravate archeologists; they evade analysis. And because beads, like ideas, are strung together, a strand is more than the sum of its beads, just as a plot is more than the sum of its elements.

Even if bead scholars could trace every single bead on the strand found in Burial 340 to its place of manufacture, they wouldn't know what those beads meant to the woman who wore them, even after death. In this, those beads are much like the details of the 1741 slave confessions. Here a wound turquoise bead, probably from Venice, traded by slave merchants to slave vendors in Ghana; here kissing Hughson's book, taken from Freemasonry; here a drawn blue bead, possibly Iroquois; here a tablecloth, connoting refinement; here a cowrie shell, from West Africa; here a slave conspiracy that looked like a political party.

Oh, but those beads, some of them are centuries old, and they come from all over the world. Who knows how they came into this woman's hands or how she carried them, across the Atlantic, on that miserable Middle Passage? But still I strain to hear, over the calls for reparations, over the rumble of barrels being pushed over cobblestones, the rattle of that long string of blue beads, wound around the waist of a woman of middle age, hidden, jangling under her clothes, as she walks down Maiden Lane.

Reconstructing New York City

When I first set about to write about the New York City slave conspiracy of 1741, I began, of course, by reading Daniel Horsmanden's *Journal of the Proceedings*. I then decided that the three most promising avenues for gaining any new understanding of the events Horsmanden documented were (1) to restore the *Journal*, and Horsmanden himself, to their cultural and political context, to avoid misreading the text; (2) to locate other contemporary sources, so as not to be forced to rely exclusively on Horsmanden's account, as other scholars have; and (3) to reconstruct the population of the city of New York, again, to avoid overreliance on Horsmanden's *Journal*. How I pursued the first two of these avenues is made explicit in each chapter of this book. How I pursued the third avenue is the subject of this appendix.

At the very end of his *Journal*, Daniel Horsmanden included a five-page "LIST *of NEGROES committed on Account of the Conspiracy*." This list is the best surviving inventory of the black population of mid-eighteenth-century New York City, and yet it has never been used as a census. When I began my research, I decided that using that list as a starting point, I would attempt to reckon with the world in which those men and women lived and died, and to find out more about them than their names and fates, not only by conducting a close literary and cultural reading of the *Journal* but also by reconstructing the city itself, using the traditional sources of social history: censuses, tax lists, court records, and maps. In undertaking this project, I was inspired both by Paul Boyer and Stephen Nissenbaum's landmark study of the 1692 witchcraft trials, *Salem Possessed,* and by my own graduate students' hunches about the 1741 conspiracy: almost every one of my students who picked up Horsmanden's *Journal* seemed to want to count something—bowls of punch, slaves with African names, confessions made on Wednesdays.[1] I decided to try counting everything.

Daniel Horsmanden wrote lists; I built a database. To reconstruct the city, I designed a database to store information about the people, places, and events of 1741. There are many different data tables in the database, but three form its back-

A LIST *of* NEGROES *committed on Account of the Conspiracy.*

Negroes.	Masters or Owners.	Committed	Arraigned	Convicted	Confessed.	Burnt.	Hanged.	Transported to	Discharged.
Antonio, ⎫	Peter De Lancey,	6 April,	13 June,	17 June,				Spanish W. Indies.	
Augustine, ⎬ Spaniards.	Macmullen,	1 April,	13 June,	17 June,					
Antonio. ⎭	Sarah Maynard,	1 April,	13 June,	17 June,				Madeira.	
Albany,	Mrs. Carpenter,	12 May,	8 June,	10 June,		12 June,			
5 Abraham, a free Negro		1 June,							
Adam,	Joseph Murray, Esq;	26 June,			27 June,			Madeira.	
Brash,	Peter Jay,	9 May,	25 June,		25 June,			Madeira.	
Baltian, alias Tom Peal,	Jacobus Vaarck,	12 May,	8 June,	10 June,	11 June,			Hispaniola.	
Ben,	Capt. Marshall,	9 June,	12 June,	13 June,		16 June,			
10 Bill, alias Will,	Coenradt Ten Eyck,	12 June,	3 July,		30 June,			Madeira.	
Bridgewater,	Abraham Van Horne,	22 June,	3 July,		27 June,			Hispaniola.	
Billy,	Mrs. Ellison,	25 June,	1 July,						
Braveboy,	Mrs. Kierstede,	27 June,	10 July,		30 June.			Madeira.	
Burlington,	Joseph Haines.	3 July,							15 July,
15 Cæsar,	Vaarck,	1 March,	24 April,	1 May, of a			11 May,		
Cuffee,	Adolph Philipse, Esq;	6 April,	28 May,	29 May,		30 May,			5 July,
Cuba, a Wench.	Mrs. Constance Lynch,	4 April,							
Curaçoa Dick,	Cornelius Tiebout,	9 May,	8 June,	10 June,		12 June.			
Cato,	Alderman Moore,	9 May,	15 July,						
20 Cæsar,	Alderman Pintard,	9 May,	3 July,		22 June,			Madeira.	
Cuffee,	Lewis Gomez,	24 May,	6 June,	8 June,	22 June.		9 June,		
Cæsar,	Benjamin Peck,	25 May,	6 June,	8 June,			9 June,		
Cato,	Joseph Cowley,	25 May,	12 June,	13 June,			16 June.		
Cook,	Gerardus Comfort,	26 May,	6 June,	8 June,			9 June.		
25 Cambridge,	Christopher Codwise,	30 May,	10 July,		30 June,			Cape François.	
Cæsar,	Israel Horsefield,	30 May,	26 June,		27 June,			St. Thomas, return'd	
Cato,	John Shurmur,	9 June,	16 June,	19 June,	27 June,		3 July,		
Cæsar,	Cornelius Kortrecht.	9 June,	3 July,		2 July,			Hispaniola.	
Cato, or Toby,	John Provoost,	9 June,	12 June,	13 June,			16 June,		
30 Cuffee,	Mrs. Fortune,	22 June,	15 July,		2 July,			Surinam.	
Cato,	Robert Benson,	23 June,	26 July,					Madeira.	
Cajoe, alias Africa.	Mordecai Gomez,	26 June,	1st July,		28 June.				
Cæsar,	Alderman Moore,	29 June,							20 July,
Cæsar,	Dr. Henderson.	29 June,	10 July,						
35 Cajoe,	Richard Baker.	30 June.							15 July,

(Vertical note in table: Robbery, but appears to have been a principal Negro Conspirator.)

The first page of Horsmanden's List of Negroes. Collection of
The New-York Historical Society.

bone. The People table is a directory of city residents; the Trial table is a chronology of legal proceedings; and the Place table is an inventory of the city's buildings, streets, and meeting places. Each data table is keyed to all the others; the database is "relational." With this data in hand, I then reconstructed the city spatially, using GIS mapping.

One of my aims in building this database was to detect patterns in the conspiracy, the fires, the confessions, and the trials that were otherwise unobservable simply by reading Horsmanden's *Journal.* As it turned out, I did discover important patterns, many of which informed my argument, especially in distinguishing among the four plots—Hughson's Plot, the "Negro Plot," the Spanish Plot, and the Priest's Plot—and in tracing their emergence over the course of the investigation. But reconstructing the city proved as much an end itself as a means to another end. The database took me to the streets, introducing me to the people and places of eighteenth-century New York. When I set about to write, I found myself referring to my database constantly: How long did it take to walk from Hogg's to Hughson's? What kind of people lived on Broadway? How many coopers worked in the West Ward? The database helped shape and refine my argument, but it also helped me to understand the city.

SOURCES AND METHODS

The People Data

The People table is a list of nearly 3,000 city residents, with fields for name, occupation, ethnicity, wealth, ward, party, and a host of other variables. I began by creating records for the 214 slaves and free blacks and 458 whites mentioned in Horsmanden's *Journal.* I then created records for people who appeared on the tax rolls, to place the trial participants in the context of the population as a whole. But before examining this data, it will be helpful to first discuss the population as described by city censuses.

Censuses

New York City censuses, providing population totals divided by race and sometimes by age and ward, are available for 1698, 1703, 1712, 1723, 1731, 1737, 1746, 1749, 1756, and 1771.[2] Because no census survives for 1741, I estimated the population for that year using an exponential growth model: $p(t) = exp\,(a*t+b)$ where p is population and t is time in years. This model is at best an approximation, since it assumes a constant rate of growth (a), but it is actually a relatively good fit with the surviving data. The extant census totals produce an average annual growth rate of 2.07% for whites and 2.29% for blacks. (The growth of the black population was due to continued importation of slaves rather than to natural increase.) Table 1 compares the actual census figures with those produced by the exponential growth model. The model white population for 1737 is the poorest fit, but its overestimation of the white population is well explained by a severe economic depression

TABLE 1. THE ACTUAL AND MODEL POPULATION OF NEW YORK, 1698–1771

Year	Actual White Population	Model White Population	Actual Black Population	Model Black Population	Actual Total Population	Sum of Model White & Model Black Populations
1698	4,237	3,607	700	692	4,937	4,299
1703	3,745	3,996	630	774	4,375	4,770
1712	n/a	4,806	n/a	949	5,840	5,755
1723	5,886	6,022	1,362	1,217	7,248	7,239
1731	7,045	7,095	1,577	1,459	8,622	8,554
1737	6,947	8,024	1,719	1,671	8,666	9,695
1741	n/a	8,709	n/a	1,829	n/a	10,538
1746	9,273	9,649	2,444	2,049	11,717	11,698
1749	10,926	10,261	2,368	2,192	13,294	12,453
1756	10,768	11,844	2,278	2,569	13,046	14,413
1771	18,726	16,108	3,137	3,607	21,863	19,715

during the period 1731–37, which was marked by significant outmigration of whites. Elsewhere, the exponential growth model is a good fit for the surviving censuses, and suggests that the population of New York in 1741 was about 10,538: 8,709 whites and 1,829 blacks.

Population density varied considerably from ward to ward, as demonstrated in the detailed census return for 1737.

TABLE 2. THE POPULATION OF NEW YORK CITY IN 1737, BY WARD, AGE, AND RACE

Ward	White Males		White Females		Black Males		Black Females		Total Whites	Total Blacks	Final Total
	over 10	under 10	over 10	under 10	over 10	under 10	over 10	under 10			
East	558	246	610	229	213	76	203	69	1,643	561	2,204
West	298	144	396	136	65	7	48	8	974	128	1,102
South	305	221	414	111	66	20	96	21	1,051	203	1,254
North	357	111	312	168	88	47	43	38	948	216	1,164
Dock	274	161	292	167	117	36	126	35	894	314	1,208
Montg.	235	136	323	147	60	19	41	14	841	134	975
Bowery	150	47	134	54	44	15	30	10	385	99	484
Harlem	76	22	87	26	21	9	22	12	211	64	275
Total	2,253	1,088	2,568	1,038	674	229	609	207	6,947	1,719	8,666

From E. B. O'Callaghan, *The Documentary History of the State of New-York* (Albany, 1851), 4:186. Arithmetic errors from the original returns, left intact by O'Callaghan, have been corrected here.

Tax Assessment Rolls

Censuses that identify individuals by name and list households by age and race are woefully lacking for mid-eighteenth-century New York. A census listing the names of white male heads of household is available for 1703 and in the first federal census in 1790, but neither is of any real use in reconstructing the city's population in 1741. And the city's first directory was not published until 1786. Because individuals are not named in any surviving censuses from 1703 to 1790, I relied on tax lists to identify individuals—although, again, only white property owners. New York City tax assessment rolls for the early eighteenth century are extant through 1734. The 1730 tax assessment roll, containing the name, ward, property description, assessment, and landlord for each of 1,902 taxpayers, was entered in the database by research assistant Kathryn Lindquist, from an available transcription.

In a Tax table in my database, programmed to populate the relevant fields in the People table, Lindquist entered the 1730 tax roll, containing the name, ward, property description, wealth, and landlord for each of 1,902 taxpayers.[3] The tax lists are arranged by ward and reveal that wealth, like population, varied by neighborhood. In her extensive analysis of the 1730 tax list in *Before the Melting Pot*, for instance, Joyce Goodfriend omits the Outward on the grounds that it was rural rather than urban. City officials also commonly excluded the Outward from city regulations, defining behavior "within this City on the South side of the fresh Water."[4] But I generally chose to include this ward because its neighborhoods, Harlem and the Bowery, were crucial sites of slave "frolicks" and also housed the city's small population of free blacks.

As a guide to the population of New York in 1741, the 1730 tax list is invaluable, but it presents an obvious problem: it is eleven years out of date. Moreover, the 1730 tax list does not include Montgomerie ward, which wasn't created until the city was granted a new charter in 1731. To better approximate the population in 1741, the manuscript 1734 tax list was also entered into the database. Most people taxed in 1734 had also been taxed in 1730, but key individuals who do not show up on the 1730 tax list do turn up in 1734, including, for instance, Daniel Horsmanden, who arrived in New York in 1732. Between the two tax lists, there is only small variation in either individual or total wealth (total wealth in 1730 was £34,910; in 1734, £36,029). And the overwhelming majority of taxpayers did not change residences between 1730 and 1734, undoubtedly because the most transient New Yorkers were also the poorest and did not own enough property to appear on either tax roll. That there was little change over the four years between 1730 and 1734 makes me reasonably confident in using the 1734 tax list to describe the city in 1741. In general, however, where I assigned residential wards to particular slaveowners, I tried to find evidence beyond the 1734 tax list to corroborate that assignment.

While the tax lists are useful in painting a portrait of the population of the city as a whole, they also provide details about individuals mentioned in the *Journal*. The two tax lists allowed me to identify property-holding city residents by both ward and wealth. And although neither tax list includes street addresses, tax assessors assessed property on a door-by-door basis, and proximity on the tax rolls reflects geographic proximity. The tax lists also provided a route to learning taxpayers' occupations and ethnicity when Joyce Goodfriend generously shared her painstaking identification of over two thirds of the 1730 taxpayers, which I then entered into my People database.[5]

Party Politics

After suspecting a link between the slave conspiracy and the Zenger trial, I began tracking party affiliations and entering them into a field in the People table. To the extent possible, individual residents of New York City who were also among the 458 white trial participants were identified as Court Party or Country Party sympathizers, based on elections, petitions, and other documents, including:

1. "Names of those agreeing to sustain Colonel Morris," James Alexander Papers, Rutherfurd Collection, New-York Historical Society, Box 2, p. 75. This is a list of 296 men who supported Lewis Morris.

2. Candidates for elected office with known party affiliations, especially in the 1734 Common Council elections and the 1737 Assembly elections.
3. The Zenger jury.
4. Signers of a petition on behalf of James Alexander, *Minutes of the Common Council of the City of New York, 1675–1776* (*MCC*), 4:314.
5. Members of the grand jury who found in favor of Alexander's good character, *MCC*, 4:326.
6. A list of men prepared to pay Zenger's bail, November 23, 1734, James Alexander Papers, the John Peter Zenger Trial Collection, New York Public Library.

Enslaved New Yorkers

While tax lists provide information about slaveowners, they are less revealing about slaves. And, although census totals document the number of blacks living in New York, and identify them by ward, age, and sex, there is no name census for slaves in the city, except for a provincial one taken in 1755, from which the New York City records are entirely missing.[6] The black men and women mentioned in Horsmanden's *Journal* offer the best name census available. I entered all of these named and anonymous individuals into the database, keyed to their owners. As the names were in many cases almost all that I knew about some slaves, I classified them by type: African, Biblical, Classical, Dutch, English, Literary, Masters (for slaves who appeared to have been named after former owners), Nouns, Place, Spanish, and Unclassifiable, and entered this data as a field in the People table.

I then built two related tables containing the names of (1) slaves who participated in the 1712 revolt; and (2) runaways, also classified by type. Participants in the 1712 revolt are taken from Kenneth Scott, "The Slave Insurrection in New York in 1712," *New-York Historical Society Quarterly* 45 (1961): 62–67. Research assistant Paul McMorrow located and photocopied advertisements for runaway slaves in five newspapers, spanning the years 1725 to 1752:

1. *New York Gazette*, 1725–44
2. *New-York Weekly Journal*, 1733–51
3. *New York Weekly Post-Boy*, 1743–47
4. *New-York Evening Post*, 1744–52
5. *New York Gazette*, 1747–52

A total of 253 ads for runaway slaves and servants appeared in New York City newspapers from 1733 to 1752. Since many of these ads were placed by owners outside New York who suspected their slaves or servants might have run to the city, most were not relevant to my inquiry. Only 21 were advertisements for runaway slaves from New York City.

In order to compare the distribution of name types across these populations, I used the 1755 slave census, containing the names of slaves outside New York City as a control population. If it represents a reasonable approximation of the names of

TABLE 3. PERCENTAGE OF CERTAIN NAME TYPES
AMONG MALE SLAVES AND FREE BLACKS

1712 Revolt	1741 Revolt	1755 Census	1725–50 Runaways	Name Type	Examples
19	8	4	14	Akan	Quash, Cuffee, Quack
2	1	5	0	Biblical	Abraham, Adam, Isaac, Jacob, Job
9	16	6	5	Classical	Pompey, Caesar, Cato, Mars, Titus
2	0	3	0	Dutch	Andries, Maat, Pieter
46	35	65	48	English	Tom, Dick, Harry
0	.5	0	0	Literary	Othello
2	2	0	0	Masters	Lowe and Jonneau*
2	8	4	5	Nouns	Fortune, Venture, Tickle, Prince
2	19	2	9	Place	Windsor, York, Jamaica, Congo
7	9	2	19	Spanish	Pedro, Antonio, Juan, Domingo
7	0	7	0	Unclassifiable	

n = 43   n = 190[†]   n = 205   n = 21

*These men appear to have borne the names of former owners.

[†]One hundred ninety-six black men were mentioned in the conspiracy; for six, no first name was given.

slaves living in Manhattan itself, the results are telling: while slaves with African names represent only 4% of the general population, they represent 8% of those named in the 1741 conspiracy, 14% of the city's runaways, and 19% of those involved in the 1712 revolt. Five of the thirteen men burned at the stake in 1741, or 38%, had African names.

Beyond these sources, much of what can be derived about the nature of the enslaved population comes from what we know about the slave trade itself, which, although it does not have a place in the database, is worth discussing here. James G. Lydon has offered a "minimum estimate" that at least 6,800 Africans were imported into the colony of New York between 1700 and 1774, 2,800 directly from Africa and 4,000 from the West Indies and other parts of North America, although "a maximum figure of 7,400 might be justified." The nature and extent of the slave trade changed dramatically after the pivotal events of 1741. Before 1741, an average of 150 slaves was imported to the colony each year; after 1741, that number dropped to 60. Before 1741, 70% of slaves imported to New York came from other parts of the Americas: of these about 30% came from Jamaica, and another 25% from Africa. Another 35% came from elsewhere in the West Indies: Barbados, Antigua, St. Eustatia, St. Thomas, Curaçao, Bermuda, and St. Kitts. Less than 3% came from South Carolina (although this data is taken from 1715 to 1764, Lydon says that "these figures emphasize the years before 1743"; after that year, 70% came directly from Africa). African historians John Thornton and Linda Heywood suggest that Lydon's figures may overestimate the prevalence of "seasoned" Caribbean imports in the early New York trade, but until more research is conducted on extant shipping records in New York, London, and Albany, Lydon's figures are by far the best available.

According to Lydon's data, taken from the naval and customs records as well as newspaper reports, there was very little slave trading in New York before 1748. But about a quarter or a third of the city's community of three or four hundred merchants took part in the trade. Where possible, I have identified which New York merchants were involved in that trade, and entered that information in the People table.[7]

The Trial Data

Having placed the people mentioned in Horsmanden's *Journal* in the context of the population as a whole, I set about processing the trial transcript itself into database form. This part of the project was inspired by the innovative work of a Boston University graduate student, Sandra Heiler, who enlisted a team of graduate students in a seminar I taught in the fall of 2001 to tabulate trial records to test her hypothesis that the more people an accused person accused, the better his chances at escaping execution. Although in the end I decided not to use the database Heiler compiled, her project was my inspiration.[8]

My work with the trial records attempted also to reconstruct tables generated by the court in 1741, including three manuscripts badly damaged by fire: "Names of negroes examined; places where examined; names of the negroes accused by them, and circumstances elicited by their testimony"; "Lists of negroes whose confessions are taken, with remarks"; and "Lists of negroes proposed to be transported, and of those proposed to be kept as witnesses."[9] I hoped that I would be able to frame queries to generate just these kinds of lists, to understand not only how the prosecution made its case but how it drew its conclusions, and with what results.

The Trial table contains a record for every legal proceeding during the investigation of the 1741 conspiracy, as recorded in Daniel Horsmanden's *Journal* and totaling more than 1,200 records: every appointment to a jury, arrest, accusation, arraignment, plea, opening or closing statement to a jury, judgment, examination, confession, deposition, trial testimony, verdict, sentence, cross-examination, execution, discharge, and pardon, beginning with April 21, 1741, the opening of the Supreme Court session, and ending with August 29, 1741, John Ury's execution. I also included a field called "trial transcript" into which I pasted the full text of confessions, testimony, and motions of the court, taken from a digital version of Horsmanden's *Journal*, available at the Library of Congress's American Memory Web site, "Slaves and the Courts." The Trial table can be sorted by any of its fields, including date, trial participant, or trial event, and can also be used for searching by keyword through Horsmanden's *Journal*. The Trial table is also keyed to the People table; for instance, the Trial record for Anthony Rutgers's appointment to the grand jury on April 21, 1741, is linked to the People table to reveal that Rutgers was a Dutch baker from the North ward who served as an Assistant Alderman from 1727 to 1734, supported the Country party, and, in 1734, owned two houses in the North ward and a farm northwest of City Hall, assessed, altogether, at a value of £255, and that his nephew, Hermanus Rutgers, Jr., owned three slaves accused of conspiracy in 1741.

To track the emergence of certain details of the conspiracy over the course of the trials, I created a Trial Detail table of 771 records, indexed to the Trial table, with a record for each detail mentioned in every substantial statement before the court, out of a list I compiled of nearly one hundred such details, e.g., "dancing," "priest," "Christmas," and "sharpening knives." To track patterns of accusation, I created an Accused table, also indexed to the Trial table, containing records for all accusations made during the investigation. It contains nearly 2,500 records.

For each slave named in the investigation, I assigned one of nine Final Outcomes—coded 1 to 9 for increasing order of severity (see Tables 8–10):

1. Unknown
2. Confessed but not arrested
3. Mentioned but not accused
4. Accused but not arrested
5. Accused but not found
6. Discharged
7. Transported
8. Hanged
9. Burned

The Place Data

The Place table is a list, with description and location information of over three hundred places in the city in 1741, coded by type: arsenal, tavern, park, street, well, warehouse, etc. A field for "Occupant" is keyed to the People table. The goal of this part of the project was to reconstruct the look and feel of the city in 1741, and to trace networks of association among both slaves and slaveowners.

Although I had initially hoped to identify the owners and residents of the majority of the city's 1,400 buildings, and thus index all buildings to the People table, that project proved both overwhelming and insufficiently relevant to my inquiry. Instead, I compiled locations and descriptions for key sites mentioned in Horsmanden's *Journal*, or otherwise important in the city. Grim's map, for instance, includes sixty named buildings or features, all entered into the Place database, along with any surviving details about date erected, owner, and description. Information about buildings and other places was also taken from I. N. Phelps Stokes's monumental labor, the Landmark Map. I also entered all places in the database keyed to Stokes's numbering system. Places were also keyed to William Burgis's detailed engraving of the city, offering a view from the south in 1716–18.[10]

With this list in hand, I set about pinpointing the location of all of these places, relying extensively on five maps depicting New York between 1731 and 1754:

1. James Lyne. *A Plan of the City of New York from an actual Survey Made by James Lyne,* 1731. New York Public Library.
2. John Carwitham. *A Plan of the City of New York,* 1740. Holkham Hall, Norfolk, UK.
3. Mrs. Buchnerd. "Plan of the City of New York In the Year 1735." New York Public Library.
4. David Grim. "Plan of the City and Environs of New York as they were in the years 1742 1743 & 1744." New-York Historical Society.
5. Francis Maerschalck. *A Plan of the City of New York from an Actual Survey,* 1754. New-York Historical Society.

Because I wanted to be able to query and display some of my database data spatially, I then turned to a GIS software program called ArcView to reconstruct a map of the city circa 1741. Digital cartographer David Rumsey helped me begin by "geo-referencing" the Carwitham map; that is, he tacked a digital image of that map onto points of latitude and longitude so that this 1740 map can be manipulated, in the same way as any modern GIS map. Robert Chavez of Tufts University then geo-referenced the other four contemporary maps for me, while generously tutoring me in ArcView. Chavez also added to my ArcView files a map from my glove compartment, *New York City, New York, Including Long Island: Downtown & Vicinity* (AAA, 2001), to provide reference to the city as it stands today. Using ArcView, it is possible to look at all of these maps more or less simultaneously, as they are stacked in layers on top of one another, and a click of the mouse moves the user from one layer to the next. To these layers, I added several more, to allow the map program to better describe the city in 1741: layers for ward divisions, streets, parks, water, markets, public buildings, residential blocks, and taverns.

I had hoped that it would be possible for my database to "talk" to my map program, so that I could, for instance, easily import the 1730 tax list to ArcView to generate a detailed scatter map depicting the distribution of wealth that year, but that proved beyond my technical savvy (which was limited to begin with). Instead, I found that I had to re-enter records from my database by hand if I wanted to use them in ArcView. I did this for some of the more interesting data; for instance, to reveal that slaves and free blacks mentioned in the investigation came from all over the city, in roughly the same proportion as they existed in the population (for more on this result, see Table 5). But, given my technical limits, this kind of work proved more useful in displaying data—creating visual aids for lectures—than in answering questions. Meanwhile, the GIS part of the project allowed me to navigate eighteenth-century New York from my desktop, to walk down a digital Broadway, and see what there was to see, on a sunny day in the spring of 1741.

Some Findings

My database and digital map served as an elaborate filing system for my research, making it possible to easily look up any given person, event, or place. But querying the data also produced important findings. The tax data, for instance, taught me that the wealthiest New Yorkers owned the most slaves and that those slaves were clustered around the neighborhoods along the East River (Table 4). The same data also allowed me to learn a good deal about individual slaveowners, and to analyze the paths and Final Outcomes of those slaves and free blacks bound up in the conspiracy. Some of what resulted is reproduced in Appendices B and C. Eventually, I hope to make all of the data available on a Web site, so that scholars and students may frame their own queries, and draw their own conclusions. Meanwhile, below I offer a very small sample of other findings.

Wards

I was able to identify the wards of 149, or 70%, of the 214 slaves and free blacks named in the conspiracy. Their numbers are roughly proportionate to those in the general population, with one exception: no slaves from the Outward were named in the conspiracy, yet 10% of the city's slaves lived there. Also, slaves from the Montgomerie and West wards—the poorest, most remote, and least densely populated wards—were slightly more likely to be involved than their presence in that population would have predicted (see Table 5).

I investigated whether slaves from certain wards fared better than others as they proceeded through the courts. Once again these outcomes proved to be, on the whole, proportionately scattered by ward (see Table 6).

Table 4. Average 1734 Tax Assessment v. Percentage of Blacks by Ward in 1737

	Average Tax (pounds)	Blacks (percentage)
East	26.6	25
West	17.5	11
South	16.9	16
North	12.2	19
Dock	21.4	25
Montgomerie	10.2	14
Outward	16.2	21

With the rural Outward omitted, there is a positive correlation (0.7) between average tax assessment and percentage of blacks in the city population.

TABLE 5. SLAVES NAMED IN 1741 BY WARD, COMPARED TO SLAVES
BY WARD IN THE 1737 CENSUS

Ward	Total Slave Population in 1737	Slaves Total %	Named in 1741	Total %
East	561	33	51	24
West	128	7	21	10
South	203	12	20	9
North	216	13	5	2
Dock	314	18	33	15
Montgomerie	124	7	19	9
Outward	163	10	—	0
Total	**1,709**	**100%**	**149***	**69%**

TABLE 6. FINAL OUTCOMES BY WARD

Ward	Mentioned but not accused	Accused but not arrested	Accused but not found	Discharged	Transported	Hanged	Burned	Total
East	2	8	1	10	19	5	4	49
West	5	1	1	1	9	2	2	21
South	3	1	0	4	10	2	0	20
North	0	2	0	0	2	1	0	5
Dock	4	3	2	7	15	0	2	33
Montgomerie	0	0	0	2	12	2	3	19
Outward	0	0	0	0	0	0	0	0
Total	**14**	**15**	**4**	**24**	**67**	**12**	**11**	**147***

*Ward locations for 149 slaves are known. Outcomes fitting these categories are known for 147 slaves. One man from the East Ward was arrested by mistake and released; another, also from the East Ward, confessed but was never arrested.

Ethnicity

I identified owner ethnicity for 168 of the 208 named slaves. Slaves owned by Dutch New Yorkers proved more likely, and those owned by English masters less likely, to be named in the conspiracy than their presence in the general population would have predicted, as shown in Table 7.

TABLE 7. OWNER ETHNICITY

Ethnicity	Total Whites in Population*	%	Owners of Named Slaves	%
Dutch		39	83	49
English		49	61	36
French		8	16	10
German		1	1	1
Jewish		2	5	3
Scottish			2	1
Total	1,087	100%	168	100%

*Owners who owned more than one named slave are counted for each slave.

Wealth

Owner wealth—the assessed value of taxable property—was identified for 134 of the named slaves. This roughly correlates with the distribution of income among taxpayers. Final Outcomes were also proportionately scattered by owner wealth. A slaveowner's wealth did not predict how his slave would fare in the courts, as shown in Table 8.

Party

I was able to identify party sympathies for the owners of only 74 named slaves. Of these, 57 were known supporters of the Country Party; 17 supported the Court Party. Almost half of those slaves owned by Country Party sympathizers were transported, compared to a fifth of those owned by supporters of the Court Party. Unfortunately, the available evidence made it easier for me to identify Country than Court Party members—the opposition was more likely to sign petitions—which renders these findings merely suggestive.

TABLE 8. FINAL OUTCOMES BY OWNER WEALTH

Owner Wealth*	Mentioned but not accused	Accused but not arrested	Accused but not found	Discharged	Transported	Hanged	Burned	Total
5–10	0	1	0	4	11	2	1	19
11–20	1	4	0	2	7	3	1	18
21–50	9	5	0	4	22	2	4	46
51–100	1	3	1	6	11	0	2	24
101–150	0	1	1	1	2	1	2	8
151–200	0	0	2	2	3	0	0	7
>200	1	1	0	3	3	1	1	10
Total	**12**	**15**	**4**	**22**	**59**	**9**	**11**	**132**

*Owners who owned more than one slave are counted for each slave.

TABLE 9. FINAL OUTCOME BY OWNER PARTY

	Party Unknown	Court Party	Country Party	Total
Burned	8	2	4	14
Hanged	9	1	6	16
Committed suicide	0	0	1	1
Transported	54	5	25	84
Accused but not found	6	0	2	8
Accused but not arrested	22	1	3	26
Confessed but not arrested	0	0	1	1
Discharged	22	4	12	38
Arrested by mistake and released	1	0	0	1
Mentioned but not accused	8	5	5	18
Unknown	1	0	0	1
Total	**131**	**18**	**58**	**208***

*This number excludes free blacks.

Accusations

One of the best predictors of an accused person's Final Outcome was the number of people who had accused him or her. The more people who accused you, the worse your fate.

TABLE 10. FINAL OUTCOME BY NUMBER OF ACCUSERS*

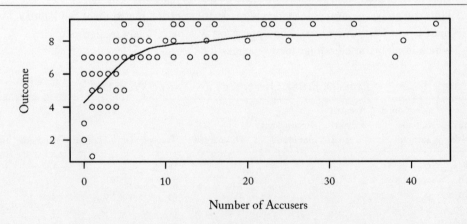

*This charts Final Outcomes versus the number of accusers, excluding the outcome for those slaves who were arrested and confessed (and whose outcome was therefore determined, most of all, by the quality of their confession). Final Outcomes are assigned numbers from 1 to 9, from least to greatest severity, as listed on p. 241. Unknown outcomes have been excluded.

APPENDIX B

The Accused

Name	Owner First Name	Owner Last Name	Arrested	Plea 1 Date	Plea 1	Plea 2 Date	Plea 2
Adam	Joseph	Murray	6/26/1741	7/30/1741	Guilty		
Albany	Elizabeth	Carpenter	5/13/1741	6/8/1741	Not guilty		
Albany	Peter	DeLancey					
Ancram	Joseph	Haines					
Anonymous	Alexander	Allair					
Anonymous	Derrick	Cook					
Anonymous	Captain	Cunningham					
Anonymous	John	Dewit					
Anonymous	Benjamin	Peck					
Anonymous	Widow	Schuyler					
Antonio de la Cruz	Sarah	Mesnard	4/6/1741	6/13/1741	Not guilty	6/17/1741	Not guilty
Antonio de St. Bendito	Peter	DeLancey	4/6/1741	6/13/1741	Not guilty	6/17/1741	Not guilty
Augustine Gutierrez	John	Macmullen	4/6/1741	6/13/1741	Not guilty	6/17/1741	Not guilty
Barbara	George	Clarke					
Bastian (alias Tom Peal)	Jacobus	Vaarck	5/13/1741	6/8/1741	Not guilty		
Ben	Stephen	Bayard					
Ben	Augustus	Jay					
Ben	Capt. Hubert	Marshall	6/9/1741	6/12/1741	Not guilty		
Bess	Frederick	Becker					
Betty	Mrs.	Clopper					
Billy	Mrs.	Ellison	6/25/1741	7/1/1741	Not guilty		
Brash	Peter	Jay	5/9/1741	6/25/1741	Not guilty	6/26/1741	Guilty
Braveboy	Mrs. Elizabeth	Kiersted	6/27/1741	7/10/1741	Guilty		
Bridgewater	Abraham	Van Horne	6/22/1741	7/3/1741	Guilty		
Burlington	Joseph	Haines	7/3/1741				
Butchell		Unknown					
Caesar	Dr. James	Henderson	6/29/1741	7/10/1741	Not guilty		
Caesar	Israel	Horsefield	5/30/1741	6/26/1741	Guilty		
Caesar	Cornelius	Kortrecht	6/9/1741	7/3/1741	Guilty		
Caesar	Col. John	Moore	6/29/1741				
Caesar	Joseph	Murray					
Caesar	Benjamin	Peck	5/25/1741	6/6/1741	Not guilty		

Trial Date*	Sentence 1 Date	Sentence 1	Confession†	Sentence 2	Sentence 2 Date	Final Outcome	Final Outcome Date
8/1/1741	7/28/1741	Transportation	6/27/1741			Transported	
6/10/1741	6/11/1741	Burning				Burned	6/12/1741
						Accused but not arrested	
						Accused but not arrested	
						Accused but not arrested	Deceased by 1741
						Accused but not arrested	
						Accused but not arrested	
						Accused but not arrested	
						Suicide	5/31/1741
						Accused but not arrested	
6/17/1741	7/1/1741	Hanging				Transported	
6/17/1741	7/1/1741	Hanging				Transported	
6/17/1741	7/1/1741	Hanging				Unknown	
						Mentioned but not accused	
6/10/1741	6/11/1741	Burning	6/11/1741	Transportation	6/13/1741	Transported	
						Accused but not found	
						Accused but not found	
6/13/1741	6/15/1741	Burning				Burned	6/16/1741
						Accused but not arrested	
						Mentioned but not accused	
						Discharged	7/30/1741
	7/15/1741	Transportation	6/25/1741			Transported	
7/10/1741	7/10/1741	Hanging	6/30/1741	Transportation	7/15/1741	Transported	
	7/9/1741	Transportation	6/27/1741			Transported	
	7/15/1741	Discharged				Discharged	
						Accused but not arrested	
						Transported	
	8/1/1741	Transportation	6/27/1741			Transported	
	7/9/1741	Transportation	7/2/1741			Transported	
	7/20/1741	Discharged				Discharged	7/20/1741
						Mentioned but not accused	
6/8/1741	6/8/1741	Burning				Burned	6/9/1741

*All trial verdicts were "guilty."
†Some of the accused confessed more than once. Only their initial confessions are noted here.

Name	Owner First Name	Owner Last Name	Arrested	Plea 1 Date	Plea 1	Plea 2 Date	Plea 2
Caesar	John	Pintard	5/9/1741	7/3/1741	Guilty		
Caesar (alias John Gwin)	John	Vaarck	3/1/1741	4/24/1741	Not guilty		
Cajoe	Richard	Baker	6/30/1741				
Cajoe	James	Favieres					
Cajoe (alias Africa)	Mordecai	Gomez	6/26/1741	7/1/1741	Guilty		
Cambridge	Christopher	Codweis	5/30/1741	7/10/1741	Not guilty		
Cataline	Mr.	Masterton					
Cato	Abraham	Alsteyn					
Cato	Robert	Benson	6/23/1741	6/26/1741	Not guilty	7/1/1741	Guilty
Cato	Joseph	Cowley	5/25/1741	6/12/1741	Not guilty		
Cato	Col. John	Moore	5/9/1741	7/15/1741	Guilty		
Cato (alias Toby)	John	Provost	6/9/1741	6/12/1741	Not guilty		
Cato	Paul	Richard					
Cato	John	Shurmur	6/9/1741	6/16/1741	Not guilty		
Congo	Joseph	Murray					
Cook (alias Acco alias Maph)	Gerardus	Comfort	5/26/1741	6/6/1741	Not guilty		
Cora	David	Van Horne	3/15/1741				
Cork	William	English					
Cuba	John	Chambers	4/13/1741				
Cuba	Mrs. Constance	Lynch	4/4/1741				
Cuffee	William	Gilbert					
Cuffee	Lewis	Gomez	5/24/1741	6/6/1741	Not guilty		
Cuffee	William	Jamison					
Cuffee	Adolph	Philipse	4/6/1741	5/28/1741	Not guilty		
Cuffee	Widow [of Michael]	Vaughton	6/22/1741	7/15/1741	Guilty		
Curacoa Dick	Cornelius	Tiebout	5/9/1741	6/8/1741	Not guilty		
Denby	George	Clarke					
Deptford	John	Cruger	6/23/1741	6/26/1741	Guilty		
Diana	David	Machado					
Dick	B.	Robins	7/8/1741				
Dick	Coenradt	Ten Eyck	6/20/1741	7/15/1741	Guilty		
Dick	Matthew	Wolf	6/23/1741	7/23/1741			

Trial Date*	Sentence 1 Date	Sentence 1	Confession†	Sentence 2	Sentence 2 Date	Final Outcome	Final Outcome Date
	7/9/1741	Transportation	6/22/1741			Transported	
5/1/1741	5/8/1741	Hanging				Hanged	5/11/1741
	7/15/1741	Discharged				Discharged	7/15/1741
						Accused but not arrested	
	7/15/1741	Transportation	6/28/1741			Transported	
		Transportation	6/30/1741			Transported	
						Accused but not arrested	
						Mentioned but not accused	
	7/9/1741	Transportation				Transported	
6/13/1741	6/15/1741	Hanging				Hanged	6/16/1741
	7/15/1741	Transportation	6/22/1741			Transported	
6/13/1741	6/15/1741	Hanging				Hanged	6/16/1741
						Accused but not arrested	
6/19/1741	7/1/1741	Hanging	6/27/1741			Hanged	7/3/1741
						Mentioned but not accused	
6/8/1741	6/8/1741	Burning				Burned	6/9/1741
						Discharged	
						Arrested by mistake and released	
						Discharged	7/6/1741
						Discharged	7/5/1741
						Accused but not arrested	
6/8/1741	6/8/1741	Burning				Burned	6/9/1741
						Accused but not arrested	
5/29/1741	5/29/1741	Burning	5/30/1741			Burned	5/30/1741
	7/15/1741	Transportation	7/2/1741			Transported	
6/10/1741	6/11/1741	Burning				Burned	6/12/1741
						Mentioned but not accused	
	7/9/1741	Transportation	6/27/1741			Transported	
						Accused but not arrested	
						Discharged	7/23/1741
	7/15/1741	Transportation	6/30/1741			Transported	
						Transported	

*All trial verdicts were "guilty."
†Some of the accused confessed more than once. Only their initial confessions are noted here.

Name	Owner First Name	Owner Last Name	Arrested	Plea 1 Date	Plea 1	Plea 2 Date	Plea 2
Dido	Joseph	Murray					
Diego	Joseph	Hildreth					
Diego	Abraham	Marschalk	Unknown				
Diego	Peter	Van Dursen	6/27/1741				
Dublin	Capt. William	Walton	7/13/1741				
Dundee	Robert	Todd	5/7/1741	7/3/1741	Guilty		
Emanuel	Thomas	Wendover	4/6/1741	6/25/1741	Not guilty	6/26/1741	Guilty
Fortune	David	Clarkson	6/25/1741	7/1/1741	Not guilty	7/9/1741	Guilty
Fortune		Cruger					
Fortune	John	Latham	6/13/1741	7/7/1741	Guilty		
Fortune	John	Vanderspiegle	5/25/1741	6/12/1741	Not guilty		
Fortune	Capt. William	Walton	6/28/1741	7/1/1741	Not guilty		
Fortune	John	Wilkins	5/22/1741	7/7/1741	Guilty		
Francis	Jasper	Bosch	4/6/1741	6/8/1741	Not guilty		
Frank		[free]					
Frank	Frederick	Philipse	6/27/1741				
Frank	Henry	Ryker	6/30/1741	7/10/1741	Not guilty		
Galloway	Hermanus, Jr.	Rutgers	7/2/1741	7/10/1741	Not guilty		
Guy (alias Gusie or Galick)	Timothy	Horsefield	5/30/1741	6/26/1741	Guilty		
Hannah		[free]					
Hanover	Henry	Cruger					
Hanover	John, Jr.	Cruger	6/29/1741				
Harry	Dr. Archibald	Fisher					
Harry	Katherine	Kipp	5/30/1741	6/16/1741	Not guilty		
Harry	John	Thurman	6/9/1741	6/19/1741	Not guilty	6/23/1741	Guilty
Dr. Harry	John	Mizreal	7/6/1741	7/10/1741	Not guilty		
Hereford	Samuel Myers	Cohen	6/29/1741				
Isabella		[free]					
Jack	Jacob	Abrahamse	6/28/1741	7/1/1741	Guilty		
Jack	Henry	Breasted	5/9/1741	6/25/1741	Not guilty	6/26/1741	Not guilty
Jack	Christopher	Codweis					
Jack	Gerardus	Comfort	5/26/1741	6/6/1741	Not guilty		
Jack	John	Dorland	6/29/1741				
Jack	Gertrude	Governeur					
Jack	Judah	Hay	7/2/1741				
Jack	Joseph	Murray	6/25/1741	7/1/1741	Guilty		
Jack	John	Roerback	6/28/1741				
Jack	Joshua	Sleydall	5/6/1741				
Jack	John	Tiebout					

Trial Date*	Sentence 1 Date	Sentence 1	Confession†	Sentence 2	Sentence 2 Date	Final Outcome	Final Outcome Date
						Mentioned but not accused	
						Accused but not arrested	
						Discharged	7/23/1741
						Discharged	7/23/1741
						Discharged	7/23/1741
	7/9/1741	Transportation	6/24/1741			Transported	
	7/15/1741	Transportation	6/27/1741			Transported	
	7/9/1741	Transportation	7/2/1741			Transported	
						Mentioned but not accused	
	7/9/1741	Transportation	7/15/1741			Transported	
6/13/1741	6/15/1741	Hanging				Hanged	6/16/1741
7/15/1741	7/17/1741	Hanging				Hanged	7/18/1741
	7/9/1741	Transportation	5/22/1741			Transported	
6/10/1741	6/11/1741	Burning				Burned	6/12/1741
						Accused but not arrested	
						Discharged	7/20/1741
7/15/1741	7/17/1741	Hanging				Hanged	7/18/1741
7/15/1741	7/17/1741	Hanging				Hanged	7/18/1741
	7/9/1741	Transportation	6/27/1741			Transported	
						Mentioned but not accused	
						Accused but not found	
						Discharged	7/15/1741
						Mentioned but not accused	
6/19/1741	7/1/1741	Hanging	6/27/1741			Hanged	7/3/1741
	8/1/1741	Transportation	6/22/1741			Transported	
7/15/1741	7/17/1741	Burning	7/18/1741			Burned	7/18/1741
						Discharged	7/2/1741
						Accused but not arrested	
	7/9/1741	Transportation	7/2/1741			Transported	
	8/1/1741	Transportation	6/27/1741			Transported	
						Accused but not found	
6/8/1741	6/8/1741	Burning	6/8/1741	Transportation	6/10/1741	Transported	
						Discharged	6/29/1741
						Accused but not found	
						Discharged	7/6/1741
	8/1/1741	Transportation	6/26/1741			Transported	
						Discharged	7/20/1741
	8/1/1741	Transportation	6/12/1741			Transported	
			6/24/1741			Confessed but not arrested	

*All trial verdicts were "guilty."
†Some of the accused confessed more than once. Only their initial confessions are noted here.

Name	Owner First Name	Owner Last Name	Arrested	Plea 1 Date	Plea 1	Plea 2 Date	Plea 2
Jacob	Hermanus, Jr.	Rutgers	6/23/1741	6/26/1741	Guilty		
Jamaica	Thomas	Ellison	5/22/1741	6/6/1741	Not guilty		
Jasper (alias Gosport)	Robert	Bound	5/29/1741	7/1/1741	Not guilty		
Jeffery	Capt. J.	Brown	6/15/1741	7/1/1741	Guilty		
Jemmy	Capt. Josiah	Bagley					
Jenny	Gerardus	Comfort					
Jenny	John	Hunt					
Joe	Henry	Holt					
John		[free]					
John	Rip	Van Dam	7/6/1741				
John	Widow	Van Ranst	6/27/1741				
John	Winant	Van Zant					
Jonneau (alias John)	Jacobus	Vaarck	5/13/1741	7/7/1741	Guilty		
Juan (alias Indian Wan)	Peter	Lowe	6/12/1741	6/19/1741	Guilty		
Juan (alias John or Wan)	Dr.	Nicols	4/24/1741				
Juan de la Silva	Capt. Jacob	Sarly	4/6/1741	6/13/1741	Not guilty	6/17/1741	Not guilty
Jupiter	Capt. William	Walton	7/13/1741				
Kid	Cornelius	Van Horne	6/29/1741				
Lewis	Adoniah	Schuyler	6/27/1741	7/1/1741	Guilty		
London	Capt. Roger	French	6/22/1741	7/3/1741	Guilty		
London	Augustine	Hicks	5/30/1741				
London	Edward	Kelly	6/12/1741	6/19/1741	Guilty		
London	Peter	Marschalk	6/9/1741	6/16/1741	Not guilty		
London	Abraham	Van Horne					
London	Benjamin	Wyncoop	6/22/1741	6/26/1741	Guilty		
Lowe	David	Provost	6/22/1741	6/25/1741	Not guilty	6/26/1741	Guilty
Lucena		Frank					
Maria		[free]					
Mars	Robert	Benson	6/12/1741	7/3/1741	Guilty		
Mink	John	Groesbeck	6/12/1741	6/16/1741	Guilty		
Neptune	Henry	Cruger					
Othello	James	DeLancey	6/27/1741	7/10/1741	Guilty		
Pablo Ventura Angel (alias Powlus)	Frederick	Becker	4/6/1741	6/13/1741	Not guilty	6/17/1741	Not guilty

Trial Date*	Sentence 1 Date	Sentence 1	Confession†	Sentence 2	Sentence 2 Date	Final Outcome	Final Outcome Date
	7/9/1741	Transportation	6/24/1741			Transported	
6/8/1741	6/8/1741	Hanging		Transportation	7/9/1741	Transported	
7/15/1741	8/1/1741	Ttransportation				Transported	
	8/1/1741	Transportation	6/27/1741			Transported	
						Mentioned but not accused	
						Accused but not arrested	
						Mentioned but not accused	
						Accused but not found	
						Accused but not arrested	
						Discharged	7/20/1741
						Discharged	7/20/1741
						Accused but not arrested	
	7/9/1741	Transportation	7/2/1741			Transported	
	7/9/1741	Transportation	6/19/1741			Transported	
						Discharged	6/30/1741
6/17/1741	7/1/1741	Hanging				Hanged	8/15/1741
	7/28/1741					Transported	
						Discharged	7/2/1741
	7/9/1741	Transportation	7/1/1741			Transported	
	7/9/1741	Transportation	6/24/1741			Transported	
						Discharged	6/4/1741
	8/1/1741	Transportation	7/2/1741			Transported	
6/19/1741	7/9/1741	Transportation	6/20/1741			Transported	
						Accused but not found	
	7/15/1741	Transportation	6/25/1741			Transported	
	8/1/1741	Transportation	6/27/1741			Transported	
						Accused but not arrested	
						Mentioned but not accused	
	7/9/1741	Transportation	6/29/1741			Transported	
	7/9/1741	Transportation	6/18/1741			Transported	
						Mentioned but not accused	
	7/10/1741	Burning	6/30/1741	Hanging	7/17/1741	Hanged	7/18/1741
6/17/1741	7/1/1741	Hanging		Transportation	Unknown	Transported	

*All trial verdicts were "guilty."
†Some of the accused confessed more than once. Only their initial confessions are noted here.

Name	Owner First Name	Owner Last Name	Arrested	Plea 1 Date	Plea 1	Plea 2 Date	Plea 2
Patrick	William	English	5/9/1741	6/25/1741	Not guilty	6/26/1741	Guilty
Pedro	Henry	Cuyler					
Pedro	Peter	DePeyster	6/13/1741	7/25/1741	Unknown		
Pedro	Richard	Stilwell					
Phaeton	Nicholas	Bayard	6/30/1741				
Pompey	Samuel	Bayard	6/23/1741	6/26/1741	Not guilty	7/1/1741	Guilty
Pompey	Peter	DeLancey	6/20/1741	7/15/1741	Guilty		
Pompey	Jane	Gilbert	6/23/1741	6/26/1741	Guilty		
Pompey	Abraham	Lefferts	6/1/1741	7/3/1741	Guilty		
Pompey	James	Searle					
Primus	James	DeBrosses	6/12/1741	7/3/1741	Guilty		
Prince	John	Auboyneau	3/2/1741	4/24/1741	Not guilty		
Prince	Gabriel	Crooke	6/13/1741	7/15/1741	Guilty		
Prince	Anthony	Duane	6/1/1741	6/25/1741	Not guilty		
Prince	Cornelius	Kortrecht	7/1/1741	7/23/1741			
Quack	Jacob	Goelet	7/4/1741				
Quack	John	Roosevelt	5/12/1741	5/28/1741	Not guilty		
Quack	John	Walter	4/6/1741	7/10/1741	Guilty		
Quamino	Ebenezer	Pemberton	6/12/1741	6/19/1741	Not guilty	6/23/1741	Guilty
Quash	Charles	LeRoux	7/2/1741				
Quash	Hermanus, Jr.	Rutgers	6/9/1741	6/12/1741	Not guilty		
Robin	Mrs.	Bickley	7/1/1741				
Robin	John	Chambers	4/13/1741	6/6/1741	Not guilty		
Robin	Justice	Willet					
Sam	Col. Frederick	Courtlandt	6/22/1741	6/26/1741	Not guilty	7/11/1741	Guilty
Sam	Peter	Lowe	6/22/1741	6/26/1741	Guilty		
Sam	George	Rappelie	5/30/1741				
Sambo	Francis	Silvester					
Samuel		Kipp					
Sandy (alias Sawney)	Thomas	Niblet	5/14/1741	7/30/1741	Guilty		
Sarah		[free]					
Sarah	[Estate of] Mary	Burk	5/25/1741	7/7/1741	Guilty		
Sarah	Thomas	Niblet	5/10/1741				
Sarah	Oliver?	Teller					
Scipio	Abraham	Abrahamse	6/25/1741	6/26/1741	Not guilty	7/9/1741	Guilty
Scipio	Robert	Bound	6/22/1741	6/26/1741	Guilty		
Scipio	Mrs.	Van Borsom	6/9/1741	6/25/1741	Guilty		
Scotland	Nathaniel	Marston	6/27/1741	7/7/1741	Guilty		
Sterling	Samuel	Lawrence	6/12/1741	7/3/1741	Guilty		
Sussex	Mrs.	Bickley	7/1/1741				
Tickle (alias Will)	Elizabeth	Carpenter	5/30/1741				

Trial Date*	Sentence 1 Date	Sentence 1	Confession†	Sentence 2	Sentence 2 Date	Final Outcome	Final Outcome Date
	7/9/1741	Transportation	6/27/1741			Transported	
						Accused but not arrested	
			6/29/1741			Discharged	7/20/1741
						Accused but not found	
						Discharged	7/15/1741
	7/15/1741	Transportation	6/30/1741			Transported	
	7/15/1741	Transportation	6/22/1741			Transported	
	7/15/1741	Transportation	6/27/1741			Transported	
	7/9/1741	Transportation	6/9/1741			Transported	
						Accused but not arrested	
	7/9/1741	Transportation	6/19/1741			Transported	
5/1/1741	5/8/1741	Hanging				Hanged	5/11/1741
	7/15/1741	Transportation	6/13/1741			Discharged	7/20/1741
6/26/1741	7/1/1741	Hanging				Hanged	7/3/1741
	7/28/1741	Transportation				Transported	
						Discharged	7/23/1741
5/29/1741	5/29/1741	Burning	5/30/1741			Burned	5/30/1741
	7/10/1741	Burning	6/23/1741	Hanging	7/17/1741	Hanged	7/18/1741
	7/9/1741	Transportation	6/22/1741			Transported	
						Discharged	7/6/1741
6/13/1741	6/15/1741	Burning				Burned	6/16/1741
						Discharged	7/20/1741
6/8/1741	6/8/1741	Burning				Burned	6/9/1741
						Accused but not arrested	
	7/15/1741	Transportation	7/1/1741			Transported	
	8/1/1741	Transportation	7/3/1741			Transported	
						Discharged	6/4/1741
						Mentioned but not accused	
						Mentioned but not accused	
	8/1/1741	Transportation	5/22/1741			Transported	
						Mentioned but not accused	
	7/7/1741	Hanging	6/1/1741	Transportation	7/15/1741	Transported	
						Discharged	7/11/1741
						Mentioned but not accused	
	7/9/1741	Transportation	6/27/1741			Transported	
	7/9/1741	Transportation	7/2/1741			Transported	
	7/9/1741	Transportation				Transported	
	7/9/1741	Transportation	6/29/1741			Transported	
	7/9/1741	Transportation	6/23/1741			Transported	
						Discharged	7/20/1741
	8/1/1741	Transportation	6/12/1741			Transported	

*All trial verdicts were "guilty."
†Some of the accused confessed more than once. Only their initial confessions are noted here.

Name	Owner First Name	Owner Last Name	Arrested	Plea 1 Date	Plea 1	Plea 2 Date	Plea 2
Titus	Capt. Jacob	Phoenix	6/27/1741	7/7/1741	Guilty		
Toby	Widow	Breasted	6/25/1741	7/1/1741	Guilty		
Toby	Thomas	Wendover	6/30/1741	7/10/1741	Not guilty		
Tom	David	Abeel					
Tom	George	Brinkerhoff					
Tom	David	Clarkson					
Tom	Walter, Sr.	Hyer	6/26/1741	7/1/1741	Not guilty		
Tom	Capt. Robert, Jr.	Livingston	6/26/1741	7/30/1741	Guilty		
Tom	Benjamin	Moore	6/1/1741	6/16/1741	Guilty		
Tom	Capt. Henry	Rowe	6/12/1741	7/3/1741	Guilty		
Tom		Ryndert					
Tom	Simeon	Soumaien	6/23/1741	6/26/1741	Guilty		
Tom	Peter	Valette	6/30/1741				
Tom	Winant	Van Zant	5/30/1741				
Tony	Judith	Brazier	6/22/1741	6/26/1741	Guilty		
Tony (alias Tonia or Jonia)	Col. Frederick	Courtlandt	6/29/1741				
Tony	John	Latham	6/13/1741	6/25/1741	Not guilty		
Venture	Adolph	Philipse					
Venture	Cornelius	Tiebout	6/28/1741	7/1/1741	Not guilty		
Warwick	Obadiah	Hunt	6/25/1741	7/1/1741	Guilty		
Will	Abraham	Filkin	4/6/1741				
Will	Johannes	Hardenbergh	6/29/1741				
Will	Capt. John	Lush	5/24/1741	6/25/1741	Not guilty	6/26/1741	Guilty
Will	Coenradt	Ten Eyck	6/12/1741	7/3/1741	Guilty		
Will	John	Tiebout	7/4/1741				
Will	Jacobus	Vaarck	6/20/1741	7/25/1741	Not guilty	6/26/1741	Guilty
Will	Anthony	Ward	6/20/1741	6/25/1741	Guilty		
Will	Samuel	Weaver					
Windsor	Samuel Myers	Cohen	6/25/1741	7/1/1741	Guilty		
Worcester	Isaac	Varyan	5/30/1741	6/19/1741	Not guilty	6/23/1741	Guilty
York	Charles	Crooke	6/22/1741	6/26/1741	Guilty		
York	Gerardus	Duyckinck	7/2/1741				
York		Ludlow					
York	Peter	Marschalk	6/9/1741	6/16/1741	Not guilty		
York	Benjamin	Peck	5/30/1741	6/25/1741	Guilty		
York	Thomas	Thomas	6/20/1741	7/6/1741			
York	Widow [of Peter]	Van Ranst	7/1/1741	7/23/1741			

Trial Date*	Sentence 1 Date	Sentence 1	Confession†	Sentence 2	Sentence 2 Date	Final Outcome	Final Outcome Date
	7/9/1741	Transportation	6/30/1741			Transported	
	7/9/1741	Transportation	6/30/1741			Transported	
	8/1/1741	Transportation				Transported	
						Mentioned but not accused	
						Mentioned but not accused	
						Mentioned but not accused	
	7/17/1741	Hanging		Transportation	8/1/1741	Transported	
	8/1/1741	Transportation	6/27/1741			Transported	
	7/9/1741	Transportation	6/18/1741			Transported	
	7/9/1741	Transportation	7/2/1741			Transported	
						Accused but not arrested	
	7/9/1741	Transportation	6/26/1741			Transported	
						Discharged	7/23/1741
						Discharged	7/2/1741
	7/9/1741	Transportation	7/2/1741			Transported	
						Discharged	7/23/1741
6/26/1741	7/1/1741	Hanging				Hanged	7/3/1741
						Accused but not arrested	
7/15/1741	7/17/1741	Hanging				Hanged	7/18/1741
	7/9/1741	Transportation	7/1/1741			Transported	
						Discharged	7/20/1741
						Discharged	6/29/1741
	7/9/1741	Transportation	6/27/1741			Transported	
	7/9/1741	Transportation	6/30/1741			Transported	
						Discharged	7/23/1741
	7/9/1741	Transportation				Transported	
	7/2/1741	Burning	7/4/1741			Burned	7/4/1741
						Accused but not arrested	
	8/1/1741	Transportation	6/30/1741			Transported	
	7/9/1741	Transportation	6/22/1741			Transported	
	7/9/1741	Transportation	6/27/1741			Transported	
						Discharged	7/13/1741
						Accused but not arrested	
6/19/1741	7/1/1741	Hanging	6/20/1741			Hanged	7/3/1741
	7/9/1741	Transportation	6/27/1741			Transported	
	8/1/1741	Transportation	6/27/1741			Transported	
	7/28/1741	Transportation				Transported	

*All trial verdicts were "guilty."
†Some of the accused confessed more than once. Only their initial confessions are noted here.

The Owners

First Name	Last Name	Wealth*	Ethnicity†	Party**
David	Abeel	50	Dutch	M
Abraham	Abrahamse	25	Dutch	
Jacob	Abrahamse		Dutch	
Alexander	Allair	30	French	M
Abraham	Alsteyn	25	Dutch	
John	Auboyneau		French	M
Capt. Josiah	Bagley	30		
Richard	Baker	10	English	
Nicholas	Bayard	70	Dutch	M
Samuel	Bayard	355	Dutch	M
Stephen	Bayard	110	Dutch	M
Frederick	Becker		English	
Robert	Benson		Dutch	
Mrs.	Bickley			
Jasper	Bosch	30	Dutch	
Robert	Bound			
Judith	Brazier			
Henry	Breasted	25	Dutch	
Widow	Breasted	15	Dutch	
George	Brinkerhoff	40	Dutch	
Capt. J.	Brown	10	English	
[Estate of] Mary	Burk	80	English	
Elizabeth	Carpenter		English	
John	Chambers	85	English	C
George	Clarke		English	C
David	Clarkson	235	Dutch	M
Mrs.	Clopper		Dutch	
Christopher	Codweis			
Samuel Myers	Cohen		Jewish	M

*Assessment of the real and personal estate of the individual in pounds, according to the 1730 or 1734 tax roll.
†Ethnicity and occupation are taken from Goodfriend's 1730 tax list database.
**M for Morrisite (Country Party); C for Cosbyite (Court Party).

Occupation	Ward	Slave's Name	Slave's Final Outcome	Slave Trader
merchant	East	Tom	Mentioned but not accused	
	East	Scipio	Transported	
	Montgomerie	Jack	Transported	
cooper	Dock	Anonymous	Accused but not arrested	
bricklayer	West	Cato	Mentioned but not accused	
merchant		Prince	Hanged	
	West	Jemmy	Mentioned but not accused	
tavernkeeper	Dock	Cajoe	Discharged	
merchant	Dock	Phaeton	Discharged	✔
merchant	Dock	Pompey	Transported	✔
merchant	Dock	Ben	Accused but not found	✔
brewer		Bess	Accused but not arrested	
		Pablo Ventura Angel (alias Powlus)	Transported	
	Montgomerie	Cato	Transported	
		Mars	Transported	
		Robin	Discharged	
		Sussex	Discharged	
mariner	East	Francis	Burned	✔
		Jasper (alias Gosport)	Transported	
		Scipio	Transported	
	East	Tony	Transported	
feltmaker	South	Jack	Transported	
	North	Toby	Transported	
merchant	Dock	Tom	Mentioned but not accused	
	Montgomerie	Jeffery	Transported	
	East	Sarah	Transported	
butcher		Albany	Burned	
		Tickle (alias Will)	Transported	
lawyer	West	Cuba	Discharged	
		Robin	Burned	
lt. governor	South	Barbara	Mentioned but not accused	
		Denby	Mentioned but not accused	
merchant	South	Fortune	Transported	✔
		Tom	Mentioned but not accused	✔
		Betty	Mentioned but not accused	
		Cambridge	Transported	
		Jack	Accused but not found	
merchant		Hereford	Discharged	
		Windsor	Transported	

First Name	Last Name	Wealth*	Ethnicity†	Party**
Gerardus	Comfort	30	Dutch	
Derrick	Cook	5	Dutch	
Col. Frederick	Courtlandt			
Joseph	Cowley			
Charles	Crooke	20	English	
Gabriel	Crooke	40	English	
Henry	Cruger		Dutch	
John	Cruger	100	Dutch	M
John, Jr.	Cruger		Dutch	C
	Cruger		Dutch	
Capt.	Cunningham		English	
Henry	Cuyler	100	Dutch	
James	DeBrosses	15	French	M
James	DeLancey	10	French	
Peter	DeLancey		French	C
Peter	DePeyster	10	Dutch	M
John	Dewit	25	Dutch	M
John	Dorland			
Anthony	Duane	110	English	C
Gerardus	Duyckinck	50	Dutch	M
Mrs.	Ellison			
Thomas	Ellison			
William	English	10		M
James	Favieres	60	French	
Abraham	Filkin	5	English	
Dr. Archibald	Fisher	55	English	M
	Frank			
Capt. Roger	French	25		
Jane	Gilbert	30	English	
William	Gilbert	30	English	
Jacob	Goelet	95	Dutch	M

*Assessment of the real and personal estate of the individual in pounds, according to the 1730 or 1734 tax roll.
†Ethnicity and occupation are taken from Goodfriend's 1730 tax list database.
**M for Morrisite (Country Party); C for Cosbyite (Court Party).

Occupation	Ward	Slave's Name	Slave's Final Outcome	Slave Trader
cooper	West	Cook	Burned	
		Jack	Transported	
		Jenny	Accused but not arrested	
	North	Anonymous	Accused but not arrested	
		Tony (alias Tonia or Jonia)	Discharged	
		Sam	Transported	
		Cato	Hanged	
bolter	East	York	Transported	
bolter	Dock	Prince	Discharged	
		Hanover	Accused but not found	✔
		Neptune	Mentioned but not accused	✔
merchant	Dock	Deptford	Transported	✔
mayor	Dock	Hanover	Discharged	
		Fortune	Mentioned but not accused	
		Anonymous	Accused but not arrested	
merchant	East	Pedro	Accused but not arrested	
distiller	Montgomerie	Primus	Transported	
lawyer	West	Othello	Hanged	
merchant		Albany	Accused but not arrested	
		Pompey	Transported	
		Antonio de St. Bendito	Transported	
merchant	East	Pedro	Discharged	
merchant	East	Anonymous	Accused but not arrested	
		Jack	Discharged	
merchant	East	Prince	Hanged	✔
house painter	Dock	York	Discharged	
		Billy	Discharged	
		Jamaica	Transported	
	East	Cork	Arrested by mistake and released	
		Patrick	Transported	
merchant	East	Cajoe	Accused but not arrested	
	Montgomerie	Will	Discharged	
doctor	Dock	Harry	Mentioned but not accused	
		Lucena	Accused but not arrested	
merchant	Dock	London	Transported	
	Dock	Pompey	Transported	
baker	Dock	Cuffee	Accused but not arrested	
shopkeeper	East	Quack	Discharged	

First Name	Last Name	Wealth*	Ethnicity†	Party**
Lewis	Gomez	80	Jewish	
Mordecai	Gomez	100	Jewish	
Gertrude	Governeur		Dutch	
John	Groesbeck	50	Dutch	M
Joseph	Haines			
Johannes	Hardenbergh	65	Dutch	C
Judah	Hay		Jewish	
Dr. James	Henderson	95	English	
Augustine	Hicks			
Joseph	Hildreth			
Henry	Holt		English	
Israel	Horsefield	5	English	M
Timothy	Horsefield		English	M
John	Hunt	30	English	M
Obadiah	Hunt	80	English	
Walter, Sr.	Hyer	15	Dutch	
William	Jamison	15	Scottish	
Augustus	Jay	175	French	
Peter	Jay	50	French	M
Edward	Kelly			
Mrs. Elizabeth	Kiersted	40	Dutch	
Katherine	Kipp		Dutch	
	Kipp	50	Dutch	M
Cornelius	Kortrecht		Dutch	M
John	Latham	15	English	
Samuel	Lawrence	25	English	M
Abraham	Lefferts	45	Dutch	
Charles	LeRoux	25	French	M
Capt. Robert, Jr.	Livingston	175	English	M
Peter	Lowe	35	Dutch	C
	Ludlow			
Capt. John	Lush	10		
Mrs. Constance	Lynch			
David	Machado	15		
John	Macmullen		Scottish	
Abraham	Marschalk	20	Dutch	
Peter	Marschalk	30	Dutch	M

*Assessment of the real and personal estate of the individual in pounds, according to the 1730 or 1734 tax roll.
†Ethnicity and occupation are taken from Goodfriend's 1730 tax list database.
**M for Morrisite (Country Party); C for Cosbyite (Court Party).

Occupation	Ward	Slave's Name	Slave's Final Outcome	Slave Trader
merchant	Montgomerie	Cuffee	Burned	
merchant	East	Cajoe (alias Africa)	Transported	✔
		Jack	Accused but not found	
merchant	East	Mink	Transported	✔
		Ancram	Accused but not arrested	
		Burlington	Discharged	
	East	Will	Discharged	
merchant		Jack	Discharged	
doctor	East	Caesar	Transported	
		London	Discharged	
schoolmaster		Diego	Accused but not arrested	
dancing master		Joe	Accused but not found	
butcher	Dock	Caesar	Transported	
butcher		Guy	Transported	
mariner	Dock	Jenny	Mentioned but not accused	
tavernkeeper	South	Warwick	Transported	✔
bricklayer	West	Tom	Transported	
lawyer	South	Cuffee	Accused but not arrested	
merchant	West	Ben	Accused but not found	✔
merchant	West	Brash	Transported	✔
butcher		London	Transported	
	East	Braveboy	Transported	
		Harry	Hanged	
cordwainer		Samuel	Mentioned but not accused	
	Montgomerie	Caesar	Transported	
		Prince	Transported	
ship's carpenter	Montgomerie	Fortune	Transported	
		Tony	Hanged	
mariner	Dock	Sterling	Transported	
merchant	East	Pompey	Transported	
silversmith	East	Quash	Discharged	
lawyer	Dock	Tom	Transported	
mariner	South	Juan (alias Indian Wan)	Transported	
		Sam	Transported	
		York	Accused but not arrested	
mariner	East	Will	Transported	✔
		Cuba	Discharged	
	East	Diana	Accused but not arrested	
		Augustine Gutierrez	Unknown	
	South	Diego	Discharged	
baker	South	London	Transported	✔
		York	Hanged	✔

First Name	Last Name	Wealth*	Ethnicity†	Party**
Capt. Hubert	Marshall			
Nathaniel	Marston	125	English	M
Mr.	Masterton			
Sarah	Mesnard		French	
John	Mizreal			
Benjamin	Moore	5	English	
Col. John	Moore	200	English	C
Joseph	Murray	50	English	C
Thomas	Niblet	70	English	
Dr.	Nicols		English	
Benjamin	Peck	30	English	M
Ebenezer	Pemberton	55	English	
Adolph	Philipse	275	Dutch	
Frederick	Philipse	210	Dutch	
Capt. Jacob	Phoenix	10	Dutch	
John	Pintard	80	French	M
David	Provost	150	Dutch	M
John	Provost	20	Dutch	M
George	Rappelie		Dutch	
Paul	Richard	125	French	
B.	Robins			
John	Roerback	5	German	M
John	Roosevelt	130	Dutch	C
Capt. Henry	Rowe	10	English	
Hermanus, Jr.	Rutgers	15	Dutch	M
Henry	Ryker			
	Ryndert			
Capt. Jacob	Sarly	30	Dutch	
Adoniah	Schuyler		Dutch	
Widow	Schuyler	40	Dutch	
James	Searle	20	English	

*Assessment of the real and personal estate of the individual in pounds, according to the 1730 or 1734 tax roll.
†Ethnicity and occupation are taken from Goodfriend's 1730 tax list database.
**M for Morrisite (Country Party); C for Cosbyite (Court Party).

Occupation	Ward	Slave's Name	Slave's Final Outcome	Slave Trader
		Ben	Burned	
merchant	East	Scotland	Transported	✔
		Cataline	Accused but not arrested	
merchant		Antonio de la Cruz	Transported	
		Dr. Harry	Burned	
sailmaker	East	Tom	Transported	
merchant	South	Caesar	Discharged	✔
		Cato	Transported	✔
lawyer	West	Adam	Transported	
		Caesar	Mentioned but not accused	
		Congo	Mentioned but not accused	
		Dido	Mentioned but not accused	
		Jack	Transported	
victualler	Dock	Sandy (alias Sawney)	Transported	
		Sarah	Discharged	
doctor		Juan	Discharged	
glover	Montgomerie	Caesar	Burned	
		York	Transported	
		Anonymous	Suicide	
minister	South	Quamino	Transported	
merchant	Dock	Cuffee	Burned	✔
		Venture	Accused but not arrested	✔
merchant	South	Frank	Discharged	
	Montgomerie	Titus	Transported	✔
merchant	Dock	Caesar	Transported	
merchant	East	Lowe	Transported	✔
cooper	North	Cato (alias Toby)	Hanged	✔
		Sam	Discharged	
merchant	East	Cato	Accused but not arrested	
		Dick	Discharged	
baker	East	Jack	Discharged	
house painter	East	Quack	Burned	
	Montgomerie	Tom	Transported	
brewer	East	Galloway	Hanged	
		Jacob	Transported	
		Quash	Burned	
		Frank	Hanged	
		Tom	Accused but not arrested	
mariner	East	Juan de la Silva	Hanged	
		Lewis	Transported	✔
	East	Anonymous	Accused but not arrested	
merchant	North	Pompey	Accused but not arrested	

First Name	Last Name	Wealth*	Ethnicity†	Party**
John	Shurmur			
Francis	Silvester	20	English	
Joshua	Sleydall			
Simeon	Soumaien	50	French	M
Richard	Stilwell	70	English	
Oliver?	Teller		English	
Coenradt	Ten Eyck	80	Dutch	
Thomas	Thomas	15	Dutch	M
John	Thurman	25	English	
Cornelius	Tiebout	10	Dutch	M
John	Tiebout	25	Dutch	M
Robert	Todd	10	English	
Jacobus	Vaarck	10	Dutch	
John	Vaarck		Dutch	
Peter	Valette	110	French	
Mrs.	Van Borsom		Dutch	
Rip	Van Dam	260	Dutch	M
John	Vanderspiegle		Dutch	
Peter	Van Dursen	20	Dutch	
Abraham	Van Horne	180	Dutch	M
Cornelius	Van Horne	180	Dutch	M
David	Van Horne		Dutch	M
Widow	Van Ranst		Dutch	
Winant	Van Zant	70	Dutch	
Isaac	Varyan			
Widow [of Michael]	Vaughton		English	
John	Walter	130	English	M
Capt. William	Walton	255	English	M
Anthony	Ward	25	English	
Samuel	Weaver	20	English	M
Thomas	Wendover	25	English	

*Assessment of the real and personal estate of the individual in pounds, according to the 1730 or 1734 tax roll.
†Ethnicity and occupation are taken from Goodfriend's 1730 tax list database.
**M for Morrisite (Country Party); C for Cosbyite (Court Party).

Occupation	Ward	Slave's Name	Slave's Final Outcome	Slave Trader
	East	Cato	Hanged	
cooper	East	Sambo	Mentioned but not accused	
		Jack	Transported	
silversmith	Dock	Tom	Transported	
mariner	Dock	Pedro	Accused but not found	
merchant	Dock	Sarah	Mentioned but not accused	
bolter	Dock	Dick	Transported	
		Will	Transported	
cordwainer	South	York	Transported	
baker	West	Harry	Transported	
carpenter	Montgomerie	Curacoa Dick	Burned	
		Venture	Hanged	
blockmaker	East	Jack	Confessed but not arrested	✔
		Will	Discharged	✔
vintner	West	Dundee	Transported	
baker	Dock	Bastian (alias Tom Peal)	Transported	
		Jonneau (alias John)	Transported	
		Will	Transported	
baker	South	Caesar (alias John Gwin)	Hanged	
merchant	East	Tom	Discharged	✔
	North	Scipio	Transported	
merchant	South	John	Discharged	✔
	West	Fortune	Hanged	
	Dock	Diego	Discharged	
merchant	East	Bridgewater	Transported	✔
		London	Accused but not found	✔
merchant	East	Kid	Discharged	✔
		Cora	Discharged	
	Montgomerie	John	Discharged	
		York	Transported	
blockmaker	East	John	Accused but not arrested	✔
		Tom	Discharged	✔
		Worcester	Transported	
sailmaker		Cuffee	Transported	
butcher	East	Quack	Hanged	✔
	East	Dublin	Discharged	✔
	East	Fortune	Hanged	✔
		Jupiter	Transported	✔
watchmaker	Dock	Will	Burned	
tanner	East	Will	Accused but not arrested	
cordwainer	West	Emanuel	Transported	
		Toby	Transported	

First Name	Last Name	Wealth*	Ethnicity†	Party**
John	Wilkins	35	English	
Justice	Willet			
Matthew	Wolf	40		
Benjamin	Wyncoop	65	Dutch	M

*Assessment of the real and personal estate of the individual in pounds, according to the 1730 or 1734 tax roll.
†Ethnicity and occupation are taken from Goodfriend's 1730 tax list database.
**M for Morrisite (Country Party); C for Cosbyite (Court Party).

Occupation	Ward	Slave's Name	Slave's Final Outcome	Slave Trader
	East	Fortune	Transported	
		Robin	Accused but not arrested	
	East	Dick	Transported	
silversmith	South	London	Transported	

Horsmanden's Journal *and the Manuscript Trial Transcripts*

All quotations from Daniel Horsmanden's *Journal* (cited as Horsmanden, *Journal*) are from the first edition, *Journal of the Proceedings in The Detection of the Conspiracy FORMED BY Some* White *People, in Conjunction with* Negro *and other* Slaves, *FOR Burning the City of* NEW-YORK *in AMERICA, and Murdering the Inhabitants* (New York, 1744). A nineteenth-century reprint, *The New York Conspiracy* (New York, 1810), contains numerous errors, as does a modern edition edited by Thomas J. Davis, *The New York Conspiracy* (Boston: Beacon, 1971), based on the flawed 1810 edition. Serena Zabin, ed., *The New York Conspiracy Trials of 1741* (New York: Bedford, 2004), is based on the 1810 edition and is greatly abridged. The 1744 edition is available both on microfiche and in digital format through Readex's *Early American Imprints;* the 1810 edition is available in digital format through the Library of Congress's American Memory Web site, "Slaves and the Courts, 1740–1860." Quotations from Horsmanden appear on nearly every page of this book, and the complete *Journal* is more readily available in digital than printed format. For these reasons, passages from Horsmanden's *Journal* are not cited in the Notes but can easily be found in the digital editions.

As discussed in chapter 4, there are two sets of trial manuscripts from 1741. The first are the records held in the New York State Archives in Albany, described by E. B. O'Callaghan in his *Calendar of Historical Manuscripts in the Office of the Secretary of State, Albany, N.Y.* (Albany, 1866), Vol. 2, originally bound in Volume 74. That bound volume was badly damaged in the Albany Capitol fire of 1911, and the fragile records of the trials have rarely been consulted since, as handling might have destroyed them. In 2003–04, archivist James Folts arranged for many of those records to be digitally scanned and made them available to me, for which I am deeply grateful. They are cited as New York Colony Council Papers (NYCCP), with reference to O'Callaghan's original index, by volume and page and in some cases with the added specification of r (recto) and v (verso), as the digital files have been titled.

The second set of manuscripts of the trial proceedings is held at The National Archives (formerly the PRO), Kew, in the Colonial Office Papers (CO), and was originally enclosed with a letter sent by George Clarke to the Lords of Trade, June 20, 1741. A transcript of Ury's trial was enclosed with a letter from Clarke to the Lords of Trade on August 24, 1741. Both can be found in CO 5/1094, and are cited by that reference in the Notes. A somewhat unreliable set of manuscript copies of these trial minutes and confessions is held at the New-York Historical Society, Parish Transcripts, folder 163.

Slave Names

Horsmanden used parentheses and the possessive to identify slaves by their owners, as in "Cuffee (Philipse's)." Some historians have copied this practice, while others have simply used the owner's last name as if it were the slave's last name, as in "Cuffee Philipse." I have tried to avoid both of these conventions. Instead, in the text, I identify slaves' owners at their slaves' initial introduction and, in subsequent discussion, refer to those slaves by their first names only. Where that creates confusion, as in the case of many slaves with the same first name, I have used owners' names in parentheses without the possessive, as in "Cuffee (Philipse)." Readers should refer to Appendices B and C for further clarification on any slave or slaveowner named in the text.

Abbreviated Names

CC   Cadwallader Colden
DH   Daniel Horsmanden
JA   James Alexander

Repositories

LOC   Library of Congress
MCNY   Museum of the City of New York
NYHS   New-York Historical Society
NYPL   New York Public Library
PRO   The National Archives (PRO), Kew, UK

Journals

JNH   *Journal of Negro History*
NYH   *New York History*
NYHSC   *New-York Historical Society Collections*
WMQ   *William and Mary Quarterly*

Newspapers

NYEP   *New York Evening Post*
NYG   *New York Gazette*
NYWJ   *New-York Weekly Journal*

Printed Public Records

Col. Laws of NY   Lincoln, Charles Z., William H. Johnson, and A. Judd Northrop. *Colonial Laws of New York from the Year 1664 to the Revolution.* Albany, 1894.

Docs. Col. NY   O'Callaghan, E. B., ed. *Documents Relative to the Colonial and Revolutionary History of New-York.* 11 vols. Albany, 1855–61.

Doc. Hist. NY	O'Callaghan, E. B., ed. *The Documentary History of the State of New-York.* 4 vols. Albany, 1849–51.
JLC	*Journal of the Legislative Council of the Colony of New-York, 1691–1775.* 2 vols. Albany, 1861.
Journal of the Assembly	*Journal of the Votes and Proceedings of the General Assembly of the Colony of New-York.* 2 vols. New York, 1764.
MCC	Osgood, Herbert L. *Minutes of the Common Council of the City of New York, 1675–1776.* 8 vols. New York, 1905.

Printed Private Papers

Colden, "History of Cosby and Clark"	Cadwallader Colden, "History of Governor William Cosby's Administration and of Lieutenant-Governor George Clarke's Administration Through 1737," *NYHSC* 68 (1935): 283, 286.
LPCC	*Letters and Papers of Cadwallader Colden,* in *New-York Historical Society Collections,* vol. 1, 1711–1729; vol. 2, 1730–1742; vol. 3, 1743–1747; vol. 8, Additional Letters and Papers, 1715–1748 (1918–37).

Other Printed Material

Hamilton, *Gentleman's Progress*	Alexander Hamilton. *Gentleman's Progress: The Itinerarium of Dr. Alexander Hamilton, 1744,* ed. Carl Bridenbaugh. Pittsburgh: University of Pittsburgh Press, 1948.
Katz, *Brief Narrative*	*A Brief Narrative of the Case and Trial of John Peter Zenger,* ed. Stanley Nider Katz. Cambridge, MA: Harvard University Press, 1963.
NYECM	Arthur Everett Peterson and George William Edwards. *New York as an Eighteenth-Century Municipality.* 2 vols. New York: Longmans, Green & Co., 1917.
SCJ	Paul M. Hamlin and Charles E. Baker. *Supreme Court of Judicature of the Province of New York, 1691–1704.* 2 vols. New York: New-York Historical Society, 1959.
Smith, Jr., *History*	William Smith, Jr. *History of the Province of New York.* 1757. 2 vols. Cambridge, MA: Harvard University Press, 1972.
Smith, Jr., *Memoirs,* 1	*Historical Memoirs of William Smith from 16 March 1763 to 9 July 1776,* ed. William H. W. Sabine. New York, 1956.
Smith, Jr., *Memoirs,* 2	*Historical Memoirs of William Smith from 12 July 1776 to 25 July 1778,* ed. William H. W. Sabine. New York, 1958.
Stokes, *Iconography*	I. N. Phelps Stokes. *Iconography of Manhattan Island, 1498–1909.* 6 vols. New York: R. H. Dodd, 1915–28; Arno Press, 1967.

NOTES

Preface

1. *NYWJ*, November 19, 1733.

2. James Thomson, "Rule, Britannia," in James Thomson, *Poetical Works*, ed. J. Logie Robertson (London: Oxford University Press, 1965), p. 422. *Massachusetts Gazette*, December 19, 1771.

3. Samuel Johnson, "Taxation Not Tryanny," in *The Yale Edition of the Works of Samuel Johnson* (New Haven: Yale University Press, 1977), 10:454. Edmund S. Morgan, *American Slavery, American Freedom: The Ordeal of Colonial Virginia* (New York: W. W. Norton, 1975, 1995), pp. 3–5.

4. *Peter Kalm's Travels in North America*, trans. Adolph B. Benson (New York, 1937), 1:131 (cited hereafter as Kalm, *Travels*).

5. DH to CC, January 24, 1734, *LPCC*, 2:104. *The Works of Alexander Pope*, ed. William Roscoe (London, 1847), 5:376. Henry St. John Bolingbroke, *Dissertation Upon Parties* (London, 1735), Letter 1. Thomas Jefferson to Francis Hopkinson, March 13, 1789, *Writings* (New York: Library of America, 1984), pp. 940–41. See also Richard Hofstadter, *The Idea of a Party System: The Rise of Legitimate Opposition in the United States, 1780–1840* (Berkeley: University of California Press, 1969).

6. George Clarke to the Lords of Trade, October 7, 1736, *Docs. Col. NY*, 6:80. Colden, "History of Cosby and Clarke," p. 349. For Van Dam and Clarke's rival administrations, see *NYWJ*, October 4, 1736.

7. DH to CC, December 22, 1736, *LPCC*, 2:164.

8. *NYG*, March 18, 1734.

9. George Clarke, Jr., to Lord De La Warr, June 20, 1740, *Docs. Col. NY*, 6:163. George Clarke to Duke of Newcastle, October 7, 1736, *Docs. Col. NY*, 6:79, 76.

10. Anonymous to CC, [July 23?], 1741, *LPCC*, 8:270–71.

11. Late eighteenth-, nineteenth-, and early twentieth-century commentators on the history of colonial New York—everyone from Oliver Wendell Holmes to Theodore Roosevelt—rarely failed to mention the trials, if only to dismiss the conspiracy as the product of widespread hysteria among panicked white New Yorkers. This view also was voiced in the Preface to an 1810 reprint of Horsmanden's *Journal*, which claimed that "no doubt can be had of the actual existence of a plot; but its extent could never have been so great as the terror of those times depicted" (Anonymous Preface to Daniel Horsmanden, *The New York Conspiracy* [New York, 1810]). Of these early accounts, one of the most influential, surprisingly, is an 89-page unpublished paper by Walter Franklin Prince, "New York 'Negro Plot' of 1741," housed at the NYPL. Parts of Prince's deeply ahistorical essay were published as "The Great Slave Conspiracy Delusion: A Sketch of the Crowning Judicial Atrocity of American History," [New Haven] *Saturday Chronicle*, June 28–August 23, 1902. For other early accounts, see also T. Wood Clarke, "The Negro Plot of 1741," *NYH* 25 (1944): 167–81, and Henry H. Ingersoll, "The New York Plot of 1741," *The Green Bag* 20 (1908). Much the

same portrait of New Yorkers in "the grip of hysteria" resurfaced in the 1960s when Winthrop Jordan concluded, "It is impossible now to tell surely whether there was *any* legitimate basis for suspecting a slave conspiracy, though clearly contemporary suspicions swelled out of all proportion to reality"—Jordan, *White over Black: American Attitudes Toward the Negro, 1550–1812* (Chapel Hill: University of North Carolina Press, 1968; New York: W. W. Norton, 1977), pp. 117–18. Herbert Aptheker agreed that the plot "provided hysteria leading to exaggeration of the extent of the actual conspiracy but that one existed is clear"—Aptheker, *A Documentary History of the Negro People in the United States* (New York: Citadel Press, 1951), p. 4. Edgar J. McManus, in his *A History of Negro Slavery in New York* (Syracuse: Syracuse University Press, 1966), dismissed the plot as a consequence of the terror with which New Yorkers viewed their slaves. In an essay noteworthy for its reasoned and thorough assessment of earlier treatments of the conspiracy, Ferenc M. Szasz argued that a conspiracy existed, "But it was not a conspiracy organized by the slaves to burn the buildings and take over the town. Instead, there existed several small groups—perhaps in contact with one another, although this is not certain—all of which were plotting to rob the richer citizens of New York City"—Szasz, "The New York Slave Revolt of 1741: A Re-Examination," *NYH* 48 (1967): 217.

A modern reprint of Horsmanden's *Journal* edited by Thomas J. Davis appeared in 1971 (*The New York Conspiracy* [Boston: Beacon]) and occasioned the publication of a number of journal articles which found extensive conspiracy somewhat more plausible. Most of these interpretations were rooted squarely in an emerging Afro-American Studies movement seeking historical precedent for slave resistance (as in Davis's essay, "The New York Slave Conspiracy of 1741 as Black Protest," *JNH* 56 [1971]: 17–30), and none looked for evidence beyond that contained in Horsmanden while, at the same time, dismissing him as unreliable. In 1979, Eugene Genovese added New York's "cloudy conspiracy" to his list of worldwide slave revolts in *From Rebellion to Revolution: Afro-American Slave Revolts in the Making of the Modern World* (New Orleans: Louisiana State University Press, 1979), pp. 26, 42. The following year, Leopold S. Launitz-Schurer, in a provocative essay influenced by the work of Genovese and John Blassingame in recovering slave resistance and slave community life, asserted that the alleged conspiracy was really an intricate black market in stolen goods and probably nothing more—Launitz-Schurer, "Slave Resistance in Colonial New York: An Interpretation of Daniel Horsmanden's New York Conspiracy," *Phylon* 41 (1980): 137–51.

Davis's reprint of Horsmanden also brought the conspiracy to the attention of literary scholar Richard Slotkin, who offered a rare interpretation of the *Journal* as a work of literature—Slotkin, "Narratives of Negro Crime in New England, 1675–1800," *American Quarterly* 25 (1973): 3–31. Thomas J. Davis published the first book-length study of the conspiracy in 1985: *A Rumor of Revolt: The "Great Negro Plot" in Colonial New York* (New York: Free Press, 1985; pbk. ed., Amherst: University of Massachusetts Press, 1990). This work, more narrative than analytical, dismissed the conspiracy question as simplistic and distorting, instead attempting to demonstrate "beyond question that blacks in New York City during 1741 clearly talked of doing damage to the society enslaving them, expressed hopes of gaining freedom and the material benefits being denied them, and acted against the laws restraining their liberty" (p. xii). In general, historians have almost entirely failed to comment on the relationship between the Zenger and conspiracy trials. One exception is B. MacDonald Steers, whose *The Counsellors, Courts and Crimes of Colonial New York* (New York: Exposition Press, 1968) is a brief narrative history of the two cases.

More recent interpretations of the 1741 conspiracy include Peter Linebaugh and Marcus Rediker's Marxist reading asserting that New York's slaves and poor whites were involved in a plot "Atlantic in scope . . . by a motley proletariat to incite an urban insurrection"—Linebaugh and Rediker, *The Many-Headed Hydra: Sailors, Slaves, Commoners, and the Hidden History of the Revolutionary Atlantic* (Boston: Beacon, 2001), pp. 174–210. In their invaluable history of New York, Edwin G. Burrows and Mike Wallace vividly tell the tale of the fires and trials and conclude, drawing heavily from Szasz and Launitz-Schurer, that although "the actual evidence" for a conspiracy "is less than convincing . . . some less widespread or well-organized coup" or arson "to cover up multiple burglaries" could have lain behind it all—Burrows and Wallace, *Gotham: A History of New York City to 1898* (New York: Oxford University Press, 1998), pp. 159–66. Most recently, legal historian Peter Hoffer has argued that the slaves "conspired," in the narrow legal sense of the term, but were innocent of the plot described by the prosecution—Hoffer, *The Great New York Conspiracy of 1741: Slavery, Crime, and Colonial Law* (Lawrence: University Press of Kansas, 2003). Serena Zabin used Horsmanden's *Journal* as a chief source in her attempt to reconstruct life in eighteenth-century New York while at the same time dismissing any genuine understanding of the conspiracy as impossible ("Places of Exchange: New York City, 1700–1763," Ph.D. diss., Rutgers University, 2000), an interpretation she also offers in the Introduction to her abridged edition of Horsmanden's *Journal*—Serena R. Zabin, ed., *The New York Conspiracy Trials of 1741* (Boston: Beacon/St. Martin's, 2004).

Prologue

1. This scene at Hughson's is reconstructed from confessions and trial testimony. For a complete list of the accused, and the dates of their confessions and trials, see Appendix B; for their owners, see Appendix C.

2. Details about the "hard winter" are taken from Horsmanden's *Journal* as well as from Smith, Jr., *History,* 2:49–50, and *NYWJ,* December 22 and 29, 1740, January 5 and 12, 1741.

3. On this literature, see Ian Watt, *The Rise of the Novel: Studies in Defoe, Richardson, and Fielding* (Berkeley: University of California Press, 1965); J. Paul Hunter, *Before Novels: The Cultural Contexts of Eighteenth-Century English Fiction* (New York: W. W. Norton, 1990); and esp. John J. Richetti, *Popular Fiction Before Richardson: Narrative Patterns, 1700–1739* (Oxford: Oxford University Press, 1969).

4. *Great Newes from the Barbados. Or, A True and Faithful Account of the Grand Conspiracy of The* Negroes *against the* English (London, 1676). The Antigua plot was reported, in brief, in the *NYWJ* on December 6, 1736, and in the *NYG* on November 29, 1736. Zenger printed another report on February 7, 1737. "A full and particular Account of the Negro Plot in Antigoa, as reported by the Committee appointed by the Government there to enquire into the same" was serialized in the *NYWJ,* March 28, April 4, April 11, April 18, and April 25, 1737 (on all but March 28, the report filled the entire front page and continued onto p. 2). In 1737, the account was published in Dublin as *A Genuine Narrative of the Intended Conspiracy of the Negroes at Antigua.* For more on the Antigua revolt, see David Barry Gaspar, *Bondmen and Rebels: A Study of Master-Slave Relations in Antigua* (Durham: Duke University Press, 1993), pp. 3–62.

5. Smith, Jr., *History,* 1:226.

6. Alexander Hamilton, *The History of the Ancient and Honorable Tuesday Club,* ed. Robert Micklus (Chapel Hill: University of North Carolina Press, 1990), 1:33, 82–83.

7. Hamilton, *Gentleman's Progress,* p. 177.

8. Hamilton, *Tuesday Club,* 1:133.

9. "The Confession of Cato a Negroe belonging to John Shurmur. Taken the 20th of June 1741," CO 5/1094, PRO.

Chapter One

1. *NYWJ*, January 5, 12, and 19, February 2, 9, and 16, 1741.

2. *NYWJ*, February 2, 1741. George Farquhar, *The Beaux' Stratagem*, ed. Charles N. Fifer (Lincoln: University of Nebraska Press, 1977). Brian Corman, "What Is the Canon of English Drama, 1660–1737?" *Eighteenth-Century Studies* 26, no. 2 (Winter 1992–93): 307–21. Farquhar's plays were well known in the colonies, as both *The Beaux' Stratagem* and *The Recruiting Officer* were performed at Williamsburg in 1736—Robert H. Land, "The First Williamsburg Theater," *WMQ* 5 (July 1948): 372–73. Farquhar's *Works* were sold in New York at the Montgomerie Library auction in 1732—Kevin J. Hayes, *The Library of John Montgomerie, Colonial Governor of New York and New Jersey* (Newark: University of Delaware Press, 2000), p. 93.

3. *MCC*, 4:172, March 12, 1733; 4:221, October 1, 1734.

4. In London in 1707, the play was an instant hit after its debut at the Queen's Theatre. "It was played twelve more times that season. For the next one hundred years, it was presented at theaters in and around London, and at Bath and Dublin, sometimes as often as fifteen or twenty times a season." It is widely acknowledged as Farquhar's best play—Fifer, ed., *The Beaux' Stratagem*, Intro. On its stage history, see Shirley Strum Kenny, ed., *The Works of George Farquhar* (Oxford: Clarendon Press, 1988), 2:136–44.

5. On Masons' theatregoing, see Richardson Wright, "Masonic Contacts with the Early American Theatre," *Transactions of the American Lodge of Research* 2 (1936): 161–64. The Charleston lodge showed up en masse for that city's May 1737 performance of Farquhar's *Recruiting Officer*, a performance essentially staged for the Masons and followed by Masonic songs (p. 164). Dancing master Henry Holt, who had been a Mason in Charleston until at least 1736, was elected junior warden of the New York Masons in January 1738. Murray married Grace Cosby Freeman, daughter of Governor Cosby and widow of Thomas Freeman, in 1738. Apparently she brought the Freeman family's slaves Adam and Jack to the marriage. For Murray's interest in drama, see his purchases from Montgomerie's library in Hayes, *The Library of John Montgomerie*. Murray's purchases included Aphra Behn's *Plays* (London, 1716 or 1724), 4 vols.; Robert Howard, *The Dramatic Works* (London, 1722); Nathaniel Lee, *Works* (London, 1722), 3 vols.; [Antoine Jacob] Montfleury, *Les Oeuvres de Monsieur Montfleury* (Paris, 1705); Nicholas Rowe, *The Works* (London, 1728), 3 vols.; and Thomas Southerne, *The Works* (London, 1713 or 1721), 2 vols. On warming pans, see Kalm, *Travels*, 1:624, 629.

6. *NYG*, December 4, 1732. George C. D. Odell, *Annals of the New York Stage* (New York: Columbia University Press, 1927), 1:8–11.

7. Daniel Horsmanden was more than a cousin to William Byrd. In 1681, when William was just seven years old, he was sent from Virginia to Purleigh, Essex, to be educated under the guidance of his mother's brother, the Reverend Daniel Horsmanden, Sr.; Byrd was still in England when his uncle's children were born: Susanna ("Suky") (1691), Ursula ("Nutty") (1692), Daniel (1694), Barrington (1695), and Samuel (1697). Byrd's early life, and his relations with Daniel Horsmanden, Sr., are best discussed in Kenneth Lockridge, *The Diary, and Life, of William Byrd II of Virginia, 1674–1744* (Chapel Hill: University of North Carolina Press, 1987). Byrd's siblings, including his sister Ursula, also visited the Horsmandens in England—see William Byrd I to Daniel Horsmanden, March 31, 1685, and William Byrd I to William Byrd II, March 31, 1685, in Tinling, ed., *The Correspondence of the Three William Byrds of Westover, Virginia, 1684–1776*, ed. Marion Tinling (Charlottesville: University Press of Virginia, 1977), 1:35–36. On the Horsmanden family, see "Purleigh, Essex, England—The Church of the Washingtons and Horsmandens," *Virginia*

Magazine of History and Biography XV (1907–08): 314–17; and "The Horsmanden Family," in Tinling, ed., *Correspondence of the Three William Byrds*, 2:830.

Daniel Horsmanden's early life is only briefly discussed in the single biography of him: Sister Mary Paula McManus, "Daniel Horsmanden: Eighteenth-Century New Yorker" (Ph.D. diss., Fordham University, 1960), pp. 1–5. *Tunbrigalia: Or, Tunbridge Miscellanies, For the Year 1719* was printed in London in 1719; the poem is reprinted in *Another Secret Diary of William Byrd of Westover, 1739–1741*, ed. Maude H. Woodfin, trans. and collated Marion Tinling (Richmond, VA: Dietz Press, 1942), p. 406. Byrd's diary was decoded from the shorthand and reprinted in William Byrd, *The London Diary (1717–1721) and Other Writings*, ed. Louis B. Wright and Marion Tinling (New York: Oxford University Press, 1958). Horsmanden appears in Byrd's diary entries regularly for 1718 and 1719. In April 1718: "I went . . . to the park with my cousin Horsmanden and then walked in St. James's Park and walked towards Will's [Coffeehouse] and picked up a girl in the street and committed uncleanness with her." In May: "Daniel and I went to see a Spaniard that made foils" (Byrd, apparently, was contemplating a duel). In August, again walking with Horsmanden in the park: "We endeavored to pick up some girls but were disappointed"—Byrd, *London Diary*, pp. 112, 119, 156. During the month of May 1718, Byrd saw Horsmanden for twenty out of thirty-one days, and for five more met with his "cousins Horsmanden," which may have been just Nutty and Suky, but may have included Daniel. On only six days in the month did he not see any Horsmandens. For Byrd and Horsmanden's exploits, including trips to Tunbridge Wells and Purleigh, see especially pp. 162–63, 170, 185. For Byrd's assessment of his estate for Mary Smith's benefit, see William Byrd II to Michael Bourke, Baron Dunkellin, February 18, 1718, in Tinling, ed., *Correspondence of the Three William Byrds*, 1:313–14.

8. Lockridge, *Diary, and Life*, p. 85. The line in *Tunbrigalia*, of course, rhymes with "more" and refers to Mary Hoar, who was also at Tunbridge Wells (see editor's note in *Another Secret Diary*, p. 407), but it remains an interesting choice. Horsmanden apparently regretted prowling for prostitutes with William Byrd. After the two men traveled to Purleigh to visit Horsmanden's father, young Daniel turned glum (disappointed by Miss B-n-y's rejection? cautioned about Byrd's depravity by his father?). One evening in November 1718 the cousins, having met "two ladies" at Will's Coffeehouse, walked with them to a tavern. "We ate some roast fowl and were merry, notwithstanding Mr. Horsmanden followed us," Byrd wrote snidely. By December, Horsmanden had become either so depressed or so pious that he had taken on a role as Byrd's conscience: "After the play I went to the coffeehouse and drank two dishes of chocolate and talked with my cousin Horsmanden, and he walked home with me lest I should pick up a whore." But by July 1719, Byrd's bad habits had prevailed: "I went to Mr. Horsmanden's lodging and carried him to Spring Garden by water, where we picked up two girls and I lay with one of them all night at the bagnio and rogered her twice"—Byrd, *London Diary*, pp. 192, 206, 289, 343.

9. Byrd, "Inamorato L'Oiseaux," in *Another Secret Diary*, p. 276. Byrd, *London Diary*, pp. 160, 311.

10. DH to Charles Cotton, New York, July 2, 1756, Horsmanden Papers, NYHS, Addenda, no. 31. "He was a Gentleman by Birth and bred at Inn," William Smith, Jr., wrote of Horsmanden, "but wasting his Fortune, & having no Hopes at the Bar he entred into a Partnership with a Chancery Collector and after a short Trial of that Business he fled from his Creditors to Virginia"—Smith, Jr., *Memoirs*, 2:39. Byrd left Horsmanden in charge of some of his business dealings—Byrd, *London Diary*, p. 343. Byrd visited England again from 1721 to 1726, but his diary for this period has never been found, and it's impossible to know how much time he spent with Horsmanden during these years. In Tunbridge Wells in 1719, at the height of enthusiasm for South Sea stock, Horsmanden dined with the wife

of the director of the South Sea Company—ibid., p. 163. Horsmanden was admitted to the Middle Temple in 1721 and to the Inner Temple in 1724.

11. Thomas Templeman, *A New Survey of the Globe: Or an Accurate Mensuration of all the Empires, Kingdoms, Countries, States, principal Provinces, Counties, & Islands in the World* (London, 1729). Horsmanden is listed as a subscriber on p. vii. Horsmanden's grandfather, a Cavalier, had once been a member of the Virginia House of Burgesses, which must have contributed to his determination to seek his fortune in that colony. The exact time of Horsmanden's departure from England is in some dispute, but it appears to have been in 1729 or 1730. Horsmanden, in a brief autobiographical statement, wrote that he "had been bred to the Bar in England, came into this Countrey in the year 1729"—DH to Robert Monckton, June 4, 1763, Chalmers Papers, Papers Relating to New York, 1608–1792, IV:22–23, NYPL. Horsmanden was in Virginia with Byrd in August 1731, when his name turns up as witness to an indenture—Tinling, ed., *Correspondence of the Three William Byrds*, 2:475.

12. William Strickland, *Journal of a Tour in the United States of America, 1794–1795,* ed. Rev. J. E. Strickland (New York: NYHS, 1971), p. 63.

13. Boston's population in 1740 was 17,000, but falling, while New York's was rising. Philadelphia's population at midcentury was nearly identical to New York's—Bureau of the Census, *A Century of Population Growth* (Washington, DC: Government Printing Office, 1909), p. 11. See also Templeman, *New Survey,* plate 1. In 1733 James Alexander's clerk, James Lyne, "counted all the houses in New York, including churches, public buildings, store houses, stables, smith shops, etc., and there were 1473"—JA to CC, June 22, 1752, quoted in Stokes, *Iconography,* 6:23–24.

14. Andrew Burnaby, *Travels through the Middle Settlements in North-America in the Years 1759 and 1760* (1775; Ithaca, NY: Great Seal Books, 1960), p. 80. The best history of the city under English rule is Joyce D. Goodfriend, *Before the Melting Pot: Society and Culture in Colonial New York City, 1664–1730* (Princeton: Princeton University Press, 1992).

15. Bayrd Still, *Mirror for Gotham: New York as Seen by Contemporaries from Dutch Days to the Present* (New York: Fordham University Press, 1994), pp. 21–22. For a full discussion of the population of New York City, including the tax and census data discussed in this chapter, see Appendix A.

16. The Assembly did vote to levy a tax on slaves in 1737 and it was first collected in 1738, at 1 shilling per slave. Records of this tax collection survive only for the single year of 1738, and only for the Outward—"Head or Title of the Tax Role," Vanderwater MS, "New York, 1700–1760," NYHS.

17. Smith, Jr., *History,* 1:226. Hamilton, *Gentleman's Progress,* pp. 43–46. On New York's trade and economy, see Michael Kammen, *Colonial New York: A History* (New York: Oxford University Press, 1975), chapter 7. *NYG,* July 24, 1732. On Adolph Philipse, see Vivienne L. Kruger, "Born to Run: The Slave Family in Early New York, 1626 to 1827" (Ph.D. diss., Columbia University, 1985), pp. 150–55.

18. In 1660 Peter Stuyvesant, having just purchased "Four Negro Boys and one Negro Girl," argued that enslaved Africans, especially "young ones," ought "to be preferred before Spaniards and unbelieving Jews"—quoted in Elizabeth Donnan, *Documents Illustrative of the History of the Slave Trade to America* (1932; New York: Octagon Books, 1969), 3:411, 420–21. On slavery in New York's Dutch period, see Joyce D. Goodfriend, "Burghers and Blacks: The Evolution of a Slave Society at New Amsterdam," *NYH* 59 (April 1978): 124–44. These unwilling immigrants were part of what Ira Berlin has called the "charter generation" of Atlantic creoles, educated, multilingual, and cosmopolitan Africans and Luso-Africans who had served as interpreters and traders for the Portuguese. See Berlin, *Many Thousands Gone: The First Two Centuries of Slavery in North America* (Cambridge,

MA: Harvard University Press, 1998), pp. 17–28. On Central Africans, see Joseph C. Miller, "Central Africa During the Era of the Slave Trade, c. 1490s–1850s," in Linda M. Heywood, ed., *Central Africans and Cultural Transformations in the American Diaspora* (Cambridge: Cambridge University Press, 2002), pp. 21–69.

19. Thelma Foote, "Black Life in Colonial Manhattan, 1664–1785" (Ph.D. diss., Harvard University, 1991), pp. 30–41. *Col. Laws of NY,* 2:768–74.

20. On the Coromantees, see John Thornton, "The Coromantees: An African Cultural Group in Colonial North America and the Caribbean," *Journal of Caribbean Studies* 32 (1998): 161–78. On naming practices, see John Thornton, "Central African Names and African-American Naming Patterns," *WMQ* 50 (1993): 727–42, and Jerome S. Handler and JoAnn Jacoby, "Slave Names and Naming in Barbados, 1650–1830," *WMQ* 53 (1996): 685–728.

21. Donnan, *Documents,* 3:440. Rip Van Dam to the Lords of Trade, November 2, 1731, *Docs. Col. NY,* 6:32–33. *NYWJ,* April 15, 1734. On death rates, see Joseph C. Miller, *The Way of Death: Merchant Capitalism and the Angolan Slave Trade, 1730–1830* (Madison: University of Wisconsin Press, 1988), pp. 440–41. And for a discussion of death rates during seasoning in Jamaica, see Vincent Brown, "Slavery and the Spirits of the Dead: Mortuary Politics in Jamaica, 1740–1834" (Ph.D. diss., Duke University, 2002), pp. 11–65. James G. Lydon has offered a "minimum estimate" that at least 6,800 Africans were imported into the colony of New York between 1700 and 1774, 2,800 directly from Africa and 4,000 from the West Indies and other parts of North America, although "a maximum figure of 7,400 might be justified"—Lydon, "New York and the Slave Trade, 1700 to 1774," *WMQ* 35 (1978): 383, 387. Although the cited data on the geographical origins of imported slaves is taken from 1715 to 1764, Lydon says that "these figures emphasize the years before 1743" (p. 383). Thornton and Heywood suggest that Lydon's figures may overestimate the prevalence of "seasoned" Caribbean imports in the New York trade—John Thornton to author, e-mail June 1, 2004.

22. Patrick M'Robert, *A Tour through Part of the North Provinces of America* (Edinburgh, 1776; New York: Arno Press, 1968), p. 5.

23. Smith, Jr., *History,* 1:226. JA to CC, March 23, 1732, *LPCC,* 2:59.

24. William Cosby to the Lords of Trade, December 18, 1732, *Docs. Col. NY,* 5:939. Cosby to the Lords of Trade, December 7, 1734, *Docs. Col. NY,* 6:24. Secretary Popple to Cosby, January 23, 1736, *Docs. Col. NY,* 6:39–40. JA to Alderman Perry, December 4, 1733, Rutherfurd Family Papers, NYHS, Box 1.

25. Lewis Morris, Jr., to the Lords of Trade, July 19, 1729, *Docs. Col. NY,* 5:887. *Memoirs of the Life and Ministerial Conduct . . . of the Late Lord Visc. Bolingbroke* (London, 1752), p. 41. Philip Livingston to Jacob Wendell, October 17, 1737, Livingston Papers, MCNY. On the overlap between "faction" and "party," see Daniel Sisson, *The American Revolution of 1800* (New York: Knopf, 1974), chap. 2.

The best accounts of the New York controversy, and of the larger context of the province's factional politics, are to be found in Bernard Bailyn, *The Origins of American Politics* (New York: Knopf, 1968), pp. 107–14; Kammen, *Colonial New York;* Stanley Nider Katz, *Newcastle's New York: Anglo-American Politics, 1732–1753* (Cambridge, MA: Harvard University Press, 1968); and Patricia U. Bonomi, *A Factious People: Politics and Society in Colonial New York* (New York: Columbia University Press, 1971). Kammen argued that "it is reasonable to assert that responsible opposition had a respectable genesis, in England and New York, during the 1730s" and concluded, "the fact and legitimacy of opposition developed in early New York" (pp. 201, 206). Bonomi maintained that the crisis of the 1730s challenged "some of the most fundamental assumptions of the imperial system—challenges which prefigured in basic ways the final rupture of 1776" (p. 135). For a more dismissive view, see

Alan Tully, *Forming American Politics: Ideals, Interests, and Institutions in Colonial New York and Pennsylvania* (Baltimore: Johns Hopkins University Press, 1994), who argues that "In attempting to import . . . 'court/country' models of political behavior from Great Britain in order to explain and give a larger legitimacy to their various cliques," New York elites "exaggerated the very factiousness they tried to explain" (p. 213).

26. Lewis Morris to the Lords of Trade, December 15, 1733, *Col. Docs. NY,* 5:957–59. *NYG,* October 7, 1734. Abigail Franks to Naphtali Franks, December 16, 1733, in Leo Hershkowitz and Isidore S. Meyer, eds., *The Lee Max Friedman Collection of American Jewish Colonial Correspondence. Letters of the Franks Family, 1733–1748* (Waltham, MA: American Jewish Historical Society, 1968), pp. 17–18. DH to CC, January 24, 1734, *LPCC,* 2:104. *NYG,* March 18, 1734. See Bailyn, *Origins of American Politics,* pp. 125–27, for a discussion of the novelty of this argument.

27. *NYG,* October 13, 1735. *NYWJ,* October 20, 1735. Archibald Kenney to CC, January 17, 1736, *LPCC,* 2:145–46. In 1734, when Daniel Horsmanden chaired a committee investigating a death threat received by James Alexander, he summoned Alexander to appear before the committee, which convened not at a room in City Hall but at Todd's tavern. Alexander refused, fearing for his safety, since the man he suspected of threatening his life—Francis Harison—was a member of Horsmanden's committee. Alexander was so terrified of entering the tavern that he proposed instead to walk along the bridge in front of Todd's, so that Horsmanden, spying Alexander from Todd's window, might realize that he wasn't defying the summons so much as afraid to obey it—copy of a letter from JA to DH, February 11, 1734; Memorandum of Lewis Morris, Jr., March 13, 1734; James Alexander Papers, the John Peter Zenger Trial Collection, Manuscripts, NYPL. It was unusual for "Ladys" to attend taverns, not least because places where men talked politics were places where women were not. At Todd's, Hamilton reported, "There were 13 gentlemen att table but not so much as one lady" (Hamilton, *Gentleman's Progress,* p. 173). Avoid "being a 'party' woman," Cadwallader Colden advised his daughter Elizabeth in 1737; "a lady never looks more ridiculous to men of sense than when she sets herself up as a politician"—CC to Elizabeth Colden DeLancey, 1737, DeLancey Papers, Box 232, MCNY.

28. "Articles of Complaint," *Doc. Col. NY,* 5:975–78. Katz, *Newcastle's New York,* p. 41. Lewis Morris to JA, February 24, 1735, in Stanley N. Katz, "A New York Mission to England: The London Letters of Lewis Morris to James Alexander, 1735 to 1736," *WMQ* 28 (July 1971): 451. On Cosby's administration, see Katz, *Newcastle's New York,* chaps. 2 and 4.

29. Kammen, *Colonial New York,* p. 201.

30. Inventory of the Estate of Governor John Montgomerie, 1732, Manuscripts Division, NYPL. The ad for the auction specified "Four Negro Men and Four Negro Women" (*NYG,* July 26, 1731). The women were Deliverance, Jenny, Betty, and Emanda. The men and boys were Andrew, Othello, Pompey, and Barbadoes.

31. James Logan to JA, May 21, 1740, quoted in Hayes, *The Library of John Montgomerie,* p. 73.

32. DH to CC, August 27, 1734, *LPCC,* 2:109–11. Lewis Morris to JA, February 24, 1735, in Katz, "A New York Mission to England," p. 457.

33. Smith, Jr., *History,* 1:226. DH to CC, April 2, 1735, *NYHSC,* LI (1918): 132. Lewis Morris to the Lords of Trade, December 15, 1733, *Docs. Col. NY,* 6:958.

34. William Byrd II to DH, February 25, 1736, in Tinling, ed., *The Correspondence of the Three William Byrds,* 2:475. The editors only tentatively identify Horsmanden as the recipient (three pages of the letter are missing, including the addressee), but the context seems to indicate him clearly.

35. According to Horsmanden, Cosby promised him the recordership in 1734—DH to CC, August 27, 1734, *LPCC,* 2:109–11.

36. The fullest treatment of Alexander is Ellen M. T. Russell's "James Alexander, 1691–1756" (Ph.D. diss., Fordham University, 1995). The description of the house Alexander built in 1739 is his great-granddaughter's, quoted in Stokes, *Iconography*, 4:560.

37. See the entry for Alexander in *American National Biography*, 11:271–72. James Alexander Papers, NYHS. On Mary's shop, see Kate Van Winkle Keller and George A. Fogg, *Country Dances from Colonial New York: James Alexander's Notebook, 1730* (Boston: Country Dance Society, Boston Centre, 2000), pp. 5–6. For an example of Alexander tending the shop when his wife was busy taking care of a sick child, see JA to CC, June 28, 1729, *LPCC*, 1:287. On the prevalence and importance of woman-run shops in the city, and on Mary Alexander's shop in particular, see Zabin, "Places of Exchange," chaps. 3 and 4.

38. *New-York Mercury*, April 2, 1756. *NYG*, June 23, 1729.

39. Yaff, who ran away from James Alexander in 1729, probably spoke English without a Dutch accent. If he was thirty-five years old when he left, he was born in New York around 1696, two years after Daniel Horsmanden was born in Purleigh, Essex, and five years after Alexander was born in Perthshire, in Scotland. Yaff's mother was probably owned by Richard Ingoldesby, governor of New York from 1691 to 1692 and again from 1709 to 1710. *NYG*, August 24, 1730.

40. Michael Blakey et al., "Biocultural Approaches to the Health and Demography of Africans in Colonial New York," unpublished paper, World Archaeological Congress 4, University of Cape Town, 1999. The scholarship on the African-descended population of colonial New York is scattered. Early essays are principally concerned with slave codes. See Edwin Vernon Morgan, "Slavery in New York with Special Reference to New York City," in Maud Wilder Goodwin et al., eds., *Historic New York* (1897; Port Washington, NY: Ira J. Friedman, 1969), I:3–29; William Renwick Riddell, "The Slave in Early New York," *JNH* 13 (1928): 53–86; A. Judd Northrup, "Slavery in New York, a Historical Sketch," *State Library Bulletin* 4 (Albany, 1900); Edwin Olson, "Social Aspects of Slave Life in New York," *JNH* 26 (1941): 66–77; Edwin Olson, "The Slave Code in Colonial New York," *JNH* 29 (1944): 147–65; and Roi Ottley and William J. Weatherby, eds., *The Negro in New York: An Informal Society History* (New York: NYPL, 1967), pp. 1–30. A book-length study was published in 1966: McManus, *A History of Negro Slavery in New York*. See also Goodfriend, *Before the Melting Pot*, chap. 6. Two dissertations provide some of the fullest accounting: Foote, "Black Life," and Kruger, "Born to Run." *NYWJ*, September 25, 1749.

41. Blakey, "Biocultural Approaches," pp. 5–7. See also Foote, "Black Life," chap. 2. *New York Post-Boy*, December 19, 1748. *NYWJ*, May 10, 1736.

42. CC to Dr. Home, December 7, 1721, *LPCC*, 1:51; CC to Mrs. Cadwallader Colden, August 29, 1744, *LPCC*, 8:307.

43. *NYG*, September 12, 1737. See also *NYWJ*, September 20, 1737, which at least mentioned a kind of remorse: "*Since it is well known that Children will mimic, I think it very imprudent to leave such dangerous Instruments in their Reach.*"

44. CC to Mr. Jordan, March 26, 1717, *LPCC*, 1:39. Colden, who was at the time in Philadelphia, regretted that he couldn't break this woman's will himself: "Were it not for her Alusive [or Abusive] Tongue her sullenness & the Custome of the Country that will not allow us to use our Negroes as you doe in Barbados when they Displeas you I would not have parted with her But I doubt not she'l make as good a slave as any in the Island after a litle of your Discipline."

45. *NYGP*, May 4, 1747. On runaway literacy rates, see Foote, "Black Life," p. 246.

46. A dance called "The Beaus Strategem" is included in *The Dancing Master* (London, 1718), p. 169, and is "possibly the one which ended the play" (Kenny, *The Works of George Farquhar*, 2:137). Alexander recorded country dances in a notebook he kept in 1730; see Keller and Fogg, *Country Dances from Colonial New York: James Alexander's Notebook,*

1730. Alexander's noteboook did not include "Beaux Stratagem" but it did include "Recruiting Officer," a dance inspired by Farquhar's earlier comedy of the same name: "Cast off, Lady follow you, turn 2d Lady, the 2d man, fig. 3d C./meet set & cast up, cast down hands wt 3d C./Set & turn single hands back again."

47. Johnson quoted in Fifer, ed., Introduction to *The Beaux' Stratagem*, p. xvii.

48. Hogg's bawdy remark about his wife is taken from Hamilton, *Gentleman's Progress*, p. 177. Hamilton lodged at the Hoggs' house during his visits to New York. Caesar and Prince were later indicted for commiting a robbery at Abraham Myers Cohen's house in the early morning hours of Sunday, March 1, and convicted.

49. *The King against Mary Lawrence*, May 4, 1738, Mayor's Court. "Mary Lawrence & Child" appear in the Poorhouse records by November 1738—"Church Wardens Accounts, 1738," NYHS. An extensive description of the Poorhouse can be found in *MCC*, 4:307–11, March 31, 1736.

Chapter Two

1. *NYWJ*, March 9 and 16, 1741.

2. On the fort, see Stokes, *Iconography*, 1:244. On its inadequacies, see, e.g., Montgomerie's plea for the Assembly to give attention to the "miserable State of the Officers Barracks in the Fort," quoted ibid., 4:516. Cosby himself most forcefully made the case for better fortifications in 1734, when various improvements were undertaken—see ibid., 4:537–38. By 1738, the Battery was still incomplete. Clarke wrote to the Lords of Trade on June 2, 1738, "In the town of New York is an old fort of very little defense cannon we have, but the carriages are good for little, we have ball but no powder. . . . There is a battery which commands the mouth of the harbour whereon may be mounted 50 cannon this is new having been built but three years but it wants finishing"—*Docs. Col. NY*, 6:120. Clarke and the Assembly battled over the appropriations for finishing construction of the Battery and repairing the barracks in August and September 1739—Stokes, *Iconography*, 4:560–61. The money fell short.

3. *NYG*, February 4, 1729.

4. Accounts of the fort fire are largely taken from Horsmanden but also from Clarke to the Lords of Trade, April 22, 1741, *Docs. Col. NY*, 6:185–86. "A Law for the Better Preventing of Fire" included the provision "That the Inhabitant or owner of every House within this City that hath three Fire Places, provide two Leather Buckets, and every House of fewer Fire Places, one Leather Bucket; every Brewer six Leather Buckets; and every Baker three Leather Buckets"—*NYWJ*, February 20, 1738.

5. *Pennsylvania Gazette*, December 20, 1733.

6. Still, *Mirror for Gotham*, p. 25.

7. Kalm, *Travels*, p. 132; Hamilton, *Gentleman's Progress*, p. 44; Still, *Mirror for Gotham*, pp. 15–16. By the end of the eighteenth century, New York City passed laws dictating that "no new houses can be built in it, or within a certain distance of it, of wood; nor any new roof made of, or old ones repaired with, shingles." Mandating building with brick and stone greatly reduced the dangers posed by fires. Between 1500 and 1700, the number and extent of fires in cities grew in proportion to population, but between 1700 and 1900, cities kept growing while the number of fires declined—Johan Goudsblom, *Fire and Civilization* (London: Penguin, 1992), pp. 143–50. William Strickland, *Journal of a Tour in the United States of America, 1794–1795* (New York: NYHS), p. 62.

8. On the use of the speaking trumpet for fire, see *MCC*, 4:228, October 11, 1734.

9. *MCC*, 4:55–56, 82–83, 436–40, May 6, June 12, and November 18, 1731, September 19,

1738. On New York firefighting, see also David T. Valentine, *Manual of the Corporation of the City of New-York for 1856* (New York, 1856), pp. 525–29; *Our Firemen: A History of the New York Fire Departments* (New York, 1887); and George W. Sheldon, *The Story of the Volunteer Fire Department of the City of New York* (New York, 1882). For eighteenth-century firefighting more broadly, see Benjamin L. Carp, "Fire of Liberty: Firefighters, Urban Voluntary Culture, and the Revolutionary Movement," *WMQ* 58, no. 4 (2001): 781–818.

10. Smith, Jr., *History*, 2:50.

11. JA to David Provost, April 22, 1741, James Alexander Papers, Rutherfurd Family Papers, NYHS, Box 2.

12. *MCC*, 5: 16–17, March 19, 1741.

13. *NYG*, May 26, 1740; *NYWJ*, May 26, 1740. On Clarke's character, see Smith, Jr., *History*, 2:28–29. Clarke to the Lords of Trade, June 20, 1741, *Docs. Col. NY*, 6:196. The plumber's "Fire-pot" explanation was reported outside the city, too. See, e.g., the *Boston Weekly News-Letter* for April 9, 1741.

14. *NYG*, December 10, 1733; *NYWJ*, February 4, 1734; *NYWJ*, November 28, 1737; *NYWJ*, January 14, 1740. *Pennsylvania Gazette*, February 4, 1734.

15. Quick owned two slaves, "One Negro man Called Sam" and "One Negro woman," but neither of them was ever accused of conspiracy ("Inventory & Apraisment of the Reall & Personall Estate of Jacobus Quick," 1741, "Inventories of Estates, NYC and Vicinity, 1717–1844," NYHS). Clarke to the Lords of Trade, June 20, 1741.

16. *American Weekly Mercury*, April 9, 1741.

17. JA to David Provost, April 22, 1741. *American Weekly Mercury*, April 9, 1741. George Clarke to the Lords of Trade, June 20, 1741.

18. "Conspiratorial events—attributing events to the concerted designs of willful individuals—became a major means by which educated men in the early modern period ordered and gave meaning to their political world," Gordon S. Wood has argued. After all, American revolutionaries' belief that Parliamentary ministers were conspiring against them inspired a good number of them to revolt—Wood, "Conspiracy and the Paranoid Style: Causality and Deceit in the Eighteenth Century," *WMQ* 39 (July 1982): 401–41. Wood attempted to historicize what Richard Hofstadter had labeled the "paranoid style in American politics" (*The Paranoid Style in American Politics and Other Essays* [New York, 1965]) and to insist that it was not particularly American but rather a mode of thinking common to the eighteenth-century Atlantic world. On conspiracy fears of American revolutionaries, see also Bernard Bailyn, *The Ideological Origins of the American Revolution* (Cambridge, MA: Harvard University Press, 1967).

19. Increase Mather, *Burnings Bewailed* (Boston, 1712).

20. Richard Savage, "Of Public Spirit in Regard to Public Works," written 1736, published 1737; reprinted in James G. Basker, ed., *Amazing Grace: An Anthology of Poems About Slavery, 1660–1810* (New Haven: Yale University Press, 2002), pp. 78–79.

21. On the 1712 revolt, see Governor Robert Hunter to the Lords of Trade, June 23, 1712, *Docs. Col. NY*, 5:341–42; Kenneth Scott, "The Slave Insurrection in New York in 1712," *New-York Historical Society Quarterly* 45 (1961): 43–74; Thelma Wills Foote, " 'Some Hard Usage': The New York City Slave Revolt of 1712," *New York Folklore* 18 (1992): 147–59; and, on the connections between 1712 and 1741, Eric W. Plaag, " 'Greater Guilt Than Theirs': New York's 1741 Slave Conspiracy in a Climate of Fear and Anxiety," *NYH* 84 (2003): 275–99. On the role of Coromantees in the revolt, see Thornton, "The Coromantees," pp. 161–78.

22. *NYWJ*, April 15, 1734. *NYG*, May 13, 1734. On the Jamaican maroon wars, see especially Orlando Patterson, "Slavery and Slave Revolts: A Sociohistorical Analysis of the

First Maroon War, 1665–1740," in Richard Price, ed., *Maroon Societies: Rebel Slave Communities in the Americas* (Baltimore: Johns Hopkins University Press, 1996), pp. 246–92.

23. See, for example, Robert Hunter, Letter of Attorney to JA, November 1, 1721; Robert Hunter to JA, January 1, 1728; Hunter to JA, September 7, 1731; JA to Hunter, November 8, 1733; Alexander Papers, NYHS, Box 1. Lydon, "New York and the Slave Trade, 1700 to 1774," p. 383.

24. See Appendix C.

25. Donnan, *Documents*, 3:498. For a list of slaves involved in the Antigua investigation, see Gaspar, *Bondmen and Rebels*, p. 36. New York's Will was probably Billy, owned by Widow Langford, in Antigua. Sentenced to death, he "came to a full Confession"—ibid., p. 24.

26. *Pennsylvania Gazette,* October 19 and 20, 1738.

27. Jonathan Swift, *Gulliver's Travels,* Part 3, chap. VI.

28. *NYWJ,* June 12, 1738.

29. *NYG,* November 2, 1730. *NYG,* December 21, 1736, and January 11, 1737. *NYWJ,* January 10 and 17, 1737.

30. New York's major provincial slave codes include laws passed in 1702 ("An Act for Regulateing of slaves," *Col. Laws of NY,* 1:519–21), 1712 ("An Act for preventing Suppressing and punishing the Conspiracy and Insurrection of Negroes and other Slaves," *Col. Laws of NY,* 1:761–67), and 1730 ("An Act for the more effectual preventing and punishing the Conspiracy of Negro and other slaves, for the better regulating them and for repealing the Acts herein mentioned relating hereto," *Col. Laws of NY,* 2:679–88). By 1731, a host of slave codes were in effect in the city of New York, including "A Law Appointing a Place for the More Convenient Hiring of Slaves," "A Law Restraining Slaves, Negroes, & Indians from Gaming with Moneys or For Moneys," "A Law Giving a Reward to Any Person or Persons who shall Apprehend any Negro, Mulatto or Indian Slaves Offending Against any of the Acts of General Assembly of this Colony," "A Law for Punishing Slaves who Shall Ride Disorderly through the Streets," "A Law for Regulating the Burial of Slaves," "A Law for Regulating Negro's & Slaves in the Night Time" (*MCC,* 4:85–90, 51–52). "A Law to Prohibit Negroes and Other Slaves Vending Indian Corn Peaches or any other Fruit with this City" was passed in 1740 (*MCC,* 4:497–98). On city slave codes, see also Oscar R. Williams, "The Regimentation of Blacks on the Urban Frontier in Colonial Albany, New York City and Philadelphia," *JNH* 63 (October 1978): 329–38. Bernard Bush, comp., *Laws of the Royal Colony of New Jersey,* (Trenton: New Jersey State Library, Archives and History Bureau, 1977–86), 2:28–30.

31. Robert Hunter to the Lords of Trade, June 23, 1712, *Docs. Col. NY,* 5:342. "An Act for preventing Suppressing and punishing the Conspiracy and Insurrection of Negroes and other Slaves," 1712.

32. Governor Robert Hunter to the Lords of Trade, March 14, 1713, *Docs. Col. NY,* 5:356; King's Instructions to Governor Thomas Donaghan, May 29, 1686, *Docs. Col. NY,* 3:374; Lords of Trade to Governor Robert Hunter, December 23, 1709, *Docs. Col. NY,* 5:157.

33. The Governor's Council met at Fort George until October 1736, when it shifted to the Council Room at City Hall.

34. *MCC,* 5:17, April 11, 1741.

Chapter Three

1. This physical description of City Hall, its history, and various improvements is taken from several sources, including Smith, Jr., *History,* 1:208–9; *SCJ,* 1:347–56; and the records of the *MCC.*

2. Abraham Van Horne, Archibald Kennedy, Philip Livingston, James DeLancey, and Cadwallader Colden constituted the New York delegation to this commission—George Clarke to CC, December 15, 1740, *LPCC,* 2:205–6. In a letter dated March 23, 1741, Alexander wrote that "the Chief Justice & the other Counsellors are going to New England next week"—JA to Vincent Pearse, James Alexander Papers, NYHS, Box 3, folder 3. Smith, Jr., *History,* 2:57.

3. Smith, Jr., *History,* 1:266–67; Smith, Jr., *Memoirs,* 2:39. New York's law courts, courtroom, and especially criminal procedure are abundantly documented in Julius Goebel, Jr., and T. Raymond Naughton, *Law Enforcement in Colonial New York: A Study in Criminal Procedure, 1664–1776* (Montclair, NJ: Patterson Smith, 1970); *SCJ,* Vol. 1; and Douglas Greenberg, *Crime and Law Enforcement in the Colony of New York, 1691–1776* (Ithaca: Cornell University Press, 1974). A useful and provocative history of the establishment of the court system is Eben Moglen, "Settling the Law" (Ph.D. diss., Yale University, 1993). On the Supreme Court officers, rules, and procedures, see especially *SJC,* Vol. 1; 2:385–86.

4. Hamilton, *Gentleman's Progress,* p. 42.

5. On the form of the judicial writ and frequency of contempt of summons, see Goebel and Naughton, *Law Enforcement,* p. 344.

6. Five of Zenger's jurors served on a grand jury or jury in other trials in 1741: John Bell, Abraham Keteltass, Edward Man, Hermanus Rutgers, and Samuel Weaver.

7. The Supreme Court, which normally met in week long sessions four times a year, would, through repeated renewals authorized by Lieutenant Governor Clarke, eventually extend its April term to August 31, 1741. The grand jury sworn on April 21 would serve until July 25; a second grand jury would serve from July 28 until the end of the proceedings.

8. Goebel and Naughton, *Law Enforcement,* esp. pp. 73–80. The best discussion of the court's establishment can be found in *SCJ,* 1:37–77.

9. As one legal historian has observed, "Tacit acceptance of each side's position that it alone could found the courts was the ordinary course, but beneath the surface of the proprieties there lay the constitutional abyss. If the contingencies of ordinary politics led one side or the other to declare its position in terms that would force the issue, the legitimacy of the courts would be the first casualty of constitutional conflict"—Eben Moglen, "Considering Zenger: Partisan Politics and the Legal Profession in Provincial New York," *Columbia Law Review* 94 (1994): 1495–1524, quoted passage at 1502. See also "Law in Colonial New York: The Legal System of 1691," *Harvard Law Review* 80 (1967): 1760–61.

10. Attorney General Richard Bradley once complained that New York juries "very rarely find for the King tho' the charge be never so well supported by evidence"—Richard Bradley to the Lords of Trade, November 23, 1734, *Docs. Col. NY,* 6:18.

11. Cosby did preside over a chancery court in 1735, to hear a case involving a complicated claim to 50,000 acres known as the Oblong or the Equivalent Lands. The land was claimed by a group of Country Party men—Lewis Morris, Cadwallader Colden, James Alexander, and William Smith—who teamed with Court Party men George Clarke and Francis Harison. Harison, however, abandoned the group and secretly acquired a royal patent for the land in 1731. Clarke took Harison's side and the English patentees hired Horsmanden as their lawyer. Cosby, as chancellor, ruled in favor of the English company in a suite filed by Harison in 1735. The case only increased tensions between the two parties, and particularly ruined the reputation of Harison, who shortly after left the province. Alexander feared that he had gone to London to assassinate Morris. See Katz, "A New York Mission to England," pp. 440, 456. In representing the English patentees, Horsmanden was put in the position of opposing Colden, whose favor he had done much to court. "I am paid for thinking," he wrote Colden in November 1734, explaining that it was his job to argue on behalf of his clients and apologizing that in the courtroom he had argued hotly

against the claim of Colden and his company. "But you know they are words of Course in Such Cases, thrown in at the will of the Clyent or in Complyance with the comon forms"—DH to CC, November 11, 1734, *LPCC,* 2:118–21; DH to CC, November 19, 1734, *LPCC,* 2:121–22. The best discussion of Horsmanden's role in this complicated dispute can be found in McManus, "Daniel Horsmanden," pp. 24–27.

12. See [James Alexander], *The Arguments of the Council for the Defendant, In Support of A Plea to the Jurisdiction . . . At the Suit of the Attorney General, Complainant, against Rip Van Dam* (New York, 1733); and Lewis Morris, *The Opinion and Argument of the Chief Justice of the Province of New-York, concerning the Jurisdiction of the Supream Court* (New York, 1733). Alexander sent copies of both to Robert Hunter in Jamaica—JA to Hunter, November 8, 1733, James Alexander Papers, Rutherfurd Family Papers, NYHS, Box 1. These events are also related in Smith, Jr., *History,* 2:chap. 1. Horsmanden sent a copy of Morris's *Opinion* to a mentor in England, who advised him that Morris's argument was sound. See copy of part of a letter from Sir John Randolph to DH, July 1734, James Alexander Papers, the John Peter Zenger Trial Collection, Manuscripts, NYPL.

13. Abigail Franks to Naphtali Franks, December 16, 1733, in Hershkowitz and Meyer, eds., *The Lee Max Friedman Collection,* pp. 17–18. JA to Mr Pope?, December 4, 1733, James Alexander Papers, Rutherfurd Family Papers, NYHS, Box 1. Colden, "History of Cosby and Clarke," p. 303.

14. On Bradford's slave Sam, see *Bradford v. Ellsworth,* January 26, 1722, Mayor's Court. In exchange for payment of £16, Bradford hired out Sam for a year to George Ellsworth, Jr. When Sam ran away, Ellsworth sued Bradford for debt. Bradford hired Murray as his defense attorney—James Parker, *A Letter to a Gentleman in the City of New-York* (New York, 1759), in Beverly McAnear, "James Parker *Versus* New York Province," *NYH* 22 (1941): 321–30. Kammen, *Colonial New York,* pp. 133–34. In 1735 Morris complained to Alexander, "Bradfords writers are no changlings; they continue their old dirty method, and wil allwaies have as little credit, and I hope in time may meet with as much disgrace as they deserve"—Lewis Morris to JA, February 24, 1735, in Katz, "A New York Mission to England," p. 457. For an early slave sale ad, see *NYG,* April 3, 1727. By colonial standards, Bradford's output was sizable; between 1732 and 1741, he printed about twenty items a year. In the half century of Bradford's tenure, the illiteracy rate among white New Yorkers dropped by half. In 1698 Bradford had printed a primer, *The Secretary's Guide,* which he wrote himself, but like all colonial printers with the notable exception of Franklin, Bradford was more mechanic than author.

15. William Cosby to the Duke of Newcastle, May 3, 1733, *Docs. Col. NY,* 5:949.

16. Jean de La Caille and James Watson, *The History of the Art of Printing* (Edinburgh, 1713). On Alexander's role in the press, see Vincent Buranelli, "Peter Zenger's Editor," *American Quarterly* 7 (1955): 174–81. *NYWJ,* November 19, 1733.

17. The debate turned on the question of whether the governor or the Assembly held the right to erect equity courts. Popular sentiment worked against Cosby. "People are Very Much Against this Court," Abigail Franks observed. An equity court acted without a jury, "that Grand Bulwark of our Freedom & Safety," against "the arbitrary power of the Crown." In the Assembly, two city attorneys presented opposing arguments. Court Party lawyer Joseph Murray, on behalf of the governor, insisted that the Assembly could not pass legislation establishing the Supreme Court's right to sit in exchequer since, even though Cosby wanted the court to do just that, he would have had to veto any such law: to sign it would concede the Assembly's right to establish courts, something Cosby was unwilling to do. For the opposition, Country Party lawyer William Smith argued that neither could the governor erect such a court, at least not without consent of the Assembly, because the English constitution protected New Yorkers against such tyranny: "'Tis the Excellency of

our *Constitution,* and the Glory of our *Princes,* that they are *Sovereign* over *Free-men,* and not *Slaves*"—Abigail Franks to Naphtali Franks, June 9, 1734, Hershkowitz and Meyer, eds., *Lee Max Friedman Collection,* pp. 24–26. The remark about the right to jury trial is quoted in Goebel and Naughton, *Law Enforcement,* p. 607. Joseph Murray, *Mr. Murray's Opinion Relating to the Courts of Justice in the Colony of New-York* (New York, 1734). William Smith, *Mr. Smith's Opinion Humbly Offered to the General Assembly of the Colony of New-York* (New York, 1734).

18. Next, in an attempt to fight paper with paper, DeLancey had William Bradford print a copy of his charge to the grand jury in the form of a six-page pamphlet. Not to be outdone, James Alexander had Zenger print a critique of DeLancey's charge, three times as long as the charge itself, arguing, not without cause, that the Chief Justice sounded more like a prosecutor than a judge. "With my Eyes shut," Alexander wrote, "I should have thought the Attorney General, with a proper Zeal natural to him, had been entertaining the Audience in the Case of some Libelor, brought to Tryal by Information or Indictment, and not a Judge giving a solemn Charge." James DeLancey, *The charge of the Honourable James DeLancey, Esq.* (New York, 1734). [James Alexander], *Some Observations on the Charge given by the Honourable* James DeLancey, *Esq* (New York, 1734). This pamphlet was once attributed to Lewis Morris; the NYPL has more reasonably attributed it to William Smith and James Alexander, but it seems most likely that Alexander is the single author.

19. Reprinted in Katz, *Brief Narrative,* pp. 109–11.

20. *JLC,* 1:637–38, October 17, 1734; 641, November 1, 1734; 642, November 2, 1734.

21. James Alexander's brief for Zenger's trial is reprinted in Katz, *Brief Narrative;* quoted passage at p. 143. The excerpt from *Cato's Letters* was reprinted in the *NYWJ,* September 15, 1735.

22. Smith, Jr., *History,* 2:18.

23. The order, or a copy of it, can be found in Alexander's papers at the NYHS: "At a Supream Court of Judicature . . . 16th Day of April 1734," James Alexander Papers, Rutherfurd Collection, NYHS, Box 2, folder 8. Colden sympathized with Alexander the week after his disbarment: "Lawyers threatning the Law when ever he is put out of Humour is as ridiculous & Scandalous as for a Fencing Master to Challenge every man that gets the better of him in Argument." CC to JA, April 23, 1735, James Alexander Papers, Rutherfurd Collection, NYHS, Box 2, folder 119. When, months later, Lewis Morris in London received news of the disbarment, he wrote Alexander, "I was surpris'd at Mr. DeLanceys silencing Smith and you. He shews himselfe a great Stranger both to the law and practice in that Case."—Lewis Morris to JA, August 9, 1735, in Katz, "A New York Mission to England," p. 467.

24. Abigail Franks to Naphtali Franks, June 15, 1735, Hershkowitz and Meyer, eds., *Lee Max Friedman Collection,* pp. 40–41. *NYG,* July 21, 1735; *NYWJ,* July 21, 1735.

25. Alexander planned that Zenger, if conducting his own defense, would not actually answer the charges against him; instead, he would argue that DeLancey was not qualified to sit as a judge in his trial, because he had "prejudged the cause." Smith, Jr., *History,* 2:19. DeLancey had in fact prejudged the case, as evidenced in the warrant he issued for Zenger's arrest; his service on the Council committee to identify the seditious passages in the *Weekly Journal;* and his earlier warning that jurors who acquitted "would go near being perjured"—Katz, *Brief Narrative,* pp. 145–48.

26. Smith, Jr., *History,* 2:19–20. *NYWJ,* December 23, 1734. Zenger's case is widely credited with establishing the right to freedom of speech in the colonies. Its importance must obviously be qualified. The most balanced assessment can be found in Katz, *Brief Narrative,* Intro. For a more dismissive view, see Leonard W. Levy, "Did the Zenger Case Really Matter? Freedom of the Press in Colonial New York," *WMQ* 17 (1960): 35–50.

27. Abigail Franks to Naphtali Franks, December 12, 1735, Hershkowitz and Meyer, eds., *Lee Max Friedman Collection*, p. 46. Colden, "History of Cosby and Clarke," p. 349. George Clarke to the Lords of Trade, September 20, 1736, *Docs. Col. NY,* 6:75. *NYG,* October 11, 1736.

28. *Journal of the Assembly,* I:707–8. Although when Smith and Alexander appeared before a committee of the Assembly to seek a reversal of their disbarment, they again insisted that their exceptions had denied "only the Legality of the Judges Commissions, and neither affirm or deny any Thing, with respect to the Supream Court." That DeLancey used their alleged challenge to the existence of the court as grounds for their disbarment, they complained, "carries with it a more heavy Imputation, than we wish we had Occasion to take notice of"—*The Complaint of* James Alexander *and* William Smith *to the Committee of the General Assembly of the Colony of* New-York (New York, 1736), p. [8].

29. Clarke to the Lords of Trade, April 22, 1741, *Doc. Hist. NY,* 6:185–86.

30. Although the colonials, unlike Horsmanden, may have been granted their membership in the Inns of Court without ever having attended. Kammen argues, "There is evidence by 1733 that the practice of law in New York did not lag much behind that of England in adeptness at dealing with common-law precedent"—Kammen, *Colonial New York,* p. 211.

31. "That when any practitioner who has obtained his License since the last day of June 1725 is employed in any Cause We or either of Us shall not directly or indirectly be concerned on that Side, by advice or otherwise and if any such practitioner or his Client or any other person shall apply to either of us to be concerned [we] shall absolutely refuse to be concern'd . . . & immediately send word thereof to the rest of us." Agreement dated July 28, 1729, quoted in Moglen, "Considering *Zenger,*" p. 14.

32. Murray's action in Supreme Court records. But note that in January 1740, Murray sued Alexander and Smith ("Chief Justice James DeLancey's Docket, 1733–1756," DeLancey Papers, MCNY).

33. Joseph Murray Form Book, 1740–1741, Law Library of Columbia University, e.g., pp. 147–49. On Smith and Chambers handling such litigation, see the Mayor's Court records for cases involving slaves, including *Provost v. Lawrence,* July 23, 1723 (Murray represented Provost); *Ham v. Ten Eyck,* November 25, 1721 (Jamison represented Ten Eyck); *Riche v. Rout,* April 5, 1728 (Smith represented Riche); and *Willett v. Tole,* July 16, 1744 (Chambers represented Willett). My thanks to Simon Middleton for sharing details of these cases with me from his database of the Mayor's Court records.

34. *NYWJ,* January 5, 1736. In a separate case, Van Zandt was later indicted for attempted rape—Goebel and Naughton, *Law Enforcement,* p. 621.

35. Stokes, *Iconography,* 4:545.

36. Greenberg, *Crime and Law Enforcement,* pp. 72–73.

37. Moglen, "Settling the Law," pp. 194–95. Hunter to Lords of Trade, March 14, 1713, and June 23, 1712, *Docs. Col. NY,* 5:356–57, 339–41. Scott, "The Slave Insurrection in New York in 1712." See also the biographical entries for May Bickley and Jacob Regnier in *SCJ,* vol. 3.

38. On Clarke's support of Bickley, see *SCJ,* 3:23.

39. On the role of the grand jury, see Goebel and Naughton, *Law Enforcement,* chap. 6; *SCJ,* 1:141–245.

40. John H. Langbein, "The Historical Origins of the Privilege Against Self-Incrimination at Common Law," *Michigan Law Review* 92 (1993–94): 1047–85.

41. Leonard W. Levy and Lawrence H. Leder, " 'Exotic Fruit': The Right Against Compulsory Self-Incrimination in Colonial New York," *WMQ* 20 (1963): 7. John H. Langbein, "Shaping the Eighteenth-Century Criminal Trial: A View from the Ryder Sources," *University of Chicago Law Review* 50 (1983): 1–136; Stephan Landsman, "The Rise of the

Contentious Spirit: Adversary Procedure in Eighteenth-Century England," *Cornell Law Review* 75 (1990). Langbein writes, "Of the main themes of the modern law, only the hearsay rule is stated recognizably" (p. 431), but even that is given many exceptions. On the lack of any real "law of evidence" in colonial New York, see Goebel and Naughton, *Law Enforcement*, pp. 628–29. See Henry Fielding, *An Enquiry into the Causes of the Late Increase of Robbers* (London, 1741; Middletown: Wesleyan University Press, 1988), and esp. Intro. by editor Malvin R. Zirker, p. liii.

42. *NYWJ*, November 25, 1734.

43. After 1737, debtors were spared the dungeon and sent to the garret instead. If the debtor's prison and apartments in the garret were squalid, they were at least well lit and well ventilated; each apartment had one window, and the common debtor's prison had six. The cellar prison was much darker, damper, and closed. City records are full of complaints about its inadequacy. As early as 1697 the sheriff asked the Supreme Court justices to motion "to the city the insufficiency of the City Hall and prison." In 1730 the legislature mandated improvements: "it appearing there is an Absolute Necessity not only to repair but to Enlarge the said Prisons and Gaols." And in 1737 the city's Common Council ordered "the Said Gaols to be Inspected and direct the same to be sufficiently repaired and Amended with all needfull and Necessary Reparations and Amendments"—October 17, 1730, *Col. Laws of NY*, 2:645; *MCC*, 4:362, January 17, 1737; Smith, Jr., *History*, 1:209. Cash, when caught, "confessed her only design was to get out of Gaol." She was ordered stripped to the waist and "whipped by the Publick Whipper Eleven Lashes on the Naked back"—Mayor's Court, May 1, 1733. See, e.g., an order paying the blacksmith "for Iron Shekells, hand Cuffs, & work done to the Prison" and another bill for "Staples" on July 15, 1731, and August 7, 1735—*MCC*, 4:61, 267.

44. Pearse himself also appeared before the Supreme Court during the April term; he was sued by George Cummings ("Chief Justice James DeLancey's Docket, 1733–1756," DeLancey Papers, MCNY). See references to *Captain Vincent Pearse v. George Cummings*, in James Alexander, "Supreme Court Register, 1721–1742," James Alexander Papers, NYHS. See also JA to [Joseph Murray?], March 25, 1741, James Alexander Papers, Box 1, folder 5; and JA to Vincent Pearse, March 23, 1741, Box 3, folder 3. Alexander served as Pearse's attorney and Murray, apparently, represented Cummings. It appears that *Pearse v. Cummings* was first heard before the Admiralty Court on April 17, 1741 (both Horsmanden and Alexander were present), and then appealed. See Admiralty Court Records, James Alexander Papers, NYHS, Box 53, folder 1.

45. See Fielding, *An Enquiry into the Causes of the Late Increase of Robbers*, esp. Intro.

46. For a specific description of the site of the gallows, see David Grim, "Notes on the City of New York," MS, NYHS. But note the discrepancies between Grim and Horsmanden. Grim says Hughson and Caesar were gibbeted in different parts of town; Horsmanden says they were next to each other.

47. Albert W. Alschuler, "Symposium on Coercion: An Interdisciplinary Examination of Coercion, Exploitation and the Law: II. Coerced Confessions: Constraint and Confession," *Denver University Law Review* 74 (1997): 957–78. *Rex v. Warwickshall* quoted on p. 968, from 168 Eng. Rep. 234, 255. Levy and Leder, " 'Exotic Fruit,' " pp. 13–15.

48. On Mills's dentistry, see *NYWJ*, January 6, 1735. On his career as jailkeeper, see *NYECM*, 2:104.

Chapter Four

1. *NYWJ*, May 31, June 8 and 15, 1741.

2. *Journal of the Assembly*, I: 823–24, November 13, 1741. Smith, Jr., *History*, 2:58. Moore would have served under the charge of the court clerk, George Clarke, Jr. The latter's posi-

tion was, effectively, a sinecure awarded to him by his father, one of many offices he held for which he provided almost no service—Stokes, *Iconography*, 4:557. On court clerks, see *SCJ*, 1:136–38; Hamlin and Baker conclude, regarding the earlier period, "No matter from what point of view the Supreme Court records of the years 1691–1704 are considered, those who wrote them down, transcribed them, or entered them in books, did a poor job." Horsmanden himself did know shorthand. In 1734, he mentioned in a letter to Colden, "My Short hand Book was lent to a Gentn"—DH to CC, January 5, 1735, *LPCC*, 2:97. CC to DH, July 29, 1742, *LPCC*, 8:288–89. See also Horsmanden's shorthand of a letter from Rip Van Dam to William Cosby, December 15, 1733, Horsmanden Papers, NYHS.

3. *Proposals for Printing by Subscription, A Journal of the Proceedings in the Detection of the Conspiracy* (New York, 1742).

4. *JLC*, I:794, November 26, 1741. The Supreme Court minutes for the years 1691–1740 and 1750–81 survive. Those for 1691–1704 are transcribed and annotated in *SCJ*, vol. 2. Originals of the minutes from 1704–40 and 1750–81 are in the County Clerk's office and have also been microfilmed: "Minute Books of the Supreme Court of Judicature," microfilm copy at Queens College Historical Documents Collection, Rolls SC1-SC8.

5. Clarke quoted in Smith, Jr., *Memoirs*, 2:41.

6. Richard Bradley to Everett Wendell, April 6, 1725, Richard Bradley Letters, Misc. MSS., NYHS.

7. Thomas D. Morris, "Slaves and the Rules of Evidence in Criminal Trials," *Chicago-Kent Law Review* 68 (1993): 1209.

8. "An Act for the more effectual preventing and punishing the Conspiracy of Negro and other slaves, for the better regulating them and for repealing the Acts herein mentioned relating hereto," *Col. Laws of NY*, 2:679–88.

9. "The King v. Quack a Negroman" and "The King v. Coffee a Negroman,' CO 5/1094, PRO. Horsmanden's version of Fortune's testimony is longer than the original courtroom minutes because Horsmanden included details from Fortune's May 23 grand jury interrogation, details the court clerk found irrelevant and failed to include in his minutes from Quack and Cuffee's trial on May 29. There is only one detail in the minutes that Horsmanden bothered to delete in his *Journal:* the reference to black Freemasons.

10. On June 27, 1741, Adam (Murray) confessed that in 1738 Hughson lived "upon the Dock next Door to *Silvester* the Cooper." The cooper Francis Silvester is listed on the 1734 tax list, residing in the South Ward, twelve buildings away from Daniel Horsmanden. Hughson does not appear on the 1734 list, and probably did not live in the city at that time. Davis (*Rumor of Revolt*, p. 3) and others say the Geneva Club was formed in 1736, because in a footnote in his *Journal,* Horsmanden wrote: "it happened about Five or Six Years ago." But Horsmanden added the footnotes not in 1741, during the trials, but in 1742 or 1743, as he prepared the *Journal* for publication.

11. Lodgemaster David Provost, Jr., was the son of David Provost, brother of Samuel Provost, James Alexander's wife's first husband. Mary Alexander also had a son named David Provost; he served in Gooch's regiment in Jamaica. On the lodgemaster Provost, see David M. McGregor, "David Provoost, Jr., of New York, Master of a Lodge in Georgia in 1739," *Transactions of the American Lodge of Research* 2 (1936): 373–76.

12. *NYG*, November 28, 1737, August 8, 1737, January 31, 1738, February 14, 1738. *NYWJ*, January 24, 1738, February 13, 1738. The case for Horsmanden's authorship of the essays in the *Gazette* is supported by the similarity of language—the language of "impudence"—with which he referred to the 1738 black Freemasons in the footnote in his *Journal,* reporting that the city's blacks had "the Impudence to assume the Style and Title of *Free Masons,* in imitation of a Society here" (Horsmanden believed that after the whipping of Caesar,

Cuffee, and Prince, "the Negroes may be supposed to have declined their Pretensions to this Title"). Zabin briefly discusses the 1738 Masonic scandal, placing it in the context of contested gender relations, in "Places of Exchange," pp. 191–96.

13. Smith, Jr., *History,* 2:34.

14. On the constable's oath, and jury withdrawal and verdict more generally, see Goebel and Naughton, *Law Enforcement,* pp. 669–79.

15. On petty treason and burning, see Frank McLynn, *Crime and Punishment in Eighteenth-Century England* (London: Routledge, 1989), p. 121. On 1712, see Scott, "The Slave Insurrection in New York in 1712."

16. *NYWJ,* May 31, 1741.

17. *NYWJ,* June 19, 1738. Grim, "Notes on the City of New York."

18. The burning of Quack and Cuffee was watched outside the city as well. See, e.g., the *Boston Weekly News-Letter,* June 11, 1741.

19. Elizabeth Colden DeLancey to CC, June 1, 1741, *LPCC,* 8:265.

20. Ibid., 8:266. Elizabeth DeLancey did not give his name, or indicate whether he was already in jail.

21. Ibid., 8:265.

22. Sarah, a twenty-four-year-old "Mullatto Servant Woman" who ran away from English merchant Joseph Reade in 1732, spoke "good English and some Dutch." John Henricus, "a Lusty Young Negro Man" who ran away from Matthew Norris in 1727, spoke "very good English and Welch"—*NYG,* November 13, 1732; *NYEP,* December 17, 1744; *NYG,* August 28, 1727. On languages spoken among New York's blacks, see Medford et al., "The Transatlantic Slave Trade to New York City: Sources and Routing of Captives," World Archaeological Conference 4 (1999), unpublished paper. On languages spoken by runaways, see Kruger, "Born to Run." Using a sample of 194 runaway slave ads from 1726 to 1814, she finds forty that specify linguistic abilities: fourteen spoke English well, five spoke it poorly, six spoke no English at all, and fifteen were bilingual (p. 86). On Gã, and on Akan as a lingua franca, see Thornton, "The Coromantees," p. 165.

23. Hamilton, *Gentleman's Progress,* pp. 40–41.

24. NYCCP, 74:54, 55.

25. Margreta de Grazia, "Sanctioning Voice: Quotation Marks, the Abolition of Torture, and the Fifth Amendment," *Cardozo Arts & Entertainment Law Journal* 10 (1992): 545–66.

26. For Kerry's mark, see "Deposition. Margaret Sarinbirr *alias* Keary," May 8, 1741, 74-35b-4; for Price's mark, see "Deposition. Arthur Price," May 7, NYCCP, 74-36b(1)-v; for Mary Burton's mark, see "Deposition. Mary Burton," June 25, 1741, 74-84a(2)-r and the addendum dated June 27, 1741, 74-84a(2)-v; for the lack of marks on slave confessions, see, e.g., "Confession. Wan, a negro belonging to Peter Lowe," June 18, 1741, 74:66-v, and "Confession of Othello," July 12, 1741, 74-121b-v. For arrest warrants signed by Horsmanden, see, e.g., "Warrant for the commitment of Sarah Hughson, single woman," May 6, 1741," NYCCP, 35-a-r; "Warrant for the commitment of Elizabeth, wife of John Roome," May 8, 1741, NYCCP, 74-36a-r; and "Warrant for arrest of John, Cambridge, Caesar, and Guise," May 30, 1741, NYCCP, 74:49a.

27. The original of Jack's confession is in very poor condition but Horsmanden's signature appears on it—e-mail from James Folts to the author, July 13, 2004.

28. *NYWJ,* November 4, 1734.

29. Katz, *Brief Narrative,* pp. 59–60, 65, 69, 78, 99.

30. *Pennsylvania Gazette,* June 18, 1741.

31. Smith, Jr., *Memoirs,* 2:40.

32. On Johnson, see *NYECM*, 2:236.

33. On the blurring of the genres of history, journalism, fiction, and memoir, see Hunter, *Before Novels*, esp. chaps. 7 and 14. Horsmanden's *Journal* might also be placed in a genre John J. Richetti calls the "criminal biography": "The criminal of popular eighteenth-century narrative moves in a world which is brutal and degrading, but which is still the medieval one of spirits, witches, the devil, and the ubiquitous operations of Providence"— Richetti, *Popular Fiction Before Richardson*, p. 34.

34. *NYWJ*, August 26, 1734.

35. *NYG*, August 12, 1728.

36. Henry Louis Gates, Jr., *Figures in Black: Words, Signs, and the "Racial" Self* (New York: Oxford University Press, 1987), p. 4.

37. This account of Williams, and all quotations, are taken from Vincent Carretta, "Who Was Francis Williams?" *Early American Literature* 38 (2003): 213–37.

38. David Hume, "Of National Characters," in *Essays Moral, Political, and Literary* (Edinburgh, 1741).

39. In 1724, young Francis Williams fell into a fistfight with a white colonist named William Brodrick. Brodrick called Williams a "black dog"; Williams called him a "white dog." Williams ripped Brodrick's shirt; Brodrick punched him in the mouth. Williams threatened to bring Brodrick to trial, and "said he was as good a man as ever stood on Brodrick's legs; that he did not stand upon the act of this country, that exempts him from such trial as other negroes." When Brodrick petitioned the court for remedy, a bill was drafted "for reducing Francis Williams, a free negro, to the same state of trial and evidence as other negroes," in which state he would no longer be allowed to testify against a white man. The provision was not passed, but it was eventually folded into Jamaica's 1730 "Act for the better regulating Slaves, and rendering free Negroes and Mulattoes more useful." Williams sent a petition to London, requesting an appeal. In 1732, it was granted.

Chapter Five

1. At the stake on May 30, Quack said that "Mary Burton *had spoke the Truth*," but neither he nor Cuffee supplied any details of the scene at Hughson's.

2. *NYG*, December 10, 1733. Comfort's house and estate are in the same location in the West Ward in both the 1730 and the 1734 tax lists.

3. This discussion of the city's water supply borrows from Diane Galusha, *Liquid Assets: A History of New York City's Water System* (Fleischmanns, NY: Purple Mountain Press, 2002), pp. 11–13; Gerard T. Koeppel, *Water for Gotham: A History* (Princeton: Princeton University Press, 2000); Nelson Manfred Blake, *Water for the Cities: A History of the Urban Water Supply Problem in the United States* (Syracuse: Syracuse University Press, 1956); *NYECM*, 2:137–41; and Edward Wegman, *The Water-Supply of the City of New York, 1658–1895* (New York, 1896), pp. 1–6.

4. Silvester owned four slaves at his death in 1769, and probably had some in 1741, although none was accused in the conspiracy—"The Personal Estate of Francis Sylvester," 1769, "Inventories of Estates, NYC and Vicinity, 1717–1844," NYHS.

5. New York Supreme Court of Judicature Minute Book, March 13, 1733–October 23, 1739, County Clerk's Office, New York City. There are three generations of Lancaster Symeses in the records of early New York, including one who lived in the East Ward in 1730, where he owned two houses assessed together at £20. He does not appear on the 1734 tax list. The man Hughson accused was probably the mariner named Lancaster Symes, not his father, a merchant, or his grandfather.

6. *MCC*, 4:423–24, April 13, 1738. Stokes, *Iconography*, 4:556–57. After 1754, the Broadway Market was called the Oswego Market.

7. The militia lists can be found in *Doc. Hist. NY*, 4:211–26.

8. *JLC*, 1:736, April 5, 1737.

9. Stokes, *Iconography*, 4:552–54. *NYWJ*, June 27, 1737.

10. CC to his wife, September 11, 1737, *LPCC*, 2:17. *Docs. Col. NY*, 3:292, September 12, 1737. On September 21 the Assembly voted that Cosby's actions had not invalidated the election. This decision was followed by a contest over the Jewish vote, with William Smith arguing that Jewish New Yorkers, who had voted overwhelmingly for Philipse, had no right to vote. Even with the Jewish votes thrown out, Van Horne still lost because the Assembly also voted to allow non-resident freeholders to vote.

11. Although a Masonic manual printed in Philadelphia in 1734 promised that "A *Mason* is a peaceable Subject to the Civil Powers, wherever he resides or works, and is never to be concerned in Plots and Conspiracies against the Peace and Welfare of the Nation." *Constitutions of the FREE-MASONS* (London, 1723; Philadelphia, 1734), p. 48.

12. *NYWJ*, November 14, 1737.

13. Melvin M. Johnson, *The Beginnings of Freemasonry in America* (Washington, DC: Masonic Service Association, 1924), p. 179.

14. *NYG*, November 28, 1737.

15. Masonry's origins have been disputed, with some arguing for the importance of earlier lodges in Scotland, only later imported to England. See, e.g., David Stevenson, *The Origins of Freemasonry: Scotland's Century, 1590–1710* (Cambridge: Cambridge University Press, 1988). On mockery of Masonry in the British North American colonies, see David S. Shields, "Clio Mocks the Masons: Joseph Gren's Anti-Masonic Satires," in J. A. Leo Lemay, ed., *Deism, Masonry, and the Enlightenment* (Newark: University of Delaware Press, 1987), pp. 109–26; Robert Micklus, "The Secret Fall of Freemasonry in Dr. Alexander Hamilton's 'The History of the Tuesday Club,'" in *Deism, Masonry*, pp. 127–36.

16. For a close examination of this story, see Steven C. Bullock, *Revolutionary Brotherhood: Freemasonry and the Transformation of the American Social Order, 1730–1840* (Chapel Hill: University of North Carolina Press, 1996), chap. 2.

17. *NYWJ*, June 29, 1741.

18. *MCC*, 5:50, March 22, 1742.

19. Hamilton, *Gentleman's Progress*, p. 88.

20. *NYWJ*, November 19, 1733.

21. *Journal of the Assembly*, I:709 (September 8, 1737), 723 (November 16, 1737).

22. *NYG*, August 17, 1730, September 14, 1730, and August 27, 1733. On slave artisans, see Foote, "Black Life," pp. 41–44.

23. Bruce M. Wilkenfeld, "New York City Neighborhoods, 1730," *NYH* (1976): 173. In 1730, of forty-two coopers in the city, eighteen were in the North Ward, twelve in the East, four in the West, four in the South, and two each in Dock and Outward (p. 174). Bruce Martin Wilkenfeld, *The Social and Economic Structure of the City of New York, 1695–1796* (New York: Arno Press, 1978), p. 92.

24. John Thornton, "War, the State, and Religious Norms in 'Coromantee' Thought: The Ideology of an African Nation," in Robert Blair St. George, ed., *Possible Pasts: Becoming Colonial in Early America* (Ithaca: Cornell University Press, 2000), pp. 192–93.

25. Thornton, "The Coromantees," pp. 170–72.

26. For the data on Akan names, see Appendix A.

27. Thornton, "War, the State, and Religious Norms," pp. 193–99.

28. Black Freemasonry may have played a role in the Haitian Revolution in 1791, and some scholars have suggested that eighteenth-century elements of Haitian *voudou*, sometimes called "a sort of religious and dancing masonry," found their way into mainstream Masonry. See Susan Buck-Morss, "Hegel and Haiti," *Critical Inquiry* 26 (2000), esp. p. 856.

29. Hamilton, *Gentleman's Progress*, pp. 175–76.

30. See Lisa C. Tolbert, *Constructing Townscapes: Space and Society in Antebellum Tennessee* (Chapel Hill: University of North Carolina Press, 1999), pp. 205–7. On slave mobility in antebellum cities, see Richard C. Wade, *Slavery in the Cities: The South, 1820–1860* (London: Oxford University Press, 1964).

31. Kruger, "Born to Run," pp. 93, 128–64. See also Olson, "Social Aspects of Slave Life," pp. 66–67. JA to CC, July 25, 1730, *LPCC*, 2:16. CC to Captain Van Pelt, in North Carolina, December 17, 1726, *LPCC*, 1:59.

32. Kruger identified family as the motivation in forty-five of sixty-nine runs, where the motivation was known—Kruger, "Born to Run," pp. 234–35.

33. Wilkenfeld, in "New York City Neighborhoods, 1730," argues that neighborhoods clustered whites by religion, wealth, and occupation: "Thus, over two-thirds of the shipwrights and half the tailors were to be found in the East Ward; silversmiths and coopers clustered in the North Ward; blacksmiths were concentrated in the nearby regions of the Out Ward" (p. 173).

34. The 1737 census counted 39 percent of the total population as black males over the age of ten. My population growth model puts the total black population in 1741 at 1,833; if the age and sex distribution remained constant between 1737 and 1741, that would make for 715 black men over the age of ten in 1741. But black males between ages ten and twenty were not likely to have participated in the conspiracy; only a handful were called "boys," and this seems to have been a term indicating black men's lowly status rather than their age. In 1746, the year of the next surviving census, the percentage of children *under age sixteen* in the total population was 43 percent. The execution and transportation of large numbers of black men in 1741 in part accounts for this discrepancy, but the different age brackets probably account for most of it. If a similar child-to-adult ratio pertained in 1741, then 862 of the 1,833 blacks in the city were adults. If the 1737 sex ratio applied in 1741, then 456 of these 862 black adults were men over age sixteen. On the age structure and the percentage of children in the population, see Kruger, "Born to Run," esp. pp. 1167–68.

35. *NYG*, October 8, 1733; *NYWJ*, April 15, 1734. November 18, 1731, *MCC*, 4:77.

36. Thomas F. DeVoe, *The Market Book* (New York: AMS Press, 1969), 1:93.

37. "An Act for the more effectual preventing and punishing the Conspiracy of Negro and other slaves, for the better regulating them and for repealing the Acts herein mentioned relating hereto," *Col. Laws of NY*, 2:679–88; "A Law for Regulating Negro's & Slaves in the Night Time," *MCC*, 4:51–52; "A Law for the Observation of the Lords Day Called Sunday," *MCC*, 4:79; "A Law for Punishing Slaves who Shall Ride Disorderly through the Streets," *MCC*, 4:89–90; "A Law to Prohibit Negroes and Other Slaves Vending Indian Corn Peaches or any other Fruit with this City," *MCC*, 4:497–98.

38. Quoted in Gaspar, *Bondmen and Rebels*, pp. 3–4, 17.

39. The reference to "Negro Peg" comes from the *Boston Weekly News-Letter*, June 25, 1741. On the Carr case, see Foote, "Black Life," pp. 270–71. On Anne Carr in the Poorhouse, see "Church Wardens Accounts, 1738," NYHS.

40. 1734 Tax Assessment Rolls. *NYWJ*, January 28, 1734, and *NYG*, January 21 and 28, 1734. For another series of episodes of sexual violence, see *NYG*, July 18, 1737: "We hear that 1st Week a Negro Man attempted to Force his Mistress, for which he is committed to Prison, and to be brought to his Tryal. Another Negro made an attempt upon a Girl about

eight years of age. The Master of the Negro deliver'd him up to the Childs Father to be corrected as he thought proper. And its said he has had suitable Correction. A third Negro for the like Crime is committed to Gaol, and put in Irons, in order to receive due Punishment."

41. *The King against Martha Cash,* Mayor's Court, February 1, 1737.

42. At his first trial on May 6, Hughson successfully challenged the impaneling of Joseph North as a juror.

43. Stephen Nissenbaum, *The Battle for Christmas* (New York: Knopf, 1996). In an analysis of slave conspiracies and revolts between 1649 and 1833 in the British Caribbean, Robert Dirks argues that 35 percent were hatched or took place in December—Dirks, "Resource Fluctuations and Competitive Transformations in West Indian Slave Societies," in C. D. Laughlin and I. A. Brady, eds., *Extinction and Survival in Human Populations* (New York: Columbia University Press, 1978), pp. 160–66.

44. Shane White, " 'It Was a Proud Day': African Americans, Festivals, and Parades in the North, 1741–1834," *Journal of American History* 81 (1994): 13–50; and Shane White, *Somewhat More Independent: The End of Slavery in New York City, 1770–1810* (Athens: University of Georgia Press, 1991), p. 95.

45. Quoted in Peter Wood, *Black Majority: Negroes in Colonial South Carolina from 1670 Through the Stono Rebellion* (New York: W. W. Norton, 1974), p. 320 n. 48.

46. *NYG,* March 11 and April 7, 1740. Howard M. Chapin, *Privateering in King George's War, 1739–1748* (Providence, RI: E. A. Johnson Co., 1928), pp. 131–33. On the status of black sailors, see also Zabin, "Places of Exchange," chap. 2. She concludes that the "Spanish Negroes" were "unwittingly drawn into the slave conspiracy" (p. 81).

47. A rare exception was the case of Joseph, "declared free (in the absence of other testimony)" in 1762. See Charles Merrill Hough, *Reports of Cases in the Vice Admiralty of the Province of New York* (New Haven: Yale University Press, 1925), pp. 199–200.

48. Deposition of Oliver Short, January 23, 1741, Admiralty Court Records, James Alexander Papers, NYHS, Box 53, folder 1. On Benjamin Kiersted, see also Chapin, *Privateering in King George's War,* pp. 138–39. Alexander clearly played a role in Kiersted's case, as Short's deposition survives among his papers.

49. George Clarke to the Duke of Newcastle, February 25, 1741, *Doc. Hist. NY,* 6:179. Hough, *Reports of Cases,* pp. 20–21.

50. Wood, *Black Majority,* pp. 312, 314.

51. George Clarke to the Lords of Trade, June 20, 1741, *Docs. Col. NY,* 6:197.

52. *NYWJ,* June 22, 1741.

53. That Alexander was in the city during most of the proceedings, and actively involved in civil cases before the Supreme Court, is confirmed by case logs and his correspondence for the period. See, e.g., JA to [Joseph Murray?], March 25, 1741 (Box 1, folder 5). On June 4, Alexander wrote a letter from Perth Amboy (Box 1, folder 2), and in his Supreme Court Register for July 1741 he refers to an extension given to a case "because of my absence in jersey" in June. But that absence appears to have been brief because he was certainly in court on June 11, as he mentions that date in his Register, and again during the "Spanish Negroes' " trial on June 17, and he wrote a letter from New York on June 30, 1741 (Supreme Court Register, 1721, 1742, pp. 49–56; JA to Richard Bradley, Box 1, folder 1). See also JA, Docket for New York Supreme Court, Box 49, folder 5.

Chapter Six

1. Kalm, *Travels,* pp. 125–32.

2. Minutes of the Council, April 27, 1741, CO 412/221, PRO.

3. Julian Gwyn, "Money Lending in New England: The Case of Admiral Sir Peter Warren and His Heirs, 1739–1805," *New England Quarterly* 44 (March 1971): 121.

4. "Scope and Content of Captain Peter Warren, *Squirrel,* New York," September 16, 1740, ADM 106/930/199, PRO; "Scope and Content of Captain Peter Warren, *Squirrel,* New York Leaving NY for Great Britain," August 19, 1741, ADM 191, PRO. Warren appears to have owned a sizable number of slaves. See "The Estate of Peter Warren Deceas'd," Warren Papers, NYHS, no. 18, which mentions, for 1741, "sending 2 Negro's to York." And also "Coll. William Johnson Due to the Estate of Sir Peter Warren," ibid., no. 19, which mentions, from 1739, "19 Negro Slaves" sent by Warren to Johnson.

5. *NYWJ,* July 6, 1741.

6. George Clarke to the Lords of Trade, June 20, 1741, *Docs. Col. NY,* 6:198.

7. A number of ships carrying slaves to be transported out of the colony are recorded in the PRO's Naval Records, although the total reported there does not add up to the number recorded by Horsmanden. Fifty slave departures are reported, as follows: July 9, 1741, on the *Mayflower,* Robert Beatty, master, carrying "8 transport Negros" to Madeira; July 15, 1741, on the *Catherine,* John Stout, master, "13 Transport Negros" bound for Madeira and Lisbon; July 18, 1741, on the *Sarah,* Abraham Brasher, master, "2 Transport Negros" bound for Newfoundland; July 31, 1741, on the *Stephen & Elisa,* Richard Langdon, master, "2 Transport Negros" bound for Curaçoa; July 31, 1741, on the *Stephen,* Elias Rice, master, carrying "with 20 Transport Negros" for St. Eustatia; August 15, on the *William & Mary,* Jacob Kiersted, master, owned by Jacob and William Walton, carrying "5 Transport Negros" to Madeira—Naval Office Records for New York, pp. 176–80, CO 5/1226.

8. DH to CC, August 7, 1741, *LPCC,* 2:224–28.

9. George Clarke to the Lords of Trade, June 20, 1741, *Docs. Col. NY,* 6:198.

10. In his *Journal,* Horsmanden notes that Burton's June 25 deposition was "*Taken before one of the Judges,*" but the original deposition bears only Burton's mark and Horsmanden's signature. The same is true for addenda to the deposition added June 27 and June 29, the latter of which reads, "Taken before me the 29th day of June 1741 Danl Horsmanden." NYCCP, 74–84a(2)-r.

11. On the eighteenth-century spread of Masonry through the British Army, see Jessica L. Harland-Jacobs, " 'The Essential Link': Freemasonry and British Imperialism, 1751–1918" (Ph.D. diss., Duke University, 2000), esp. pp. 63–70.

12. The ad for Jones appeared in the *NYWJ,* July 13, 20, 27, and August 24, 1741. He ran away on July 11. Wilson, Horsmanden said, had "Acquaintance with two white Servants belonging to Gentlemen who lodged at Mr. *Hogg's* House."

13. *NYG,* October 8, 1733. Linebaugh and Rediker see the Irish as "another cell in New York's insurrectionary movement"—Linebaugh and Rediker, *Many-Headed Hydra,* pp. 186–88.

14. *NYWJ,* March 30, 1741.

15. Pierre Jurieu (1637–1713) wrote dozens of anti-Catholic tracts and histories.

16. Farquhar, *Beaux' Stratagem,* Act III, scene iii.

17. Thornton, "Central African Names," pp. 729–30. "Lawes . . . 1664," *NYHSC* 1 (1809): 322–23; *Laws of New York* (New York, 1757), p. 69; Earl of Bellomont to the Lords of Trade, April 27, 1699, *Docs. Col. NY,* 4:510–11; "An Act to Incourage the Baptizing of Negro, Indian and Mulatto Slaves," *Col. Laws of NY,* 1:597–98.

18. Jon Butler, *The Huguenots in America: A Refugee People in a New World Society* (Cambridge, MA: Harvard University Press, 1983), pp. 161–69.

19. "A List of Slaves taught by Mr. Neau since the year 1704, Enclosed in his Letter of the 10 November 1714," Society for the Propagation of the Gospel in Foreign Parts (SPG)

Letterbooks, LOC, series A, Vol. 10, 220–23. "A List of Negroes Taught by Mr Neau December the 23 1719," ibid., Vol. 14, pp. 141–43.

20. David Humphreys, *An Historical Account of the Incorporated Society for the Propagation of the Gospel in Foreign Parts* (London, 1730), pp. 232–44; Graham Russell Hodges, *Root and Branch: African Americans in New York and East Jersey, 1613–1863* (Chapel Hill: University of North Carolina Press, 1999), pp. 55–63. William Taylor to Elias Neau, November 6, 1712, and Elias Neau to William Taylor, October 15, 1712, in Letters and Reports of Missionaries and Other Correspondents, SPG Papers, LOC, series A, Vol. 7 (1711–12), Box 5450, pp. 276–77 and 226–27.

21. *NYG*, November 30, 1730.

22. Summary of Charlton to the SPG, November 11, 1740; summary dated March 20, 1741, SPG General Meeting Journals, Vol. 8 (1738–39/1741–42); Transcript, Box 5503, 231, SPG Papers, LOC.

23. See Stokes, *Iconography*, 4:563.

24. Anonymous, "A Poem, on the Joyful News of the Rev. Mr. Whitefield's Visit to Boston," 1754, in Basker, ed., *Amazing Grace*, p. 109.

25. George Whitefield, *Three Letters from the Reverend Mr. G. Whitefield* (Philadelphia, 1740), pp. 13–16. See also Alan Gallay, "The Great Sellout: George Whitefield on Slavery," in Winfred B. Moore, Jr., and Joseph F. Tripp, eds., *Looking South: Chapters in the Story of an American Region* (New York: Greenwood Press, 1989). See also Whitefield's sermons discussed in *NYWJ*, March 10, 1740, and *NYG*, February 12, 1740.

26. James Mascoparran to Philip Bearcroft, May 4, 1741, SPG Papers, LOC, Vol. 9, Box 5473; Richard Charlton to Philip Bearcroft, October 30, 1741, ibid.

27. Cambridge's recanting, Horsmanden says, took place on June 9, but he includes it in the day's events for July 10. As Cambridge did not confess until June 30, "June" must be a mistake for July.

28. Again, in the *Journal,* Horsmanden indicates only that Othello confessed *"Before One of the Judges,"* but the original MS confession reads "before me Danl Horsmanden." NYCCP, 74:121:b:v.

29. Frederick Philipse and Daniel Horsmanden to George Clarke, July 16, 1741, NYCCP, 74:128a and b.

30. For Harry's confession, see NYCCP, 74:129a:4.

31. *NYWJ*, July 27, 1741.

32. George Clarke to the Lords of Trade, August 24, 1741, *Docs. Col. NY*, 6:202.

33. *NYWJ*, August 17, 1741.

34. *NYWJ*, August 31, 1741.

Chapter Seven

1. DH to CC, August 7, 1741, *LPCC*, 2:224–28.

2. On August 24, Clarke reported to the Lords of Trade, "great industry has been used through out the town to discredit the witnesses and prejudice the people against them." In this, as in everything relating to the conspiracy, Clarke took his lead from Horsmanden— George Clarke to the Lords of Trade, August 24, 1741, *Docs. Col. NY*, 6:202.

3. *MCC*, 5:23, July 28, 1741; 5:31, October 7, 1741; 5:67, October 22, 1742; 5:50, March 22, 1742; and 5:86, March 30, 1743. Clarke to the Lords of Trade, August 24, 1741, *Docs. Col. NY*, 6:203. Clarke to the Duke of Newcastle, October 19, 1741, *Docs. Col. NY*, 6:205. Clarke to the Lords of Trade, December 15, 1741, *Docs. Col. NY*, 6:209. *MCC*, 5:67, October 22, 1742.

4. Anonymous to CC, [July 23?] 1741, *LLPC*, 8:270–71. Anonymous to Elizabeth

DeLancey, undated, c. July 1741, *LPCC*, 8:269–72. CC to Clarke, August 15, 1741, *LPCC*, 8:272–73.

5. George Clarke to CC, August 18, 1741, *LPCC*, 8:273–74.

6. Thomas Hutchinson, *A History of the Colony of Massachusetts Bay* (Boston, 1767), 2:400–401.

7. Miller quoted in Mary Beth Norton, *In the Devil's Snare: The Salem Witchcraft Crisis of 1692* (New York: Knopf, 2002), p. 287. My thanks to Norton for her invaluable assistance in thinking about the links between 1692 and 1741.

8. John Hale, *A Modest Inquiry into the Nature of Witchcraft* (Boston, 1702). The complete text reads as follows: "that which chiefly carried on this matter to such an height, was the increasing of confessors till they amounted to near about Fifty: and four or six of them upon their tryals owned their guilt of this crime, and were condemned for the same, but not Executed. And many of the confessors confirmed their confessions with very strong circumstances: As their exact agreement with the accusations of the afflicted; their punctual agreement with their fellow confessors; their relating the times when they covenanted with Satan, and the reasons that moved them thereunto; their Witch meetings, and that they had their mock Sacraments of Baptism and the Supper, in some of them; their signing the Devils book."

9. Thomas E. Drake, *Quakers and Slavery in America* (1950; Gloucester, MA: Peter Smith, 1965); J. William Frost, ed., *The Quaker Origins of Antislavery* (Norwood, PA: Norwood Editions, 1980). *The Journal and Major Essays of John Woolman*, ed. Phillips P. Moulton (Richmond, IN: Friends United Press, 1971), pp. 200, 93.

10. Two of the Massachusetts commissioners appear to have had a Salem connection. Among the members was a man referred to in the records only as "Doctor Hale," whose possible relationship to John Hale is difficult to determine. Another commissioner almost as likely to have owned a copy of Hale's *Modest Enquiry* was Nathaniel Hubbard. Hubbard, born in Ipswich, Massachusetts, in 1680, was the grandson of Ipswich's minister, William Hubbard, who had written an impassioned defense of the colonists' conduct in King Philip's War, *A Narrative of the Troubles with the Indians in New-England* (Boston, 1677). Nathaniel Hubbard knew his Massachusetts history, and he had lived in Ipswich while witches were hanged in Salem, just a few miles away. A girl named Elizabeth Hubbard was one of the "afflicted girls" whose "spectral evidence" sent so many to the gallows (although her relation to Nathaniel Hubbard is unclear). Hubbard could easily have spoken intimately and passionately about Salem witchcraft. And beyond resenting, in principle, New Yorkers sitting in judicature about his colony's affairs, Hubbard had another reason to resent Colden's argument on behalf of Rhode Island; as an adult, Hubbard made his home in Bristol (he died there in 1748).

11. *The Diaries of Benjamin Lynde and of Benjamin Lynde, Jr.* (Boston, 1880): Barns trial, pp. 88–89; London rape case, p. 61; Sumners murder case, p. 116; "Negro halloday," p. 109; Scipio, pp. 84, 106.

12. Still, Cadwallader Colden believed that the letter was actually written by a New Yorker disguising himself as a Bostonian. In addition to meeting all the other criteria—he would have had to understand legal matters, know Latin, have read about the Antiguan slave revolt, and be familiar with the central tenets of early anti-slavery sentiment—that New Yorker would have to be an avid book collector in order to own a copy of *Modest Enquiry*, which was much rarer in New York than in Boston. He would also have to have, ready at hand, the most recent Boston newspapers. And herein lies another clue. The author wrote, "I observe in one of the Boston News letters dated July 13th that 5 Negros were executed in one day at the Gallows, a favour indeed, for one next day was burnt at the stake, where he impeached several others, & amongst them some whites." That can only

describe the executions of July 3 and 4. And, indeed, on July 23, the *Boston Weekly News-Letter* did print a report from New York with a dateline of July 13. But the report does not describe five hangings followed, the next day, by one burning. Instead, it recounts only the burning of Will, on July 4 (which the newspaper misreports as having taken place on July 11); the sentencing of two more slaves to be burnt; and the pardoning of forty-two. The *Weekly News-Letter* said nothing at all about the five black men hanged on July 3.

What the author says he read actually appeared in the *Boston Gazette*, on July 13: "On Fryday last Five Negroes were executed at the Gallows. . . . And on Saturday one was burnt; at the Stake he made a Confession and impeach'd several, and among them some Whites." This account, in turn, was an exact reprinting of the account Zenger had published in the *New-York Weekly Journal* on July 6. Colonial newspapers swapped stories all the time, cutting and pasting local news from other papers. Both the *Boston Weekly News-Letter*, printed by B. Green, and the *Boston Gazette*, printed by James Franklin, republished New York news taken from Zenger's *New-York Weekly Journal*—as Zenger and anyone else at his printshop well knew. But Green cut his copy from Franklin's reprinting of Zenger, and not directly from Zenger (instead, Green swapped papers with New York's other printer, William Bradford). Zenger sent his July 6 *Weekly Journal*—with its account of the July 3 and 4 executions—to Franklin the day he printed it. In his July 13 *Boston Gazette*, Franklin reprinted Zenger's report about the executions, word for word. That Green took his news not from Zenger but from Franklin accounts for his error in dating Will's execution to July 11, not July 4. For on Monday, July 6, Zenger's paper reported that Will was burned at the stake the previous Saturday (July 4); one week later, on July 13, Franklin printed the identical story—the execution had taken place on the previous Saturday—which Green took to mean July 11 (and which also explains why Green used the dateline, "NEW-YORK, July 13").

If someone from New York wrote the letter to Colden hoping to disguise himself as a Bostonian, he either received and read a copy of the *Boston Gazette* very soon after it was printed on July 13 (and confused it with the *Boston News-Letter*), or else he guessed which Boston newspaper would reprint Zenger's report of the July 3 and 4 executions, and on what date. To make such a guess, he would need to know something of the newspaper business, but not too much, because he confused the *Boston Gazette* with the *Boston News-Letter*. One New Yorker who fits the description—a book collector, with knowledge of Latin, law, and the newspaper business, and who had cause to complain about the trials—is James Alexander.

13. CC to George Clarke, August, 1741, *LPCC*, 8:272.

14. Smith, *History*, 2:57–58.

15. The events of 1742 bear further inquiry but lie outside the scope of this study, as does a related incident, in Kingston, New York, in the summer of 1741. See Leo Hershkowitz, "Tom's Case: An Incident, 1741," *NYH* 52 (1971): 63–71.

16. *MCC*, 5:22, 48, 52–53, 60–61. On Burton's April petition and its being referred to the Supreme Court, see NYCCP, 74:142 and 143. The depositions of Kannady, Hogg, and Masters, along with several others, appear in the Appendix to Horsmanden's *Journal*.

17. *Proposals for Printing by Subscription, a Journal of the Proceedings in The Detection of the Conspiracy* (New York, 1742).

18. James Parker, *A Letter to a Gentleman in the City of New-York* (New York, 1759), reprinted in Beverly McAnear, "James Parker *Versus* New York Province," *NYH* 22 (1941): 321–30. Bradford placed an ad for Parker's return in the *Gazette* on May 14, 1733.

19. Horsmanden's personal copy of the *Journal* is described in Randy F. Weinstein, ed., *Against the Tide: Commentaries on a Collection of African Americana, 1711–1987* (New York: Glenn Horowitz Bookseller, 1996), p. 4.

20. Smith, Jr., *Memoirs*, 2:41.

21. *Journal of the Assembly*, 2:70, July 5, 1745. George Clinton to the Lords of Trade, September 27, 1747, *Docs. Col. NY*, 6:380–82.

22. George Clinton to the Duke of Newcastle, December 9, 1746, *Docs. Col. NY*, 6:312; Clinton to the Lords of Trade, September 27, 1747, *Docs. Col. NY*, 6:378–79, 386. Horsmanden's troubled years in Clinton's administration are chronicled in chapter 3 of McManus's "Daniel Horsmanden."

23. Smith, Jr., *History*, 2:100. CC to George Clinton, February 14, 1748, *LPCC*, 4:13–14. Clinton to CC, April 1, 1748, *LPCC*, 4:32. A week later Colden wrote, "it is impossible to save your Excellency's honour if Mr H_____n be thought worthy to be inploy'd in places of the greatest trust after the publication of such libelous papers as have been printed & of which no one can doubt of his being the author"—CC to Clinton, April 9, 1748, *LPCC*, 4:45. *The New York Gazette, revivied in the Weekly Post-Boy*, January 18, 1748.

24. See McManus, "Daniel Horsmanden," pp. 134–61.

25. *NYG*, March 18, 1734.

26. Thomas Hobbes, *De Cive*, chapter 13, para. 13.

27. Clarke quoted in Smith, Jr., *Memoirs*, 2:41.

Epilogue

1. The Last Will and Testament of Daniel Horsmanden, February 5, 1777, in *Abstracts of Wills, NYHSC* 33 (1900): 57–58.

2. Smith, Jr., *Memoirs*, 2:40–41. In 1757, when William Smith, Jr., set about writing his *History of the Province of New York*, he dismissed the conspiracy altogether: "That a few slaves would hope to effect a massacre of their masters, or thus vindicate their liberties, was the height of absurdity: but the fears of the multitude, led them to presume nothing less; and perhaps that extravagance then gave birth to the proof by which it was afterwards supposed to be incontestably confirmed." Billy Smith was thirteen years old in 1741, when his father participated in the prosecution of those plotters. In 1756 and 1757, when Smith was writing, his father was still alive. Yet his source for much of his *History* came not from the senior William Smith, but from his close associate, James Alexander. As Smith was writing, he corresponded with Alexander, read books in Alexander's library, and consulted his friend's collection of historical manuscripts. Only Alexander's death in April 1756 prevented him from checking Smith's manuscript for accuracy, as he had agreed to. It is fair to say that Smith's assessment of the trials was Alexander's as much as his own: "Every new trial led to further accusations: a coincidence of slight circumstances, was magnified by the general terror into violent presumptions, tales collected without doors, mingling with the proofs given at the bar, poisoned the minds of the jurors, and the sanguinary spirit of the day suffered no check till Mary, the capital informer, bewildered by frequent examinations and suggestions, lost her first impressions, and began to touch characters, which malice itself did not dare to suspect"—Smith, Jr., *History*, 2:52–53; 1:xxii–xxiv, xxxiv, lxii.

3. Smith, Jr., *History*, 2:100–101.

4. John Watts to Sir Charles Hardy, August 13, 1763, *Letter Book of John Watts, NYHSC* 61 (1928): 172. Robert Livingston, Jr., to Robert Livingston, July 6, 1763, Robert Livingston Papers, Box 1, NYHS.

5. William Smith, Jr., to Philip Schuyler, September 12, 1769, in Smith, *Memoirs*, 1:54. He had bought the chariot in 1763, the year he married Ann, but only paid for it months later. "The Old Gentleman has not paid for the Charriot," his creditor complained. "No Cash," Horsmanden explained. Horsmanden's coach, chariot, and conduct with his creditor is detailed in McManus, "Daniel Horsmanden," pp. 166–67.

6. On the commandeering of Frog Hall, see McManus, "Daniel Horsmanden," p. 162.

7. Miles Sherbrook was a friend of Horsmanden's wife's family. In 1763, Ann's brother-in-law, Joseph Haynes, wrote a will, witnessed by Sherbrook, making Ann his executor—Joseph Haynes will, codicil dated March 9, 1763, New York City Wills, 1760–66.

8. *Proclamation, The Number of Fires,* September 23, 1776, New York.

9. Horsmanden's final years are best documented in McManus, "Daniel Horsmanden," chap. 5.

10. The full text of all these New York wills can be found at Ancestry.com.

11. "A Law for Regulating the Burial of Slaves," *MCC,* 4:88–89, November 18, 1731. For a fascinating discussion of slavery and deathways, see Vincent Brown, "Slavery and the Spirits of the Dead: Mortuary Politics in Jamaica, 1740–1834" (Ph.D. diss., Duke University, 2002).

12. Betty M. Kuyk, "The African Derivation of Black Fraternal Orders in the United States," *Comparative Studies in Society and History* 25, no. 4 (October 1983): 559–92. John P. McCarthy, "African-Influenced Burial Practices and Sociocultural Identity in Antebellum Philadelphia," unpublished paper, World Archaeological Congress 4, University of Cape Town, 1999.

13. Bruce Frankel, "Black Cemetery in New York City New Key to Colonial Times," *New York Times,* September 15, 1992. See also Michael L. Blaakey, "The New York African Burial Ground Project: An Examination of Enslaved Lives, A Construction of Ancestral Ties," *Transforming Anthropology* 7 (1998): 53–58. None of the studies conducted of the African Burial Ground remains and artifacts have been made available to the public so far, and my repeated requests to read draft reports were denied.

14. Christopher R. DeCorse, "An African Bead in New York City," *Newsletter of the African Burial Ground* 3, no. 1 (Winter 2000): 6–7; Cheryl Laroche, "Beads from the African Burial Ground, New York City: A Preliminary Assessment," *Beads: Journal of the Society of Bead Researchers* 6 (1994): 3–20; Linda France Stine, Melanie A. Cabak, and Mark D. Groover, "Blue Beads as African-American Cultural Symbols," *Historical Archaeology* 30 (1996): 49–75; Christopher R. DeCorse, "Culture Contact, Continuity, and Change on the Gold Coast, AD 1400–1900," *African Archaeological Review* 10 (1992): 163–96.

Appendix A

1. Paul Boyer and Stephen Nissenbaum, *Salem Possessed: The Social Origins of Witchcraft* (Cambridge, MA: Harvard University Press, 1974).

2. They can be found in Evarts B. Greene and Virginia D. Harrington, *American Population Before the Federal Census of 1790* (New York, 1932), pp. 97–98. I have altered the 1731 and 1737 censuses according to corrections offered by Robert V. Wells ("The New York Census of 1731," *New-York Historical Society Quarterly* 57 [1973]: 255–59) and Gary Nash ("The New York Census of 1737: A Critical Note on the Integration of Statistical and Literary Sources," *WMQ* 36 [1979]: 428–35).

3. David Franks, *The New-York Directory* (New York, 1786). The transcription of the 1730 tax list was made by Julius M. Block, Leo Hershkowitz, and Kenneth Scott, and published in *New York Genealogical and Biographical Record* 95 (1964): 27–32, 166–74, 195–202. (Because it has been transcribed, the 1730 tax list has also been used extensively by other historians of the city; see esp. Wilkenfeld, "New York City Neighborhoods, 1730.")

4. Goodfriend, *Before the Melting Pot.* "A Law for Punishing Slaves who Shall Ride Disorderly through the Streets," *MCC,* 4:89–90.

5. Goodfriend to the author, personal communication, May 23, 2002. Scattered occupations were also taken from Valentine, "List of Citizens Admitted as Freemen of the City

of New York, from 1749 to the Revolutionary War," *Manual of the Corporation of the City of New-York for 1856,* pp. 477–502, as well as from other miscellaneous sources. I entered additional biographical information for many of the 458 white trial participants from biographical encyclopedias (the *Dictionary of American Biography,* the *Encyclopedia of New York City,* and the *American National Biography*), as well as from print and online genealogical reference tools, including Ancestry.com and the *New York Genealogical and Biographical Record.* The list of white trial participants was checked against a surviving list of the city's militia companies (printed in *Doc. Hist. NY,* 4:211–26), which I entered in the database, along with the list of city firemen appointed in 1738. Public offices held are taken from E. B. O'Callaghan, "Officials of the Province of New York, 1630–1775," O'Callaghan Papers, NYHS; and from David T. Valentine, *Manual of the Corporation of the City of New-York for 1854* (New York, 1854), pp. 400–440.

6. "Census of Slaves, 1755," in *Doc. Hist. NY,* 3: (1850): 843–68.

7. John Thornton to author, e-mail, June 1, 2004. James G. Lydon, "New York and the Slave Trade, 1700 to 1774," pp. 377, 383–84, 387–88.

8. Sandra Heiler, " 'May It Please the Court . . .': Confessional Strategies in the New York Conspiracy Trials of 1741," unpublished paper, 2001. A related method was employed by a Boston University undergraduate, Greg O'Malley, in his 1999 honors thesis, " 'These Enemies of Their Own Household': New York's Slave Conspiracy and White Anxiety of 1741," in which he measured pleas of guilty and not guilty before and after Clarke's June 19 proclamation of amnesty.

9. New York Colony Council Papers, 74:88, 99, 100, 105, 108, 109.

10. Stokes, *Iconography,* 3:922–1025. I also consulted a handful of eighteenth-century travel narratives, and Nan Rothschild's *New York City Neighborhoods: The 18th Century* (San Diego: Academic Press, 1990), pp. 185–227. William Burgis, "A South Prospect of ye Flourishing City of New York in the Province of New York in America," 1719–21, is described at length in Stokes, *Iconography,* 1:239–77. Issued in 1719–21, the Burgis view depicts the city in 1716–18, and identifies 103 buildings along the East River.

ACKNOWLEDGMENTS

Years before I began writing this book I assigned excerpts from Daniel Horsmanden's *Journal* to undergraduates and graduate students at Boston University, whose fascination with the text served as a once-a-semester reminder that the murky events of 1741 were worth investigating. Greg O'Malley wrote a wonderful senior honors thesis on the topic in 1999. In the fall of 2001, I taught a graduate research seminar on the *Journal,* whose students brought to their work so much enthusiasm that I want to thank them all: Andrew Black, Susannah Black, Eoin Cannon, Hannah Carlson, Antonios Clapsis, Jennifer Coval, Steven Crowther, Sandra Heiler, Christina Kopp, Tara Kraenzlin, Carney Maley, Darrell Morey, Emily Murphy, Eric Plaag, Vanessa Pool, Satoka Sawauchi, Jeanette Sedgwick, Katherine Stebbins-McCaffrey, and Peter Surfin. I, for one, will never forget the cold December night, near Christmastime, when we made a pilgrimage to Cambridge to view Horsmanden's portrait at the Harvard Law School, and then retired to drink and feast in the warmth of a nearby tavern.

Two of my BU students, Kathryn Lindquist and Hannah Carlson, became my indefatigable research assistants, working long hours at the painstaking labor of entering data into tables. My thanks to both of them and to everyone else who helped me reconstruct New York: James Dutton tutored me in database design, Kashid Mohammed helped set up my first database, Paul McMorrow photocopied runaway ads, Albert Sutton helped analyze the data, David Rumsey supplied a geo-referenced eighteenth-century map, and Robert Chavez taught me how to work in GIS.

At Harvard, I benefited immensely from the research assistance of Mark Hanna and especially Michelle Jarrett Morris, who saved me from a barrel of errors. I'd also like to thank Harvard graduate students and faculty in the Early American History Workshop, including Richard Bell, Vincent Brown, Joyce Chaplin, Brian DeLay, Judy Kertesz, and Margot Minardi.

I presented portions of this research at seminars, lectures, and conferences, including meetings hosted by the Charles Warren Center at Harvard, the Legal History Workshop at Harvard Law School, the American Studies Program at the City University of New York, the New-York Historical Society, the American Studies Association, the History and Literature Program at Harvard University, the University of Toronto Centre for the Study of the United States, Cambridge University, the University of Southern Maine, Yale University, Boston University, Columbia University, and Boston College. I thank all who offered comments at those sessions.

Several scholars offered very specific assistance: Ann Fabian attended the reburial ceremonies with me, sharing her boundless knowledge of what happens to old bones; Mary Beth Norton and Mark Peterson provided clues to the New York–Salem connection;

Simon Middleton shared his digitized Mayor's Court records; and Joyce Goodfriend, displaying exceptional scholarly generosity, mailed me a printout of her assiduously researched 1730 tax list. Others read portions of the manuscript and supplied helpful corrections, including Vincent Brown, Stanley Katz, Corey Robin, Erik Seeman, John Thornton, David Waldstreicher, and Shane White. Don Lamm read the first half, and shared with me his sage advice. A hardy few friends and colleagues read an early draft of the whole book: John Demos, Jane Kamensky, Daniel Penrice, Bruce Schulman, and Laurel Ulrich, along with my editor, Jane Garrett, and my agent, Andrew Wylie. I thank each for their generosity and insight. And I want to thank the editorial production staff at Knopf for their careful work and patience with my pile of last-minute changes.

I wrote most of this book during a leave jointly funded by the National Endowment for the Humanities and Harvard University. I am deeply grateful for the time that made writing possible, and especially for the support of my dean and department at Harvard. I also thank the Gilder Lehrman Institute of American History for providing a much-needed research grant early on. And I'm grateful to the librarians and archivists at the New-York Historical Society, the New York Public Library, and the Museum of the City of New York, whose efforts greatly aided my research. I want especially to thank James Folts at the New York State Archives for arranging document scanning of the fragile New York Colony Council Records.

On bleaker days, it has seemed to me as though there have been only a few hours over the last few years that I've escaped eighteenth-century New York. Mercifully, that hasn't actually been the case. To everyone who rescued me from my work with coffee and phone calls, runs along the river and walks through the woods: bless you. For every conversation, for every excursion, I thank Adrianna Alty, Kathleen Dalton, Deborah Favreau, Benjamin Filene, Jane Kamensky, Lisa Lovett, Elizabeth McNerney, Bruce Schulman, Rachel Seidman, Ariadne Valsamis, Denise Webb, and Wendy Weitzner. Finally, my thanks to the people who wake me up in the morning, the best part of every day: Timothy, Gideon, Simon, and Oliver Leek.

Cambridge, March 2005

INDEX

Italicized page numbers indicate illustrations; names in parentheses indicate slaves' owners. Appendices B and C are not indexed here.

Adam (Murray), 8, 9, 25, 35, 80, 138, 150, 167, 168–9, 172, 177, 181–2, 190, 226
Afonso I, Kongolese King, 183
Albany (Carpenter), 8, 44, 119, 120, 151, 153
Alexander, James, xv, 13, 17, *32*, 35, 40, 52, 54, 67, 93, 149, 219
   bar of New York and, 79–80
   black Masons incident, 100, 101
   book purchases, 28–9
   death of, 223
   death threat against, 286*n*27
   early years, 31
   fires of 1741, 46, 50–51
   on liberty and slavery, xi
   Masons and, 139, 140, 141
   Oblong or the Equivalent Lands case, 291*n*11
   personal qualities, 32
   political crisis of 1730s, xiii, xv–xvi, 26, 71, 77–8, 286*n*27
   prosecution of conspirators, 79, 121; Alexander's involvement, 200; attorneys' agreement to assist with, 82; criticism of, 200, 305*n*12; Priest's Plot investigation, 180; prominent whites, accusations against, 201; resumption of prosecutions in 1742, efforts toward, 212; Smith Jr.'s account of, 306*n*2; "Spanish Negroes" trial, 165–6
   as slaveowner, 32–3
   Vice Admiralty Court, 162
   wealth of, 31
   Zenger trial, xiii, 72, 73, 74, 75–7, 115–17, 293*nn*18, 23, 25

Alexander, Lewis Morris, 33
Alexander, Mary Spratt Provost, 31, 35, 36
Alexander, William, 223, 224
All Slave-Keepers, That keep the Innocent in Bondage (Lay), 208
Amba (Philipse), 59
Amelia (Fielding), 123
American Philosophical Society, 32
American Revolution, xvii, 221–2, 223–5
Anne, Queen, 59
Antigua slave rebellion (1736), 11, 53, 91, 92, 98, 104, 105
anti-slavery movement, 208, 219
Antonio de la Cruz (Mesnard), 50, 160–1, 164, 165, 166
Antonio de St. Bendito (DeLancey), 15, 50, 160, 164, 165, 166
Aptheker, Herbert, 280*n*11
Arding, Charles, 96, 108
Ashfield, Richard, 30
Auboyneau, John, 85
Augustine Gutierrez (Macmullen), 50, 161, 164, 165, 166

Bacon, Nathaniel, 52
Baker, Richard, 138
Baker's Tavern robbery, 99, 137–8, 141
Barbados slave rebellion (1676), 10–11
Barbara (Clarke), 93, 105–6, 107
Barns, John, 209
bar of New York, 79–80, 294*nn*30, 31
Bastian (Vaarck), 5, 6, 7, 110, 119, 120, 147, 163, 166
beads owned by blacks, 231–2

Beaux' Stratagem, The (Farquhar), 16–18, 30–1, 35–6, 55, 183, 282*n*4
Becker, Frederick, 166
Beekman, Andries, 53, 104
Beekman, Gerardus, 59
Before the Melting Pot (Goodfriend), 237
Bell, John, 208
Ben (Jay), 8
Ben (Marshall), 5, 6, 9, 111, 120, 124, 133, 149–50, 151, 162, 164, 165
Bickley, May, 82
Black Horse Tavern, 27
black Masons incident, 99–102, 296*n*12
blacks
    artisans, 146
    beads owned by, 231–2
    birth and death patterns, 33–4
    burial of, 226–8
    celebrating by, 154–5, 158–60
    child care for whites, 34
    childhood and family life, 34–5
    election of leaders of black community, 159
    humanity issue, 207–8
    languages of, 110–11
    literacy among, 35, 123–6
    markings on, 33
    marriages of, 156
    population information on, 238–40, 300*n*34
    religion among, 183
    remains and artifacts of colonial-era blacks discovered in 1991, 228–32
    social connections, 148–57
    see also slavery
black saturnalia, 159–60
Bohenna, Thomas, 96
Bolingbroke, Viscount St. John, xv, 26
Bonett, Daniel, 96
Bosch, Jasper, 54
Boston Gazette, 305*n*12
Boston Weekly News-Letter, 305*n*12
Boyer, Paul, 233
Bradford, Andrew, 142, 143
Bradford, William, 72, 99, 139, 140–1, 142–3, 214, 292*n*14, 293*n*18
Bradley, Richard, 79, 165
    death of, 223
    Hogg's shop robbery trials, 85

prosecution of conspirators:
    Hughson/Kerry trial, 108–9, 128;
    Priest's Plot trial, 192, 194–5;
    prosecution's trial strategy, 131;
    Quack/Cuffee trial, 96, 103; six black men's trial, 131; "white leadership of conspiracy" issue, 126, 128
    Vice Admiralty Court, 162
    Zenger trial, 74, 76, 117, 118
Bradt, Divertie, 212
Brash (Jay), 8, 89, 168
Braveboy (Kiersted), 154–5
Bridgewater (Van Horne), 151, 226
Brief Examination of the Practice of the Times, A (Sandiford), 208
Brief Narrative of the Case and Trial of John Peter Zenger (Alexander), xiii, xiv
Broadway Market House, 137
Brodrick, William, 298*n*39
Browne, William, 209
Burgis, William, 242
Burnings Bewailed (Mather), 51
Burns, George, 49
Burrows, Edwin G., 281*n*11
Burton, Mary, 7, 15, 122, 129, 132, 133, 147, 156, 158
    Hogg's shop robbery, 37, 38, 85
    prosecution of conspirators: Burton's lying, concerns about, 201–2; Burton's reward, 211–12, 213–14; confessions of the accused, 78–9, 113; criticism of, 200, 202; Hughson/Kerry trial, 109; investigations by judges and grand jury, 78–9, 84–5, 90; last slave trial, 191; Priest's Plot investigation, 177, 178, 182; Priest's Plot trial, 192–3; prominent whites, accusations against, 200–2; Quack/Cuffee trial, 96–7; six black men's trial, 131; "Spanish Negroes" trial, 163–4, 165, 166, 167
Byrd, Maria Horsmanden, 221
Byrd, William, II, 18–19, 25, 30, 282*n*7, 283*n*8

Caesar (Morin), 185
Caesar (Murray), 167, 226
Caesar (Peck), 110, 119, 131, 132, 151
Caesar (Pintard), 89, 150–1

Caesar (Vaarck), 6, 7, 138, 143, 147, 151, 156
  Baker's Tavern robbery, 99, 137, 141
  decay of exposed corpse, 170–1
  Hogg's shop robbery, 36, 37–8
  trial and execution, 85–6, 89–90
Cajoe (Gomez), 7
Cambridge (Codweis), 189
Campbell, John, 182
Caribbean Christmas, 159–60
Carlson, Hannah, 241–2
Carr, William, 156
Cash, Martha, 86, 295*n*43
Catholicism, *see* Priest's Plot
Cato (Cowley), 144, 151, 164, 165
Cato (Moore), 6, 89, 150–1, 163, 175, 189
Cato (Provost), 151, 164, 165
Cato (Shurmur), 14, 168, 173
Cato's Letters (Trenchard and Gordon), 72
Cesar (Moore), 123
Chambers, Anna, 17
Chambers, John, 28, 29, 137
  bar of New York and, 79–80
  death of, 223
  prosecution of conspirators, 79, 121;
    attorneys' agreement to assist with, 82;
    last slave trial, 191; Priest's Plot trial,
    192–3, 195; six black men's trial, 131, 132;
    "Spanish Negroes" trial, 165, 166
  Zenger trial, 75, 76
Charlton, Richard, 186, 188
Chavez, Robert, 242
Christmastime, 158–60
City Hall, 64–6, *65*
Clarke, George, xvi, 60, 61, 73, 106, 163, 203,
  220
  background of, 47
  death of, 223
  elevation to governor at Cosby's death,
    77
  fires of 1741, 43, 45, 46, 47–8, 49, 51
  General Assembly elections of 1737, 139
  Oblong or the Equivalent Lands case,
    291*n*11
  political crisis of 1730s, xv, xvi, 77–8
  Priest's Plot, 176, 177, 196
  prosecution of conspirators, 78; criticism
    of, 205–6; executions of the
    condemned, 175; pardoning of
    convicts, 121, 191; records of, 95–6;

  resumption of prosecutions in 1742,
    efforts toward, 212; termination of, 211
Clarke, George, Jr., 295–6*n*2
Clarkson, David, 54
Claus, 104
Clinton, George, 215, 217, 218, 222
Coffin, John, 180, 181, 211
Cohen, Samuel Myers, 189, 226
Colden, Cadwallader, 29, 31, 34, 35, 66, 71,
  77, 93, 94–5, 136, 139, 149, 198, 199, 201,
  203, 205, 206, 210, 214, 217, 223, 287*n*44,
  291*n*11, 306*n*23
Comfort, Gerardus, 48, 130–1, 133, 135, 146
Committee for the Detection of
  Conspiracies, 222, 223, 224
Common Council, 30, 45, 47, 57, 61–2, 64,
  135–6, 137, 144, 185, 203, 211, 212, 213, 227
Congo (Murray), 167
Connolly, Peter, 180, 181, 211
conspiracy
  colonists' fears regarding, 51–2, 55–6,
    289*n*18
  see also slave conspiracy of 1712; slave
    conspiracy of 1741
Cook (Comfort), 110, 111, 119, 130, 131, 132,
  133
coopering trade, 146
Corker, Jerry, 180, 181
Coromantees, 24, 53, 147–8
Corry, John, 211
Corwin, Jonathan, 209
Cosby, William, xiii, xv, 13, 41, 47
  arrival in New York, 25
  death of, 77
  Horsmanden, assistance for, 30
  Oblong or the Equivalent Lands case,
    291*n*11
  political crisis of 1730s, 25–6, 27, 70–2,
    292*n*17
  Zenger trial, 72, 73, 115
Cosby, William, Jr., 139–40
Country Party, xv, xvi, xvii, 13, 26, 27, 100,
  139, 140
Court, 104
Court Party, xv, xvii, 13, 26, 27, 139, 140, 218
criminal biography, 298*n*33
criminal trial procedure, 83–4, 88, 91
  "Negro Evidence," 97–8
Cruger, Henry, 54

Cruger, John, 54, 60
Cuba (Chambers), 17, 62–3, 80, 149
Cudjoe, 53–4
Cuffee (Gomez), 110, 119, 131, 132
Cuffee (Jamison), 80
Cuffee (Philipse), 7, 22, 35, 87, 89, 92, 110,
    123, 129, 130, 131, 137, 138, 141, 143, 176–7,
    182
  Baker's Tavern robbery, 99
  execution of, 104–6
  fires of 1741, 43, 44, 46, 50
  Hogg's shop robbery, 37, 38–9
  trial of, 59–60, 93, 96–9, 102–3, 104,
    296*n*9
Curacoa Dick (Tiebout), 89, 119, 120, 151,
    154

dancing, 35, 287*n*46
Davis, Thomas J., 280*n*11
De Cive (Hobbes), 219
Declaration of Independence, 223–4
Defoe, Daniel, 122
DeLancey, Elizabeth Colden, 93, 105, 106,
    107, 109–10, 203
DeLancey, James, 12, 13, 28, 40, 47, 66, 83,
    137, *174*, 206, 217
  bar of New York and, 79–80
  death of, 223
  governorship of, 218
  political crisis of 1730s, 26, 71
  prosecution of conspirators: confessions
    of the accused, 171–2; criticism of, 205;
    executions of the condemned, 173, 174,
    175; last slave trial, 190; pardoning of
    conspirators, 175, 191; Priest's Plot
    investigation, 177, 178, 180, 181, 194;
    Priest's Plot trial, 196; prominent
    whites, accusations against, 201;
    resumption of prosecutions in 1742,
    efforts toward, 213; termination of, 211
  Zenger trial, 72–3, 74, 75, 117, 118, 293*nn*18,
    23, 25
DeLancey, Oliver, 224
DeLancey, Peter, 166
DeLancey, Stephen, 64
Delawarr, Baron, 77
Diana (Machado), 15, 34
Dido (Murray), 167

Dimmock, Mrs., 17
Dinkins, David, 229
disease problem, 136
"Dissertation upon Parties" (Bolingbroke),
    xv
Dromo (Hamilton), 111
Dundee (Todd), 8, 9, 43, 49, 87, 138, 144,
    147, 163
Dunscomb, John, 158
DuPuy, Francis, 166
DuPuy, Francis, Jr., 166
Dutch West India Company, 23

Earle, Abigail, 49
Ellsworth, George, Jr., 292*n*14
Emanuel (Wendover), 5, 6
Enquiry into the Cause of the late Increase of
    Robbers, An (Fielding), 123
Equiano, Olaudah, 124
Evans, Griffith, 46
Evans, Thomas, 191

Fagan, David, 180, 181
Farmer, Jaspar, 54
Farquhar, George, *see Beaux' Stratagem, The*
Fielding, Henry, 88, 122–3
Fielding, John, 88
firefighting, 42–4, *43*, 45, 46
fires of 1741, xii, xvi
  "accident" explanation for, 47–8
  March 18 fire, 40–7
  March 25–April 6 fires, 48–50
  Priest's Plot and, 181
  "slave conspiracy" explanation for, 49–51,
    60–2
  slaves' reactions, 43, 44, 46, 49, 50
  "witchcraft" explanation for, 51
Fort George, xv, xvi, 40–3, *41*, 44, 46, 47, 53,
    95, 288*n*2
Fortune (Clarkson), 144
Fortune (Vanderspiegle), 107, 109, 129, 131,
    144, 151, 164, 165
Fortune (Wilkins), 92, 97, 98, 99, 102
Francis (Bosch), 90, 91, 119, 120, 163–4
Frank (Philipse), 80
Franklin, Benjamin, 32, 72, 142, 187, 208,
    214–15

Franklin, James, 305*n*12
Franks, Abigail, 26, 71, 75, 292*n*17
Freemasons, *see* Masons
frolicks (black parties), 154–5

Gabriel (Colden), 149
Galloway (Rutgers), 226
Gardner, Isaac, 43, 44
Garrick, David, 36
General Assembly, 13, 45, 56, 57, 58, 64, 70,
    73, 144, 184, 203, 215, 217
  elections of 1737, 139–40, 299*n*10
Geneva Club, 99–102, 137–8, 141, 143, 180–1,
    296*n*10
Genovese, Eugene, 280*n*11
Gilbert, Jane, 226
Gomez, Mordecai, 54, 166
Goodfriend, Joyce, 237
Gordon, Thomas, 72
Green, B., 305*n*12
Grim, David, 2, 105
Groesbeck, John, 54
Gulliver's Travels (Swift), 55–6, 122

Haitian Revolution of 1791, 300*n*28
Hale, John, 207, 304*n*8
Hale, Nathan, 225
Hamilton, Dr. Alexander, 12, 22, 46, 111, 126,
    142, 145
Hamilton, Andrew, 76, 117–18
Hanover (Cruger), 173
Harison, Francis, 72, 73, 76, 77, 99, 286*n*27,
    291*n*11
Harlem Boys Choir, 229
Harry (Kipp), 144, 151, 168, 173
Harry, Dr. (Mizreal), 192
Hawkins, William, 84
Hearly, Thomas, 17
Heiler, Sandra, 240
Hereford (Cohen), 189, 226
Heywood, Linda, 239–40
Hilton, Mrs., 49
"History of the Ancient and Honorable
    Tuesday Club" (Hamilton), 12, 142
History of the Province of New York
    (Smith), 12, 67, 74–5, 86, 94, 306*n*2
Hobbes, Thomas, 219

Hobbs, Abigail, 209
Hoffer, Peter, 281*n*11
Hogg, Rebecca, 36, 37–8, 85, 213
Hogg, Robert, 36, 85, 181
Hogg's shop robbery, 78, 181
  executions of the condemned, 89–90
  slave conspiracy of 1741 and, 36–9
  trials of robbers, 85–6, 87
Hoghlandt, Adrian, 53, 104
Holmes, Oliver Wendell, 279*n*11
Holt, Henry, 139, 180, 182, 282*n*5
Horsmanden, Ann Jevon, 222–3, 224
Horsmanden, Daniel, xvi, 12, 13–14, 25, 37,
    55, *68*, 84, 86, 125, 133, 136, 137, 138, 148,
    150, 152, 155, 158, 160, 168, 169, 188
  arrival in New York, 20, 25
  black Masons incident, 99, 102, 296*n*12
  career vicissitudes in 1740s and 1750s,
    217–18
  chief justiceship, 222
  City Recorder position, 30
  courtroom style, 66–7
  death of, 225
  early years, 18–20, 283*nn*7, 8, 10, 284*n*11
  equine enthusiasm, 223
  financial situation, 28, 29–30, 215, 217
  fires of 1741, 46, 47, 48, 60
  Hogg's shop robbery executions, 89, 90
  later years, 221–5
  Oblong or the Equivalent Lands case,
    291*n*11
  physical appearance, 67
  political crisis of 1730s, xiii, xv, 25, 26,
    27–8, 71, 77, 78, 286*n*27
  prosecution of conspirators: attorneys'
    agreement to assist with, 82; Burton's
    lying, concerns about, 201–2; Burton's
    reward, 213–14; confessions of the
    accused, 10, 106, 110, 111–13, 115, 121–2,
    123, 171, 172–3, 189–90; criticism of,
    199, 202; executions of the
    condemned, 106, 164; fixing the
    meaning of conspirators' words, 113,
    115, 118; Horsmanden's assessment of,
    198–9; Horsmanden's control of, 122;
    Horsmanden's personal interest in,
    82–3; Hughson/Kerry trial, 108, 109,
    130–1; investigations by judges and
    grand jury, 60, 61, 66–7, 78, 79, 83, 85,

Horsmanden, Daniel, prosecution of
conspirators *(continued)*
87, 88, 89, 90, 92, 107, 108; "list of
conspirators" rumor, 120; pardoning of
convicts, 175, 191; party politics and,
220; Priest's Plot designated as master
plot, 198; Priest's Plot investigation,
177, 178, 180, 181, 182, 191, 194; Priest's
Plot trial, 195; prominent whites,
accusations against, 201–2;
Quack/Cuffee trial, 93, 96, 97, 99, 103,
104, 296n9; recantations of
confessions, 190; resumption of
prosecutions in 1742, efforts toward,
212–13, 214; slaves designated as
primary suspects in arson fires, 61–2;
"Spanish Negroes" trial, 162, 165, 167;
Supreme Court's jurisdiction over,
81–3; termination of, 211; "white
leadership of conspiracy" issue, 126,
128
Vice Admiralty Court, 162
will of, 221
Zenger trial, 73, 115, 117, 118
*see also Journal of the Proceedings in The
Detection of the Conspiracy*
Horsmanden, Lucretia, 221
Horsmanden, Mary Reade Vesey, 222
Horsmanden, Susanna, 18
Horsmanden, Ursula, 18, 221
Howard University, 229
Hubbard, Nathaniel, 304n10
Hughson, John, xvi, 15, 21, 61, 99, 103, 133,
141, 143
Baker's Tavern robbery, 137–8
decay of exposed corpse, 170–1
execution of, 119–20
Hogg's shop robbery, 36, 38, 87
legal problems in 1737, 137
move to West Ward, 136–8
Priest's Plot, 179, 180, 181, 196
prosecution of conspirators:
Hughson/Kerry trial, 108–10, 128,
130–1; investigations by judges and
grand jury, 107–8; "white leadership of
conspiracy" issue, 126, 128
slave conspiracy of 1741: as joke, 143;
plotting of, 5, 6, 7, 8, 9; "three years in
preparation" issue, 137–8

Hughson, Nathaniel, 180
Hughson, Richard, 180
Hughson, Sarah (daughter), 6, 87, 108, 119,
193–5
Hughson, Sarah (mother), 6, 38, 61, 87, 108,
109, 120, 136
Hughson, Thomas, 180
Hughson, Walter, 180
Hughson, William, 180
Hume, David, 125
Hunt, Obadiah, 54
Hunter, Robert, 53, 54, 58, 59, 82, 185

Indian uprisings, 11, 55

Jack (Breasted), 89, 151, 189
Jack (Comfort), 5, 110, 119, 130, 131, 132, 133,
145, 151, 162–4, 166
confession of, 111–15, *114, 116*
leadership role in slave conspiracy, 146–7,
148
Jack (Hayes), 189
Jack (Murray), 8, 9, 80, 167, 168–9, 226
Jack (Sleydall), 7, 144, 150, 153
Jackson, Jesse, 229
jail facilities, 86, 295n43
Jamaica, 131, 132
Jamaica (Ellison), 7, 110
Jamaica slave rebellion (1730s), 53–4
Jamison, William, 67–9, 79, 82, 104–5, 106,
121
Jay, Peter and Augustus, 54
Jefferson, Thomas, xii, xv
Jeffrey (Brown), 149–50
Jenny (Comfort), 111, 133
Joe (Holt), 9, 17, 87, 182
John (Van Dam), 59
Johnson, David, 180, 181, 211
Johnson, Samuel, xii, 36, 187
Johnson, Simon, 122
Jones, Evan, 142
Jones, Francis, 181
Jonneau (Carr), 156
Jonneau (Vaarck), 6
Jordan, Winthrop, 280n11
*Journal of the Proceedings in The Detection
of the Conspiracy* (Horsmanden),

xviii–xx, *xix,* 81, 83, 88, 91, 93, 97, 99,
    104, 106, 107, 111, 112, 113, *116,* 162, 183,
    194, 198, *216,* 280*n*11
  credibility as historical document, 95–6
  database of trial transcript from, 240–1
  Horsmanden's hiding of his role in
    prosecution of conspirators, 122–3
  List of Negroes, 233, *234*
  quotation marks used in, 112–13
  sales of, 220
  writing and publication of, 94–5, 210–11,
    214–15
Juan (Lowe), 7
Juan de la Silva (Sarly), 49–50, 160, 164, 165,
    166–7, 176, 196–7
judiciary of New York, 69, 70–1, 291*n*9

Kane, William, 174, 176, 178–80, 181, 182,
    191, 193, 194, 201
Kannady, Ann, 38, 213, 214
Kannady, James, 38
Kelly, Edward, 174, 180, 181, 211
Kennedy, Archibald, 206
Kerry, Peggy, 6, 22, 132, 150, 156
  execution of, 119–20
  Hogg's shop robbery, 37, 38, 87
  prosecution of conspirators: confessions
    of the accused, 89, 113;
    Hughson/Kerry trial, 108–10;
    investigations by judges and grand
    jury, 85, 86, 87, 89, 90
  as prostitute, 37
Keteltass, Abraham, 69
Kiersted, Capt. Benjamin, 161–2
King, Adam, 109
King Philip's War, 11
Kortreicht, Cornelius, 54

Lashier, John, 96, 108
Launitz-Schurer, Leopold S., 280*n*11
Law of Evidence (treatise), 91
Lawrence, Mary, 37
Lay, Benjamin, 208
Leisler, Jacob, 52, 70
*Letter to the Masters and Mistresses of
    Families in the English Plantations
    abroad* (pamphlet), 185–6

Lindquist, Kathryn, 236
Linebaugh, Peter, 280*n*11
Livingston, Philip, 206
Lodge, Abraham, 79, 82, 121, 123, 132
London (French), 144, 151
London (Kelly), 189
London (Marschalk), 9, 168
London (Van Horne), 226
London (Wyncoop), 151, 158
Luckstead, Elizabeth, 180
Lurting, George, 79
Lush, John, 49, 50, 54, 161
Lydon, James G., 239–40, 285*n*21
Lynch, Peter, 158
Lynde, Benjamin, 209–10

Macmullen, John, 166
manumission, 58, 226
Maria (Richards), 150
Mars (Benson), 151
Mars (Regnier), 82
Marschalk, Joris, 53
Marston, Nathaniel, 54
Masons, 17, 179, 282*n*5
  black Masons incident, 99–102, 296*n*12
  mockery directed at, 141–3
  party politics and, 139–41
  slave conspiracy of 1741 and, 12–13, 143–4
Massachusetts–Rhode Island boundary
    dispute, 205–7
Masters, Susannah, 214
Mather, Increase, 51
McManus, Edgar J., 280*n*11
McMorrow, Paul, 238
Mesnard, Sarah, 166
Milborne, Jacob, 70
Mills, James, 38, 86, 87, 90, 91–2, 103, 107,
    108, 113, 171, 178, 194, 202, 211
Mingo (Barberie), 185
*Modest Enquiry into the Nature of
    Witchcraft* (Hale), 207, 304*n*8
Moglen, Eben, 291*n*9
Montague, Duke of, 125
Montgomerie, John, 25, 57
  estate of, 28–9
Moore, Clement, 159
Moore, George Joseph, 94, 105, 106, 109,
    192

Moore, John, 54

Morgan, Edmund, xii

Morris, Gouverneur, 225

Morris, Lewis, 29, 30, 31, 52, 292n14
  Oblong or the Equivalent Lands case,
    291n11
  political crisis of 1730s, 25, 26, 28, 71, 77
  Zenger trial, 75, 76–7

Morris, Lewis, Jr., 139, 162, 224

Murphy, Edward, 180, 181, 211

Murray, Grace, 17

Murray, Joseph, 17, 25, 28, 49, 167–9, 282n5
  bar of New York and, 79–80
  death of, 223
  Hogg's shop robbery trials, 85
  political crisis of 1730s, 71, 72, 292n17
  prosecution of conspirators, 79, 121;
    attorneys' agreement to assist with, 82;
    last slave trial, 191; Priest's Plot trial,
    195; Quack/Cuffee trial, 96, 98; six
    black men's trial, 131, 132; "Spanish
    Negroes" trial, 165, 166
  will of, 226

Nail, William, 189

"National Characters" (Hume), 125

Neau, Elias, 184–5

Negro Election Day, 159, 209

Negroes Burial Ground, 226–9

"Negro Evidence," xix–xx, 97–8, 103, 109,
  125–6

New Englander's letter about prosecution
  of conspirators, xvi–xvii, 203–10,
  304n12

Newsham, Richard, 45

New Survey of the Globe, A (Templeman),
  19–20, 21

New York City, 20
  American Revolution, 224–5
  anti-Catholic legislation, 182–3
  beauty of, xii
  buildings of, 44–5, 288n7
  cultural diversity, 21
  disease problem, 136
  early history, 21
  economic conditions, 22
  English fashions, 20
  enlightenment outlook, 29

fire of 1776, 224–5
historical reconstruction of, 233–46
maps of, *2, 3*
place data regarding, 241–2
population of, 21, 235–40, 300n34
slavery in, 22–5
wards of, 21–2, 150, 243–4, 300n33
water for drinking, 135–6, 144–5
winter of 1740–41, 5–7, 15
see also fires of 1741

New York Gazette, 27, 32, 34, 42, 53, 56–7, 93,
  140–1, 142–3, 161, 186, 218
  black Masons incident, 99–102
  founding of, 72

New-York Weekly Journal, xi, xiii, 5, 6, 11, 15,
  16, 34, 40, 47, 53, 56, 77, 140, 164, 192,
  197, 305n12
  black Masons incident, 100, 101, 102
  founding of, 72
  reporting on prosecution of conspirators,
    93–4

New York Weekly Post-Boy, 215

Nichols, Richard, 79, 82, 121, 123, 132, 166

Nissenbaum, Stephen, 233

Norris, Capt. Matthew, 76, 100

North, Joseph, 158, 159

novel, the, 122

Oblong or the Equivalent Lands case,
  291n11

O'Brien, James, 191

"Of Public Spirit in Regard to Public
  Works" (Savage), 52

Oglethorpe, Gen. James, 176

Osborne, Sir Danvers, 218

Othello (DeLancey), 9, 14, 80, 171–3, 175,
  176, 189–90, 191–2, 227

Pablo Ventura Angel (Becker), 50, 161, 162,
  164, 165, 166

Pagano, Daniel, 228

Parker, James, 95, 112–13, 214–15, 220

party politics, xiii, xv, 218–19
  affiliations of people involved in Zenger
    trial and slave conspiracy of 1741, 237–8
  Masons and, 139–41
  party sympathies of slaveowners, 245–6

political crisis of 1730s and, 26–7
slave conspiracy of 1741 and, xvii–xviii,
219–20
Patrick (English), 43, 49, 89, 163
Pearse, Vincent, 88, 162
Pedro (DePeyster), 8–9, 144, 152–3, 188–9
Pennsylvania Gazette, 44, 48, 55
Peter the Porter (Marschalk), 53, 185
Philipse, Adolph, 59, 139, 140
Philipse, Frederick, 31, 50, 59, 133, 137, 159,
168
death of, 223
Hogg's shop robbery trials, 85
political crisis of 1730s, 71
prosecution of conspirators: confessions
of the accused, 110, 111, 113, 121, 171;
Hughson/Kerry trial, 109, 110, 130–1;
investigations by judges and grand
jury, 66, 67, 69–70, 78, 79, 83, 85, 87, 89,
90; pardoning of conspirators, 175;
Quack/Cuffee trial, 93, 96, 103;
"Spanish Negroes" trial, 164, 165, 167;
termination of, 211
Zenger trial, 74, 118
Phips, Sir William, 207
Phoenix, Jacob, 54
Pinkster holiday, 158, 159
Pleas of the Crown (Hawkins), 84
political crisis of 1730s, xiii, xv–xvi, 285n25
Alexander's death threat, 286n27
complaints regarding Cosby's actions,
27–8
Cosby's abuses of power, 25–6, 70–2,
292n17
party politics and, 26–7
resolution of, 77–8
rival governments, 77
slave conspiracy of 1741 and, xvii
Zenger trial, 72–7, 115–18, 293nn18, 23, 25
Pompey (DeLancey), 106, 150–1, 172
Pompey (Gilbert), 226
Poorhouse, 37
poor whites, 180–1
Pope, Alexander, xv
press freedom, 71–2
Zenger trial, 73–7, 115–18, 293nn18, 23,
25
Price, Arthur, 86, 87–8, 89, 97, 109, 113,
181

Priest's Plot, 169
anti-Catholicism in New York and,
182–3
investigation into, 177–82, 189–90, 191,
194
"master plot" designation, 198
trial and execution of Ury, 192–7
warnings about, 176–7
Primus (DeBrosses), 8, 151
Prince (Auboyneau), 36–7, 38, 60, 85–6,
89–90, 99, 137, 138, 141, 143
Prince (Crooke), 105, 151
Prince (Duane), 168, 173
Prince, Walter Franklin, 279n11
privateering, 161–2
prosecution of conspirators, xii, xvi
Alexander's involvement, 200
arrests of first suspects, 60–1, 62–3
attorneys' agreement to assist with, 82
black Masons incident and, 99–102
Boston newspapers' coverage of, 305n12
Burton's lying, concerns about, 201–2
Burton's reward, 211–12, 213–14
confessions of the accused, 7, 9–10, 14,
78–9, 89, 105–6, 107, 110, 111–15, *114, 116,*
119, 120, 121–2, 123–4, *124,* 132–3, *134,*
150–1, 158, 171–3, 174–5, 178–80, 189–90,
194. *see also* recantations of confessions
below
costs of, 202–3
criticism of, xvi–xvii, 99, 199–200,
202–10, 304n12
data of trial transcript, 240–1
executions of the condemned, 103,
104–6, 119–20, 164–5, 173–5, 176, 191–2,
196–7
fixing the meaning of conspirators'
words, 113, 115, 118
four black men's trial, 119
Horsmanden's assessment of, 198–9
Horsmanden's control of, 122
Horsmanden's personal interest in, 82–3
Hughson/Kerry trial, 108–10, 128, 130–1
investigations by judges and grand jury,
60–1, 62–3, 66–70, 78–9, 83, 84–5, 86,
87–92, 107–8, 130, 291n7. *see also*
Priest's Plot investigation *below*
last slave trial, 190–1
"list of conspirators" rumor, 120

prosecution of conspirators *(continued)*
"Negro Evidence" and, xix–xx, 97–8, 103, 109
New Englander's letter about, xvi–xvii, 203–10, 304n12
pardoning of convicts, 119, 121, 175, 191, 194–5
party politics and, 220
Priest's Plot designated as master plot, 198
Priest's Plot investigation, 177–82, 189–90, 191, 194
Priest's Plot trial, 192–7
proceedings of trials, *see Journal of the Proceedings in The Detection of the Conspiracy*
prominent whites, accusations against, 200–2
prosecution's trial strategy, 131
Quack/Cuffee trial, 59–60, 93, 96–9, 102–3, 104, 296n9
recantations of confessions, 188–90, 194
records of, 93–6
resumption of prosecutions in 1742, efforts toward, 212–13, 214
reward for information on conspirators, 62
six black men's trial, 110, 131–2
slaves designated as primary suspects in arson fires, 61–2
Smith Jr.'s account of, 306n2
social connections of accusers and accused, 150–7
"Spanish Negroes" trial, 162–4, 165–7
Supreme Court's jurisdiction over, 80, 81–3
termination of, 211
torture of suspects, 91–2
water regulations and, 144–5
"white leadership of conspiracy" issue, 126, 128
prostitution, 37
Provost, David, 40, 54, 93
Provost, David, Jr., 100

Quack (Roosevelt), 60, 87, 89, 92, 129, 130, 131, 149, 151, 152, 154
execution of, 104–6

trial of, 59–60, 93, 96–9, 102–3, 104, 296n9
Quack (Walter), 49, 61, 150, 174, 191
Quakers, 208
Quash (LeRoux), 189
Quash (Rutgers), 5, 164, 165, 226
Quick, Jacobus, 48

Rediker, Marcus, 280n11
Rees, Daniel, 142
Regnier, Jacob, 82
religion and slavery, 183–8
religious revival of 1740s, 186–7
Rex v. Warwickshall, 91
Richetti, John J., 298n33
Robin (Chambers), 9, 62–3, 80, 110, 119, 131–2, 149
Robin (Hoghlandt), 53, 104
Robins, John, 96
Robinson Crusoe (Defoe), 122
Romme, Elizabeth, 89
Romme, John, 89
Roosevelt, Jacobus, 59
Roosevelt, John, 59, 60, 105, 109, 152
Roosevelt, Theodore, 279n11
Royal African Company, 23
Rumsey, David, 242
Rutgers, Hermanus, Jr., 226
Ryan, Andrew, 211
Ryan, Eleanor, 109

St. John's slave rebellion (1733), 53
Salem Possessed (Boyer and Nissenbaum), 233
Salem witchcraft trials, xvi–xvii, xix–xx, 203–4, 207, 209, 304n8
Sancho, Ignatius, 124
Sandiford, Ralph, 208
Sandy (Niblet), 90–1, 92, 97, 98–9, 107, 109, 119, 129–30, 131, 144, 147, 150, 162, 166
Sarah (Burk), 107, 129, 130, 131, 144, 150, 191, 194
Sarly, Jacob, 49, 50, 54, 167
Savage, Richard, 52
Saxon, Andrew, 146
Schultz, John, 188–9, 191
Scipio (Abrahamse), 158

Scipio (Nichols), 123, 188
Scott, Kenneth, 238
Secretary's Office building, 45, 46, 47
Sewall, Samuel, 207–8
sex, interracial, 156–7, 300n40
Sherbrook, Elizabeth, 221, 224
Sherbrook, Miles, 224
Shurmur, John, 96
Silvester, Francis, 136
slave conspiracy of 1712, 52–3
  African ceremonies and, 147
  executions of the condemned, 104
  prosecution of conspirators, 82
  religious training for slaves and, 184–5
  slave conspiracy of 1741 and, 59–60
  torture of suspects, 92
slave conspiracy of 1741, xii, xvi
  African ceremonies and, 147–8
  black celebrations and, 158–60
  economic motivations, 22
  English ideas about slave plots and,
    10–11
  fires in New York attributed to, 49–51,
    60–2
  as fraternity, 150–7
  historical perspectives on, 279n11
  Hogg's shop robbery and, 36–9
  Hughson's Plot and "Negro Plot,"
    129–33, 145–8, 157, 158, 163
  as imaginary plot, xviii, 203–5
  Jack's leadership role, 146–7, 148
  as joke, 13–14, 138, 143–4, 190
  Masons and, 12–13, 143–4
  owners of accused slaves, 54
  party politics and, xvii–xviii, 219–20
  plotting of, 5–14
  political crisis of 1730s and, xvii
  religious training for slaves and, 188
  slave conspiracy of 1712 and, 59–60
  "Spanish Plot," 160–4, 165–7
  "three years in preparation" issue, 137–8
  War of Jenkins's Ear and, 163
  see also Priest's Plot; prosecution of
    conspirators
"Slave Insurrection in New York in 1712,
  The" (Scott), 238
slave rebellions
  Antigua (1736), 11, 53, 91, 92, 98, 104, 105
  Barbados (1676), 10–11

false alarms, 56
Haiti (1791), 300n28
Jamaica (1730s), 53–4
New Yorkers' fears regarding, 52–5, 58
religious training for slaves and, 184–5,
  187–8
St. John's (1733), 53
Stono Rebellion (1739), 53, 163
Virginia (1730), 186
see also slave conspiracy of 1712; slave
  conspiracy of 1741
slavery
  abolition in New York, 228
  anti-slavery movement, 208, 219
  bequeathing of slaves in wills, 225–6
  criminal trials of slaves, 81
  ethnicity, wealth, and party of
    slaveowners, 244–6
  laws regarding (slave codes), 56–9, 80, 81,
    153–4, 183–4, 185, 227, 290n30
  manumission, 58, 226
  names for slaves, 24, 29
  in New York City, 22–5
  number of Africans imported into New
    York colony, 285n21
  paradox of liberty and slavery, xi–xii,
    xx
  political slavery of tyranny, xi
  population information on slaves,
    238–40, 300n34
  punishment of slaves, 80–1
  religion and, 183–8
  runaways, 32–3, 35, 149
  "seasoning" of slaves, 24
  sexual issues, 156–7, 300n40
  tax on slaves, 284n16
  see also slave conspiracy of 1712; slave
    conspiracy of 1741; slave rebellions
Slotkin, Richard, 280n11
Sloughter, Henry, 70
Smith, Alexander Murray, 29
Smith, Mary, 18
Smith, William, 29
  bar of New York and, 79–80
  death of, 223
  Oblong or the Equivalent Lands case,
    291n11
  political crisis of 1730s, 71, 72, 77–8,
    292n17

Smith, William *(continued)*
　prosecution of conspirators, 10, 79, 121;
　　attorneys' agreement to assist with, 82;
　　Hughson/Kerry trial, 109; last slave
　　trial, 191; Priest's Plot trial, 195, 196;
　　Quack/Cuffee trial, 59–60, 96, 103
　Vice Admiralty Court, 162
　Zenger trial, 74, 75
Smith, William, Jr., 12, 22, 25, 46, 47, 76,
　103, 222, 223, 283n10, 306n2
　*see also History of the Province of New
　York*
Society for the Propagation of the Gospel,
　184, 185, 186
"Some Considerations on the Keeping of
　Negroes" (Woolman), 208
Spanish (slave), 163
"Spanish Negroes," 6, 49–50, 196–7
　slave conspiracy of 1741, 160–4, 165–7
Steers, B. MacDonald, 280n11
Sterling (Lawrence), 158
Stokes, I. N. Phelps, 241
Stono Rebellion (1739), 53, 163
Stoutenburgh, Jacobus, 50
Stuyvesant, Peter, 135, 284n18
Supreme Court of Judicature of the
　Province of New York, xiii, 64, 70, 78,
　137
　Zenger trial, 72–7, 115–18
　see also prosecution of conspirators
Swift, Jonathan, 55–6, 58, 122
Symes, John, 74, 75
Symes, Lancaster, 137, 298n5
Szasz, Ferenc M., 280n11

"Tea-Water Men," 145
Templeman, Thomas, 19–20, 21
theatre-going, 16–18, 35–6
Thomas, Ben, 49, 119
Thornton, John, 239–40
Tickle (Carpenter), 120, 145, 151, 166
Tiebout, John, 54
Todd, Robert, 144
Todd's tavern, 27
Tom (Bradt), 212, 213
Tom (Moore), 176–7, 182
Tom (Roosevelt), 53, 59, 60, 104
Tom (Rowe), 158

Tom (Soumaien), 9
Tom Jones (Fielding), 123
Tony (Brazier), 151
Tony (Latham), 168, 173
torture, 91–2
Trenchard, John, 72
Trinity Church, 221, 224–5, 227
Tunbrigalia (Byrd), 18, 19
"'Twas the Night Before Christmas"
　(Moore), 159

Ury, John, 177–8, 181–2
　trial and execution, 192–7

Vallet, Peter, 156–7
Van Cortlandt, Jacobus, 146
Van Dam, Rip, 25, 26, 27–8, 48, 54, 59, 70, 77
Vanderspiegle, John, 107, 151
Van Horne, Abraham, 54, 206, 226
Van Horne, Cornelius ("Major Drum"), 46,
　139, 155
Van Zant, John, 80
Van Zant, Winant, 48, 54, 69
Vice Admiralty Court, 162
Virginia slave rebellion (1730), 186

Wallace, Mike, 281n11
Waller, John, 88
Walton, William, 54
War of Jenkins's Ear, 9, 40, 46
　privateering in, 161–2
　slave conspiracy of 1741 and, 163
Warren, Capt. Peter, 28, 40, 48, 172
Warren, Susannah DeLancey, 172
Washington, George, 221, 223, 224
water for drinking, 135–6, 144–5
Watts, Robert, 69
Weaver, Samuel, 96
Webb, Joseph, 195
Wheatley, Phillis, 124
Whitefield, George, 186–8, 190
Whitsuntide, 158, 159
Will (Ten Eyck), 8, 151
Will (Vaarck), 151
Will (Ward), 54–5, 155–6, 173, 174–5, 188–9
William (Lush), 161, 162

William III, King, 183
Williams, Francis, 125–6, *127,* 298*n*39
Williams, John, 126
Wilson, Christopher ("Yorkshire"), 36–8,
    85, 88, 181
Wilson, Sherrill, 229
Wilson, Thomas, 211
Wimbleton, Lt., 162
Windsor (Cohen), 226
winter of 1740–41, 5–7, 15
witchcraft
    fires of 1741 and, 51
    Salem trials, xvi–xvii, xix–xx, 203–4, 207,
        209, 304*n*8
Witts, George, 96
Wood, Gordon S., 289*n*18
Woolman, John, 208

Yaff (Alexander), 32–3, 35, 287*n*39
York (Crooke), 7, 8, 9
York (Ludlow), 189
York (Marschalk), 105, 145, 168, 173,
    174
York (Peck), 151
York, Duke of, 59

Zabin, Serena, 281*n*11
Zenger, John Peter, 11, 86, 139, 164, 165,
    173–4, 197, 305*n*12
    reporting on prosecution of
        conspirators, 93–4
    trial of, xiii, 72–7, 115–18, 293*nn*18, 23,
        25
    see also New-York Weekly Journal

ABOUT THE AUTHOR

Jill Lepore is Professor of History at Harvard University and the author of *The Name of War: King Philip's War and the Origins of American Identity* (winner of the Bancroft Prize and Phi Beta Kappa's Ralph Waldo Emerson Award) and *A Is for American: Letters and Other Characters in the Newly United States*. She lives in Cambridge with her husband and three sons.

A NOTE ON THE TYPE

This book was set in a modern adaptation of a type designed by the first William Caslon (1692–1766). The Caslon face, an artistic, easily read type, has enjoyed over two centuries of popularity in our own county. It is of interest to note that the first copies of the Declaration of Independence and the first paper currency distributed to the citizens of the newborn nation were printed in this typeface.

Composed by North Market Street Graphics,
Lancaster, Pennsylvania
Printed and bound by Berryville Graphics,
Berryville, Virginia
Designed by Virginia Tan
Map of New York in 1741 by David Lindroth